American Attitudes

American Attitudes

Who Thinks What about the Issues That Shape Our Lives

BY THE EDITORS OF NEW STRATEGIST PRESS **7**th EDITION

New Strategist Press, LLC
Amityville, New York

New Strategist Press, LLC
P.O. Box 635, Amityville, New York 11701
800/848-0842; 631/608-8795
www.newstrategist.com

ISBN 978-1-940308-29-6 (hardcover)
ISBN 978-1-940308-36-4 (paper)

Printed in the United States of America

Table of Contents

List of Tables

Chapter 2: Government and Politics

Chapter 3: Science and Information

Chapter 6: Family

Chapter 7: Diversity

Chapter 8: Personal Outlook

Chapter 9: Sexuality

Introduction

Surveys and polls have become fixtures of American life, each day bringing new findings and making headlines. Some of the results are enlightening, while others serve only to muddy the water. Many surveys do not segment their findings by demographic characteristic, and most cannot reveal trends in attitudes over time because methodologies and questions vary from survey to survey.

The General Social Survey is different. It has a long history. For 40 years, it has asked Americans many of the same questions, allowing researchers to compare attitudes not just over time, but also by demographic characteristic. The General Social Survey is one of the few resources that allow attitudinal differences and changes in attitudes to be explored in depth, often permitting researchers to pinpoint why change has occurred. The General Social Survey is the mirror of America. The National Academy of Science has described it as a "national resource" and the National Science Foundation as a "public utility for the community at large." The survey may not always show us a pretty picture of ourselves, but it is a more accurate picture than can be gleaned from snapshot surveys carried out by a multitude of organizations, each with a different agenda.

The seventh edition of *American Attitudes: Who Thinks What about the Issues That Shape Our Lives* brings you the results from the latest General Social Survey, fielded in 2012. In six previous editions of *American Attitudes,* New Strategist has coaxed General Social Survey results out of the shadows of academia and placed them solidly in public view. This edition does even more with General Social Survey results, not only examining changes in the public's attitudes over the past four decades, but also providing a demographic profile of the most recent attitudes question by question. In hundreds of tables, the seventh edition of *American Attitudes* taps into the General Social Survey gold mine, revealing what the public thinks about topics ranging from gay marriage to the American Dream, how Americans feel about their financial status, their hopes for their children, how often they socialize and with whom, their religious beliefs, political leanings, family life, and standard of living. This reference reveals the attitudes of Americans in two ways. First, it provides 2012 attitudes by demographic characteristic—sex, generation, race and Hispanic origin, region of residence, and education. Second, for every 2012 question for which historical data are available, *American Attitudes* shows you the history of response all the way back to the first appearance of the question on the General Social Survey.

Changing Attitudes

On most issues, Americans are surprisingly constant in their views. Over the decades that the General Social Survey has been administered, the majority of Americans consistently claim to be at least "pretty happy," and most husbands and wives describe their marriage as "very happy." Religion remains highly important to the majority, although religious diversity has increased. Most favor the death penalty, but also gun control. Most support abortion, at least in some circumstances.

On some issues, however, there have been important shifts over time. Attitudes toward sex roles, sexual behavior, and race relations have changed profoundly as younger generations with different attitudes replaced older ones. Overall, only 32 percent of Americans still favor traditional sex roles, for example, down from 66 percent in 1977. In 2012, only 25 percent of Millennials supported traditional roles compared with 47 percent of Americans aged 67 or older.

Other issues that have experienced significant attitudinal shifts in the past few decades include a decline in the percentage of people who identify themselves as Protestant, a sharp drop in daily newspaper readership, a decline in the percentage of people who think two is the ideal number of children, and a drop in the percentage of people who believe their income is average—the latter falling from 58 percent in 1972 to 46 percent in 2012. The percentage of Americans who believe their income is below average relative to others has grown from 24 to 33 percent. Most disturbing, perhaps, is the loss of faith in the American Dream. The percentage of people who agree with the statement, "The way things are in America, people like me and my family have a good chance of improving our standard of living," has fallen from a high of 77 percent in 2000 to 55 percent in 2012. Fortunately, nearly two-thirds of Millennials and more than 70 percent of blacks and Hispanics still believe in the American Dream. Among older Americans, however, the figure is just 43 percent.

Differences by Demographics

Demographics do not necessarily divide Americans. On many issues, men and women think alike, blacks and whites agree, young and old are on the same side, and college graduates are in accord with their less educated counterparts. Every demographic segment, for example, overwhelmingly supports gun control. Regardless of their demographics, few people have much confidence in Congress, television, or the press.

On some issues, however, there are large differences by demographic characteristic. Women are more likely than men to pray at least once a day (67 versus 50 percent). Non-Hispanic whites are more likely than blacks to favor capital punishment (71 versus 48 percent). The Millennial generation is more likely than older Americans to think gays and lesbians should have the right to marry (62 versus 30 percent). The college-educated are much more likely than those without a bachelor's degree to be interested in science and understand scientific concepts. Mix these diverse attitudes and values together, and you get the American perspective. That perspective is revealed in *American Attitudes*.

About the Book

The seventh edition of *American Attitudes* is organized into nine topical chapters: Public Arena, Government and Politics, Science and Information, Religion, Work and Money, Family and Friends, Diversity, Personal Outlook, and Sexuality.

All but one chapter (Science and Information is the lone exception) has two sections of tables: 2012 responses by demographic characteristic and historical data back to the first appearance of the question on the General Social Survey. The exact wording of survey questions is shown above each table—

minus instructional details. The 2012 profile tables show attitudes by sex, generation (Millennials, aged 18 to 35; Generation X, aged 36 to 47; Baby Boomers, aged 48 to 66; and older Americans, aged 67 or older), race and Hispanic origin (black, Hispanic, and non-Hispanic white—the sample size is too small to allow for a breakout of Asian attitudes), the four geographic regions, and education (not a college graduate and bachelor's degree or more). Each chapter also includes an introductory text that examines what has—and has not—changed over the four decades.

About the General Social Survey

The University of Chicago's National Opinion Research Center fields the General Social Survey. The National Opinion Research Center is the oldest nonprofit, university-affiliated national survey research facility in the nation. It conducts the General Social Survey through face-to-face interviews with an independently drawn, nationally representative sample of about 3,000 people aged 18 or older living in households in the United States. The center fielded the first survey in 1972, conducted it annually through 1994 (except for the years 1979, 1981, and 1992), and has fielded the survey every two years since then.

Although social scientists frequently use the General Social Survey to study trends, the survey's results are not published comprehensively or regularly. Most General Social Survey analysis appears in academic papers and journals, which are not readily available to the average person. Several years ago, the Computer-assisted Survey Methods Program of the University of California, Berkeley created a web-based tool for analyzing the General Social Survey. The online tool allows users to create custom tables of survey data. Using the tool, researchers at New Strategist extracted General Social Survey results like gold from a mine. With the publication of the seventh edition of *American Attitudes*, New Strategist is placing the gold in the hands of the public.

For More Information

Those who would like Excel spreadsheets of the General Social Survey attitudinal data presented here should visit New Strategist's web site (newstrategist.com) and download the PDF of *American Attitudes*, which has links to the Excel version of each table.

Those who would like more information about General Social Survey methodology should visit the National Opinion Research Center site at http://www.norc.org/Research/Projects/Pages/general -social-survey.aspx.

Those who want to explore the General Social Survey extraction tool should visit the Computer-assisted Survey Methods Program site at http://sda.berkeley.edu/cgi-bin/hsda?harcsda+gss12.

Executive Summary: What Americans Think

Although Americans disagree about some things, they find common ground on many important issues. These common attitudes and values define the American people. But knowing the issues on which we agree can hinder as much as further an understanding of the American psyche. That is because many of our attitudes are contradictory, causing confusion for those who try to explain the American perspective.

How can we be so optimistic about our lives but so cynical about our leaders? How can we so avidly want to cut government spending but support an increase in spending on so many government programs? How can we be so enthusiastic about science yet pray every day, think the Bible is the word of God, and believe in life after death? Here is a look at what Americans think about some of the most important issues of the day, revealing our many contradictions.

Chapter 1: Public Arena

The death penalty is supported...

"Do you favor or oppose the death penalty for persons convicted of murder?"

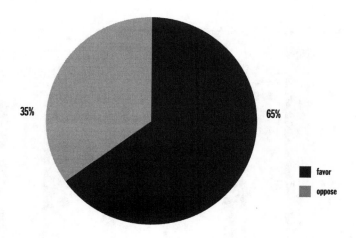

35%   65%

■ favor
■ oppose

And so is gun control...

"Would you favor or oppose a law which would require a person to obtain a police permit before he or she could buy a gun?"

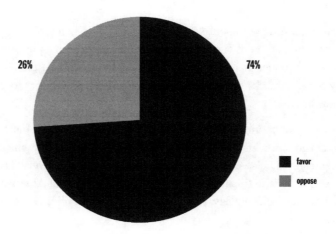

26%   74%

- ■ favor
- ■ oppose

Chapter 2: Government and Politics

Most think taxes are too high, but they want the government to spend more...

"Do you think we're spending too much money, too little money, or about the right amount on...?"   (percent saying "too little")

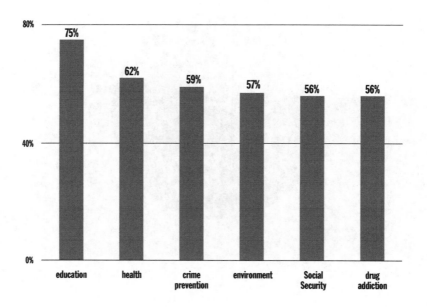

Chapter 3. Science and Information

Most think science creates opportunities for younger generations...

"Because of science and technology, there will be more
opportunities for the next generation?"

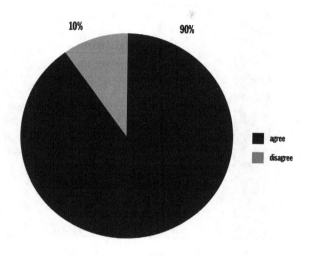

But interest in science lags...

"There are a lot of issues in the news, and it is hard to keep up with every area.
How interested are you in new scientific discoveries?"

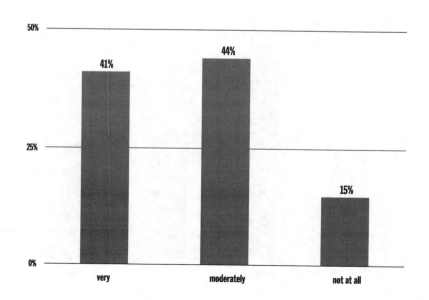

Most pray at least once a day...

"About how often do you pray?"

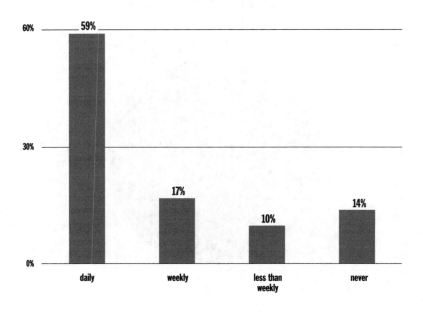

But few consider themselves "very religious"...

"To what extent do you consider yourself a religious person?"

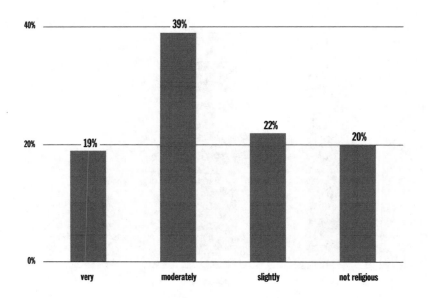

Chapter 5. Work and Money

Older Americans enjoyed a rising standard of living...

"Compared to your parents when they were the age you are now, do you think your own standard of living now is...?" (percent of people aged 67 or older responding)

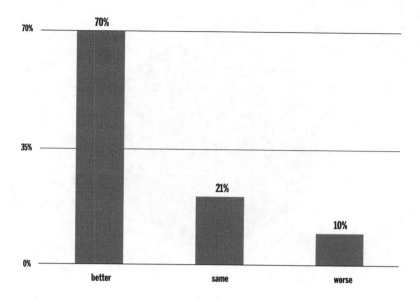

But they don't think the trend will continue...

"The way things are in America, people like me and my family have a good chance of improving our standard of living. Do you agree or disagree?"
(percent of people aged 67 or older responding)

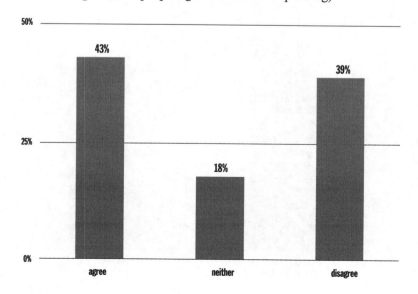

Most think spanking children is OK...

"Do you agree that it is sometimes necessary to discipline
a child with a good, hard spanking?"

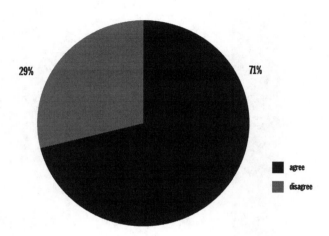

29%   71%

■ agree
■ disagree

But few think obedience is the most important trait in a child...

"How important is it for a child to learn to think for self/obey
to prepare him or her for life?"

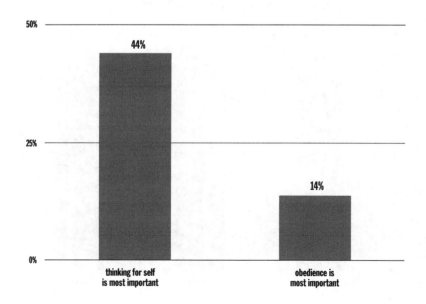

Chapter 7. Diversity

American society is more integrated...

Percent who say blacks live in their neighborhood...

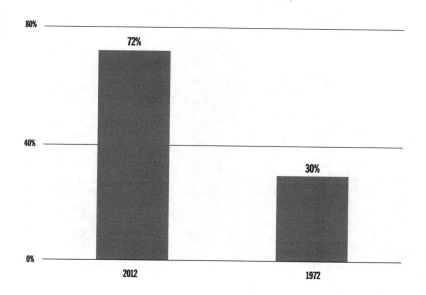

But racism lurks...

Percent of Americans aged 67 or older who think...

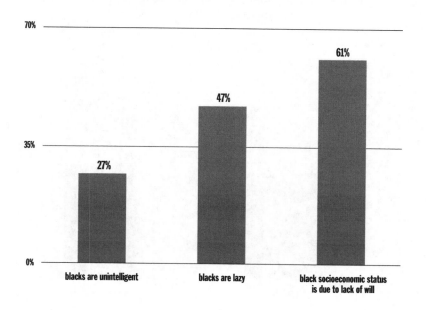

Most Americans are at least pretty happy...

"Would you say that you are...?"

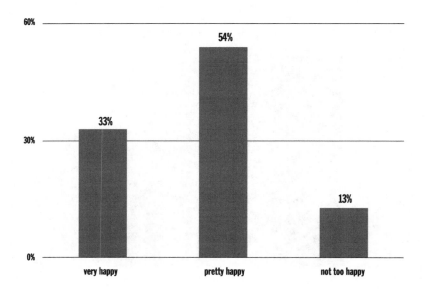

But nearly three out of four do not trust other people...

"Generally speaking, would you say that most people can be trusted or that you can't be too careful in life?"

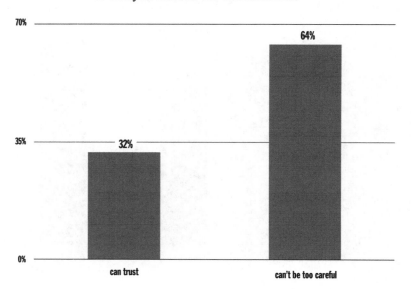

Chapter 9. Sexuality

Most support abortion if a woman is raped or her health is endangered...

"Do you think it should be possible for a pregnant woman to obtain a legal abortion if she became pregnant as a result of rape/the woman's health is seriously endangered by the pregnancy?" (percent saying "yes")

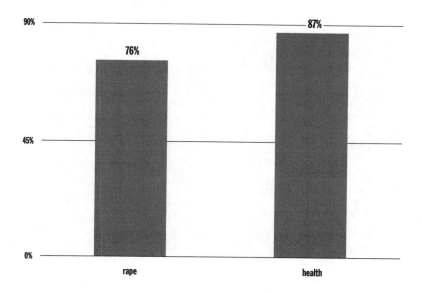

But most do not support abortion for any reason...

"Should it be possible for a pregnant woman to obtain a legal abortion if the woman wants it for any reason?"

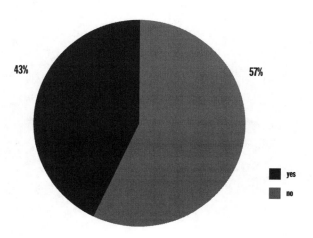

1

The Public Arena

Public opinion on some issues has been remarkably stable over the years. On other issues, changes in public opinion can—or should—raise alarm bells. Here is a synopsis of how attitudes regarding public institutions and public issues have changed—or not—over the past four decades.

Little or No Change

• **Most support gun control.** Politicians may argue about gun regulation, but the public firmly supports requiring a police permit before someone can buy a gun. In 2012, 74 percent of Americans favored gun permits, up slightly from the 72 percent of 1972.

• **Most want the courts to treat criminals more harshly.** Although the United States has more prisoners per capita than any other country, most Americans still think the courts in their area are not tough enough on criminals. Most also favor the death penalty, with little change in support for capital punishment over the years.

Big Changes

• **Less confidence in institutions.** Confidence in most institutions has declined over the decades. Only the military has seen an increase. Confidence in banks and financial institutions, major companies, medicine, religion, and education has taken a hit in recent years. The public has never expressed much confidence in the legislative branch of government, and in 2012 only 7 percent had a "great deal" of confidence in Congress. The press is the only other institution in which less than 10 percent of the public has a great deal of confidence.

• **Higher taxes for someone.** A shrinking share of the public believes taxes are too high, the figure falling from a high of 74 percent in 1982 to just 52 percent in 2012. Nearly half the public now thinks taxes are "about right," up from a low of 25 percent in 1982. Fewer than 3 percent think taxes are too low.

• **Legalizing marijuana.** A growing share of Americans favor legalizing marijuana, the figure rising from just 20 percent in 1973 to 47 percent in 2012. The majority of men, Millennials, non-Hispanic whites, and college graduates favor the legalization of marijuana.

The Public Arena: 2012 Profiles

Table 1.1 Confidence in Executive Branch of Government, 2012

"As far as the people running these institutions are concerned, would you say you have a great deal of confidence, only some confidence, or hardly any confidence at all in them: the executive branch of the federal government?"

(percent of people aged 18 or older responding by selected characteristics, 2012)

	total	a great deal	only some	hardly any
Total people	**100.0%**	**14.6%**	**49.4%**	**36.1%**
Men	100.0	13.3	49.6	37.1
Women	100.0	15.7	49.2	35.2
Millennials	100.0	15.5	58.0	26.4
Generation Xers	100.0	15.1	51.0	33.9
Baby Boomers	100.0	14.5	42.7	42.9
Older Americans	100.0	12.0	42.8	45.1
Black	100.0	20.0	55.3	24.7
Hispanic	100.0	20.1	57.9	22.1
Non-Hispanic white	100.0	12.0	45.0	42.9
Northeast	100.0	14.7	56.4	28.9
Midwest	100.0	14.2	50.5	35.2
South	100.0	12.6	44.9	42.4
West	100.0	17.9	50.1	32.0
Not a college graduate	100.0	13.2	48.4	38.4
Bachelor's degree or more	100.0	17.8	51.6	30.6

Note: Millennials are aged 18 to 35; Generation Xers are aged 36 to 47; Baby Boomers are aged 48 to 66; Older Americans are aged 67 or older.
Source: Survey Documentation and Analysis, Computer-assisted Survey Methods Program, University of California, Berkeley, General Social Survey, 1972–2012 Cumulative Data Files, Internet site http://sda.berkeley.edu/cgi-bin/hsda?harcsda+gss12; calculations by New Strategist

Table 1.2 Confidence in Legislative Branch of Government, 2012

"As far as the people running these institutions are concerned, would you say you have a great deal of confidence, only some confidence, or hardly any confidence at all in them: the legislative branch of the federal government?"

(percent of people aged 18 or older responding by selected characteristics, 2012)

	total	a great deal	only some	hardly any
Total people	**100.0%**	**6.8%**	**45.9%**	**47.3%**
Men	100.0	6.9	40.3	52.8
Women	100.0	6.8	50.7	42.5
Millennials	100.0	8.6	57.2	34.2
Generation Xers	100.0	6.4	44.9	48.7
Baby Boomers	100.0	6.1	40.2	53.7
Older Americans	100.0	5.6	35.0	59.4
Black	100.0	6.7	49.5	43.9
Hispanic	100.0	12.6	55.9	31.6
Non-Hispanic white	100.0	5.8	40.8	53.4
Northeast	100.0	7.3	48.9	43.8
Midwest	100.0	7.1	43.0	49.9
South	100.0	6.8	45.6	47.6
West	100.0	6.3	46.8	46.8
Not a college graduate	100.0	8.5	47.2	44.3
Bachelor's degree or more	100.0	3.0	42.6	54.4

Note: Millennials are aged 18 to 35; Generation Xers are aged 36 to 47; Baby Boomers are aged 48 to 66; Older Americans are aged 67 or older.
Source: Survey Documentation and Analysis, Computer-assisted Survey Methods Program, University of California, Berkeley, General Social Survey, 1972–2012 Cumulative Data Files, Internet site http://sda.berkeley.edu/cgi-bin/hsda?harcsda+gss12; calculations by New Strategist

Table 1.3 Confidence in the United States Supreme Court, 2012

"As far as the people running these institutions are concerned, would you say
you have a great deal of confidence, only some confidence, or hardly
any confidence at all in them: the United States Supreme Court?"

(percent of people aged 18 or older responding by selected characteristics, 2012)

	total	a great deal	only some	hardly any
Total people	**100.0%**	**29.5%**	**54.3%**	**16.1%**
Men	100.0	32.3	52.0	15.7
Women	100.0	27.2	56.3	15.5
Millennials	100.0	28.8	58.2	13.0
Generation Xers	100.0	31.7	50.0	18.3
Baby Boomers	100.0	32.4	51.2	16.5
Older Americans	100.0	21.5	59.4	19.1
Black	100.0	21.3	61.5	17.2
Hispanic	100.0	38.0	43.6	18.4
Non-Hispanic white	100.0	28.1	55.9	16.0
Northeast	100.0	30.1	56.4	13.4
Midwest	100.0	31.9	53.7	14.4
South	100.0	24.4	56.6	19.0
West	100.0	35.1	49.8	15.1
Not a college graduate	100.0	26.6	55.5	17.9
Bachelor's degree or more	100.0	36.6	51.5	11.9

Note: Millennials are aged 18 to 35; Generation Xers are aged 36 to 47; Baby Boomers are aged 48 to 66; Older Americans are aged 67 or older.
Source: Survey Documentation and Analysis, Computer-assisted Survey Methods Program, University of California, Berkeley, General Social Survey, 1972–2012 Cumulative Data Files, Internet site http://sda.berkeley.edu/cgi-bin/hsda?harcsda+gss12; calculations by New Strategist

Table 1.4 Confidence in Banks and Financial Institutions, 2012

"As far as the people running these institutions are concerned, would you say you have a great deal of confidence, only some confidence, or hardly any confidence at all in them: banks and financial institutions?"

(percent of people aged 18 or older responding by selected characteristics, 2012)

	total	a great deal	only some	hardly any
Total people	**100.0%**	**11.9%**	**51.8%**	**36.3%**
Men	100.0	11.8	49.9	38.3
Women	100.0	12.0	53.4	34.6
Millennials	100.0	17.9	50.7	31.4
Generation Xers	100.0	8.4	52.9	38.6
Baby Boomers	100.0	7.8	52.6	39.6
Older Americans	100.0	13.5	50.4	36.1
Black	100.0	14.1	54.8	31.1
Hispanic	100.0	14.8	54.9	30.4
Non-Hispanic white	100.0	10.8	50.3	38.8
Northeast	100.0	10.3	53.8	35.9
Midwest	100.0	11.1	50.1	38.8
South	100.0	14.6	52.7	32.7
West	100.0	9.7	50.4	40.0
Not a college graduate	100.0	13.9	50.6	35.5
Bachelor's degree or more	100.0	7.0	54.7	38.3

Note: Millennials are aged 18 to 35; Generation Xers are aged 36 to 47; Baby Boomers are aged 48 to 66; Older Americans are aged 67 or older.
Source: Survey Documentation and Analysis, Computer-assisted Survey Methods Program, University of California, Berkeley, General Social Survey, 1972–2012 Cumulative Data Files, Internet site http://sda.berkeley.edu/cgi-bin/hsda?harcsda+gss12; calculations by New Strategist

Table 1.5 Confidence in Major Companies, 2012

"As far as the people running these institutions are concerned, would you say you have a great deal of confidence, only some confidence, or hardly any confidence at all in them: major companies?"

(percent of people aged 18 or older responding by selected characteristics, 2012)

	total	a great deal	only some	hardly any
Total people	**100.0%**	**17.6%**	**62.0%**	**20.4%**
Men	100.0	19.0	61.5	19.5
Women	100.0	16.4	62.4	21.2
Millennials	100.0	19.2	61.5	19.3
Generation Xers	100.0	16.7	64.9	18.4
Baby Boomers	100.0	17.1	61.3	21.7
Older Americans	100.0	17.1	60.4	22.5
Black	100.0	14.1	63.1	22.8
Hispanic	100.0	16.2	64.6	19.3
Non-Hispanic white	100.0	18.2	61.1	20.7
Northeast	100.0	17.2	60.4	22.3
Midwest	100.0	18.1	59.0	23.0
South	100.0	18.6	62.5	19.0
West	100.0	16.1	65.3	18.6
Not a college graduate	100.0	15.8	62.9	21.4
Bachelor's degree or more	100.0	22.2	59.8	18.0

Note: Millennials are aged 18 to 35; Generation Xers are aged 36 to 47; Baby Boomers are aged 48 to 66; Older Americans are aged 67 or older.
Source: Survey Documentation and Analysis, Computer-assisted Survey Methods Program, University of California, Berkeley, General Social Survey, 1972–2012 Cumulative Data Files, Internet site http://sda.berkeley.edu/cgi-bin/hsda?harcsda+gss12; calculations by New Strategist

Table 1.6 Confidence in Organized Labor, 2012

"As far as the people running these institutions are concerned, would you say you have a great deal of confidence, only some confidence, or hardly any confidence at all in them: organized labor?"

(percent of people aged 18 or older responding by selected characteristics, 2012)

	total	a great deal	only some	hardly any
Total people	**100.0%**	**11.9%**	**58.0%**	**30.1%**
Men	100.0	12.8	51.7	35.5
Women	100.0	11.1	63.5	25.4
Millennials	100.0	16.1	66.3	17.6
Generation Xers	100.0	9.1	60.1	30.8
Baby Boomers	100.0	10.5	53.2	36.3
Older Americans	100.0	9.7	47.5	42.7
Black	100.0	13.6	67.8	18.6
Hispanic	100.0	17.6	64.0	18.4
Non-Hispanic white	100.0	9.4	54.9	35.7
Northeast	100.0	13.7	58.7	27.6
Midwest	100.0	11.6	58.5	29.9
South	100.0	11.4	55.5	33.1
West	100.0	11.5	61.1	27.5
Not a college graduate	100.0	11.7	61.1	27.2
Bachelor's degree or more	100.0	12.3	50.4	37.3

Note: Millennials are aged 18 to 35; Generation Xers are aged 36 to 47; Baby Boomers are aged 48 to 66; Older Americans are aged 67 or older.
Source: Survey Documentation and Analysis, Computer-assisted Survey Methods Program, University of California, Berkeley, General Social Survey, 1972–2012 Cumulative Data Files, Internet site http://sda.berkeley.edu/cgi-bin/hsda?harcsda+gss12; calculations by New Strategist

Table 1.7 Confidence in the Scientific Community, 2012

"As far as the people running these institutions are concerned, would you say you have a great deal of confidence, only some confidence, or hardly any confidence at all in them: the scientific community?"

(percent of people aged 18 or older responding by selected characteristics, 2012)

	total	a great deal	only some	hardly any
Total people	**100.0%**	**41.8%**	**51.0%**	**7.2%**
Men	100.0	47.1	46.6	6.3
Women	100.0	37.2	54.9	8.0
Millennials	100.0	46.1	47.0	6.9
Generation Xers	100.0	40.8	51.5	7.7
Baby Boomers	100.0	39.2	53.2	7.6
Older Americans	100.0	38.9	54.9	6.2
Black	100.0	28.0	58.9	13.2
Hispanic	100.0	47.8	45.1	7.1
Non-Hispanic white	100.0	43.4	50.4	6.2
Northeast	100.0	40.8	51.9	7.3
Midwest	100.0	51.8	42.5	5.7
South	100.0	34.1	56.2	9.7
West	100.0	44.9	50.4	4.7
Not a college graduate	100.0	38.0	53.3	8.7
Bachelor's degree or more	100.0	50.5	45.8	3.7

Note: Millennials are aged 18 to 35; Generation Xers are aged 36 to 47; Baby Boomers are aged 48 to 66; Older Americans are aged 67 or older.
Source: Survey Documentation and Analysis, Computer-assisted Survey Methods Program, University of California, Berkeley, General Social Survey, 1972–2012 Cumulative Data Files, Internet site http://sda.berkeley.edu/cgi-bin/hsda?harcsda+gss12; calculations by New Strategist

Table 1.8 Confidence in Medicine, 2012

"As far as the people running these institutions are concerned, would you say
you have a great deal of confidence, only some confidence, or hardly
any confidence at all in them: medicine?"

(percent of people aged 18 or older responding by selected characteristics, 2012)

	total	a great deal	only some	hardly any
Total people	**100.0%**	**39.2%**	**50.6%**	**10.2%**
Men	100.0	43.0	47.5	9.6
Women	100.0	36.0	53.3	10.8
Millennials	100.0	43.2	49.2	7.6
Generation Xers	100.0	36.4	52.2	11.4
Baby Boomers	100.0	35.8	53.2	10.9
Older Americans	100.0	42.0	45.5	12.5
Black	100.0	37.9	49.8	12.2
Hispanic	100.0	45.1	47.2	7.7
Non-Hispanic white	100.0	38.4	51.1	10.6
Northeast	100.0	38.9	51.6	9.5
Midwest	100.0	43.7	47.3	9.0
South	100.0	36.8	52.2	11.0
West	100.0	38.8	50.5	10.7
Not a college graduate	100.0	39.1	49.3	11.6
Bachelor's degree or more	100.0	39.4	53.8	6.9

Note: Millennials are aged 18 to 35; Generation Xers are aged 36 to 47; Baby Boomers are aged 48 to 66; Older Americans are aged 67 or older.
Source: Survey Documentation and Analysis, Computer-assisted Survey Methods Program, University of California, Berkeley, General Social Survey, 1972–2012 Cumulative Data Files, Internet site http://sda.berkeley.edu/cgi-bin/hsda?harcsda+gss12; calculations by New Strategist

Table 1.9 Confidence in Education, 2012

"As far as the people running these institutions are concerned, would you say you have a great deal of confidence, only some confidence, or hardly any confidence at all in them: education?"

(percent of people aged 18 or older responding by selected characteristics, 2012)

	total	a great deal	only some	hardly any
Total people	**100.0%**	**25.8%**	**58.3%**	**15.9%**
Men	100.0	24.3	59.1	16.6
Women	100.0	27.1	57.6	15.3
Millennials	100.0	31.1	52.7	16.3
Generation Xers	100.0	24.7	59.6	15.7
Baby Boomers	100.0	20.6	63.5	15.8
Older Americans	100.0	27.9	56.3	15.8
Black	100.0	36.1	53.0	10.9
Hispanic	100.0	39.0	49.6	11.4
Non-Hispanic white	100.0	19.1	62.3	18.6
Northeast	100.0	24.9	61.1	14.0
Midwest	100.0	24.3	64.3	11.4
South	100.0	24.7	60.1	15.2
West	100.0	29.7	47.6	22.8
Not a college graduate	100.0	28.8	56.4	14.8
Bachelor's degree or more	100.0	18.4	62.9	18.7

Note: Millennials are aged 18 to 35; Generation Xers are aged 36 to 47; Baby Boomers are aged 48 to 66; Older Americans are aged 67 or older.
Source: Survey Documentation and Analysis, Computer-assisted Survey Methods Program, University of California, Berkeley, General Social Survey, 1972–2012 Cumulative Data Files, Internet site http://sda.berkeley.edu/cgi-bin/hsda?harcsda+gss12; calculations by New Strategist

Table 1.10 Confidence in Organized Religion, 2012

"As far as the people running these institutions are concerned, would you say you have a great deal of confidence, only some confidence, or hardly any confidence at all in them: organized religion?"

(percent of people aged 18 or older responding by selected characteristics, 2012)

	total	a great deal	only some	hardly any
Total people	**100.0%**	**20.6%**	**55.0%**	**24.3%**
Men	100.0	19.9	54.2	25.9
Women	100.0	21.3	55.8	23.0
Millennials	100.0	17.2	56.5	26.3
Generation Xers	100.0	18.0	55.5	26.5
Baby Boomers	100.0	22.6	56.0	21.4
Older Americans	100.0	27.5	58.8	23.7
Black	100.0	25.7	58.9	15.4
Hispanic	100.0	19.3	55.3	25.4
Non-Hispanic white	100.0	22.5	48.7	28.8
Northeast	100.0	14.3	57.5	28.2
Midwest	100.0	19.4	58.9	21.7
South	100.0	23.8	55.0	21.2
West	100.0	21.6	49.5	29.0
Not a college graduate	100.0	21.8	53.0	25.3
Bachelor's degree or more	100.0	17.8	60.0	22.2

Note: Millennials are aged 18 to 35; Generation Xers are aged 36 to 47; Baby Boomers are aged 48 to 66; Older Americans are aged 67 or older.
Source: Survey Documentation and Analysis, Computer-assisted Survey Methods Program, University of California, Berkeley, General Social Survey, 1972–2012 Cumulative Data Files, Internet site http://sda.berkeley.edu/cgi-bin/hsda?harcsda+gss12; calculations by New Strategist

Table 1.11 Confidence in the Military, 2012

"As far as the people running these institutions are concerned, would you say you have a great deal of confidence, only some confidence, or hardly any confidence at all in them: the military?"

(percent of people aged 18 or older responding by selected characteristics, 2012)

	total	a great deal	only some	hardly any
Total people	**100.0%**	**55.2%**	**36.9%**	**7.9%**
Men	100.0	58.5	33.7	7.8
Women	100.0	52.4	39.6	8.0
Millennials	100.0	53.6	38.1	8.4
Generation Xers	100.0	56.2	37.8	6.0
Baby Boomers	100.0	56.5	36.1	7.4
Older Americans	100.0	54.5	34.4	11.2
Black	100.0	49.9	43.1	7.1
Hispanic	100.0	57.5	35.3	7.1
Non-Hispanic white	100.0	50.3	38.1	11.7
Northeast	100.0	46.8	44.2	9.0
Midwest	100.0	59.8	31.0	9.2
South	100.0	58.2	36.6	5.2
West	100.0	52.2	37.5	10.4
Not a college graduate	100.0	56.4	35.3	8.4
Bachelor's degree or more	100.0	52.2	40.9	6.9

Note: Millennials are aged 18 to 35; Generation Xers are aged 36 to 47; Baby Boomers are aged 48 to 66; Older Americans are aged 67 or older.
Source: Survey Documentation and Analysis, Computer-assisted Survey Methods Program, University of California, Berkeley, General Social Survey, 1972–2012 Cumulative Data Files, Internet site http://sda.berkeley.edu/cgi-bin/hsda?harcsda+gss12; calculations by New Strategist

Table 1.12 Confidence in the Press, 2012

"As far as the people running these institutions are concerned, would you say you have a great deal of confidence, only some confidence, or hardly any confidence at all in them: the press?"

(percent of people aged 18 or older responding by selected characteristics, 2012)

	total	a great deal	only some	hardly any
Total people	**100.0%**	**8.9%**	**44.1%**	**46.9%**
Men	100.0	8.7	42.8	48.5
Women	100.0	9.1	45.3	45.6
Millennials	100.0	10.3	43.1	46.7
Generation Xers	100.0	7.9	48.5	43.6
Baby Boomers	100.0	8.2	41.2	50.6
Older Americans	100.0	9.2	46.3	44.5
Black	100.0	13.4	45.3	41.3
Hispanic	100.0	6.5	42.8	50.6
Non-Hispanic white	100.0	9.8	46.6	43.6
Northeast	100.0	8.6	54.2	37.3
Midwest	100.0	9.5	43.6	47.0
South	100.0	8.9	39.7	51.3
West	100.0	8.8	44.0	47.3
Not a college graduate	100.0	8.5	45.1	46.3
Bachelor's degree or more	100.0	9.9	41.6	48.5

Note: Millennials are aged 18 to 35; Generation Xers are aged 36 to 47; Baby Boomers are aged 48 to 66; Older Americans are aged 67 or older.
Source: Survey Documentation and Analysis, Computer-assisted Survey Methods Program, University of California, Berkeley, General Social Survey, 1972–2012 Cumulative Data Files, Internet site http://sda.berkeley.edu/cgi-bin/hsda?harcsda+gss12; calculations by New Strategist

Table 1.13 Confidence in Television, 2012

"As far as the people running these institutions are concerned, would you say you have a great deal of confidence, only some confidence, or hardly any confidence at all in them: television?"

(percent of people aged 18 or older responding by selected characteristics, 2012)

	total	a great deal	only some	hardly any
Total people	**100.0%**	**10.4%**	**48.3%**	**41.4%**
Men	100.0	12.3	47.3	40.3
Women	100.0	8.7	49.1	42.2
Millennials	100.0	14.4	49.4	36.2
Generation Xers	100.0	10.1	45.2	44.7
Baby Boomers	100.0	6.8	48.0	45.2
Older Americans	100.0	10.1	50.6	39.2
Black	100.0	14.7	50.6	34.6
Hispanic	100.0	9.6	55.5	34.9
Non-Hispanic white	100.0	8.7	46.7	44.5
Northeast	100.0	9.9	49.0	41.1
Midwest	100.0	9.4	48.6	42.1
South	100.0	9.7	47.9	42.4
West	100.0	12.8	48.0	39.2
Not a college graduate	100.0	12.3	50.4	37.3
Bachelor's degree or more	100.0	5.7	42.9	51.4

Note: Millennials are aged 18 to 35; Generation Xers are aged 36 to 47; Baby Boomers are aged 48 to 66; Older Americans are aged 67 or older.
Source: Survey Documentation and Analysis, Computer-assisted Survey Methods Program, University of California, Berkeley, General Social Survey, 1972–2012 Cumulative Data Files, Internet site http://sda.berkeley.edu/cgi-bin/hsda?harcsda+gss12; calculations by New Strategist

Table 1.14 Federal Income Tax Level, 2012

"Do you consider the amount of federal income tax which you
have to pay as too high, about right, or too low?"

(percent of people aged 18 or older responding by selected characteristics, 2012)

	total	too high	about right	too low
Total people	**100.0%**	**52.0%**	**45.5%**	**2.5%**
Men	100.0	49.7	46.6	3.7
Women	100.0	53.9	44.6	1.5
Millennials	100.0	50.8	46.0	3.2
Generation Xers	100.0	52.3	44.9	2.7
Baby Boomers	100.0	57.1	40.9	2.0
Older Americans	100.0	40.2	58.1	1.8
Black	100.0	53.1	42.5	4.5
Hispanic	100.0	52.2	45.9	1.9
Non-Hispanic white	100.0	49.7	48.3	2.1
Northeast	100.0	61.6	37.5	0.9
Midwest	100.0	48.7	49.2	2.1
South	100.0	50.9	46.2	2.9
West	100.0	49.5	47.0	3.5
Not a college graduate	100.0	54.0	43.8	2.2
Bachelor's degree or more	100.0	46.8	49.8	3.4

Note: Millennials are aged 18 to 35; Generation Xers are aged 36 to 47; Baby Boomers are aged 48 to 66; Older Americans are aged 67 or older.
Source: Survey Documentation and Analysis, Computer-assisted Survey Methods Program, University of California, Berkeley, General Social Survey, 1972–2012 Cumulative Data Files, Internet site http://sda.berkeley.edu/cgi-bin/hsda?harcsda+gss12; calculations by New Strategist

Table 1.15 Should Marijuana Be Made Legal, 2012

"Do you think the use of marijuana should be made legal or not?"

(percent of people aged 18 or older responding by selected characteristics, 2012)

	total	legal	not legal
Total people	**100.0%**	**46.9%**	**53.1%**
Men	100.0	52.5	47.5
Women	100.0	42.3	57.7
Millennials	100.0	55.3	44.7
Generation Xers	100.0	41.7	58.3
Baby Boomers	100.0	49.0	51.0
Older Americans	100.0	33.0	67.0
Black	100.0	40.8	59.2
Hispanic	100.0	32.9	67.1
Non-Hispanic white	100.0	52.5	47.5
Northeast	100.0	49.1	50.9
Midwest	100.0	48.2	51.8
South	100.0	44.3	55.7
West	100.0	48.5	51.5
Not a college graduate	100.0	45.7	54.3
Bachelor's degree or more	100.0	50.1	49.9

Note: Millennials are aged 18 to 35; Generation Xers are aged 36 to 47; Baby Boomers are aged 48 to 66; Older Americans are aged 67 or older.
Source: Survey Documentation and Analysis, Computer-assisted Survey Methods Program, University of California, Berkeley, General Social Survey, 1972–2012 Cumulative Data Files, Internet site http://sda.berkeley.edu/cgi-bin/hsda?harcsda+gss12; calculations by New Strategist

Table 1.16 Favor or Oppose Gun Permits, 2012

"Would you favor or oppose a law which would require a person
to obtain a police permit before he or she could buy a gun?"

(percent of people aged 18 or older responding by selected characteristics, 2012)

	total	favor	oppose
Total people	**100.0%**	**73.7%**	**26.3%**
Men	100.0	66.9	33.1
Women	100.0	79.5	20.5
Millennials	100.0	67.7	32.3
Generation Xers	100.0	75.7	24.3
Baby Boomers	100.0	77.0	23.0
Older Americans	100.0	77.5	22.5
Black	100.0	82.9	17.1
Hispanic	100.0	72.2	27.8
Non-Hispanic white	100.0	72.2	27.8
Northeast	100.0	82.5	17.5
Midwest	100.0	75.6	24.4
South	100.0	69.6	30.4
West	100.0	72.0	28.0
Not a college graduate	100.0	74.2	25.8
Bachelor's degree or more	100.0	72.5	27.5

Note: Millennials are aged 18 to 35; Generation Xers are aged 36 to 47; Baby Boomers are aged 48 to 66; Older Americans are aged 67 or older.
Source: Survey Documentation and Analysis, Computer-assisted Survey Methods Program, University of California, Berkeley, General Social Survey, 1972–2012 Cumulative Data Files, Internet site http://sda.berkeley.edu/cgi-bin/hsda?harcsda+gss12; calculations by New Strategist

Table 1.17 Courts Deal Too Harshly with Criminals, 2012

"In general, do you think the courts in this area deal too harshly
or not harshly enough with criminals?"

(percent of people aged 18 or older responding by selected characteristics, 2012)

	total	too harsh	not harsh enough	about right
Total people	**100.0%**	**15.5%**	**62.5%**	**22.1%**
Men	100.0	17.6	60.1	22.3
Women	100.0	13.6	64.5	21.9
Millennials	100.0	20.8	56.8	22.3
Generation Xers	100.0	16.7	63.6	19.7
Baby Boomers	100.0	13.3	65.0	21.7
Older Americans	100.0	6.5	68.6	24.9
Black	100.0	23.9	57.4	18.8
Hispanic	100.0	24.3	55.8	20.0
Non-Hispanic white	100.0	10.9	65.4	23.6
Northeast	100.0	13.2	58.3	28.5
Midwest	100.0	11.5	69.9	18.7
South	100.0	15.4	62.0	22.6
West	100.0	21.1	59.1	19.8
Not a college graduate	100.0	15.7	66.1	18.2
Bachelor's degree or more	100.0	14.8	52.6	32.6

Note: Millennials are aged 18 to 35; Generation Xers are aged 36 to 47; Baby Boomers are aged 48 to 66; Older Americans are aged 67 or older.
Source: Survey Documentation and Analysis, Computer-assisted Survey Methods Program, University of California, Berkeley, General Social Survey, 1972–2012 Cumulative Data Files, Internet site http://sda.berkeley.edu/cgi-bin/hsda?harcsda+gss12; calculations by New Strategist

Table 1.18 Favor or Oppose Death Penalty for Murder, 2012

"Do you favor or oppose the death penalty for persons convicted of murder?"

(percent of people aged 18 or older responding by selected characteristics, 2012)

	total	favor	oppose
Total people	**100.0%**	**65.1%**	**34.9%**
Men	100.0	70.6	29.4
Women	100.0	60.3	39.7
Millennials	100.0	62.8	37.2
Generation Xers	100.0	67.2	32.8
Baby Boomers	100.0	66.6	33.4
Older Americans	100.0	64.1	35.9
Black	100.0	47.9	52.1
Hispanic	100.0	55.8	44.2
Non-Hispanic white	100.0	71.1	28.9
Northeast	100.0	60.0	40.0
Midwest	100.0	69.9	30.1
South	100.0	64.5	35.5
West	100.0	64.8	35.2
Not a college graduate	100.0	67.1	32.9
Bachelor's degree or more	100.0	59.8	40.2

Note: Millennials are aged 18 to 35; Generation Xers are aged 36 to 47; Baby Boomers are aged 48 to 66; Older Americans are aged 67 or older.
Source: Survey Documentation and Analysis, Computer-assisted Survey Methods Program, University of California, Berkeley, General Social Survey, 1972–2012 Cumulative Data Files, Internet site http://sda.berkeley.edu/cgi-bin/hsda?harcsda+gss12; calculations by New Strategist

Table 1.19 Allow Patients with Incurable Disease to Die, 2012

"When a person has a disease that cannot be cured, do you think doctors should be allowed by law to end the patient's life by some painless means if the patient and his family request it?"

(percent of people aged 18 or older responding by selected characteristics, 2012)

	total	yes	no
Total people	**100.0%**	**68.3%**	**31.7%**
Men	100.0	74.1	25.9
Women	100.0	63.1	36.9
Millennials	100.0	73.0	27.0
Generation Xers	100.0	64.7	35.3
Baby Boomers	100.0	68.4	31.6
Older Americans	100.0	60.7	39.3
Black	100.0	48.7	51.3
Hispanic	100.0	60.6	39.4
Non-Hispanic white	100.0	73.7	26.3
Northeast	100.0	78.6	21.4
Midwest	100.0	70.9	29.1
South	100.0	59.6	40.4
West	100.0	72.3	27.7
Not a college graduate	100.0	67.8	32.2
Bachelor's degree or more	100.0	69.7	30.3

Note: Millennials are aged 18 to 35; Generation Xers are aged 36 to 47; Baby Boomers are aged 48 to 66; Older Americans are aged 67 or older.
Source: Survey Documentation and Analysis, Computer-assisted Survey Methods Program, University of California, Berkeley, General Social Survey, 1972–2012 Cumulative Data Files, Internet site http://sda.berkeley.edu/cgi-bin/hsda?harcsda+gss12; calculations by New Strategist

Table 1.20 Expect World War in 10 Years, 2012

"Do you expect the United States to fight in another
world war within the next 10 years?"

(percent of people aged 18 or older responding by selected characteristics, 2012)

	total	yes	no
Total people	**100.0%**	**50.4%**	**49.6%**
Men	100.0	50.0	50.0
Women	100.0	50.9	49.1
Millennials	100.0	53.7	46.3
Generation Xers	100.0	52.8	47.2
Baby Boomers	100.0	44.5	55.5
Older Americans	100.0	50.0	50.0
Black	100.0	53.0	47.0
Hispanic	100.0	51.2	48.8
Non-Hispanic white	100.0	49.2	50.8
Northeast	100.0	33.7	66.3
Midwest	100.0	48.8	51.2
South	100.0	59.6	40.4
West	100.0	48.1	51.9
Not a college graduate	100.0	55.9	44.1
Bachelor's degree or more	100.0	35.1	64.9

Note: Millennials are aged 18 to 35; Generation Xers are aged 36 to 47; Baby Boomers are aged 48 to 66; Older Americans are aged 67 or older.
Source: Survey Documentation and Analysis, Computer-assisted Survey Methods Program, University of California, Berkeley, General Social Survey, 1972–2012 Cumulative Data Files, Internet site http://sda.berkeley.edu/cgi-bin/hsda?harcsda+gss12; calculations by New Strategist

Table 1.21 Allow Antireligious Book in Local Library, 2012

"There are always some people whose ideas are considered bad or dangerous by other people. For instance, somebody who is against all churches and religion: If some people in your community suggested that a book he wrote against churches and religion should be taken out of your public library, would you favor removing this book, or not?"

(percent of people aged 18 or older responding by selected characteristics, 2012)

	total	remove	not remove
Total people	**100.0%**	**23.1%**	**76.9%**
Men	100.0	22.6	77.4
Women	100.0	23.5	76.5
Millennials	100.0	20.2	79.8
Generation Xers	100.0	15.4	84.6
Baby Boomers	100.0	26.7	73.3
Older Americans	100.0	34.0	66.0
Black	100.0	40.6	59.4
Hispanic	100.0	22.0	78.0
Non-Hispanic white	100.0	18.7	81.3
Northeast	100.0	15.5	84.5
Midwest	100.0	19.5	80.5
South	100.0	32.1	67.9
West	100.0	17.0	83.0
Not a college graduate	100.0	27.3	72.7
Bachelor's degree or more	100.0	12.3	87.7

Note: Millennials are aged 18 to 35; Generation Xers are aged 36 to 47; Baby Boomers are aged 48 to 66; Older Americans are aged 67 or older.
Source: Survey Documentation and Analysis, Computer-assisted Survey Methods Program, University of California, Berkeley, General Social Survey, 1972–2012 Cumulative Data Files, Internet site http://sda.berkeley.edu/cgi-bin/hsda?harcsda+gss12; calculations by New Strategist

Table 1.22 Allow Someone Who Is Against Religion to Speak, 2012

"There are always some people whose ideas are considered bad or dangerous by other people. For instance, somebody who is against all churches and religion: If such a person wanted to make a speech in your (city/town/community) against churches and religion, should he be allowed to speak, or not?"

(percent of people aged 18 or older responding by selected characteristics, 2012)

	total	allow	disallow
Total people	**100.0%**	**77.2%**	**22.8%**
Men	100.0	77.9	22.1
Women	100.0	76.7	23.3
Millennials	100.0	79.1	20.9
Generation Xers	100.0	83.8	16.2
Baby Boomers	100.0	75.9	24.1
Older Americans	100.0	64.9	35.1
Black	100.0	67.9	32.1
Hispanic	100.0	66.2	33.8
Non-Hispanic white	100.0	83.1	16.9
Northeast	100.0	81.2	18.8
Midwest	100.0	80.9	19.1
South	100.0	71.4	28.6
West	100.0	80.6	19.4
Not a college graduate	100.0	71.4	28.6
Bachelor's degree or more	100.0	92.3	7.7

Note: Millennials are aged 18 to 35; Generation Xers are aged 36 to 47; Baby Boomers are aged 48 to 66; Older Americans are aged 67 or older.
Source: Survey Documentation and Analysis, Computer-assisted Survey Methods Program, University of California, Berkeley, General Social Survey, 1972–2012 Cumulative Data Files, Internet site http://sda.berkeley.edu/cgi-bin/hsda?harcsda+gss12; calculations by New Strategist

Table 1.23 Allow Someone Who Is Against Religion to Teach College, 2012

"There are always some people whose ideas are considered bad or dangerous by
other people. For instance, somebody who is against all churches and religion:
Should such a person be allowed to teach in a college or university, or not?"

(percent of people aged 18 or older responding by selected characteristics, 2012)

	total	allow	disallow
Total people	**100.0%**	**64.9%**	**35.1%**
Men	100.0	63.7	36.3
Women	100.0	66.0	34.0
Millennials	100.0	75.1	24.9
Generation Xers	100.0	70.0	30.0
Baby Boomers	100.0	60.7	39.3
Older Americans	100.0	41.3	58.7
Black	100.0	56.6	43.3
Hispanic	100.0	67.5	32.5
Non-Hispanic white	100.0	67.2	32.8
Northeast	100.0	67.0	33.0
Midwest	100.0	66.0	34.0
South	100.0	61.4	38.6
West	100.0	68.4	31.6
Not a college graduate	100.0	58.9	41.1
Bachelor's degree or more	100.0	80.2	19.8

*Note: Millennials are aged 18 to 35; Generation Xers are aged 36 to 47; Baby Boomers are aged 48 to 66; Older Americans
are aged 67 or older.*
*Source: Survey Documentation and Analysis, Computer-assisted Survey Methods Program, University of California, Berkeley,
General Social Survey, 1972–2012 Cumulative Data Files, Internet site http://sda.berkeley.edu/cgi-bin/hsda?harcsda+gss12;
calculations by New Strategist*

Table 1.24 Allow a Communist's Book in the Local Library, 2012

"Suppose a man who admits he is a communist wrote a book which is in your public library. Somebody in your community suggests that the book should be removed from the library. Would you favor removing it, or not?"

(percent of people aged 18 or older responding by selected characteristics, 2012)

	total	remove	not remove
Total people	**100.0%**	**26.6%**	**73.4%**
Men	100.0	24.5	75.5
Women	100.0	28.4	71.6
Millennials	100.0	26.3	73.7
Generation Xers	100.0	19.1	80.9
Baby Boomers	100.0	28.0	72.0
Older Americans	100.0	36.2	63.8
Black	100.0	40.0	60.0
Hispanic	100.0	33.7	66.3
Non-Hispanic white	100.0	22.1	77.9
Northeast	100.0	22.4	77.6
Midwest	100.0	22.9	77.1
South	100.0	32.1	67.9
West	100.0	24.2	75.8
Not a college graduate	100.0	32.5	67.5
Bachelor's degree or more	100.0	11.9	88.1

Note: Millennials are aged 18 to 35; Generation Xers are aged 36 to 47; Baby Boomers are aged 48 to 66; Older Americans are aged 67 or older.
Source: Survey Documentation and Analysis, Computer-assisted Survey Methods Program, University of California, Berkeley, General Social Survey, 1972–2012 Cumulative Data Files, Internet site http://sda.berkeley.edu/cgi-bin/hsda?harcsda+gss12; calculations by New Strategist

Table 1.25 Allow a Communist to Speak, 2012

"Suppose an admitted communist wanted to make a speech in your community.
Should he be allowed to speak, or not?"

(percent of people aged 18 or older responding by selected characteristics, 2012)

	total	allow	disallow
Total people	**100.0%**	**67.2%**	**32.8%**
Men	100.0	68.2	31.8
Women	100.0	66.3	33.7
Millennials	100.0	67.4	32.6
Generation Xers	100.0	79.3	20.7
Baby Boomers	100.0	64.9	35.1
Older Americans	100.0	52.6	47.4
Black	100.0	62.0	38.0
Hispanic	100.0	59.2	40.8
Non-Hispanic white	100.0	71.7	28.3
Northeast	100.0	70.9	29.1
Midwest	100.0	69.9	30.1
South	100.0	60.8	39.2
West	100.0	72.5	27.5
Not a college graduate	100.0	58.5	41.5
Bachelor's degree or more	100.0	88.9	11.1

Note: Millennials are aged 18 to 35; Generation Xers are aged 36 to 47; Baby Boomers are aged 48 to 66; Older Americans are aged 67 or older.
Source: Survey Documentation and Analysis, Computer-assisted Survey Methods Program, University of California, Berkeley, General Social Survey, 1972–2012 Cumulative Data Files, Internet site http://sda.berkeley.edu/cgi-bin/hsda?harcsda+gss12; calculations by New Strategist

Table 1.26 Allow a Communist to Teach College, 2012

"What about a man who admits he is a communist? Suppose he
is teaching in a college. Should he be fired, or not?"

(percent of people aged 18 or older responding by selected characteristics, 2012)

	total	fired	not fired
Total people	**100.0%**	**34.6%**	**65.4%**
Men	100.0	33.2	66.8
Women	100.0	35.9	64.1
Millennials	100.0	30.8	69.2
Generation Xers	100.0	25.7	74.3
Baby Boomers	100.0	38.6	61.4
Older Americans	100.0	49.0	51.0
Black	100.0	44.0	56.0
Hispanic	100.0	35.0	65.0
Non-Hispanic white	100.0	31.7	68.3
Northeast	100.0	29.0	71.0
Midwest	100.0	32.7	67.3
South	100.0	38.8	61.2
West	100.0	33.6	66.4
Not a college graduate	100.0	41.6	58.4
Bachelor's degree or more	100.0	16.8	83.2

Note: Millennials are aged 18 to 35; Generation Xers are aged 36 to 47; Baby Boomers are aged 48 to 66; Older Americans are aged 67 or older.
Source: Survey Documentation and Analysis, Computer-assisted Survey Methods Program, University of California, Berkeley, General Social Survey, 1972–2012 Cumulative Data Files, Internet site http://sda.berkeley.edu/cgi-bin/hsda?harcsda+gss12; calculations by New Strategist

Table 1.27 Allow a Homosexual's Book in the Local Library, 2012

"What about a man who admits that he is a homosexual? If some people in your community suggested that a book he wrote in favor of homosexuality should be taken out of your public library, would you favor removing this book, or not?"

(percent of people aged 18 or older responding by selected characteristics, 2012)

	total	remove	not remove
Total people	**100.0%**	**20.3%**	**79.7%**
Men	100.0	22.0	78.0
Women	100.0	18.9	81.1
Millennials	100.0	17.0	83.0
Generation Xers	100.0	17.1	82.9
Baby Boomers	100.0	18.4	81.6
Older Americans	100.0	39.5	60.5
Black	100.0	30.2	69.8
Hispanic	100.0	23.3	76.7
Non-Hispanic white	100.0	17.1	82.9
Northeast	100.0	14.6	85.4
Midwest	100.0	18.9	81.1
South	100.0	27.5	72.5
West	100.0	13.7	86.3
Not a college graduate	100.0	24.6	75.4
Bachelor's degree or more	100.0	9.6	90.4

Note: Millennials are aged 18 to 35; Generation Xers are aged 36 to 47; Baby Boomers are aged 48 to 66; Older Americans are aged 67 or older.
Source: Survey Documentation and Analysis, Computer-assisted Survey Methods Program, University of California, Berkeley, General Social Survey, 1972–2012 Cumulative Data Files, Internet site http://sda.berkeley.edu/cgi-bin/hsda?harcsda+gss12; calculations by New Strategist

Table 1.28 Allow a Homosexual to Speak, 2012

"What about a man who admits that he is a homosexual? Suppose this admitted homosexual wanted to make a speech in your community. Should he be allowed to speak, or not?"

(percent of people aged 18 or older responding by selected characteristics, 2012)

	total	allow	disallow
Total people	**100.0%**	**86.6%**	**13.4%**
Men	100.0	82.7	17.3
Women	100.0	89.9	10.1
Millennials	100.0	89.6	10.4
Generation Xers	100.0	91.3	8.7
Baby Boomers	100.0	85.9	14.1
Older Americans	100.0	73.4	26.6
Black	100.0	83.0	17.0
Hispanic	100.0	88.3	11.7
Non-Hispanic white	100.0	88.7	11.3
Northeast	100.0	87.0	13.0
Midwest	100.0	90.6	9.4
South	100.0	82.5	17.5
West	100.0	89.6	10.4
Not a college graduate	100.0	82.2	17.8
Bachelor's degree or more	100.0	97.9	2.1

Note: Millennials are aged 18 to 35; Generation Xers are aged 36 to 47; Baby Boomers are aged 48 to 66; Older Americans are aged 67 or older.
Source: Survey Documentation and Analysis, Computer-assisted Survey Methods Program, University of California, Berkeley, General Social Survey, 1972–2012 Cumulative Data Files, Internet site http://sda.berkeley.edu/cgi-bin/hsda?harcsda+gss12; calculations by New Strategist

Table 1.29 Allow a Homosexual to Teach College, 2012

"What about a man who admits that he is a homosexual? Should such a person be allowed to teach in a college or university, or not?"

(percent of people aged 18 or older responding by selected characteristics, 2012)

	total	allow	disallow
Total people	**100.0%**	**84.3%**	**15.7%**
Men	100.0	80.1	19.9
Women	100.0	87.8	12.2
Millennials	100.0	88.7	11.3
Generation Xers	100.0	88.7	11.3
Baby Boomers	100.0	83.3	16.7
Older Americans	100.0	67.5	32.5
Black	100.0	80.8	19.2
Hispanic	100.0	86.7	13.3
Non-Hispanic white	100.0	86.2	13.8
Northeast	100.0	85.6	14.4
Midwest	100.0	86.2	13.8
South	100.0	82.5	17.5
West	100.0	84.4	15.6
Not a college graduate	100.0	79.7	20.3
Bachelor's degree or more	100.0	95.9	4.1

Note: Millennials are aged 18 to 35; Generation Xers are aged 36 to 47; Baby Boomers are aged 48 to 66; Older Americans are aged 67 or older.
Source: Survey Documentation and Analysis, Computer-assisted Survey Methods Program, University of California, Berkeley, General Social Survey, 1972–2012 Cumulative Data Files, Internet site http://sda.berkeley.edu/cgi-bin/hsda?harcsda+gss12; calculations by New Strategist

Table 1.30 Allow a Militarist's Book in the Local Library, 2012

"Consider a person who advocates doing away with elections and letting
the military run the country. Suppose he wrote a book advocating doing away
with elections and letting the military run the country. Somebody in your
community suggests that the book should be removed from
the library. Would you favor removing it, or not?"

(percent of people aged 18 or older responding by selected characteristics, 2012)

	total	remove	not remove
Total people	**100.0%**	**27.1%**	**72.9%**
Men	100.0	27.0	73.0
Women	100.0	27.2	72.8
Millennials	100.0	24.5	75.5
Generation Xers	100.0	19.2	80.8
Baby Boomers	100.0	28.2	71.8
Older Americans	100.0	44.1	55.9
Black	100.0	39.0	61.0
Hispanic	100.0	34.9	65.1
Non-Hispanic white	100.0	22.3	77.7
Northeast	100.0	22.3	77.7
Midwest	100.0	24.6	75.4
South	100.0	32.7	67.3
West	100.0	23.8	76.2
Not a college graduate	100.0	33.1	66.9
Bachelor's degree or more	100.0	12.0	88.0

Note: Millennials are aged 18 to 35; Generation Xers are aged 36 to 47; Baby Boomers are aged 48 to 66; Older Americans are aged 67 or older.
Source: Survey Documentation and Analysis, Computer-assisted Survey Methods Program, University of California, Berkeley, General Social Survey, 1972–2012 Cumulative Data Files, Internet site http://sda.berkeley.edu/cgi-bin/hsda?harcsda+gss12; calculations by New Strategist

Table 1.31 Allow a Militarist to Speak, 2012

"Consider a person who advocates doing away with elections and letting the military run the country. If such a person wanted to make a speech in your community, should he be allowed to speak, or not?"

(percent of people aged 18 or older responding by selected characteristics, 2012)

	total	allow	disallow
Total people	**100.0%**	**68.9%**	**31.1%**
Men	100.0	68.7	31.3
Women	100.0	69.2	30.8
Millennials	100.0	68.8	31.2
Generation Xers	100.0	79.9	20.1
Baby Boomers	100.0	67.3	32.7
Older Americans	100.0	55.1	44.9
Black	100.0	66.2	33.8
Hispanic	100.0	61.2	38.8
Non-Hispanic white	100.0	73.5	26.5
Northeast	100.0	69.9	30.1
Midwest	100.0	74.1	25.9
South	100.0	63.7	36.3
West	100.0	72.2	27.8
Not a college graduate	100.0	62.2	37.8
Bachelor's degree or more	100.0	86.4	13.6

Note: Millennials are aged 18 to 35; Generation Xers are aged 36 to 47; Baby Boomers are aged 48 to 66; Older Americans are aged 67 or older.
Source: Survey Documentation and Analysis, Computer-assisted Survey Methods Program, University of California, Berkeley, General Social Survey, 1972–2012 Cumulative Data Files, Internet site http://sda.berkeley.edu/cgi-bin/hsda?harcsda+gss12; calculations by New Strategist

Table 1.32 Allow a Militarist to Teach College, 2012

"Consider a person who advocates doing away with elections and letting
the military run the country. Should such a person be allowed
to teach in a college or university, or not?"

(percent of people aged 18 or older responding by selected characteristics, 2012)

	total	allow	disallow
Total people	**100.0%**	**57.3%**	**42.7%**
Men	100.0	57.6	42.4
Women	100.0	57.0	43.0
Millennials	100.0	60.6	39.4
Generation Xers	100.0	68.4	31.6
Baby Boomers	100.0	54.8	45.2
Older Americans	100.0	37.1	62.9
Black	100.0	49.4	50.6
Hispanic	100.0	56.1	43.9
Non-Hispanic white	100.0	60.9	39.1
Northeast	100.0	60.2	39.8
Midwest	100.0	58.0	42.0
South	100.0	54.3	45.7
West	100.0	59.4	40.6
Not a college graduate	100.0	51.5	48.5
Bachelor's degree or more	100.0	72.1	27.9

Note: Millennials are aged 18 to 35; Generation Xers are aged 36 to 47; Baby Boomers are aged 48 to 66; Older Americans are aged 67 or older.
Source: Survey Documentation and Analysis, Computer-assisted Survey Methods Program, University of California, Berkeley, General Social Survey, 1972–2012 Cumulative Data Files, Internet site http://sda.berkeley.edu/cgi-bin/hsda?harcsda+gss12; calculations by New Strategist

Table 1.33 Allow a Racist's Book in the Local Library, 2012

"Consider a person who believes that blacks are genetically inferior. If some people in your community suggested that a book he wrote which said blacks are inferior should be taken out of your public library, would you favor removing this book, or not?"

(percent of people aged 18 or older responding by selected characteristics, 2012)

	total	remove	not remove
Total people	**100.0%**	**35.5%**	**64.5%**
Men	100.0	32.8	67.2
Women	100.0	37.8	62.2
Millennials	100.0	42.6	57.4
Generation Xers	100.0	28.1	71.9
Baby Boomers	100.0	33.6	66.4
Older Americans	100.0	34.8	65.2
Black	100.0	50.5	49.5
Hispanic	100.0	48.8	51.2
Non-Hispanic white	100.0	29.6	70.4
Northeast	100.0	39.6	60.4
Midwest	100.0	28.9	71.1
South	100.0	38.7	61.3
West	100.0	33.5	66.5
Not a college graduate	100.0	39.2	60.8
Bachelor's degree or more	100.0	26.2	73.8

Note: Millennials are aged 18 to 35; Generation Xers are aged 36 to 47; Baby Boomers are aged 48 to 66; Older Americans are aged 67 or older.
Source: Survey Documentation and Analysis, Computer-assisted Survey Methods Program, University of California, Berkeley, General Social Survey, 1972–2012 Cumulative Data Files, Internet site http://sda.berkeley.edu/cgi-bin/hsda?harcsda+gss12; calculations by New Strategist

Table 1.34 Allow a Racist to Speak, 2012

"Consider a person who believes that blacks are genetically inferior. If such
a person wanted to make a speech in your community claiming that
blacks are inferior, should he be allowed to speak, or not?"

(percent of people aged 18 or older responding by selected characteristics, 2012)

	total	allow	disallow
Total people	**100.0%**	**58.2%**	**41.8%**
Men	100.0	60.7	39.3
Women	100.0	56.0	44.0
Millennials	100.0	53.6	46.4
Generation Xers	100.0	64.8	35.2
Baby Boomers	100.0	59.8	40.2
Older Americans	100.0	53.7	46.3
Black	100.0	55.0	45.0
Hispanic	100.0	43.4	56.6
Non-Hispanic white	100.0	64.5	35.5
Northeast	100.0	57.2	42.8
Midwest	100.0	61.8	38.2
South	100.0	56.7	43.3
West	100.0	57.9	42.1
Not a college graduate	100.0	52.5	47.5
Bachelor's degree or more	100.0	72.5	27.5

Note: Millennials are aged 18 to 35; Generation Xers are aged 36 to 47; Baby Boomers are aged 48 to 66; Older Americans are aged 67 or older.
Source: Survey Documentation and Analysis, Computer-assisted Survey Methods Program, University of California, Berkeley, General Social Survey, 1972–2012 Cumulative Data Files, Internet site http://sda.berkeley.edu/cgi-bin/hsda?harcsda+gss12; calculations by New Strategist

Table 1.35 Allow a Racist to Teach College, 2012

"Consider a person who believes that blacks are genetically inferior. Should such a person be allowed to teach in a college or university, or not?"

(percent of people aged 18 or older responding by selected characteristics, 2012)

	total	allow	disallow
Total people	**100.0%**	**46.8%**	**53.2%**
Men	100.0	46.6	53.4
Women	100.0	46.9	53.1
Millennials	100.0	44.9	55.1
Generation Xers	100.0	54.2	45.8
Baby Boomers	100.0	46.7	53.3
Older Americans	100.0	39.7	60.3
Black	100.0	39.8	60.2
Hispanic	100.0	40.3	59.7
Non-Hispanic white	100.0	51.0	49.0
Northeast	100.0	42.8	57.2
Midwest	100.0	48.2	51.8
South	100.0	46.4	53.6
West	100.0	49.1	50.9
Not a college graduate	100.0	43.4	56.6
Bachelor's degree or more	100.0	55.6	44.4

Note: Millennials are aged 18 to 35; Generation Xers are aged 36 to 47; Baby Boomers are aged 48 to 66; Older Americans are aged 67 or older.
Source: Survey Documentation and Analysis, Computer-assisted Survey Methods Program, University of California, Berkeley, General Social Survey, 1972–2012 Cumulative Data Files, Internet site http://sda.berkeley.edu/cgi-bin/hsda?harcsda+gss12; calculations by New Strategist

Table 1.36 Suicide if Person Has an Incurable Disease, 2012

"Do you think a person has the right to end his or her own life
if this person has an incurable disease?"

(percent of people aged 18 or older responding by selected characteristics, 2012)

	total	yes	no
Total people	**100.0%**	**58.8%**	**41.2%**
Men	100.0	64.4	35.6
Women	100.0	53.9	46.1
Millennials	100.0	59.6	40.4
Generation Xers	100.0	60.8	39.2
Baby Boomers	100.0	60.0	40.0
Older Americans	100.0	50.8	49.2
Black	100.0	44.6	55.4
Hispanic	100.0	41.3	58.7
Non-Hispanic white	100.0	65.6	34.4
Northeast	100.0	67.1	32.9
Midwest	100.0	59.0	41.0
South	100.0	51.4	48.6
West	100.0	64.6	35.4
Not a college graduate	100.0	55.9	44.1
Bachelor's degree or more	100.0	66.9	33.1

Note: Millennials are aged 18 to 35; Generation Xers are aged 36 to 47; Baby Boomers are aged 48 to 66; Older Americans are aged 67 or older.
Source: Survey Documentation and Analysis, Computer-assisted Survey Methods Program, University of California, Berkeley, General Social Survey, 1972–2012 Cumulative Data Files, Internet site http://sda.berkeley.edu/cgi-bin/hsda?harcsda+gss12; calculations by New Strategist

Table 1.37 Suicide if Bankrupt, 2012

"Do you think a person has the right to end his or her own life
if this person has gone bankrupt?"

(percent of people aged 18 or older responding by selected characteristics, 2012)

	total	yes	no
Total people	**100.0%**	**11.2%**	**88.8%**
Men	100.0	14.5	85.5
Women	100.0	8.4	91.6
Millennials	100.0	13.3	86.7
Generation Xers	100.0	12.3	87.7
Baby Boomers	100.0	9.6	90.4
Older Americans	100.0	7.7	92.3
Black	100.0	10.6	89.4
Hispanic	100.0	5.1	94.9
Non-Hispanic white	100.0	13.0	87.0
Northeast	100.0	11.5	88.5
Midwest	100.0	7.8	92.2
South	100.0	12.5	87.5
West	100.0	12.4	87.6
Not a college graduate	100.0	9.2	90.8
Bachelor's degree or more	100.0	16.6	83.4

Note: Millennials are aged 18 to 35; Generation Xers are aged 36 to 47; Baby Boomers are aged 48 to 66; Older Americans are aged 67 or older.
Source: Survey Documentation and Analysis, Computer-assisted Survey Methods Program, University of California, Berkeley, General Social Survey, 1972–2012 Cumulative Data Files, Internet site http://sda.berkeley.edu/cgi-bin/hsda?harcsda+gss12; calculations by New Strategist

Table 1.38 Suicide if Person Has Dishonored Family, 2012

"Do you think a person has the right to end his or her own life
if this person has dishonored his or her family?"

(percent of people aged 18 or older responding by selected characteristics, 2012)

	total	yes	no
Total people	**100.0%**	**10.9%**	**89.1%**
Men	100.0	13.1	86.9
Women	100.0	8.9	91.1
Millennials	100.0	13.7	86.3
Generation Xers	100.0	12.1	87.9
Baby Boomers	100.0	8.7	91.3
Older Americans	100.0	6.0	94.0
Black	100.0	8.3	91.7
Hispanic	100.0	6.0	94.0
Non-Hispanic white	100.0	12.6	87.4
Northeast	100.0	11.3	88.7
Midwest	100.0	8.1	91.9
South	100.0	11.2	88.8
West	100.0	12.7	87.3
Not a college graduate	100.0	8.5	91.5
Bachelor's degree or more	100.0	17.1	82.9

Note: Millennials are aged 18 to 35; Generation Xers are aged 36 to 47; Baby Boomers are aged 48 to 66; Older Americans are aged 67 or older.
Source: Survey Documentation and Analysis, Computer-assisted Survey Methods Program, University of California, Berkeley, General Social Survey, 1972–2012 Cumulative Data Files, Internet site http://sda.berkeley.edu/cgi-bin/hsda?harcsda+gss12; calculations by New Strategist

Table 1.39 Suicide if Ready to Die, 2012

"Do you think a person has the right to end his or her own life
if this person is tired of living and ready to die?"

(percent of people aged 18 or older responding by selected characteristics, 2012)

	total	yes	no
Total people	**100.0%**	**18.9%**	**81.1%**
Men	100.0	21.7	78.3
Women	100.0	16.5	83.5
Millennials	100.0	20.2	79.8
Generation Xers	100.0	18.6	81.4
Baby Boomers	100.0	18.1	81.9
Older Americans	100.0	18.2	81.8
Black	100.0	11.8	88.2
Hispanic	100.0	13.0	87.0
Non-Hispanic white	100.0	21.6	78.4
Northeast	100.0	20.6	79.4
Midwest	100.0	14.1	85.9
South	100.0	19.1	80.9
West	100.0	22.2	77.8
Not a college graduate	100.0	17.2	82.8
Bachelor's degree or more	100.0	23.5	76.5

Note: Millennials are aged 18 to 35; Generation Xers are aged 36 to 47; Baby Boomers are aged 48 to 66; Older Americans are aged 67 or older.
Source: Survey Documentation and Analysis, Computer-assisted Survey Methods Program, University of California, Berkeley, General Social Survey, 1972–2012 Cumulative Data Files, Internet site http://sda.berkeley.edu/cgi-bin/hsda?harcsda+gss12; calculations by New Strategist

The Public Arena: Historical Trends

Table 1.40 Confidence in Executive Branch of Government, 1973 to 2012

"As far as the people running these institutions are concerned, would you say you have a great deal of confidence, only some confidence, or hardly any confidence at all in them: the executive branch of the federal government?"

(percent distribution of people aged 18 or older by response for selected years)

	total	a great deal	only some	hardly any
2012	100.0%	14.6%	49.4%	36.1%
2010	100.0	17.0	45.7	37.3
2008	100.0	10.9	50.3	38.9
2006	100.0	16.0	45.9	38.1
2004	100.0	22.0	47.2	30.8
2002	100.0	27.8	51.6	20.6
2000	100.0	14.1	50.7	35.2
1998	100.0	13.7	49.7	36.6
1996	100.0	10.2	46.2	43.6
1994	100.0	11.5	52.8	35.7
1993	100.0	11.7	54.7	33.6
1991	100.0	27.2	51.0	21.8
1990	100.0	24.7	51.4	23.9
1989	100.0	21.5	57.2	21.3
1988	100.0	17.1	55.4	27.5
1987	100.0	19.3	53.3	27.4
1986	100.0	21.8	55.0	23.1
1984	100.0	20.0	52.2	27.8
1983	100.0	13.6	56.2	30.2
1982	100.0	20.8	54.7	24.5
1980	100.0	12.7	52.6	34.7
1978	100.0	12.0	61.9	26.2
1977	100.0	28.3	57.3	14.4
1976	100.0	13.4	61.2	25.4
1975	100.0	13.4	56.8	29.7
1974	100.0	13.9	43.2	42.9
1973	100.0	29.4	52.0	18.6

Source: Survey Documentation and Analysis, Computer-assisted Survey Methods Program, University of California, Berkeley, General Social Survey, 1972–2012 Cumulative Data Files, Internet site http://sda.berkeley.edu/cgi-bin/hsda?harcsda+gss12; calculations by New Strategist

Table 1.41 Confidence in Legislative Branch of Government, 1973 to 2012

"As far as the people running these institutions are concerned, would you say you have a great deal of confidence, only some confidence, or hardly any confidence at all in them: the legislative branch of the federal government?"

(percent distribution of people aged 18 or older by response for selected years)

	total	a great deal	only some	hardly any
2012	100.0%	6.8%	45.9%	47.3%
2010	100.0	10.1	46.9	43.0
2008	100.0	10.5	51.9	37.6
2006	100.0	11.9	54.1	34.0
2004	100.0	14.8	59.3	25.9
2002	100.0	14.0	60.3	25.6
2000	100.0	13.3	57.6	29.1
1998	100.0	10.7	58.1	31.3
1996	100.0	7.4	48.5	44.1
1994	100.0	8.2	51.5	40.2
1993	100.0	6.6	51.3	42.1
1991	100.0	18.1	55.6	26.3
1990	100.0	16.2	60.4	23.4
1989	100.0	18.1	60.2	21.7
1988	100.0	16.5	63.7	19.9
1987	100.0	17.0	63.9	19.1
1986	100.0	16.6	63.3	20.1
1984	100.0	14.1	64.7	21.2
1983	100.0	9.9	67.0	23.1
1982	100.0	13.5	63.5	23.1
1980	100.0	9.6	56.0	34.4
1978	100.0	12.8	66.1	21.1
1977	100.0	19.7	62.8	17.5
1976	100.0	13.7	59.7	26.7
1975	100.0	13.6	60.2	26.2
1974	100.0	17.5	61.0	21.5
1973	100.0	23.9	60.3	15.7

Source: Survey Documentation and Analysis, Computer-assisted Survey Methods Program, University of California, Berkeley, General Social Survey, 1972–2012 Cumulative Data Files, Internet site http://sda.berkeley.edu/cgi-bin/hsda?harcsda+gss12; calculations by New Strategist

Table 1.42 Confidence in the United States Supreme Court, 1973 to 2012

"As far as the people running these institutions are concerned, would you say
you have a great deal of confidence, only some confidence, or hardly
any confidence at all in them: the United States Supreme Court?"

(percent distribution of people aged 18 or older by response for selected years)

	total	a great deal	only some	hardly any
2012	100.0%	29.5%	54.3%	16.1%
2010	100.0	30.5	52.1	17.4
2008	100.0	31.6	54.2	14.2
2006	100.0	33.9	50.8	15.4
2004	100.0	32.1	53.0	14.9
2002	100.0	37.4	51.4	11.2
2000	100.0	34.4	52.3	13.3
1998	100.0	32.7	52.7	14.6
1996	100.0	29.8	52.1	18.2
1994	100.0	32.2	51.5	16.3
1993	100.0	31.4	54.7	13.9
1991	100.0	39.0	47.9	13.1
1990	100.0	36.0	50.7	13.3
1989	100.0	36.3	53.3	10.4
1988	100.0	36.6	52.9	10.5
1987	100.0	38.9	50.4	10.7
1986	100.0	31.4	54.3	14.3
1984	100.0	36.3	50.9	12.8
1983	100.0	28.3	57.7	14.0
1982	100.0	31.2	56.0	12.8
1980	100.0	25.8	53.3	20.9
1978	100.0	30.9	54.6	14.5
1977	100.0	37.3	51.8	10.9
1976	100.0	36.1	47.6	16.3
1975	100.0	31.7	49.0	19.2
1974	100.0	34.4	50.0	15.6
1973	100.0	31.9	52.4	15.7

Source: Survey Documentation and Analysis, Computer-assisted Survey Methods Program, University of California, Berkeley, General Social Survey, 1972–2012 Cumulative Data Files, Internet site http://sda.berkeley.edu/cgi-bin/hsda?harcsda+gss12; calculations by New Strategist

Table 1.43 Confidence in Banks and Financial Institutions, 1975 to 2012

"As far as the people running these institutions are concerned, would you say
you have a great deal of confidence, only some confidence, or hardly
any confidence at all in them: banks and financial institutions?"

(percent distribution of people aged 18 or older by response for selected years)

	total	a great deal	only some	hardly any
2012	100.0%	11.9%	51.8%	36.3%
2010	100.0	10.6	47.5	41.9
2008	100.0	19.2	60.5	20.3
2006	100.0	30.1	56.5	13.4
2004	100.0	29.6	57.3	13.1
2002	100.0	22.7	59.4	17.9
2000	100.0	30.2	55.8	14.0
1998	100.0	26.6	57.1	16.3
1996	100.0	25.1	58.1	16.8
1994	100.0	18.3	61.7	20.0
1993	100.0	14.8	57.8	27.4
1991	100.0	12.2	53.0	34.8
1990	100.0	17.2	60.1	22.7
1989	100.0	19.1	61.1	19.8
1988	100.0	27.6	58.7	13.7
1987	100.0	28.0	57.9	14.0
1986	100.0	21.1	61.6	17.3
1984	100.0	31.4	57.6	11.0
1983	100.0	23.3	60.8	15.9
1982	100.0	26.3	56.9	16.9
1980	100.0	33.0	50.7	16.3
1978	100.0	31.1	57.0	12.0
1977	100.0	42.6	48.8	8.6
1976	100.0	39.8	50.1	10.1
1975	100.0	32.3	56.7	10.9

*Source: Survey Documentation and Analysis, Computer-assisted Survey Methods Program, University of California, Berkeley,
General Social Survey, 1972–2012 Cumulative Data Files, Internet site http://sda.berkeley.edu/cgi-bin/hsda?harcsda+gss12;
calculations by New Strategist*

Table 1.44 Confidence in Major Companies, 1973 to 2012

"As far as the people running these institutions are concerned, would you say you have a great deal of confidence, only some confidence, or hardly any confidence at all in them: major companies?"

(percent distribution of people aged 18 or older by response for selected years)

	total	a great deal	only some	hardly any
2012	100.0%	17.6%	62.0%	20.4%
2010	100.0	13.3	62.2	24.5
2008	100.0	16.0	67.4	16.6
2006	100.0	18.3	63.5	18.3
2004	100.0	18.7	63.8	17.5
2002	100.0	17.7	65.4	17.0
2000	100.0	29.5	59.9	10.6
1998	100.0	27.6	59.1	13.3
1996	100.0	25.0	61.5	13.5
1994	100.0	27.0	63.4	9.5
1993	100.0	22.0	65.4	12.6
1991	100.0	20.8	65.4	13.8
1990	100.0	26.5	62.1	11.4
1989	100.0	26.3	63.7	10.0
1988	100.0	25.9	63.0	11.1
1987	100.0	31.7	59.2	9.1
1986	100.0	25.6	64.5	9.9
1984	100.0	31.6	60.0	8.4
1983	100.0	24.3	60.6	15.1
1982	100.0	23.2	61.9	14.9
1980	100.0	28.3	56.9	14.8
1978	100.0	22.4	61.9	15.7
1977	100.0	28.2	59.0	12.9
1976	100.0	22.1	55.0	22.9
1975	100.0	20.5	56.7	22.9
1974	100.0	32.4	52.8	14.8
1973	100.0	31.1	56.9	12.0

Source: Survey Documentation and Analysis, Computer-assisted Survey Methods Program, University of California, Berkeley, General Social Survey, 1972–2012 Cumulative Data Files, Internet site http://sda.berkeley.edu/cgi-bin/hsda?harcsda+gss12; calculations by New Strategist

Table 1.45 Confidence in Organized Labor, 1973 to 2012

"As far as the people running these institutions are concerned, would you say you have a great deal of confidence, only some confidence, or hardly any confidence at all in them: organized labor?"

(percent distribution of people aged 18 or older by response for selected years)

	total	a great deal	only some	hardly any
2012	100.0%	11.9%	58.0%	30.1%
2010	100.0	12.3	59.4	28.2
2008	100.0	12.7	59.1	28.1
2006	100.0	12.4	58.5	29.1
2004	100.0	13.5	56.8	29.6
2002	100.0	12.3	63.0	24.8
2000	100.0	14.4	56.7	28.9
1998	100.0	11.8	56.8	31.4
1996	100.0	12.1	55.1	32.8
1994	100.0	11.1	55.3	33.6
1993	100.0	8.3	57.2	34.5
1991	100.0	12.0	51.4	36.6
1990	100.0	11.3	56.5	32.2
1989	100.0	9.9	54.5	35.6
1988	100.0	11.4	52.9	35.7
1987	100.0	11.3	53.7	35.0
1986	100.0	9.3	50.0	40.7
1984	100.0	9.1	53.8	37.1
1983	100.0	9.2	49.9	40.9
1982	100.0	13.5	55.2	31.3
1980	100.0	15.2	54.5	30.3
1978	100.0	11.3	48.7	40.0
1977	100.0	15.3	52.7	32.0
1976	100.0	12.5	52.4	35.2
1975	100.0	10.2	58.2	31.6
1974	100.0	19.4	54.7	25.8
1973	100.0	16.1	56.8	27.0

Source: Survey Documentation and Analysis, Computer-assisted Survey Methods Program, University of California, Berkeley, General Social Survey, 1972–2012 Cumulative Data Files, Internet site http://sda.berkeley.edu/cgi-bin/hsda?harcsda+gss12; calculations by New Strategist

Table 1.46 Confidence in the Scientific Community, 1973 to 2012

"As far as the people running these institutions are concerned, would you say you have a great deal of confidence, only some confidence, or hardly any confidence at all in them: the scientific community?"

(percent distribution of people aged 18 or older by response for selected years)

	total	a great deal	only some	hardly any
2012	100.0%	41.8%	51.0%	7.2%
2010	100.0	42.3	51.2	6.5
2008	100.0	40.4	53.8	5.8
2006	100.0	43.0	50.6	6.4
2004	100.0	43.2	50.3	6.5
2002	100.0	39.6	51.4	9.0
2000	100.0	44.8	47.3	7.9
1998	100.0	42.7	48.6	8.7
1996	100.0	42.9	48.7	8.4
1994	100.0	41.0	51.8	7.2
1993	100.0	40.6	51.9	7.5
1991	100.0	42.7	50.1	7.2
1990	100.0	41.3	51.4	7.3
1989	100.0	44.6	48.8	6.6
1988	100.0	42.5	51.8	5.7
1987	100.0	46.9	46.3	6.8
1986	100.0	41.6	51.0	7.4
1984	100.0	49.1	44.9	6.0
1983	100.0	44.4	49.2	6.4
1982	100.0	41.8	51.7	6.5
1980	100.0	44.1	48.5	7.4
1978	100.0	40.8	51.7	7.5
1977	100.0	44.7	49.9	5.4
1976	100.0	48.0	43.5	8.5
1975	100.0	41.7	50.9	7.4
1974	100.0	50.5	41.9	7.5
1973	100.0	40.9	52.5	6.6

Source: Survey Documentation and Analysis, Computer-assisted Survey Methods Program, University of California, Berkeley, General Social Survey, 1972–2012 Cumulative Data Files, Internet site http://sda.berkeley.edu/cgi-bin/hsda?harcsda+gss12; calculations by New Strategist

Table 1.47 Confidence in Medicine, 1973 to 2012

"As far as the people running these institutions are concerned, would you say you have a great deal of confidence, only some confidence, or hardly any confidence at all in them: medicine?"

(percent distribution of people aged 18 or older by response for selected years)

	total	a great deal	only some	hardly any
2012	100.0%	39.2%	50.6%	10.2%
2010	100.0	41.5	47.2	11.3
2008	100.0	39.2	50.3	10.5
2006	100.0	40.1	49.3	10.7
2004	100.0	37.9	50.0	12.1
2002	100.0	37.5	51.4	11.1
2000	100.0	45.2	45.7	9.1
1998	100.0	45.6	45.4	8.9
1996	100.0	45.8	45.7	8.5
1994	100.0	42.8	47.2	10.0
1993	100.0	40.8	50.8	8.3
1991	100.0	48.4	43.9	7.7
1990	100.0	45.8	47.5	6.8
1989	100.0	48.0	45.2	6.9
1988	100.0	53.2	40.9	5.9
1987	100.0	52.7	42.0	5.3
1986	100.0	47.3	45.3	7.4
1984	100.0	51.6	43.1	5.3
1983	100.0	51.9	41.0	7.1
1982	100.0	45.2	47.4	7.3
1980	100.0	54.3	38.1	7.7
1978	100.0	47.6	43.6	8.7
1977	100.0	53.5	40.9	5.6
1976	100.0	55.2	35.4	9.4
1975	100.0	51.8	40.3	7.9
1974	100.0	61.8	33.6	4.6
1973	100.0	54.2	39.9	5.9

Source: Survey Documentation and Analysis, Computer-assisted Survey Methods Program, University of California, Berkeley, General Social Survey, 1972–2012 Cumulative Data Files, Internet site http://sda.berkeley.edu/cgi-bin/hsda?harcsda+gss12; calculations by New Strategist

Table 1.48 Confidence in Education, 1973 to 2012

"As far as the people running these institutions are concerned, would you say you have a great deal of confidence, only some confidence, or hardly any confidence at all in them: education?"

(percent distribution of people aged 18 or older by response for selected years)

	total	a great deal	only some	hardly any
2012	100.0%	25.8%	58.3%	15.9%
2010	100.0	27.8	56.6	15.5
2008	100.0	29.5	55.2	15.2
2006	100.0	28.3	56.8	14.9
2004	100.0	28.8	56.9	14.3
2002	100.0	26.0	58.4	15.6
2000	100.0	27.5	56.8	15.7
1998	100.0	27.2	55.7	17.1
1996	100.0	23.6	57.7	18.7
1994	100.0	25.8	57.0	17.2
1993	100.0	22.7	58.7	18.7
1991	100.0	30.2	55.9	13.8
1990	100.0	27.1	59.5	13.4
1989	100.0	30.5	59.2	10.3
1988	100.0	30.3	60.8	8.9
1987	100.0	34.6	56.4	9.0
1986	100.0	28.4	60.5	11.1
1984	100.0	28.8	60.4	10.8
1983	100.0	28.2	57.2	14.6
1982	100.0	33.7	53.2	13.1
1980	100.0	30.6	57.2	12.2
1978	100.0	28.5	56.9	14.6
1977	100.0	40.8	50.6	8.6
1976	100.0	38.4	45.9	15.7
1975	100.0	31.6	55.4	13.0
1974	100.0	49.5	42.2	8.3
1973	100.0	37.3	54.7	8.0

Source: Survey Documentation and Analysis, Computer-assisted Survey Methods Program, University of California, Berkeley, General Social Survey, 1972–2012 Cumulative Data Files, Internet site http://sda.berkeley.edu/cgi-bin/hsda?harcsda+gss12; calculations by New Strategist

Table 1.49 Confidence in Organized Religion, 1973 to 2012

"As far as the people running these institutions are concerned, would you say you have a great deal of confidence, only some confidence, or hardly any confidence at all in them: organized religion?"

(percent distribution of people aged 18 or older by response for selected years)

	total	a great deal	only some	hardly any
2012	100.0%	20.6%	55.0%	24.3%
2010	100.0	20.3	54.7	25.1
2008	100.0	20.4	54.1	25.5
2006	100.0	24.7	53.0	22.2
2004	100.0	23.9	53.2	22.8
2002	100.0	19.3	57.2	23.5
2000	100.0	28.9	51.8	19.2
1998	100.0	27.5	53.6	18.9
1996	100.0	26.6	53.5	20.0
1994	100.0	25.5	53.0	21.5
1993	100.0	23.3	51.6	25.1
1991	100.0	25.6	54.3	20.1
1990	100.0	23.8	51.2	25.0
1989	100.0	22.4	47.3	30.3
1988	100.0	21.2	49.1	29.8
1987	100.0	30.3	50.5	19.2
1986	100.0	25.8	52.8	21.4
1984	100.0	30.9	49.2	19.9
1983	100.0	29.7	50.6	19.7
1982	100.0	32.5	52.3	15.2
1980	100.0	36.4	44.3	19.3
1978	100.0	30.9	51.0	18.1
1977	100.0	41.0	47.4	11.6
1976	100.0	32.2	48.3	19.5
1975	100.0	25.5	51.6	22.9
1974	100.0	45.4	43.6	11.1
1973	100.0	35.7	47.9	16.4

Source: Survey Documentation and Analysis, Computer-assisted Survey Methods Program, University of California, Berkeley, General Social Survey, 1972–2012 Cumulative Data Files, Internet site http://sda.berkeley.edu/cgi-bin/hsda?harcsda+gss12; calculations by New Strategist

Table 1.50 Confidence in the Military, 1973 to 2012

"As far as the people running these institutions are concerned, would you say
you have a great deal of confidence, only some confidence, or hardly
any confidence at all in them: the military?"

(percent distribution of people aged 18 or older by response for selected years)

	total	a great deal	only some	hardly any
2012	100.0%	55.2%	36.9%	7.9%
2010	100.0	54.3	36.5	9.2
2008	100.0	51.9	37.7	10.4
2006	100.0	47.8	39.7	12.5
2004	100.0	58.6	33.1	8.3
2002	100.0	56.7	36.6	6.7
2000	100.0	41.0	49.1	9.8
1998	100.0	37.2	49.8	13.0
1996	100.0	39.9	49.3	10.8
1994	100.0	38.4	49.6	12.0
1993	100.0	41.9	46.5	11.6
1991	100.0	61.7	32.6	5.7
1990	100.0	34.4	51.2	14.4
1989	100.0	34.0	52.3	13.7
1988	100.0	35.9	51.4	12.7
1987	100.0	36.6	50.8	12.6
1986	100.0	32.0	54.4	13.6
1984	100.0	36.8	50.6	12.6
1983	100.0	29.6	56.3	14.1
1982	100.0	31.6	53.6	14.8
1980	100.0	29.4	53.6	17.0
1978	100.0	31.2	55.5	13.2
1977	100.0	37.3	52.3	10.4
1976	100.0	42.3	43.6	14.1
1975	100.0	36.2	49.0	14.8
1974	100.0	40.2	45.6	14.2
1973	100.0	32.7	50.3	17.0

*Source: Survey Documentation and Analysis, Computer-assisted Survey Methods Program, University of California, Berkeley,
General Social Survey, 1972–2012 Cumulative Data Files, Internet site http://sda.berkeley.edu/cgi-bin/hsda?harcsda+gss12;
calculations by New Strategist*

Table 1.51 Confidence in the Press, 1973 to 2012

"As far as the people running these institutions are concerned, would you say you have a great deal of confidence, only some confidence, or hardly any confidence at all in them: the press?"

(percent distribution of people aged 18 or older by response for selected years)

	total	a great deal	only some	hardly any
2012	100.0%	8.9%	44.1%	46.9%
2010	100.0	10.8	45.7	43.4
2008	100.0	8.6	46.3	45.1
2006	100.0	10.3	48.6	41.1
2004	100.0	8.9	47.5	43.6
2002	100.0	10.1	47.5	42.4
2000	100.0	10.2	47.8	42.0
1998	100.0	9.2	47.2	43.6
1996	100.0	10.9	48.1	41.0
1994	100.0	10.2	50.0	39.8
1993	100.0	10.8	49.8	39.3
1991	100.0	16.3	54.0	29.8
1990	100.0	14.9	58.8	26.3
1989	100.0	17.0	55.7	27.3
1988	100.0	19.5	55.1	25.4
1987	100.0	18.4	56.9	24.7
1986	100.0	18.9	54.6	26.4
1984	100.0	18.4	60.4	21.3
1983	100.0	13.7	61.1	25.1
1982	100.0	18.0	61.1	20.8
1980	100.0	23.4	59.5	17.1
1978	100.0	20.6	59.5	19.9
1977	100.0	25.3	59.1	15.6
1976	100.0	28.8	52.7	18.5
1975	100.0	24.5	56.6	18.9
1974	100.0	25.7	56.5	17.8
1973	100.0	23.1	62.3	14.6

Source: Survey Documentation and Analysis, Computer-assisted Survey Methods Program, University of California, Berkeley, General Social Survey, 1972–2012 Cumulative Data Files, Internet site http://sda.berkeley.edu/cgi-bin/hsda?harcsda+gss12; calculations by New Strategist

Table 1.52 Confidence in Television, 1973 to 2012

"As far as the people running these institutions are concerned, would you say
you have a great deal of confidence, only some confidence, or hardly
any confidence at all in them: television?"

(percent distribution of people aged 18 or older by response for selected years)

	total	a great deal	only some	hardly any
2012	100.0%	10.4%	48.3%	41.4%
2010	100.0	12.8	50.7	36.5
2008	100.0	9.3	51.9	38.7
2006	100.0	9.1	49.5	41.5
2004	100.0	10.2	47.1	42.7
2002	100.0	9.5	48.0	42.5
2000	100.0	10.5	47.4	42.2
1998	100.0	10.2	50.6	39.2
1996	100.0	10.7	46.8	42.5
1994	100.0	9.7	50.6	39.7
1993	100.0	11.7	51.7	36.7
1991	100.0	14.8	54.6	30.6
1990	100.0	13.9	58.7	27.4
1989	100.0	14.1	55.4	30.6
1988	100.0	14.3	59.3	26.4
1987	100.0	11.1	59.9	29.1
1986	100.0	15.0	56.2	28.8
1984	100.0	13.8	57.6	28.6
1983	100.0	12.5	56.9	30.7
1982	100.0	14.2	59.1	26.7
1980	100.0	16.1	54.6	29.3
1978	100.0	15.0	53.3	31.7
1977	100.0	17.8	56.9	25.3
1976	100.0	18.4	53.6	28.0
1975	100.0	18.3	58.3	23.3
1974	100.0	23.2	58.8	18.0
1973	100.0	18.4	59.8	21.8

Source: Survey Documentation and Analysis, Computer-assisted Survey Methods Program, University of California, Berkeley, General Social Survey, 1972–2012 Cumulative Data Files, Internet site http://sda.berkeley.edu/cgi-bin/hsda?harcsda+gss12; calculations by New Strategist

Table 1.53 Federal Income Tax Level, 1976 to 2012

"Do you consider the amount of federal income tax which you
have to pay as too high, about right, or too low?"

(percent distribution of people aged 18 or older by response for selected years)

	total	too high	about right	too low
2012	100.0%	52.0%	45.5%	2.5%
2010	100.0	52.1	46.4	1.5
2008	100.0	56.8	41.8	1.4
2006	100.0	58.3	40.9	0.9
2004	100.0	60.6	38.2	1.3
2002	100.0	61.9	37.0	1.0
2000	100.0	66.7	32.4	0.9
1998	100.0	66.8	32.4	0.8
1996	100.0	68.0	31.1	0.9
1994	100.0	65.7	33.6	0.8
1993	100.0	56.3	42.4	1.3
1991	100.0	58.5	40.5	1.0
1990	100.0	62.6	36.8	0.6
1989	100.0	58.3	38.5	1.0
1988	100.0	57.8	39.2	1.1
1987	100.0	61.4	35.9	0.8
1985	100.0	63.0	33.2	0.3
1984	100.0	65.0	32.3	0.5
1982	100.0	73.7	24.9	0.5
1980	100.0	73.2	26.4	0.3
1977	100.0	69.1	28.0	0.9
1976	100.0	61.6	34.1	0.6

Source: Survey Documentation and Analysis, Computer-assisted Survey Methods Program, University of California, Berkeley, General Social Survey, 1972–2012 Cumulative Data Files, Internet site http://sda.berkeley.edu/cgi-bin/hsda?harcsda+gss12; calculations by New Strategist

Table 1.54 Should Marijuana Be Made Legal, 1973 to 2012

"Do you think the use of marijuana should be made legal or not?"

(percent distribution of people aged 18 or older by response for selected years)

	total	legal	not legal
2012	100.0%	46.9%	53.1%
2010	100.0	48.4	51.6
2008	100.0	38.3	61.7
2006	100.0	34.9	65.1
2004	100.0	35.9	64.1
2002	100.0	34.5	65.5
2000	100.0	32.9	67.1
1998	100.0	29.1	70.9
1996	100.0	26.6	73.4
1994	100.0	23.2	76.8
1993	100.0	23.5	76.6
1991	100.0	18.0	82.0
1990	100.0	16.4	83.6
1989	100.0	16.6	83.4
1988	100.0	17.5	82.5
1987	100.0	16.5	83.6
1986	100.0	17.6	82.4
1984	100.0	22.7	77.3
1983	100.0	19.9	80.1
1980	100.0	24.6	75.4
1978	100.0	31.3	68.7
1976	100.0	28.7	71.3
1975	100.0	21.4	78.6
1973	100.0	19.6	80.4

Source: Survey Documentation and Analysis, Computer-assisted Survey Methods Program, University of California, Berkeley, General Social Survey, 1972–2012 Cumulative Data Files, Internet site http://sda.berkeley.edu/cgi-bin/hsda?harcsda+gss12; calculations by New Strategist

Table 1.55 Favor or Oppose Gun Permits, 1972 to 2012

"Would you favor or oppose a law which would require a person
to obtain a police permit before he or she could buy a gun?"

(percent distribution of people aged 18 or older by response for selected years)

	total	favor	oppose
2012	100.0%	73.7%	26.3%
2010	100.0	74.3	25.7
2008	100.0	79.1	20.9
2006	100.0	80.6	19.4
2004	100.0	80.7	19.3
2002	100.0	81.4	18.6
2000	100.0	81.0	19.0
1998	100.0	83.7	16.3
1996	100.0	81.8	18.2
1994	100.0	79.0	21.0
1993	100.0	82.1	17.9
1991	100.0	81.5	18.5
1990	100.0	80.3	19.7
1989	100.0	79.4	20.6
1988	100.0	75.4	24.6
1987	100.0	71.0	29.0
1985	100.0	73.8	26.2
1984	100.0	70.4	29.6
1982	100.0	72.6	27.4
1980	100.0	70.0	30.0
1977	100.0	72.0	28.0
1976	100.0	72.5	27.5
1975	100.0	74.4	25.6
1974	100.0	76.2	23.8
1973	100.0	74.9	25.1
1972	100.0	72.5	27.5

Source: Survey Documentation and Analysis, Computer-assisted Survey Methods Program, University of California, Berkeley, General Social Survey, 1972–2012 Cumulative Data Files, Internet site http://sda.berkeley.edu/cgi-bin/hsda?harcsda+gss12; calculations by New Strategist

Table 1.56 Courts Deal Too Harshly with Criminals, 1972 to 2012

"In general, do you think the courts in this area deal too harshly
or not harshly enough with criminals?"

(percent distribution of people aged 18 or older by response for selected years)

	total	too harsh	not harsh enough	about right
2012	100.0%	15.5%	62.5%	22.1%
2010	100.0	14.4	66.6	19.0
2008	100.0	11.9	67.3	20.9
2006	100.0	9.4	68.3	22.3
2004	100.0	9.3	69.3	21.4
2002	100.0	10.0	71.5	18.5
2000	100.0	8.1	75.2	16.7
1998	100.0	6.5	79.9	13.7
1996	100.0	4.9	83.9	11.2
1994	100.0	2.9	89.0	8.1
1993	100.0	3.8	86.3	9.9
1991	100.0	4.4	84.0	11.6
1990	100.0	3.9	85.9	10.2
1989	100.0	3.0	88.1	9.0
1988	100.0	4.3	85.8	9.9
1987	100.0	3.7	84.0	12.3
1986	100.0	3.2	88.6	8.1
1985	100.0	3.2	87.0	9.7
1984	100.0	3.1	85.4	11.6
1983	100.0	3.4	90.3	6.2
1982	100.0	2.7	90.1	7.2
1980	100.0	3.1	89.3	7.5
1978	100.0	2.8	90.2	7.0
1977	100.0	3.3	88.2	8.5
1976	100.0	3.3	86.6	10.1
1975	100.0	4.9	84.8	10.3
1974	100.0	5.7	83.6	10.7
1973	100.0	5.0	80.3	14.6
1972	100.0	8.6	73.1	18.2

Source: Survey Documentation and Analysis, Computer-assisted Survey Methods Program, University of California, Berkeley, General Social Survey, 1972–2012 Cumulative Data Files, Internet site http://sda.berkeley.edu/cgi-bin/hsda?harcsda+gss12; calculations by New Strategist

Table 1.57 Favor or Oppose Death Penalty for Murder, 1974 to 2012

"Do you favor or oppose the death penalty for persons convicted of murder?"

(percent distribution of people aged 18 or older by response for selected years)

	total	favor	oppose
2012	100.0%	65.1%	34.9%
2010	100.0	67.8	32.2
2008	100.0	67.6	32.4
2006	100.0	69.1	30.9
2004	100.0	68.3	31.7
2002	100.0	69.8	30.2
2000	100.0	69.6	30.4
1998	100.0	73.5	26.5
1996	100.0	77.8	22.2
1994	100.0	79.7	20.3
1993	100.0	77.5	22.5
1991	100.0	76.1	23.9
1990	100.0	79.2	20.8
1989	100.0	77.9	22.1
1988	100.0	76.3	23.7
1987	100.0	73.5	26.5
1986	100.0	75.6	24.4
1985	100.0	79.5	20.5
1984	100.0	74.9	25.1
1983	100.0	78.0	22.0
1982	100.0	78.3	21.7
1980	100.0	70.9	29.1
1978	100.0	71.3	28.7
1977	100.0	72.1	27.9
1976	100.0	69.7	30.3
1975	100.0	64.4	35.6
1974	100.0	66.4	33.6

Source: Survey Documentation and Analysis, Computer-assisted Survey Methods Program, University of California, Berkeley, General Social Survey, 1972–2012 Cumulative Data Files, Internet site http://sda.berkeley.edu/cgi-bin/hsda?harcsda+gss12; calculations by New Strategist

Table 1.58 Allow Patients with Incurable Disease to Die, 1977 to 2012

"When a person has a disease that cannot be cured, do you think doctors should be allowed by law to end the patient's life by some painless means if the patient and his family request it?"

(percent distribution of people aged 18 or older by response for selected years)

	total	yes	no
2012	100.0%	68.3%	31.7%
2010	100.0	68.4	31.6
2008	100.0	66.2	33.8
2006	100.0	67.6	32.4
2004	100.0	66.8	33.2
2002	100.0	67.2	32.8
2000	100.0	68.0	32.0
1998	100.0	70.7	29.3
1996	100.0	71.0	29.0
1994	100.0	70.7	29.3
1993	100.0	68.9	31.1
1991	100.0	73.1	26.9
1990	100.0	72.4	27.6
1989	100.0	68.3	31.7
1988	100.0	70.2	29.8
1986	100.0	68.9	31.1
1985	100.0	65.5	34.5
1983	100.0	64.3	35.7
1982	100.0	63.9	36.1
1978	100.0	59.3	40.7
1977	100.0	61.6	38.4

Source: Survey Documentation and Analysis, Computer-assisted Survey Methods Program, University of California, Berkeley, General Social Survey, 1972–2012 Cumulative Data Files, Internet site http://sda.berkeley.edu/cgi-bin/hsda?harcsda+gss12; calculations by New Strategist

Table 1.59 Expect World War in 10 Years, 1976 to 2012

"Do you expect the United States to fight in another
world war within the next 10 years?"

(percent distribution of people aged 18 or older by response for selected years)

	total	yes	no
2012	100.0%	50.4%	49.6%
2010	100.0	53.5	46.5
2008	100.0	52.7	47.3
2006	100.0	61.0	39.0
2004	100.0	55.2	44.8
2002	100.0	68.1	31.9
2000	100.0	37.8	62.2
1998	100.0	49.7	50.3
1996	100.0	40.4	59.6
1994	100.0	44.3	55.7
1993	100.0	47.2	52.8
1991	100.0	47.0	53.0
1990	100.0	28.6	71.4
1989	100.0	32.1	67.9
1988	100.0	40.7	59.3
1986	100.0	47.5	52.5
1985	100.0	43.6	56.4
1976	100.0	47.1	52.9

Source: Survey Documentation and Analysis, Computer-assisted Survey Methods Program, University of California, Berkeley, General Social Survey, 1972–2012 Cumulative Data Files, Internet site http://sda.berkeley.edu/cgi-bin/hsda?harcsda+gss12; calculations by New Strategist

Table 1.60 Allow Antireligious Book in Local Library, 1972 to 2012

"There are always some people whose ideas are considered bad or dangerous by
other people. For instance, somebody who is against all churches and religion:
If some people in your community suggested that a book he wrote against
churches and religion should be taken out of your public library,
would you favor removing this book, or not?"

(percent distribution of people aged 18 or older by response for selected years)

	total	remove	not remove
2012	100.0%	23.1%	76.9%
2010	100.0	25.1	74.9
2008	100.0	27.1	72.9
2006	100.0	27.2	72.8
2004	100.0	26.7	73.3
2002	100.0	25.9	74.1
2000	100.0	29.1	70.9
1998	100.0	27.9	72.1
1996	100.0	29.3	70.7
1994	100.0	28.5	71.5
1993	100.0	29.7	70.3
1991	100.0	29.9	70.1
1990	100.0	30.6	69.4
1989	100.0	29.8	70.2
1988	100.0	34.6	65.4
1987	100.0	31.7	68.3
1985	100.0	36.8	63.2
1984	100.0	33.0	67.0
1982	100.0	37.3	62.7
1980	100.0	37.4	62.6
1977	100.0	40.3	59.7
1976	100.0	38.7	61.3
1974	100.0	38.2	61.8
1973	100.0	37.2	62.8
1972	100.0	36.4	63.6

Source: Survey Documentation and Analysis, Computer-assisted Survey Methods Program, University of California, Berkeley, General Social Survey, 1972–2012 Cumulative Data Files, Internet site http://sda.berkeley.edu/cgi-bin/hsda?harcsda+gss12; calculations by New Strategist

Table 1.61 Allow Someone Who Is Against Religion to Speak, 1972 to 2012

"There are always some people whose ideas are considered bad or dangerous by
other people. For instance, somebody who is against all churches and religion:
If such a person wanted to make a speech in your (city/town/community)
against churches and religion, should he be allowed to speak, or not?"

(percent distribution of people aged 18 or older by response for selected years)

	total	allow	disallow
2012	100.0%	77.2%	22.8%
2010	100.0	76.6	23.4
2008	100.0	76.6	23.4
2006	100.0	78.2	21.8
2004	100.0	77.0	23.0
2002	100.0	77.0	23.0
2000	100.0	76.1	23.9
1998	100.0	75.9	24.1
1996	100.0	75.0	25.0
1994	100.0	73.9	26.1
1993	100.0	72.4	27.6
1991	100.0	73.6	26.4
1990	100.0	74.4	25.6
1989	100.0	73.1	26.9
1988	100.0	71.7	28.3
1987	100.0	69.9	30.1
1985	100.0	67.1	32.9
1984	100.0	69.0	31.0
1982	100.0	64.7	35.3
1980	100.0	65.1	34.9
1977	100.0	63.9	36.1
1976	100.0	65.4	34.6
1974	100.0	63.3	36.7
1973	100.0	66.7	33.3
1972	100.0	67.7	32.3

*Source: Survey Documentation and Analysis, Computer-assisted Survey Methods Program, University of California, Berkeley,
General Social Survey, 1972–2012 Cumulative Data Files, Internet site http://sda.berkeley.edu/cgi-bin/hsda?harcsda+gss12;
calculations by New Strategist*

Table 1.62 Allow Someone Who Is Against Religion to Teach College, 1972 to 2012

"There are always some people whose ideas are considered bad or dangerous by other people. For instance, somebody who is against all churches and religion: Should such a person be allowed to teach in a college or university, or not?"

(percent distribution of people aged 18 or older by response for selected years)

	total	allow	disallow
2012	100.0%	64.9%	35.1%
2010	100.0	61.8	38.2
2008	100.0	62.1	37.9
2006	100.0	62.7	37.3
2004	100.0	65.7	34.3
2002	100.0	60.5	39.5
2000	100.0	59.6	40.4
1998	100.0	60.9	39.1
1996	100.0	58.3	41.7
1994	100.0	55.3	44.7
1993	100.0	55.3	44.7
1991	100.0	53.0	47.0
1990	100.0	53.9	46.2
1989	100.0	54.3	45.7
1988	100.0	47.6	52.4
1987	100.0	48.0	52.0
1985	100.0	47.4	52.6
1984	100.0	48.0	52.1
1982	100.0	47.5	52.5
1980	100.0	46.4	53.6
1977	100.0	40.5	59.5
1976	100.0	42.6	57.4
1974	100.0	43.6	56.4
1973	100.0	43.1	56.9
1972	100.0	43.5	56.5

Source: Survey Documentation and Analysis, Computer-assisted Survey Methods Program, University of California, Berkeley, General Social Survey, 1972–2012 Cumulative Data Files, Internet site http://sda.berkeley.edu/cgi-bin/hsda?harcsda+gss12; calculations by New Strategist

Table 1.63 Allow a Communist's Book in the Local Library, 1972 to 2012

"Suppose a man who admits he is a communist wrote a book which is in your public library. Somebody in your community suggests that the book should be removed from the library. Would you favor removing it, or not?"

(percent distribution of people aged 18 or older by response for selected years)

	total	remove	not remove
2012	100.0%	26.6%	73.4%
2010	100.0	29.3	70.7
2008	100.0	30.3	69.7
2006	100.0	30.3	69.7
2004	100.0	29.2	70.8
2002	100.0	29.3	70.7
2000	100.0	31.5	68.5
1998	100.0	30.0	70.0
1996	100.0	32.1	67.9
1994	100.0	31.5	68.5
1993	100.0	29.4	70.6
1991	100.0	31.0	69.0
1990	100.0	34.0	66.0
1989	100.0	35.1	64.9
1988	100.0	38.0	62.0
1987	100.0	37.2	62.8
1985	100.0	39.5	60.5
1984	100.0	37.4	62.6
1982	100.0	40.1	59.9
1980	100.0	40.9	59.1
1977	100.0	42.9	57.1
1976	100.0	41.5	58.5
1974	100.0	39.0	61.0
1973	100.0	39.4	60.6
1972	100.0	44.0	56.0

Source: Survey Documentation and Analysis, Computer-assisted Survey Methods Program, University of California, Berkeley, General Social Survey, 1972–2012 Cumulative Data Files, Internet site http://sda.berkeley.edu/cgi-bin/hsda?harcsda+gss12; calculations by New Strategist

Table 1.64 Allow a Communist to Speak, 1972 to 2012

"Suppose an admitted communist wanted to make a speech in your community.
Should he be allowed to speak, or not?"

(percent distribution of people aged 18 or older by response for selected years)

	total	allow	disallow
2012	100.0	67.2	32.8
2010	100.0	65.7	34.3
2008	100.0	67.4	32.6
2006	100.0	69.1	30.9
2004	100.0	70.3	29.7
2002	100.0	70.4	29.6
2000	100.0	67.8	32.2
1998	100.0	68.1	31.9
1996	100.0	66.1	33.9
1994	100.0	68.6	31.4
1993	100.0	71.9	28.1
1991	100.0	68.9	31.1
1990	100.0	67.0	33.0
1989	100.0	66.0	34.0
1988	100.0	62.8	37.2
1987	100.0	59.8	40.2
1985	100.0	59.9	40.1
1984	100.0	61.5	38.5
1982	100.0	57.9	42.1
1980	100.0	55.6	44.4
1977	100.0	57.1	42.9
1976	100.0	56.2	43.8
1974	100.0	60.0	40.0
1973	100.0	62.4	37.6
1972	100.0	54.7	45.3

Source: Survey Documentation and Analysis, Computer-assisted Survey Methods Program, University of California, Berkeley, General Social Survey, 1972–2012 Cumulative Data Files, Internet site http://sda.berkeley.edu/cgi-bin/hsda?harcsda+gss12; calculations by New Strategist

Table 1.65 Allow a Communist to Teach College, 1972 to 2012

"What about a man who admits he is a communist? Suppose he
is teaching in a college. Should he be fired, or not?"

(percent distribution of people aged 18 or older by response for selected years)

	total	fired	not fired
2012	100.0%	34.6%	65.4%
2010	100.0	36.8	63.2
2008	100.0	38.8	61.2
2006	100.0	37.2	62.8
2004	100.0	34.4	65.6
2002	100.0	38.5	61.5
2000	100.0	38.4	61.6
1998	100.0	38.8	61.2
1996	100.0	38.7	61.3
1994	100.0	42.0	58.0
1993	100.0	38.4	61.6
1991	100.0	42.7	57.3
1990	100.0	44.2	55.8
1989	100.0	45.9	54.1
1988	100.0	48.7	51.3
1987	100.0	51.9	48.1
1985	100.0	52.3	47.7
1984	100.0	49.6	50.4
1982	100.0	53.5	46.5
1980	100.0	56.5	43.5
1977	100.0	59.8	40.2
1976	100.0	55.9	44.1
1974	100.0	55.6	44.4
1973	100.0	57.4	42.6
1972	100.0	64.3	35.7

Source: Survey Documentation and Analysis, Computer-assisted Survey Methods Program, University of California, Berkeley, General Social Survey, 1972–2012 Cumulative Data Files, Internet site http://sda.berkeley.edu/cgi-bin/hsda?harcsda+gss12; calculations by New Strategist

Table 1.66 Allow a Homosexual's Book in the Local Library, 1973 to 2012

"What about a man who admits that he is a homosexual? If some people in your community suggested that a book he wrote in favor of homosexuality should be taken out of your public library, would you favor removing this book, or not?"

(percent distribution of people aged 18 or older by response for selected years)

	total	remove	not remove
2012	100.0%	20.3%	79.7%
2010	100.0	21.3	78.7
2008	100.0	22.7	77.3
2006	100.0	24.1	75.9
2004	100.0	26.1	73.9
2002	100.0	23.4	76.6
2000	100.0	26.7	73.3
1998	100.0	26.4	73.6
1996	100.0	29.0	71.0
1994	100.0	28.9	71.1
1993	100.0	30.0	70.0
1991	100.0	29.5	70.5
1990	100.0	32.7	67.3
1989	100.0	32.5	67.5
1988	100.0	37.0	63.0
1987	100.0	41.0	59.0
1985	100.0	41.5	58.5
1984	100.0	38.0	62.0
1982	100.0	41.3	58.7
1980	100.0	40.6	59.4
1977	100.0	43.0	57.0
1976	100.0	41.8	58.2
1974	100.0	41.9	58.1
1973	100.0	44.5	55.5

Source: Survey Documentation and Analysis, Computer-assisted Survey Methods Program, University of California, Berkeley, General Social Survey, 1972–2012 Cumulative Data Files, Internet site http://sda.berkeley.edu/cgi-bin/hsda?harcsda+gss12; calculations by New Strategist

Table 1.67 Allow a Homosexual to Speak, 1973 to 2012

"What about a man who admits that he is a homosexual? Suppose this admitted homosexual wanted to make a speech in your community. Should he be allowed to speak, or not?"

(percent distribution of people aged 18 or older by response for selected years)

	total	allow	disallow
2012	100.0%	86.6%	13.4%
2010	100.0	87.0	13.0
2008	100.0	83.1	16.9
2006	100.0	83.4	16.6
2004	100.0	83.4	16.6
2002	100.0	84.2	15.8
2000	100.0	83.3	16.7
1998	100.0	83.7	16.3
1996	100.0	82.5	17.5
1994	100.0	81.6	18.4
1993	100.0	81.4	18.6
1991	100.0	78.5	21.5
1990	100.0	78.2	21.8
1989	100.0	78.9	21.1
1988	100.0	72.7	27.3
1987	100.0	70.3	29.7
1985	100.0	71.1	28.9
1984	100.0	71.2	28.8
1982	100.0	67.7	32.3
1980	100.0	67.8	32.2
1977	100.0	64.2	35.8
1976	100.0	65.1	34.9
1974	100.0	65.9	34.1
1973	100.0	63.9	36.1

Source: Survey Documentation and Analysis, Computer-assisted Survey Methods Program, University of California, Berkeley, General Social Survey, 1972–2012 Cumulative Data Files, Internet site http://sda.berkeley.edu/cgi-bin/hsda?harcsda+gss12; calculations by New Strategist

Table 1.68 Allow a Homosexual to Teach College, 1973 to 2012

"What about a man who admits that he is a homosexual? Should such a person be allowed to teach in a college or university, or not?"

(percent distribution of people aged 18 or older by response for selected years)

	total	allow	disallow
2012	100.0%	84.3%	15.7%
2010	100.0	85.4	14.6
2008	100.0	80.5	19.5
2006	100.0	79.3	20.7
2004	100.0	79.8	20.2
2002	100.0	80.2	19.8
2000	100.0	79.6	20.4
1998	100.0	77.7	22.3
1996	100.0	77.0	23.0
1994	100.0	73.2	26.8
1993	100.0	72.0	28.0
1991	100.0	65.6	34.4
1990	100.0	67.8	32.2
1989	100.0	67.0	33.0
1988	100.0	59.5	40.5
1987	100.0	59.4	40.6
1985	100.0	60.5	39.5
1984	100.0	61.2	38.8
1982	100.0	57.1	42.9
1980	100.0	57.4	42.6
1977	100.0	51.9	48.1
1976	100.0	54.5	45.5
1974	100.0	54.1	45.9
1973	100.0	50.1	49.9

Source: Survey Documentation and Analysis, Computer-assisted Survey Methods Program, University of California, Berkeley, General Social Survey, 1972–2012 Cumulative Data Files, Internet site http://sda.berkeley.edu/cgi-bin/hsda?harcsda+gss12; calculations by New Strategist

Table 1.69 Allow a Militarist's Book in the Local Library, 1976 to 2012

"Consider a person who advocates doing away with elections and letting
the military run the country. Suppose he wrote a book advocating doing away
with elections and letting the military run the country. Somebody in your
community suggests that the book should be removed from
the library. Would you favor removing it, or not?"

(percent distribution of people aged 18 or older by response for selected years)

	total	remove	not remove
2012	100.0%	27.1%	72.9%
2010	100.0	27.8	72.2
2008	100.0	28.7	71.3
2006	100.0	30.0	70.0
2004	100.0	30.8	69.2
2002	100.0	27.8	72.2
2000	100.0	33.2	66.8
1998	100.0	30.0	70.0
1996	100.0	33.3	66.7
1994	100.0	33.7	66.3
1993	100.0	29.2	70.8
1991	100.0	32.5	67.5
1990	100.0	36.6	63.4
1989	100.0	37.2	62.8
1988	100.0	41.4	58.6
1987	100.0	40.0	60.0
1985	100.0	42.1	57.9
1984	100.0	39.4	60.6
1982	100.0	41.4	58.6
1980	100.0	41.0	59.0
1977	100.0	44.2	55.8
1976	100.0	41.4	58.6

Source: Survey Documentation and Analysis, Computer-assisted Survey Methods Program, University of California, Berkeley, General Social Survey, 1972–2012 Cumulative Data Files, Internet site http://sda.berkeley.edu/cgi-bin/hsda?harcsda+gss12; calculations by New Strategist

Table 1.70 Allow a Militarist to Speak, 1976 to 2012

"Consider a person who advocates doing away with elections and letting
the military run the country. If such a person wanted to make a speech
in your community, should he be allowed to speak, or not?"

(percent distribution of people aged 18 or older by response for selected years)

	total	allow	disallow
2012	100.0%	68.9%	31.1%
2010	100.0	69.5	30.5
2008	100.0	66.7	33.3
2006	100.0	66.7	33.3
2004	100.0	67.3	32.7
2002	100.0	69.6	30.4
2000	100.0	65.0	35.0
1998	100.0	68.1	31.9
1996	100.0	64.5	35.5
1994	100.0	65.9	34.1
1993	100.0	67.0	33.0
1991	100.0	63.4	36.6
1990	100.0	60.0	40.0
1989	100.0	61.6	38.4
1988	100.0	58.8	41.2
1987	100.0	56.4	43.6
1985	100.0	56.7	43.3
1984	100.0	58.6	41.4
1982	100.0	55.1	44.9
1980	100.0	57.4	42.6
1977	100.0	52.0	48.0
1976	100.0	55.4	44.6

*Source: Survey Documentation and Analysis, Computer-assisted Survey Methods Program, University of California, Berkeley,
General Social Survey, 1972–2012 Cumulative Data Files, Internet site http://sda.berkeley.edu/cgi-bin/hsda?harcsda+gss12;
calculations by New Strategist*

Table 1.71 Allow a Militarist to Teach College, 1976 to 2012

"Consider a person who advocates doing away with elections and letting
the military run the country. Should such a person be allowed
to teach in a college or university, or not?"

(percent distribution of people aged 18 or older by response for selected years)

	total	allow	disallow
2012	100.0%	57.3%	42.7%
2010	100.0	58.4	41.6
2008	100.0	52.6	47.4
2006	100.0	54.5	45.5
2004	100.0	54.3	45.7
2002	100.0	56.8	43.2
2000	100.0	50.2	49.8
1998	100.0	53.8	46.2
1996	100.0	50.4	49.6
1994	100.0	48.8	51.2
1993	100.0	50.9	49.1
1991	100.0	45.2	54.8
1990	100.0	46.1	53.9
1989	100.0	44.6	55.4
1988	100.0	39.2	60.8
1987	100.0	41.0	59.0
1985	100.0	41.1	58.9
1984	100.0	42.5	57.5
1982	100.0	41.2	58.8
1980	100.0	40.4	59.6
1977	100.0	35.2	64.8
1976	100.0	38.8	61.2

Source: Survey Documentation and Analysis, Computer-assisted Survey Methods Program, University of California, Berkeley, General Social Survey, 1972–2012 Cumulative Data Files, Internet site http://sda.berkeley.edu/cgi-bin/hsda?harcsda+gss12; calculations by New Strategist

Table 1.72 Allow a Racist's Book in the Local Library, 1976 to 2012

"Consider a person who believes that blacks are genetically inferior. If some
people in your community suggested that a book he wrote which said
blacks are inferior should be taken out of your public library,
would you favor removing this book, or not?"

(percent distribution of people aged 18 or older by response for selected years)

	total	remove	not remove
2012	100.0%	35.5%	64.5%
2010	100.0	33.9	66.1
2008	100.0	34.9	65.1
2006	100.0	34.5	65.5
2004	100.0	34.0	66.0
2002	100.0	33.8	66.2
2000	100.0	34.7	65.3
1998	100.0	34.6	65.4
1996	100.0	33.8	66.2
1994	100.0	31.8	68.2
1993	100.0	32.4	67.6
1991	100.0	33.8	66.2
1990	100.0	32.8	67.2
1989	100.0	33.6	66.4
1988	100.0	36.9	63.1
1987	100.0	35.3	64.7
1985	100.0	37.3	62.7
1984	100.0	35.0	65.0
1982	100.0	37.4	62.6
1980	100.0	35.2	64.8
1977	100.0	36.7	63.3
1976	100.0	38.1	61.9

Source: Survey Documentation and Analysis, Computer-assisted Survey Methods Program, University of California, Berkeley, General Social Survey, 1972–2012 Cumulative Data Files, Internet site http://sda.berkeley.edu/cgi-bin/hsda?harcsda+gss12; calculations by New Strategist

Table 1.73 Allow a Racist to Speak, 1976 to 2012

"Consider a person who believes that blacks are genetically inferior. If such a person wanted to make a speech in your community claiming that blacks are inferior, should he be allowed to speak, or not?"

(percent distribution of people aged 18 or older by response for selected years)

	total	allow	disallow
2012	100.0%	58.2%	41.8%
2010	100.0	58.6	41.4
2008	100.0	59.4	40.6
2006	100.0	62.9	37.1
2004	100.0	62.4	37.6
2002	100.0	63.3	36.7
2000	100.0	61.2	38.8
1998	100.0	63.7	36.3
1996	100.0	62.2	37.8
1994	100.0	63.4	36.6
1993	100.0	63.0	37.0
1991	100.0	63.0	37.0
1990	100.0	65.0	35.0
1989	100.0	62.5	37.5
1988	100.0	62.1	37.9
1987	100.0	61.1	38.9
1985	100.0	58.8	41.2
1984	100.0	58.8	41.2
1982	100.0	61.3	38.7
1980	100.0	61.9	38.1
1977	100.0	60.3	39.7
1976	100.0	62.6	37.4

Source: Survey Documentation and Analysis, Computer-assisted Survey Methods Program, University of California, Berkeley, General Social Survey, 1972–2012 Cumulative Data Files, Internet site http://sda.berkeley.edu/cgi-bin/hsda?harcsda+gss12; calculations by New Strategist

Table 1.74 Allow a Racist to Teach College, 1976 to 2012

"Consider a person who believes that blacks are genetically inferior. Should such a person be allowed to teach in a college or university, or not?"

(percent distribution of people aged 18 or older by response for selected years)

	total	allow	disallow
2012	100.0%	46.8%	53.2%
2010	100.0	49.1	50.9
2008	100.0	46.3	53.7
2006	100.0	48.4	51.6
2004	100.0	47.0	53.0
2002	100.0	52.7	47.3
2000	100.0	47.4	52.6
1998	100.0	47.8	52.2
1996	100.0	48.0	52.0
1994	100.0	44.4	55.6
1993	100.0	46.8	53.2
1991	100.0	43.0	57.0
1990	100.0	48.1	51.9
1989	100.0	47.4	52.6
1988	100.0	42.3	57.7
1987	100.0	44.2	55.8
1985	100.0	43.7	56.3
1984	100.0	42.5	57.5
1982	100.0	44.4	55.6
1980	100.0	43.5	56.5
1977	100.0	41.8	58.3
1976	100.0	42.0	58.0

Source: Survey Documentation and Analysis, Computer-assisted Survey Methods Program, University of California, Berkeley, General Social Survey, 1972–2012 Cumulative Data Files, Internet site http://sda.berkeley.edu/cgi-bin/hsda?harcsda+gss12; calculations by New Strategist

Table 1.75 Suicide if Person Has an Incurable Disease, 1977 to 2012

"Do you think a person has the right to end his or her own life
if this person has an incurable disease?"

(percent distribution of people aged 18 or older by response for selected years)

	total	yes	no
2012	100.0%	58.8%	41.2%
2010	100.0	60.7	39.3
2008	100.0	61.1	38.9
2006	100.0	61.7	38.3
2004	100.0	59.5	40.5
2002	100.0	58.7	41.3
2000	100.0	57.4	42.6
1998	100.0	62.7	37.3
1996	100.0	64.0	36.0
1994	100.0	64.2	35.8
1993	100.0	60.0	40.0
1991	100.0	58.3	41.7
1990	100.0	60.6	39.4
1989	100.0	48.4	51.6
1988	100.0	53.1	46.9
1986	100.0	53.8	46.2
1985	100.0	44.8	55.2
1983	100.0	48.4	51.6
1982	100.0	46.7	53.3
1978	100.0	40.2	59.8
1977	100.0	39.3	60.7

Source: Survey Documentation and Analysis, Computer-assisted Survey Methods Program, University of California, Berkeley, General Social Survey, 1972–2012 Cumulative Data Files, Internet site http://sda.berkeley.edu/cgi-bin/hsda?harcsda+gss12; calculations by New Strategist

Table 1.76 Suicide if Bankrupt, 1977 to 2012

"Do you think a person has the right to end his or her own life
if this person has gone bankrupt?"

(percent distribution of people aged 18 or older by response for selected years)

	total	yes	no
2012	100.0%	11.2%	88.8%
2010	100.0	10.0	90.0
2008	100.0	7.5	92.5
2006	100.0	9.4	90.6
2004	100.0	10.7	89.3
2002	100.0	8.7	91.3
2000	100.0	8.6	91.4
1998	100.0	9.5	90.5
1996	100.0	9.3	90.7
1994	100.0	8.9	91.1
1993	100.0	8.4	91.6
1991	100.0	6.1	93.9
1990	100.0	7.2	92.8
1989	100.0	6.3	93.7
1988	100.0	6.0	94.0
1986	100.0	6.1	93.9
1985	100.0	7.7	92.3
1983	100.0	5.9	94.1
1982	100.0	7.7	92.3
1978	100.0	4.7	95.3
1977	100.0	6.2	93.8

Source: Survey Documentation and Analysis, Computer-assisted Survey Methods Program, University of California, Berkeley, General Social Survey, 1972–2012 Cumulative Data Files, Internet site http://sda.berkeley.edu/cgi-bin/hsda?harcsda+gss12; calculations by New Strategist

Table 1.77 Suicide if Person Has Dishonored Family, 1977 to 2012

"Do you think a person has the right to end his or her own life
if this person has dishonored his or her family?"

(percent distribution of people aged 18 or older by response for selected years)

	total	yes	no
2012	100.0%	10.9%	89.1%
2010	100.0	9.6	90.4
2008	100.0	8.9	91.1
2006	100.0	9.1	90.9
2004	100.0	11.3	88.7
2002	100.0	9.0	91.0
2000	100.0	8.3	91.7
1998	100.0	9.6	90.4
1996	100.0	9.6	90.4
1994	100.0	9.0	91.0
1993	100.0	7.5	92.5
1991	100.0	5.5	94.5
1990	100.0	7.6	92.4
1989	100.0	6.5	93.5
1988	100.0	7.1	92.9
1986	100.0	5.5	94.5
1985	100.0	7.8	92.2
1983	100.0	6.6	93.4
1982	100.0	8.0	92.0
1978	100.0	5.7	94.3
1977	100.0	7.0	93.0

Source: Survey Documentation and Analysis, Computer-assisted Survey Methods Program, University of California, Berkeley, General Social Survey, 1972–2012 Cumulative Data Files, Internet site http://sda.berkeley.edu/cgi-bin/hsda?harcsda+gss12; calculations by New Strategist

Table 1.78 Suicide if Ready to Die, 1977 to 2012

"Do you think a person has the right to end his or her own life
if this person is tired of living and ready to die?"

(percent distribution of people aged 18 or older by response for selected years

	total	yes	no
2012	100.0%	18.9%	81.1%
2010	100.0	17.1	82.9
2008	100.0	16.5	83.5
2006	100.0	16.5	83.5
2004	100.0	16.5	83.5
2002	100.0	15.1	84.9
2000	100.0	16.6	83.4
1998	100.0	16.0	84.0
1996	100.0	17.1	82.9
1994	100.0	17.2	82.8
1993	100.0	16.2	83.8
1991	100.0	11.7	88.3
1990	100.0	15.0	85.0
1989	100.0	12.6	87.4
1988	100.0	12.0	88.0
1986	100.0	14.5	85.5
1985	100.0	12.5	87.5
1983	100.0	13.4	86.6
1982	100.0	13.3	86.7
1978	100.0	11.5	88.5
1977	100.0	13.0	87.0

*Source: Survey Documentation and Analysis, Computer-assisted Survey Methods Program, University of California, Berkeley,
General Social Survey, 1972–2012 Cumulative Data Files, Internet site http://sda.berkeley.edu/cgi-bin/hsda?harcsda+gss12;
calculations by New Strategist*

2

Government and Politics

The media talk about the growing partisan divide among Americans, and the General Social Survey reveals it. But the gap is not all that big, nor has it changed all that much. Our shared beliefs about government and politics have been relatively stable over the decades, despite the rancor of the 24-hour news cycle.

No Change

• **Americans want government to spend more.** Whether it's education, the environment, fighting crime, or Social Security, the majority of the public has long thought the federal government spends too little on these causes. The public's appetite for spending is not matched by its willingness to levy taxes, however.

Little Change

• **Political leanings have drifted.** Political perspectives have changed somewhat over the decades, but by 2012 they were almost back to where they had been four decades ago. Twenty-seven percent of Americans considered themselves liberal in 2012, up from only 23 percent in the 1980s but down from the 30 percent of 1974. Thirty-five percent identified themselves as conservative in 2012, up from the 30 percent who felt that way in 1974.

• **Political affiliation has shifted.** In 2012, 46 percent of Americans considered themselves Democrats, down from more than half who identified with the Democratic Party until the mid-1980s. A smaller 32 percent identified themselves as Republicans in 2012, down from a high of 43 percent in 1990 but more than the 27 percent of 1972.

Big Change

•**Americans believe women are suited for politics.** In the 1970s, about half the public agreed that men were better suited emotionally for politics than women. Today, only 20 percent agree that men are better suited. Those most likely to feel that way are older Americans (27 percent).

Government and Politics: 2012 Profiles

Table 2.1 Political Leanings, 2012

"We hear a lot of talk these days about liberals and conservatives. On a seven-point scale from extremely liberal (1) to extremely conservative (7), where would you place yourself?"

(percent of people aged 18 or older responding by selected characteristics, 2012)

	total	1 extremely liberal	2 liberal	3 slightly liberal	4 moderate	5 slightly conservative	6 conservative	7 extremely conservative
Total people	100.0%	4.0%	11.8%	11.2%	38.5%	15.4%	15.5%	3.7%
Men	100.0	3.9	11.0	10.0	38.2	17.9	15.7	3.4
Women	100.0	4.2	12.4	12.2	38.7	13.2	15.3	4.0
Millennials	100.0	3.1	12.8	13.1	42.7	15.0	10.7	2.5
Generation Xers	100.0	5.7	11.4	13.3	35.4	15.9	13.9	4.5
Baby Boomers	100.0	4.3	11.3	9.3	37.6	14.4	20.1	3.2
Older Americans	100.0	3.1	10.6	7.7	36.1	18.0	17.6	6.8
Black	100.0	6.1	10.1	13.6	46.2	10.7	10.2	3.1
Hispanic	100.0	4.6	11.8	10.8	41.0	12.7	12.5	6.7
Non-Hispanic white	100.0	3.2	12.0	11.1	35.5	16.7	18.0	3.5
Northeast	100.0	3.6	20.1	11.4	34.0	16.9	11.5	2.5
Midwest	100.0	3.0	9.7	12.6	41.7	15.5	14.2	3.4
South	100.0	4.4	7.7	9.6	39.6	14.9	19.2	4.5
West	100.0	5.0	14.2	12.0	36.8	14.8	13.7	3.6
Not a college graduate	100.0	3.8	9.9	10.8	41.3	14.4	15.4	4.4
Bachelor's degree or more	100.0	4.6	16.4	12.0	31.5	17.7	15.6	2.0

Note: Millennials are aged 18 to 35; Generation Xers are aged 36 to 47; Baby Boomers are aged 48 to 66; Older Americans are aged 67 or older.
Source: Survey Documentation and Analysis, Computer-assisted Survey Methods Program, University of California, Berkeley, General Social Survey, 1972–2012 Cumulative Data Files, Internet site http://sda.berkeley.edu/cgi-bin/hsda?harcsda+gss12; calculations by New Strategist

Table 2.2 Political Party Affiliation, 2012

"Generally speaking, do you usually think of yourself as a Republican, Democrat, Independent, or what?"

(percent of people aged 18 or older responding by selected characteristics, 2012)

	total	strong Democrat	not strong Democrat	independent, near Democrat	independent	independent, near Republican	not strong Republican	strong Republican	other party
Total people	**100.0%**	**16.7%**	**17.0%**	**12.4%**	**19.8%**	**8.2%**	**13.7%**	**9.8%**	**2.3%**
Men	100.0	15.1	14.3	15.6	17.6	10.2	14.5	9.5	3.3
Women	100.0	18.0	19.3	9.7	21.8	6.6	13.1	10.1	1.5
Millennials	100.0	13.5	17.9	13.6	26.2	6.9	14.7	5.2	2.1
Generation Xers	100.0	13.5	17.3	14.1	20.4	10.3	15.3	7.0	2.1
Baby Boomers	100.0	20.1	14.9	12.0	16.7	7.8	11.6	13.9	3.0
Older Americans	100.0	21.2	18.9	8.2	10.5	9.4	13.8	16.0	2.0
Black	100.0	45.1	22.5	13.1	13.7	2.2	0.7	1.2	1.4
Hispanic	100.0	10.8	22.5	12.3	31.5	7.0	10.1	5.3	0.6
Non-Hispanic white	100.0	11.7	14.6	12.3	17.5	10.0	18.0	12.9	3.1
Northeast	100.0	18.5	19.1	13.9	24.0	6.0	9.4	5.8	3.3
Midwest	100.0	17.4	17.8	13.3	18.1	7.6	13.5	10.3	2.1
South	100.0	17.5	14.3	11.3	17.5	9.8	15.2	12.5	1.8
West	100.0	13.3	18.8	12.4	22.2	8.0	14.7	7.9	2.7
Not a college graduate	100.0	15.9	16.5	11.9	22.9	8.2	12.6	9.8	2.1
Bachelor's degree or more	100.0	18.5	18.2	13.8	11.9	8.3	16.6	9.7	3.0

Note: Millennials are aged 18 to 35; Generation Xers are aged 36 to 47; Baby Boomers are aged 48 to 66; Older Americans are aged 67 or older.
Source: Survey Documentation and Analysis, Computer-assisted Survey Methods Program, University of California, Berkeley, General Social Survey, 1972–2012 Cumulative Data Files, Internet site http://sda.berkeley.edu/cgi-bin/hsda?harcsda+gss12; calculations by New Strategist

Table 2.3 Average Citizen Influence on Politics, 2012

"How much influence does the average citizen have on politics:
none, a little, some, quite a bit, or a great deal?"

(percent of people aged 18 or older responding by selected characteristics, 2012)

	total	none	a little	some	quite a bit	great deal
Total people	**100.0%**	**14.5%**	**34.2%**	**31.1%**	**11.3%**	**9.0%**
Men	100.0	18.9	34.2	29.8	10.4	6.8
Women	100.0	9.8	34.2	32.5	12.2	11.3
Millennials	100.0	13.7	37.1	30.9	13.6	4.7
Generation Xers	100.0	15.9	33.3	29.9	11.7	9.2
Baby Boomers	100.0	12.4	32.1	33.2	10.8	11.6
Older Americans	100.0	17.8	33.7	29.8	7.7	11.0
Black	100.0	11.6	18.9	35.6	13.5	20.4
Hispanic	100.0	9.3	24.0	29.8	21.7	15.1
Non-Hispanic white	100.0	15.6	39.6	30.2	10.0	4.6
Northeast	100.0	11.2	28.1	41.6	12.4	6.8
Midwest	100.0	18.1	38.4	28.3	7.4	7.9
South	100.0	13.5	35.9	30.9	10.3	9.5
West	100.0	14.9	31.6	26.3	16.3	11.0
Not a college graduate	100.0	17.1	33.3	27.5	12.4	9.8
Bachelor's degree or more	100.0	8.4	36.3	39.4	8.8	7.1

Note: Millennials are aged 18 to 35; Generation Xers are aged 36 to 47; Baby Boomers are aged 48 to 66; Older Americans are aged 67 or older.
Source: Survey Documentation and Analysis, Computer-assisted Survey Methods Program, University of California, Berkeley, General Social Survey, 1972–2012 Cumulative Data Files, Internet site http://sda.berkeley.edu/cgi-bin/hsda?harcsda+gss12; calculations by New Strategist

Table 2.4 How Much Say about What Government Does, 2012

"How much say do people like you have about what the government does:
none, a little, some, quite a bit, or a great deal?"

(percent of people aged 18 or older responding by selected characteristics, 2012)

	total	none	a little	some	quite a bit	great deal
Total people	**100.0%**	**25.6%**	**34.8%**	**29.6%**	**6.2%**	**3.7%**
Men	100.0	27.6	34.3	27.5	6.0	4.6
Women	100.0	23.5	35.4	31.8	6.5	2.8
Millennials	100.0	25.7	37.0	31.1	3.6	2.5
Generation Xers	100.0	23.5	31.7	33.1	7.1	4.7
Baby Boomers	100.0	23.4	35.6	27.9	8.9	4.2
Older Americans	100.0	32.7	33.8	25.8	4.0	3.7
Black	100.0	24.1	24.3	35.9	4.9	10.8
Hispanic	100.0	17.5	34.8	27.1	17.4	3.3
Non-Hispanic white	100.0	27.4	37.6	28.5	4.7	1.7
Northeast	100.0	15.0	29.7	43.9	9.0	2.3
Midwest	100.0	32.8	34.4	28.2	4.4	0.3
South	100.0	29.1	35.2	25.5	4.4	5.8
West	100.0	20.5	38.7	26.7	9.0	5.1
Not a college graduate	100.0	31.8	32.9	26.7	4.9	3.8
Bachelor's degree or more	100.0	11.5	39.3	36.2	9.3	3.7

Note: Millennials are aged 18 to 35; Generation Xers are aged 36 to 47; Baby Boomers are aged 48 to 66; Older Americans are aged 67 or older.
Source: Survey Documentation and Analysis, Computer-assisted Survey Methods Program, University of California, Berkeley, General Social Survey, 1972–2012 Cumulative Data Files, Internet site http://sda.berkeley.edu/cgi-bin/hsda?harcsda+gss12; calculations by New Strategist

Table 2.5 How Good Is Your Understanding of Political Issues, 2012

"How good is your understanding of the important political issues facing the country: not at all, a little, somewhat, very, or extremely?"

(percent of people aged 18 or older responding by selected characteristics, 2012)

	total	not at all	a little	somewhat	very good	extremely good
Total people	**100.0%**	**4.9%**	**19.6%**	**45.2%**	**24.0%**	**6.4%**
Men	100.0	4.4	16.2	44.1	28.1	7.3
Women	100.0	5.4	23.2	46.4	19.6	5.5
Millennials	100.0	7.1	29.2	39.7	20.1	3.9
Generation Xers	100.0	6.6	14.6	51.3	19.0	8.5
Baby Boomers	100.0	2.4	13.5	43.4	33.6	7.1
Older Americans	100.0	3.7	21.8	50.3	17.8	6.4
Black	100.0	5.7	15.8	45.6	22.9	10.0
Hispanic	100.0	5.4	33.2	40.4	17.3	3.8
Non-Hispanic white	100.0	4.8	18.8	43.3	27.0	6.1
Northeast	100.0	4.2	21.3	50.0	21.5	3.1
Midwest	100.0	3.9	21.1	40.3	29.2	5.6
South	100.0	5.8	19.4	43.3	23.2	8.3
West	100.0	4.7	17.0	49.7	21.7	6.8
Not a college graduate	100.0	6.6	23.3	46.2	19.2	4.7
Bachelor's degree or more	100.0	0.9	10.9	42.9	34.9	10.4

Note: Millennials are aged 18 to 35; Generation Xers are aged 36 to 47; Baby Boomers are aged 48 to 66; Older Americans are aged 67 or older.
Source: Survey Documentation and Analysis, Computer-assisted Survey Methods Program, University of California, Berkeley, General Social Survey, 1972–2012 Cumulative Data Files, Internet site http://sda.berkeley.edu/cgi-bin/hsda?harcsda+gss12; calculations by New Strategist

Table 2.6 How Informed Are You about Politics, 2012

"Compared to most people, how informed are you about politics: not at all, a little, somewhat, very, or extremely?"

(percent of people aged 18 or older responding by selected characteristics, 2012)

	total	not at all	a little	somewhat	very	extremely
Total people	**100.0%**	**8.2%**	**22.3%**	**40.6%**	**21.8%**	**7.1%**
Men	100.0	7.1	18.1	41.8	24.2	8.8
Women	100.0	9.3	26.8	39.2	19.3	5.4
Millennials	100.0	12.4	30.4	36.6	16.7	3.9
Generation Xers	100.0	5.8	25.5	38.2	20.8	9.8
Baby Boomers	100.0	6.0	13.5	46.4	25.0	9.0
Older Americans	100.0	7.1	22.5	39.7	25.8	4.9
Black	100.0	6.6	15.6	48.4	22.4	7.0
Hispanic	100.0	14.8	33.8	37.3	9.4	4.6
Non-Hispanic white	100.0	6.3	21.9	40.1	24.3	7.4
Northeast	100.0	11.4	21.2	44.3	17.8	5.3
Midwest	100.0	7.0	21.6	43.0	21.4	7.0
South	100.0	8.4	21.2	38.6	23.0	8.9
West	100.0	6.4	25.9	38.5	23.4	5.8
Not a college graduate	100.0	10.1	26.3	40.6	18.7	4.2
Bachelor's degree or more	100.0	3.6	13.0	40.3	29.0	14.0

Note: Millennials are aged 18 to 35; Generation Xers are aged 36 to 47; Baby Boomers are aged 48 to 66; Older Americans are aged 67 or older.
Source: Survey Documentation and Analysis, Computer-assisted Survey Methods Program, University of California, Berkeley, General Social Survey, 1972–2012 Cumulative Data Files, Internet site http://sda.berkeley.edu/cgi-bin/hsda?harcsda+gss12; calculations by New Strategist

Table 2.7 How Often Does Congress Keep Promises, 2012

"How often do the people we elect to Congress try to keep the promises they have made during the election: never, rarely, sometimes, very often, or extremely often?"

(percent of people aged 18 or older responding by selected characteristics, 2012)

	total	never	very rarely	sometimes	often	extremely often
Total people	**100.0%**	**10.3%**	**35.7%**	**45.2%**	**7.8%**	**1.0%**
Men	100.0	12.6	38.9	39.1	8.2	1.2
Women	100.0	7.8	32.4	51.7	7.4	0.7
Millennials	100.0	12.9	33.9	45.4	5.9	1.8
Generation Xers	100.0	12.4	26.8	51.9	7.4	1.5
Baby Boomers	100.0	6.0	41.9	41.4	10.2	0.4
Older Americans	100.0	12.4	37.9	43.4	6.3	0.0
Black	100.0	7.7	28.1	45.7	14.5	4.1
Hispanic	100.0	15.4	31.1	46.7	5.7	1.1
Non-Hispanic white	100.0	10.6	37.1	45.3	6.8	0.3
Northeast	100.0	8.1	34.3	51.2	4.5	2.0
Midwest	100.0	11.7	30.2	50.9	5.9	1.2
South	100.0	12.9	40.0	39.2	7.7	0.2
West	100.0	6.1	35.3	44.9	12.4	1.3
Not a college graduate	100.0	13.5	38.1	39.7	7.3	1.4
Bachelor's degree or more	100.0	2.9	30.2	58.0	8.8	0.0

Note: Millennials are aged 18 to 35; Generation Xers are aged 36 to 47; Baby Boomers are aged 48 to 66; Older Americans are aged 67 or older.
Source: Survey Documentation and Analysis, Computer-assisted Survey Methods Program, University of California, Berkeley, General Social Survey, 1972–2012 Cumulative Data Files, Internet site http://sda.berkeley.edu/cgi-bin/hsda?harcsda+gss12; calculations by New Strategist

Table 2.8 How Many Government Administrators Can Be Trusted, 2012

"How many government administrators can be trusted to do what
is best for the country: none, a few, some, most, or all?"

(percent of people aged 18 or older responding by selected characteristics, 2012)

	total	none	a few	some	most	all
Total people	**100.0%**	**9.6%**	**42.0%**	**38.2%**	**9.7%**	**0.5%**
Men	100.0	8.5	43.2	35.6	11.8	0.8
Women	100.0	10.7	40.7	41.0	7.4	0.3
Millennials	100.0	12.8	45.8	29.8	10.6	1.0
Generation Xers	100.0	12.7	31.0	49.4	6.3	0.6
Baby Boomers	100.0	4.6	44.8	41.2	9.3	0.2
Older Americans	100.0	8.7	46.8	29.6	14.4	0.5
Black	100.0	8.0	47.6	31.8	12.6	0.0
Hispanic	100.0	16.2	38.7	35.7	7.8	1.6
Non-Hispanic white	100.0	8.8	39.4	41.5	9.7	0.5
Northeast	100.0	6.9	37.5	45.6	9.2	0.8
Midwest	100.0	9.6	48.6	31.5	10.2	0.0
South	100.0	13.5	39.1	38.4	8.0	1.1
West	100.0	5.0	43.4	39.3	12.4	0.0
Not a college graduate	100.0	12.9	44.9	33.5	8.0	0.7
Bachelor's degree or more	100.0	1.9	35.1	49.3	13.6	0.2

Note: Millennials are aged 18 to 35; Generation Xers are aged 36 to 47; Baby Boomers are aged 48 to 66; Older Americans are aged 67 or older.
Source: Survey Documentation and Analysis, Computer-assisted Survey Methods Program, University of California, Berkeley, General Social Survey, 1972–2012 Cumulative Data Files, Internet site http://sda.berkeley.edu/cgi-bin/hsda?harcsda+gss12; calculations by New Strategist

Table 2.9 Women Not Suited for Politics, 2012

"Tell me if you agree or disagree with this statement: Most men are better suited emotionally for politics than are most women."

(percent of people aged 18 or older responding by selected characteristics, 2012)

	total	agree	disagree
Total people	**100.0%**	**20.1%**	**79.9%**
Men	100.0	21.3	78.7
Women	100.0	19.2	80.8
Millennials	100.0	23.4	76.6
Generation Xers	100.0	20.0	80.0
Baby Boomers	100.0	12.5	87.5
Older Americans	100.0	27.4	72.6
Black	100.0	19.4	80.6
Hispanic	100.0	24.6	75.4
Non-Hispanic white	100.0	17.1	82.9
Northeast	100.0	18.2	81.8
Midwest	100.0	16.3	83.7
South	100.0	22.6	77.4
West	100.0	21.3	78.7
Not a college graduate	100.0	22.7	77.3
Bachelor's degree or more	100.0	13.4	86.6

Note: Millennials are aged 18 to 35; Generation Xers are aged 36 to 47; Baby Boomers are aged 48 to 66; Older Americans are aged 67 or older.
Source: Survey Documentation and Analysis, Computer-assisted Survey Methods Program, University of California, Berkeley, General Social Survey, 1972–2012 Cumulative Data Files, Internet site http://sda.berkeley.edu/cgi-bin/hsda?harcsda+gss12; calculations by New Strategist

Table 2.10 Should Government Do More or Less, 2012

"Some people think that the government in Washington is trying to do too many things that should be left to individuals and private business; they are at point 5. Others disagree and think the government should do even more to solve our country's problems; they are at point 1. Where would you place yourself on the scale?"

(percent of people aged 18 or older responding by selected characteristics, 2012)

	total	1 government should do more	2	3 agree with both	4	5 government does too much
Total people	100.0%	15.0%	12.1%	41.0%	12.7%	19.2%
Men	100.0	14.4	12.3	39.6	12.1	21.5
Women	100.0	15.6	11.8	42.3	13.1	17.2
Millennials	100.0	13.0	17.6	43.6	15.6	10.2
Generation Xers	100.0	16.2	10.1	45.5	11.8	16.4
Baby Boomers	100.0	14.3	10.6	38.6	11.1	25.4
Older Americans	100.0	19.5	6.7	34.8	11.0	28.1
Black	100.0	30.0	12.3	44.2	5.7	7.8
Hispanic	100.0	24.2	10.4	47.4	7.6	10.4
Non-Hispanic white	100.0	8.8	12.5	38.4	15.5	24.8
Northeast	100.0	20.2	12.8	45.8	5.9	15.3
Midwest	100.0	14.6	11.5	40.4	14.0	19.6
South	100.0	13.9	10.6	40.2	12.2	23.1
West	100.0	13.2	14.5	39.3	17.4	15.6
Not a college graduate	100.0	17.6	10.6	42.4	10.9	18.5
Bachelor's degree or more	100.0	9.0	15.5	37.8	16.7	21.0

Note: Millennials are aged 18 to 35; Generation Xers are aged 36 to 47; Baby Boomers are aged 48 to 66; Older Americans are aged 67 or older.
Source: Survey Documentation and Analysis, Computer-assisted Survey Methods Program, University of California, Berkeley, General Social Survey, 1972–2012 Cumulative Data Files, Internet site http://sda.berkeley.edu/cgi-bin/hsda?harcsda+gss12; calculations by New Strategist

Table 2.11 Government Should Help Pay for Medical Care, 2012

"In general, some people think that it is the responsibility of the government in Washington to see to it that people have help in paying for doctors and hospital bills; they are at point 1. Others think that these matters are not the responsibility of the federal government and that people should take care of these things themselves; they are at point 5. Where would you place yourself on the scale?"

(percent of people aged 18 or older responding by selected characteristics, 2012)

	total	1 government should help	2	3 agree with both	4	5 people should help themselves
Total people	100.0%	28.4%	18.1%	31.4%	12.4%	9.7%
Men	100.0	22.2	19.5	33.5	16.1	8.8
Women	100.0	33.6	17.0	29.6	9.3	10.5
Millennials	100.0	29.4	25.2	26.9	13.8	4.6
Generation Xers	100.0	24.3	17.7	36.3	12.6	9.2
Baby Boomers	100.0	31.3	15.3	29.3	11.8	12.3
Older Americans	100.0	25.4	9.7	38.7	10.4	15.7
Black	100.0	44.8	17.4	30.4	2.0	5.4
Hispanic	100.0	33.3	14.9	34.6	8.3	9.0
Non-Hispanic white	100.0	23.8	19.5	30.2	15.4	10.9
Northeast	100.0	33.4	22.5	30.1	9.1	4.9
Midwest	100.0	26.2	19.9	28.7	12.9	12.4
South	100.0	26.4	14.0	33.8	13.7	12.1
West	100.0	29.9	19.7	31.1	12.3	7.0
Not a college graduate	100.0	30.7	16.8	31.9	10.0	10.6
Bachelor's degree or more	100.0	22.8	21.4	30.1	18.2	7.4

Note: Millennials are aged 18 to 35; Generation Xers are aged 36 to 47; Baby Boomers are aged 48 to 66; Older Americans are aged 67 or older.
Source: Survey Documentation and Analysis, Computer-assisted Survey Methods Program, University of California, Berkeley, General Social Survey, 1972–2012 Cumulative Data Files, Internet site http://sda.berkeley.edu/cgi-bin/hsda?harcsda+gss12; calculations by New Strategist

Table 2.12 Should Government Improve the Standard of Living, 2012

"Some people think that the government in Washington should do everything possible to improve the standard of living of all poor Americans. Other people think it is not the government's responsibility, and that each person should take care of himself. Where would you place yourself on this scale?"

(percent of people aged 18 or older responding by selected characteristics, 2012)

	total	1 government should act	2	3 agree with both	4	5 people should help themselves
Total people	100.0%	14.9%	11.9%	44.6%	14.9%	13.7%
Men	100.0	11.6	11.4	45.4	16.8	14.8
Women	100.0	17.7	12.3	43.9	13.2	12.8
Millennials	100.0	13.0	17.6	47.3	15.4	6.6
Generation Xers	100.0	14.3	10.0	45.9	15.2	14.5
Baby Boomers	100.0	16.3	11.4	40.8	14.0	17.5
Older Americans	100.0	16.4	3.3	45.2	15.1	20.0
Black	100.0	28.8	10.2	48.5	5.2	7.3
Hispanic	100.0	23.1	10.6	43.3	11.2	11.9
Non-Hispanic white	100.0	9.7	12.5	43.9	17.7	16.1
Northeast	100.0	22.2	16.7	39.6	12.0	9.5
Midwest	100.0	11.8	10.2	44.0	16.8	17.2
South	100.0	14.9	7.8	44.5	15.7	17.2
West	100.0	12.1	16.4	49.4	13.9	8.1
Not a college graduate	100.0	18.4	10.8	45.8	10.8	14.1
Bachelor's degree or more	100.0	6.4	14.6	41.6	24.6	12.8

Note: Millennials are aged 18 to 35; Generation Xers are aged 36 to 47; Baby Boomers are aged 48 to 66; Older Americans are aged 67 or older.
Source: Survey Documentation and Analysis, Computer-assisted Survey Methods Program, University of California, Berkeley, General Social Survey, 1972–2012 Cumulative Data Files, Internet site http://sda.berkeley.edu/cgi-bin/hsda?harcsda+gss12; calculations by New Strategist

Table 2.13 Should Government Reduce Income Differences, 2012

"Some people think that the government in Washington ought to reduce the income differences between the rich and the poor, perhaps by raising the taxes of wealthy families or by giving income assistance to the poor. Others think that the government should not concern itself with reducing this income difference between the rich and the poor. Think of a score of 1 as meaning that the government ought to reduce the income differences between rich and poor, and a score of 7 meaning that the government should not concern itself with reducing income differences. What score between 1 and 7 comes closest to the way you feel?"

(percent of people aged 18 or older responding by selected characteristics, 2012)

	total	1 government should reduce	2	3	4	5	6	7 no government involvement
Total people	100.0%	24.3%	10.1%	15.3%	18.0%	11.2%	6.6%	14.5%
Men	100.0	22.4	11.8	13.9	17.1	10.6	7.8	16.4
Women	100.0	25.9	8.7	16.5	18.8	11.7	5.6	12.8
Millennials	100.0	23.6	12.3	21.3	19.6	11.9	4.1	7.2
Generation Xers	100.0	20.3	12.5	16.4	16.4	12.9	7.7	13.8
Baby Boomers	100.0	27.4	8.1	11.9	16.4	10.3	7.8	18.2
Older Americans	100.0	24.2	6.6	8.3	21.0	9.2	7.8	22.9
Black	100.0	46.8	10.3	12.1	16.4	7.8	0.4	6.1
Hispanic	100.0	28.5	8.5	16.6	23.7	7.5	3.6	11.6
Non-Hispanic white	100.0	17.8	11.3	14.8	17.2	12.5	8.8	17.7
Northeast	100.0	29.9	10.6	17.9	17.4	9.3	5.6	9.3
Midwest	100.0	20.9	13.3	12.3	13.5	15.1	8.2	16.8
South	100.0	25.5	8.0	15.0	19.1	9.1	6.8	16.5
West	100.0	21.4	10.1	16.8	21.1	12.2	5.5	12.9
Not a college graduate	100.0	28.8	9.0	14.7	18.5	10.5	5.1	13.2
Bachelor's degree or more	100.0	13.2	12.7	16.7	16.8	12.8	10.2	17.6

Note: Millennials are aged 18 to 35; Generation Xers are aged 36 to 47; Baby Boomers are aged 48 to 66; Older Americans are aged 67 or older.
Source: Survey Documentation and Analysis, Computer-assisted Survey Methods Program, University of California, Berkeley, General Social Survey, 1972–2012 Cumulative Data Files, Internet site http://sda.berkeley.edu/cgi-bin/hsda?harcsda+gss12; calculations by New Strategist

Table 2.14 Spending on Education, 2012

"We are faced with many problems in this country, none of which can be solved easily or inexpensively. Are we spending too much, too little money, or about the right amount on improving the nation's education system?"

(percent of people aged 18 or older responding by selected characteristics, 2012)

	total	too little	about right	too much
Total people	**100.0%**	**74.9%**	**17.4%**	**7.7%**
Men	100.0	71.0	20.3	8.7
Women	100.0	77.6	15.4	7.1
Millennials	100.0	77.5	19.7	2.8
Generation Xers	100.0	78.6	12.6	8.8
Baby Boomers	100.0	72.9	15.0	12.1
Older Americans	100.0	64.0	25.2	10.7
Black	100.0	77.3	19.2	3.5
Hispanic	100.0	65.5	30.5	4.0
Non-Hispanic white	100.0	76.5	13.9	9.6
Northeast	100.0	78.6	14.4	7.0
Midwest	100.0	77.8	17.9	4.3
South	100.0	70.4	20.4	9.2
West	100.0	77.0	14.0	9.0
Not a college graduate	100.0	72.8	20.4	6.8
Bachelor's degree or more	100.0	80.2	9.6	10.2

Note: Millennials are aged 18 to 35; Generation Xers are aged 36 to 47; Baby Boomers are aged 48 to 66; Older Americans are aged 67 or older.
Source: Survey Documentation and Analysis, Computer-assisted Survey Methods Program, University of California, Berkeley, General Social Survey, 1972–2012 Cumulative Data Files, Internet site http://sda.berkeley.edu/cgi-bin/hsda?harcsda+gss12; calculations by New Strategist

Table 2.15 Spending on the Environment, 2012

"We are faced with many problems in this country, none of which can be solved easily or inexpensively. Are we spending too much, too little money, or about the right amount on improving and protecting the environment?"

(percent of people aged 18 or older responding by selected characteristics, 2012)

	total	too little	about right	too much
Total people	**100.0%**	**57.1%**	**31.2%**	**11.7%**
Men	100.0	59.0	28.1	12.9
Women	100.0	55.8	33.3	10.9
Millennials	100.0	64.0	29.4	6.6
Generation Xers	100.0	54.7	32.9	12.4
Baby Boomers	100.0	53.6	29.8	16.6
Older Americans	100.0	49.4	35.9	14.7
Black	100.0	63.7	31.8	4.5
Hispanic	100.0	55.2	37.8	7.0
Non-Hispanic white	100.0	55.5	29.5	14.9
Northeast	100.0	63.6	23.5	12.9
Midwest	100.0	58.1	34.8	7.1
South	100.0	55.0	31.2	13.9
West	100.0	54.9	33.7	11.4
Not a college graduate	100.0	58.0	32.0	10.0
Bachelor's degree or more	100.0	54.9	29.1	16.1

Note: Millennials are aged 18 to 35; Generation Xers are aged 36 to 47; Baby Boomers are aged 48 to 66; Older Americans are aged 67 or older.
Source: Survey Documentation and Analysis, Computer-assisted Survey Methods Program, University of California, Berkeley, General Social Survey, 1972–2012 Cumulative Data Files, Internet site http://sda.berkeley.edu/cgi-bin/hsda?harcsda+gss12; calculations by New Strategist

Table 2.16 Spending on Drug Addiction, 2012

"We are faced with many problems in this country, none of which can be solved easily or inexpensively. Are we spending too much, too little money, or about the right amount on dealing with drug addiction?"

(percent of people aged 18 or older responding by selected characteristics, 2012)

	total	too little	about right	too much
Total people	**100.0%**	**55.8%**	**31.9%**	**12.3%**
Men	100.0	54.4	29.5	16.1
Women	100.0	56.8	33.5	9.7
Millennials	100.0	52.0	34.7	13.3
Generation Xers	100.0	54.0	34.1	11.9
Baby Boomers	100.0	58.8	28.3	12.9
Older Americans	100.0	63.1	28.2	8.7
Black	100.0	69.6	23.4	7.0
Hispanic	100.0	51.8	34.9	13.3
Non-Hispanic white	100.0	52.9	34.3	12.8
Northeast	100.0	54.1	29.5	16.4
Midwest	100.0	54.3	37.5	8.2
South	100.0	57.2	27.1	15.7
West	100.0	56.1	36.4	7.4
Not a college graduate	100.0	59.5	30.1	10.3
Bachelor's degree or more	100.0	46.2	36.3	17.5

Note: Millennials are aged 18 to 35; Generation Xers are aged 36 to 47; Baby Boomers are aged 48 to 66; Older Americans are aged 67 or older.
Source: Survey Documentation and Analysis, Computer-assisted Survey Methods Program, University of California, Berkeley, General Social Survey, 1972–2012 Cumulative Data Files, Internet site http://sda.berkeley.edu/cgi-bin/hsda?harcsda+gss12; calculations by New Strategist

Table 2.17 Spending on Halting the Rising Crime Rate, 2012

"We are faced with many problems in this country, none of which can be solved easily or inexpensively. Are we spending too much, too little money, or about the right amount on halting the rising crime rate?"

(percent of people aged 18 or older responding by selected characteristics, 2012)

	total	too little	about right	too much
Total people	**100.0%**	**59.0%**	**33.9%**	**7.1%**
Men	100.0	53.4	38.7	7.9
Women	100.0	62.8	30.6	6.6
Millennials	100.0	53.8	36.8	9.4
Generation Xers	100.0	57.4	38.1	4.5
Baby Boomers	100.0	64.3	29.5	6.3
Older Americans	100.0	64.7	28.4	7.0
Black	100.0	67.8	27.1	5.1
Hispanic	100.0	56.9	34.5	8.6
Non-Hispanic white	100.0	58.5	35.0	6.5
Northeast	100.0	49.5	41.2	9.3
Midwest	100.0	61.3	33.1	5.6
South	100.0	59.7	33.7	6.5
West	100.0	62.7	29.5	7.9
Not a college graduate	100.0	64.5	28.9	6.5
Bachelor's degree or more	100.0	44.8	46.6	8.6

Note: Millennials are aged 18 to 35; Generation Xers are aged 36 to 47; Baby Boomers are aged 48 to 66; Older Americans are aged 67 or older.
Source: Survey Documentation and Analysis, Computer-assisted Survey Methods Program, University of California, Berkeley, General Social Survey, 1972–2012 Cumulative Data Files, Internet site http://sda.berkeley.edu/cgi-bin/hsda?harcsda+gss12; calculations by New Strategist

Table 2.18 Spending on Solving the Problems of Big Cities, 2012

"We are faced with many problems in this country, none of which can be solved easily or inexpensively. Are we spending too much, too little money, or about the right amount on solving the problems of big cities?"

(percent of people aged 18 or older responding by selected characteristics, 2012)

	total	too little	about right	too much
Total people	**100.0%**	**42.3%**	**39.4%**	**18.2%**
Men	100.0	42.3	41.1	16.7
Women	100.0	42.4	38.3	19.3
Millennials	100.0	40.9	43.4	15.7
Generation Xers	100.0	44.9	39.6	15.5
Baby Boomers	100.0	40.0	37.4	22.6
Older Americans	100.0	48.3	30.7	21.1
Black	100.0	54.7	27.6	17.7
Hispanic	100.0	42.5	44.3	13.2
Non-Hispanic white	100.0	38.1	41.6	20.3
Northeast	100.0	45.0	44.4	10.5
Midwest	100.0	45.9	38.9	15.2
South	100.0	41.8	35.3	22.8
West	100.0	37.8	43.3	19.0
Not a college graduate	100.0	43.2	36.2	20.6
Bachelor's degree or more	100.0	40.3	47.5	12.3

Note: Millennials are aged 18 to 35; Generation Xers are aged 36 to 47; Baby Boomers are aged 48 to 66; Older Americans are aged 67 or older.
Source: Survey Documentation and Analysis, Computer-assisted Survey Methods Program, University of California, Berkeley, General Social Survey, 1972–2012 Cumulative Data Files, Internet site http://sda.berkeley.edu/cgi-bin/hsda?harcsda+gss12; calculations by New Strategist

Table 2.19 Spending on Improving the Nation's Health, 2012

"We are faced with many problems in this country, none of which can be solved easily or inexpensively. Are we spending too much, too little money, or about the right amount on improving and protecting the nation's health?"

(percent of people aged 18 or older responding by selected characteristics, 2012)

	total	too little	about right	too much
Total people	**100.0%**	**61.7%**	**26.3%**	**12.0%**
Men	100.0	56.7	31.0	12.2
Women	100.0	65.1	23.0	11.9
Millennials	100.0	64.1	27.3	8.7
Generation Xers	100.0	63.1	24.5	12.4
Baby Boomers	100.0	64.3	21.4	14.3
Older Americans	100.0	45.5	37.9	16.6
Black	100.0	78.8	18.6	2.6
Hispanic	100.0	58.8	31.1	10.0
Non-Hispanic white	100.0	57.3	27.3	15.4
Northeast	100.0	63.6	27.3	9.1
Midwest	100.0	57.8	31.6	10.5
South	100.0	62.9	23.5	13.6
West	100.0	61.8	25.2	13.0
Not a college graduate	100.0	64.9	25.0	10.0
Bachelor's degree or more	100.0	53.4	29.4	17.2

Note: Millennials are aged 18 to 35; Generation Xers are aged 36 to 47; Baby Boomers are aged 48 to 66; Older Americans are aged 67 or older.
Source: Survey Documentation and Analysis, Computer-assisted Survey Methods Program, University of California, Berkeley, General Social Survey, 1972–2012 Cumulative Data Files, Internet site http://sda.berkeley.edu/cgi-bin/hsda?harcsda+gss12; calculations by New Strategist

Table 2.20 Spending on Improving the Condition of Blacks, 2012

"We are faced with many problems in this country, none of which can be solved easily or inexpensively. Are we spending too much, too little money, or about the right amount on improving the condition of blacks?"

(percent of people aged 18 or older responding by selected characteristics, 2012)

	total	too little	about right	too much
Total people	**100.0%**	**36.0%**	**49.0%**	**15.0%**
Men	100.0	31.3	53.0	15.7
Women	100.0	39.4	46.1	14.5
Millennials	100.0	35.5	54.3	10.2
Generation Xers	100.0	34.6	50.4	15.0
Baby Boomers	100.0	35.3	44.3	20.4
Older Americans	100.0	41.8	41.9	16.4
Black	100.0	66.5	32.0	1.5
Hispanic	100.0	31.8	56.4	11.8
Non-Hispanic white	100.0	29.3	51.0	19.7
Northeast	100.0	40.7	52.8	6.6
Midwest	100.0	40.6	47.2	12.2
South	100.0	33.2	45.1	21.7
West	100.0	32.9	54.7	12.4
Not a college graduate	100.0	35.3	47.1	17.6
Bachelor's degree or more	100.0	37.8	53.8	8.4

Note: Millennials are aged 18 to 35; Generation Xers are aged 36 to 47; Baby Boomers are aged 48 to 66; Older Americans are aged 67 or older.
Source: Survey Documentation and Analysis, Computer-assisted Survey Methods Program, University of California, Berkeley, General Social Survey, 1972–2012 Cumulative Data Files, Internet site http://sda.berkeley.edu/cgi-bin/hsda?harcsda+gss12; calculations by New Strategist

Table 2.21 Spending on the Military, 2012

"We are faced with many problems in this country, none of which can be solved easily or inexpensively. Are we spending too much, too little money, or about the right amount on military, armaments, and defense?"

(percent of people aged 18 or older responding by selected characteristics, 2012)

	total	too little	about right	too much
Total people	**100.0%**	**24.7%**	**42.9%**	**32.4%**
Men	100.0	20.0	42.5	37.5
Women	100.0	28.0	43.2	28.8
Millennials	100.0	20.0	46.6	33.5
Generation Xers	100.0	21.0	43.8	35.2
Baby Boomers	100.0	30.3	36.5	33.2
Older Americans	100.0	33.2	45.5	21.3
Black	100.0	19.5	52.1	28.4
Hispanic	100.0	17.4	45.4	37.2
Non-Hispanic white	100.0	27.4	41.6	31.0
Northeast	100.0	15.9	43.0	41.0
Midwest	100.0	21.6	48.7	29.7
South	100.0	28.1	44.8	27.1
West	100.0	28.4	34.2	37.4
Not a college graduate	100.0	27.4	43.8	28.8
Bachelor's degree or more	100.0	17.8	40.6	41.6

Note: Millennials are aged 18 to 35; Generation Xers are aged 36 to 47; Baby Boomers are aged 48 to 66; Older Americans are aged 67 or older.
Source: Survey Documentation and Analysis, Computer-assisted Survey Methods Program, University of California, Berkeley, General Social Survey, 1972–2012 Cumulative Data Files, Internet site http://sda.berkeley.edu/cgi-bin/hsda?harcsda+gss12; calculations by New Strategist

Table 2.22 Spending on Foreign Aid, 2012

"We are faced with many problems in this country, none of which can be solved easily or inexpensively. Are we spending too much, too little money, or about the right amount on foreign aid?"

(percent of people aged 18 or older responding by selected characteristics, 2012)

	total	too little	about right	too much
Total people	**100.0%**	**9.3%**	**26.9%**	**63.8%**
Men	100.0	10.4	26.2	63.4
Women	100.0	8.5	27.4	64.1
Millennials	100.0	11.9	37.0	51.1
Generation Xers	100.0	6.8	24.5	68.6
Baby Boomers	100.0	7.9	19.4	72.8
Older Americans	100.0	9.4	19.0	71.6
Black	100.0	15.8	32.0	52.2
Hispanic	100.0	18.5	33.5	48.0
Non-Hispanic white	100.0	5.4	24.0	70.6
Northeast	100.0	13.3	28.3	58.4
Midwest	100.0	5.5	21.0	73.5
South	100.0	7.6	30.2	62.2
West	100.0	12.7	25.7	61.5
Not a college graduate	100.0	10.0	24.8	65.2
Bachelor's degree or more	100.0	7.5	32.1	60.4

Note: Millennials are aged 18 to 35; Generation Xers are aged 36 to 47; Baby Boomers are aged 48 to 66; Older Americans are aged 67 or older.
Source: Survey Documentation and Analysis, Computer-assisted Survey Methods Program, University of California, Berkeley, General Social Survey, 1972–2012 Cumulative Data Files, Internet site http://sda.berkeley.edu/cgi-bin/hsda?harcsda+gss12; calculations by New Strategist

Table 2.23 Spending on Welfare, 2012

"We are faced with many problems in this country, none of which can be solved easily or inexpensively. Are we spending too much, too little money, or about the right amount on welfare?"

(percent of people aged 18 or older responding by selected characteristics, 2012)

	total	too little	about right	too much
Total people	**100.0%**	**19.1%**	**33.3%**	**47.6%**
Men	100.0	16.8	35.6	47.6
Women	100.0	20.7	31.7	47.5
Millennials	100.0	16.9	34.9	48.2
Generation Xers	100.0	21.4	31.5	47.1
Baby Boomers	100.0	21.2	29.6	49.3
Older Americans	100.0	16.3	40.5	43.2
Black	100.0	25.2	39.3	35.5
Hispanic	100.0	19.6	39.2	41.2
Non-Hispanic white	100.0	16.0	30.0	54.0
Northeast	100.0	19.9	29.1	50.9
Midwest	100.0	15.4	34.9	49.7
South	100.0	20.5	31.5	48.0
West	100.0	19.6	37.9	42.4
Not a college graduate	100.0	19.9	30.7	49.4
Bachelor's degree or more	100.0	17.2	40.0	42.9

Note: Millennials are aged 18 to 35; Generation Xers are aged 36 to 47; Baby Boomers are aged 48 to 66; Older Americans are aged 67 or older.
Source: Survey Documentation and Analysis, Computer-assisted Survey Methods Program, University of California, Berkeley, General Social Survey, 1972–2012 Cumulative Data Files, Internet site http://sda.berkeley.edu/cgi-bin/hsda?harcsda+gss12; calculations by New Strategist

Table 2.24 Spending on Space Exploration, 2012

"We are faced with many problems in this country, none of which can be solved easily or inexpensively. Are we spending too much, too little money, or about the right amount on space exploration?"

(percent of people aged 18 or older responding by selected characteristics, 2012)

	total	too little	about right	too much
Total people	**100.0%**	**21.7%**	**45.9%**	**32.5%**
Men	100.0	27.3	44.6	28.1
Women	100.0	17.6	46.8	35.6
Millennials	100.0	21.6	51.9	26.5
Generation Xers	100.0	24.4	38.4	37.2
Baby Boomers	100.0	20.0	45.7	34.3
Older Americans	100.0	21.1	41.2	37.8
Black	100.0	11.1	38.6	50.3
Hispanic	100.0	20.1	43.9	36.0
Non-Hispanic white	100.0	25.5	47.0	27.5
Northeast	100.0	19.8	47.7	32.6
Midwest	100.0	20.1	49.0	30.8
South	100.0	23.2	42.5	34.4
West	100.0	22.0	47.4	30.7
Not a college graduate	100.0	17.3	46.9	35.8
Bachelor's degree or more	100.0	32.3	43.5	24.3

Note: Millennials are aged 18 to 35; Generation Xers are aged 36 to 47; Baby Boomers are aged 48 to 66; Older Americans are aged 67 or older.
Source: Survey Documentation and Analysis, Computer-assisted Survey Methods Program, University of California, Berkeley, General Social Survey, 1972–2012 Cumulative Data Files, Internet site http://sda.berkeley.edu/cgi-bin/hsda?harcsda+gss12; calculations by New Strategist

Table 2.25 Spending on Mass Transportation, 2012

"We are faced with many problems in this country, none of which can be solved easily or inexpensively. Are we spending too much, too little money, or about the right amount on mass transportation?"

(percent of people aged 18 or older responding by selected characteristics, 2012)

	total	too little	about right	too much
Total people	**100.0%**	**39.9%**	**50.1%**	**10.0%**
Men	100.0	44.0	44.9	11.1
Women	100.0	36.2	54.8	9.1
Millennials	100.0	36.7	55.0	8.2
Generation Xers	100.0	39.5	49.5	11.0
Baby Boomers	100.0	42.2	45.9	11.9
Older Americans	100.0	43.2	48.3	8.4
Black	100.0	47.0	44.5	8.6
Hispanic	100.0	32.6	57.4	10.0
Non-Hispanic white	100.0	39.4	50.1	10.5
Northeast	100.0	40.5	48.8	10.7
Midwest	100.0	35.0	57.3	7.7
South	100.0	40.4	48.6	11.0
West	100.0	43.2	46.5	10.3
Not a college graduate	100.0	35.9	53.4	10.6
Bachelor's degree or more	100.0	49.4	42.0	8.5

Note: Millennials are aged 18 to 35; Generation Xers are aged 36 to 47; Baby Boomers are aged 48 to 66; Older Americans are aged 67 or older.
Source: Survey Documentation and Analysis, Computer-assisted Survey Methods Program, University of California, Berkeley, General Social Survey, 1972–2012 Cumulative Data Files, Internet site http://sda.berkeley.edu/cgi-bin/hsda?harcsda+gss12; calculations by New Strategist

Table 2.26 Spending on Highways and Bridges, 2012

"We are faced with many problems in this country, none of which can be solved easily or inexpensively. Are we spending too much, too little money, or about the right amount on highways and bridges?"

(percent of people aged 18 or older responding by selected characteristics, 2012)

	total	too little	about right	too much
Total people	**100.0%**	**43.0%**	**43.9%**	**13.1%**
Men	100.0	50.2	40.1	9.7
Women	100.0	36.7	47.2	16.1
Millennials	100.0	32.4	50.6	17.0
Generation Xers	100.0	42.0	42.8	15.2
Baby Boomers	100.0	48.6	40.5	11.0
Older Americans	100.0	57.0	37.4	5.6
Black	100.0	42.3	34.9	22.9
Hispanic	100.0	22.8	56.4	20.8
Non-Hispanic white	100.0	49.2	41.6	9.1
Northeast	100.0	50.2	40.3	9.6
Midwest	100.0	46.8	42.0	11.1
South	100.0	41.3	45.3	13.4
West	100.0	36.6	46.2	17.3
Not a college graduate	100.0	40.7	44.0	15.4
Bachelor's degree or more	100.0	48.9	43.8	7.3

Note: Millennials are aged 18 to 35; Generation Xers are aged 36 to 47; Baby Boomers are aged 48 to 66; Older Americans are aged 67 or older.
Source: Survey Documentation and Analysis, Computer-assisted Survey Methods Program, University of California, Berkeley, General Social Survey, 1972–2012 Cumulative Data Files, Internet site http://sda.berkeley.edu/cgi-bin/hsda?harcsda+gss12; calculations by New Strategist

Table 2.27 Spending on Social Security, 2012

"We are faced with many problems in this country, none of which can be solved easily or inexpensively. Are we spending too much, too little money, or about the right amount on Social Security?"

(percent of people aged 18 or older responding by selected characteristics, 2012)

	total	too little	about right	too much
Total people	**100.0%**	**55.9%**	**35.8%**	**8.3%**
Men	100.0	50.3	40.5	9.2
Women	100.0	60.7	31.7	7.6
Millennials	100.0	56.9	31.4	11.7
Generation Xers	100.0	56.9	34.7	8.4
Baby Boomers	100.0	60.6	33.4	6.1
Older Americans	100.0	42.3	52.8	4.9
Black	100.0	73.8	23.4	2.8
Hispanic	100.0	57.5	31.2	11.3
Non-Hispanic white	100.0	52.1	39.1	8.7
Northeast	100.0	52.9	34.2	12.8
Midwest	100.0	55.9	36.7	7.5
South	100.0	61.3	31.7	7.1
West	100.0	49.5	42.7	7.8
Not a college graduate	100.0	61.9	30.8	7.2
Bachelor's degree or more	100.0	40.6	48.4	11.0

Note: Millennials are aged 18 to 35; Generation Xers are aged 36 to 47; Baby Boomers are aged 48 to 66; Older Americans are aged 67 or older.
Source: Survey Documentation and Analysis, Computer-assisted Survey Methods Program, University of California, Berkeley, General Social Survey, 1972–2012 Cumulative Data Files, Internet site http://sda.berkeley.edu/cgi-bin/hsda?harcsda+gss12; calculations by New Strategist

Table 2.28 Spending on Parks and Recreation, 2012

"We are faced with many problems in this country, none of which can be solved easily or inexpensively. Are we spending too much, too little money, or about the right amount on parks and recreation?"

(percent of people aged 18 or older responding by selected characteristics, 2012)

	total	too little	about right	too much
Total people	100.0%	32.6%	61.3%	6.1%
Men	100.0	34.9	59.4	5.7
Women	100.0	30.7	62.9	6.4
Millennials	100.0	34.7	60.7	4.6
Generation Xers	100.0	36.0	57.4	6.7
Baby Boomers	100.0	33.2	59.8	7.0
Older Americans	100.0	21.1	72.1	6.8
Black	100.0	43.2	49.3	7.5
Hispanic	100.0	35.1	59.5	5.4
Non-Hispanic white	100.0	28.3	65.6	6.0
Northeast	100.0	35.0	59.0	6.0
Midwest	100.0	26.9	67.9	5.2
South	100.0	32.7	60.4	6.9
West	100.0	36.1	58.2	5.7
Not a college graduate	100.0	35.2	58.4	6.4
Bachelor's degree or more	100.0	26.0	68.6	5.4

Note: Millennials are aged 18 to 35; Generation Xers are aged 36 to 47; Baby Boomers are aged 48 to 66; Older Americans are aged 67 or older.
Source: Survey Documentation and Analysis, Computer-assisted Survey Methods Program, University of California, Berkeley, General Social Survey, 1972–2012 Cumulative Data Files, Internet site http://sda.berkeley.edu/cgi-bin/hsda?harcsda+gss12; calculations by New Strategist

Table 2.29 Spending on Scientific Research, 2012

"We are faced with many problems in this country, none of which can be solved easily or inexpensively. Are we spending too much, too little money, or about the right amount on supporting scientific research?"

(percent of people aged 18 or older responding by selected characteristics, 2012)

	total	too little	about right	too much
Total people	**100.0%**	**39.9%**	**45.9%**	**14.2%**
Men	100.0	44.6	42.5	12.9
Women	100.0	35.7	49.0	15.3
Millennials	100.0	40.0	47.4	12.6
Generation Xers	100.0	39.5	42.5	18.0
Baby Boomers	100.0	39.5	45.5	15.0
Older Americans	100.0	41.8	48.2	10.0
Black	100.0	34.1	50.2	15.7
Hispanic	100.0	36.0	48.6	15.4
Non-Hispanic white	100.0	41.1	45.7	13.3
Northeast	100.0	41.7	43.0	15.3
Midwest	100.0	41.7	47.5	10.8
South	100.0	36.8	46.6	16.6
West	100.0	42.0	45.4	12.7
Not a college graduate	100.0	38.2	46.0	15.9
Bachelor's degree or more	100.0	44.3	45.8	9.9

Note: Millennials are aged 18 to 35; Generation Xers are aged 36 to 47; Baby Boomers are aged 48 to 66; Older Americans are aged 67 or older.
Source: Survey Documentation and Analysis, Computer-assisted Survey Methods Program, University of California, Berkeley, General Social Survey, 1972–2012 Cumulative Data Files, Internet site http://sda.berkeley.edu/cgi-bin/hsda?harcsda+gss12; calculations by New Strategist

Table 2.30 Spending on Assistance for Child Care, 2012

"We are faced with many problems in this country, none of which can be solved easily or inexpensively. Are we spending too much, too little money, or about the right amount on assistance for child care?"

(percent of people aged 18 or older responding by selected characteristics, 2012)

	total	too little	about right	too much
Total people	**100.0%**	**48.1%**	**41.9%**	**10.1%**
Men	100.0	44.9	43.7	11.4
Women	100.0	50.7	40.3	8.9
Millennials	100.0	51.9	41.2	7.0
Generation Xers	100.0	47.6	41.7	10.7
Baby Boomers	100.0	47.9	40.0	12.1
Older Americans	100.0	40.8	47.5	11.7
Black	100.0	65.6	29.8	4.6
Hispanic	100.0	51.6	40.3	8.1
Non-Hispanic white	100.0	43.5	45.3	11.2
Northeast	100.0	54.1	37.1	8.9
Midwest	100.0	39.8	51.2	8.9
South	100.0	51.6	39.3	9.1
West	100.0	46.0	40.4	13.6
Not a college graduate	100.0	51.1	39.8	9.1
Bachelor's degree or more	100.0	40.2	47.3	12.5

Note: Millennials are aged 18 to 35; Generation Xers are aged 36 to 47; Baby Boomers are aged 48 to 66; Older Americans are aged 67 or older.
Source: Survey Documentation and Analysis, Computer-assisted Survey Methods Program, University of California, Berkeley, General Social Survey, 1972–2012 Cumulative Data Files, Internet site http://sda.berkeley.edu/cgi-bin/hsda?harcsda+gss12; calculations by New Strategist

Government and Politics: Historical Trends

Table 2.31 Political Leanings, 1974 to 2012

"We hear a lot of talk these days about liberals and convervatives. On a seven-point scale from extremely liberal—point 1—to extremely conservative—point 7—where would you place yourself?"

(percent distribution of people aged 18 or older by response for selected years)

	total	extremely liberal	liberal	slightly liberal	moderate	slightly conservative	conservative	extremely conservative
2012	100.0%	4.0%	11.8%	11.2%	38.5%	15.4%	15.5%	3.7%
2010	100.0	3.8	12.9	11.9	37.6	12.8	16.6	4.4
2008	100.0	2.9	12.2	10.6	38.6	15.1	16.7	3.9
2006	100.0	3.0	11.5	11.8	39.0	14.9	16.1	3.7
2004	100.0	2.9	9.1	12.3	37.5	16.6	17.5	4.3
2002	100.0	3.2	11.0	11.9	38.7	15.5	16.6	3.0
2000	100.0	3.9	11.5	10.8	39.9	14.5	15.9	3.6
1998	100.0	2.4	12.2	12.7	37.6	15.9	15.7	3.4
1996	100.0	2.2	10.6	12.1	37.9	16.8	17.1	3.3
1994	100.0	2.6	10.8	13.3	36.3	16.8	16.6	3.6
1993	100.0	1.9	12.3	13.1	36.3	17.7	16.0	2.6
1991	100.0	2.5	10.6	14.5	40.2	14.7	14.5	3.0
1990	100.0	3.0	10.5	13.8	35.8	18.6	14.5	3.8
1989	100.0	2.7	12.7	13.2	39.0	16.7	13.5	2.1
1988	100.0	2.3	12.2	12.9	35.9	17.6	16.6	2.5
1987	100.0	2.6	12.0	12.9	39.6	16.9	13.2	2.7
1986	100.0	1.8	9.4	11.9	41.1	17.6	15.6	2.6
1985	100.0	1.9	10.9	11.8	39.6	18.6	14.1	3.0
1984	100.0	2.0	9.0	12.4	39.7	20.4	13.9	2.6
1983	100.0	2.4	8.5	13.8	42.1	16.8	14.4	2.0
1982	100.0	2.6	9.6	13.7	41.4	14.6	14.0	4.1
1980	100.0	2.6	7.9	14.0	41.9	18.6	12.1	2.8
1978	100.0	1.4	10.4	15.5	40.0	18.9	11.5	2.2
1977	100.0	2.6	11.9	14.5	39.1	17.2	12.1	2.5
1976	100.0	2.0	13.2	13.2	39.9	16.3	13.5	1.9
1975	100.0	3.2	12.8	13.5	40.4	16.4	11.3	2.4
1974	100.0	1.6	13.9	14.9	40.0	16.0	11.1	2.4

Source: Survey Documentation and Analysis, Computer-assisted Survey Methods Program, University of California, Berkeley, General Social Survey, 1972–2012 Cumulative Data Files, Internet site http://sda.berkeley.edu/cgi-bin/hsda?harcsda+gss12; calculations by New Strategist

Table 2.32 Political Party Affiliation, 1972 to 2012

"Generally speaking, do you usually think of yourself as a Republican, Democrat, Independent, or what?"

(percent distribution of people aged 18 or older by response for selected years)

	total	strong Democrat	not strong Democrat	independent, near Democrat	independent	independent, near Republican	not strong Republican	strong Republican	other party
2012	100.0%	16.7%	17.0%	12.4%	19.8%	8.2%	13.7%	9.8%	2.3%
2010	100.0	16.5	15.7	13.5	18.8	10.0	13.4	9.6	2.6
2008	100.0	18.9	17.1	12.1	15.7	8.1	15.7	10.5	1.8
2006	100.0	14.4	15.9	11.4	23.2	7.4	15.0	11.3	1.4
2004	100.0	15.4	18.6	9.9	16.0	9.0	15.8	14.1	1.1
2002	100.0	14.1	19.0	9.5	19.7	7.7	16.6	11.6	1.7
2000	100.0	13.8	17.9	11.5	20.4	9.3	14.9	10.6	1.7
1998	100.0	12.4	20.6	12.3	17.4	8.9	17.4	8.6	2.3
1996	100.0	13.2	19.2	12.2	16.1	9.6	17.6	10.7	1.4
1994	100.0	14.0	21.6	11.2	12.8	9.6	17.8	11.5	1.4
1993	100.0	14.6	19.8	11.5	12.3	10.5	18.6	11.7	1.0
1991	100.0	14.9	20.9	8.1	13.0	11.4	19.0	12.0	0.7
1990	100.0	12.7	22.8	9.6	11.0	10.5	21.2	11.4	0.8
1989	100.0	14.4	22.1	9.2	12.9	7.8	21.5	11.4	0.7
1988	100.0	15.3	21.3	12.1	12.6	9.5	18.7	10.2	0.2
1987	100.0	17.5	21.2	11.2	11.1	10.3	17.3	10.2	1.1
1986	100.0	16.5	22.3	10.6	13.1	10.0	17.0	9.9	0.7
1985	100.0	16.9	22.2	10.3	9.1	10.6	17.2	12.6	1.2
1984	100.0	17.8	18.0	14.2	10.7	12.7	16.5	8.2	1.9
1983	100.0	15.7	24.6	12.7	12.3	8.7	16.5	8.9	0.6
1982	100.0	15.1	25.3	13.1	13.2	9.4	14.2	9.0	0.7
1980	100.0	13.5	25.3	13.4	16.5	8.4	15.1	7.2	0.7
1978	100.0	13.3	25.1	12.8	14.9	9.7	16.5	7.1	0.6
1977	100.0	18.0	26.7	13.1	11.1	8.7	14.6	7.6	0.2
1976	100.0	14.5	27.0	14.2	16.3	7.1	14.9	5.8	0.2
1975	100.0	17.2	23.8	14.0	13.6	8.4	15.9	6.2	0.8
1974	100.0	16.9	25.8	13.9	10.1	7.4	14.7	7.0	4.1
1973	100.0	15.2	25.4	12.7	9.7	9.4	14.8	8.3	4.5
1972	100.0	20.8	26.8	10.7	10.1	6.1	14.0	7.2	4.3

Source: Survey Documentation and Analysis, Computer-assisted Survey Methods Program, University of California, Berkeley, General Social Survey, 1972–2012 Cumulative Data Files, Internet site http://sda.berkeley.edu/cgi-bin/hsda?harcsda+gss12; calculations by New Strategist

Table 2.33 Women Not Suited for Politics, 1974 to 2012

"Tell me if you agree or disagree with this statement: Most men are better suited emotionally for politics than are most women."

(percent distribution of people aged 18 or older by response for selected years)

	total	agree	disagree
2012	100.0%	20.1%	79.9%
2010	100.0	21.6	78.4
2008	100.0	25.9	74.1
2006	100.0	24.2	75.8
2004	100.0	25.5	74.5
2002	100.0	22.6	77.4
2000	100.0	24.0	76.0
1998	100.0	23.3	76.7
1996	100.0	21.3	78.7
1994	100.0	21.3	78.7
1993	100.0	21.8	78.2
1991	100.0	25.7	74.3
1990	100.0	26.2	73.8
1989	100.0	30.9	69.1
1988	100.0	32.4	67.6
1986	100.0	37.3	62.7
1985	100.0	39.1	60.9
1983	100.0	37.8	62.2
1982	100.0	37.6	62.4
1978	100.0	44.4	55.6
1977	100.0	50.5	49.5
1975	100.0	49.8	50.2
1974	100.0	47.0	53.0

Source: Survey Documentation and Analysis, Computer-assisted Survey Methods Program, University of California, Berkeley, General Social Survey, 1972–2012 Cumulative Data Files, Internet site http://sda.berkeley.edu/cgi-bin/hsda?harcsda+gss12; calculations by New Strategist

Table 2.34 Should Government Do More or Less, 1975 to 2012

"Some people think that the government in Washington is trying to do too many things that should be left to individuals and private business; they are at point 5. Others disagree and think the government should do even more to solve our country's problems; they are at point 1. Where would you place yourself on the scale?"

(percent distribution of people aged 18 or older by response for selected years)

	total	1 government should do more	2	3 agree with both	4	5 government does too much
2012	100.0%	15.0%	12.1%	41.0%	12.7%	19.2%
2010	100.0	15.7	12.4	37.2	14.7	20.2
2008	100.0	16.7	14.5	40.9	13.1	14.9
2006	100.0	17.2	10.1	44.3	15.7	12.7
2004	100.0	16.1	10.8	43.9	13.5	15.7
2002	100.0	14.4	11.0	48.4	14.5	11.7
2000	100.0	11.1	13.0	39.9	18.5	17.5
1998	100.0	11.1	12.5	41.7	19.5	15.2
1996	100.0	12.3	13.3	38.6	18.7	17.2
1994	100.0	12.5	14.4	37.6	18.6	16.9
1993	100.0	13.9	15.5	40.0	15.4	15.3
1991	100.0	14.4	16.4	41.0	16.4	11.8
1990	100.0	14.5	16.3	43.1	14.8	11.3
1989	100.0	13.2	16.2	40.3	16.8	13.5
1988	100.0	14.0	14.8	42.1	15.7	13.3
1987	100.0	15.4	14.6	40.9	15.6	13.6
1986	100.0	12.7	13.6	43.7	16.3	13.7
1984	100.0	14.9	13.5	38.2	18.3	15.2
1983	100.0	13.7	11.0	38.7	20.3	16.3
1975	100.0	27.5	12.1	30.4	12.3	17.7

Source: Survey Documentation and Analysis, Computer-assisted Survey Methods Program, University of California, Berkeley, General Social Survey, 1972–2012 Cumulative Data Files, Internet site http://sda.berkeley.edu/cgi-bin/hsda?harcsda+gss12; calculations by New Strategist

Table 2.35 Government Should Help Pay for Medical Care, 1975 to 2012

"In general, some people think that it is the responsibility of the government in Washington to see to it that people have help in paying for doctors and hospital bills; they are at point 1. Others think that these matters are not the responsibility of the federal government and that people should take care of these things themselves; they are at point 5. Where would you place yourself on the scale?"

(percent distribution of people aged 18 or older by response for selected years)

	total	1 government should help	2	3 agree with both	4	5 people should help themselves
2012	100.0%	28.4%	18.1%	31.4%	12.4%	9.7%
2010	100.0	30.5	16.4	31.9	11.1	10.1
2008	100.0	34.9	18.7	30.0	9.3	7.2
2006	100.0	33.4	19.1	31.9	8.9	6.7
2004	100.0	32.1	21.1	30.7	7.7	8.3
2002	100.0	31.9	19.6	34.5	6.8	7.1
2000	100.0	29.2	22.4	31.4	10.9	6.1
1998	100.0	25.5	23.4	32.9	10.1	8.3
1996	100.0	27.0	21.6	33.7	11.4	6.3
1994	100.0	25.7	21.0	31.9	11.8	9.5
1993	100.0	28.9	23.6	31.5	9.4	6.5
1991	100.0	32.7	24.2	27.2	9.8	6.1
1990	100.0	31.6	26.5	30.0	7.5	4.4
1989	100.0	31.7	22.7	30.4	7.8	7.5
1988	100.0	26.3	21.5	37.0	8.7	6.6
1987	100.0	26.6	20.9	35.6	8.9	8.0
1986	100.0	29.3	20.0	32.5	11.9	6.4
1984	100.0	24.3	21.1	34.1	12.7	7.8
1983	100.0	27.0	19.4	31.7	11.5	10.4
1975	100.0	36.6	12.9	29.6	7.4	13.6

Source: Survey Documentation and Analysis, Computer-assisted Survey Methods Program, University of California, Berkeley, General Social Survey, 1972–2012 Cumulative Data Files, Internet site http://sda.berkeley.edu/cgi-bin/hsda?harcsda+gss12; calculations by New Strategist

Table 2.36 Should Government Improve the Standard of Living, 1975 to 2012

"Some people think that the government in Washington should do everything possible to improve the standard of living of all poor Americans. Other people think it is not the government's responsibility, and that each person should take care of himself. Where would you place yourself on this scale?"

(percent distribution of people aged 18 or older by response for selected years)

	total	1 government should act	2	3 agree with both	4	5 people should help themselves
2012	100.0%	14.9%	11.9%	44.6%	14.9%	13.7%
2010	100.0	16.3	12.2	44.0	14.8	12.6
2008	100.0	20.1	12.9	41.5	14.8	10.7
2006	100.0	17.5	10.9	47.7	13.7	10.3
2004	100.0	16.7	9.6	47.5	15.0	11.1
2002	100.0	17.9	10.2	46.4	13.6	11.9
2000	100.0	13.9	13.2	42.9	17.4	12.7
1998	100.0	13.1	13.1	44.3	17.8	11.8
1996	100.0	13.1	12.3	46.4	17.3	11.0
1994	100.0	12.9	14.1	45.3	16.3	11.3
1993	100.0	12.3	14.7	48.7	14.2	10.1
1991	100.0	17.0	16.6	44.1	13.3	8.9
1990	100.0	19.8	15.2	43.7	12.8	8.5
1989	100.0	17.0	15.4	44.4	14.4	8.8
1988	100.0	16.7	12.2	46.1	13.0	12.0
1987	100.0	18.0	12.4	45.8	13.6	10.2
1986	100.0	19.0	12.9	45.5	12.4	10.2
1984	100.0	16.8	10.9	46.9	16.0	9.5
1983	100.0	18.6	15.6	40.1	15.4	10.4
1975	100.0	30.3	10.4	35.9	10.5	13.0

Source: Survey Documentation and Analysis, Computer-assisted Survey Methods Program, University of California, Berkeley, General Social Survey, 1972–2012 Cumulative Data Files, Internet site http://sda.berkeley.edu/cgi-bin/hsda?harcsda+gss12; calculations by New Strategist

Table 2.37 Should Government Reduce Income Differences, 1978 to 2012

"Some people think that the government in Washington ought to reduce the income differences between the rich and the poor, perhaps by raising the taxes of wealthy families or by giving income assistance to the poor. Others think that the government should not concern itself with reducing this income difference between the rich and the poor. Think of a score of 1 as meaning that the government ought to reduce the income differences between rich and poor, and a score of 7 meaning that the government should not concern itself with reducing income differences. What score between 1 and 7 comes closest to the way you feel?"

(percent distribution of people aged 18 or older by response for selected years)

	total	1 government should reduce	2	3	4	5	6	7 no government involvement
2012	100.0%	24.3%	10.1%	15.3%	18.0%	11.2%	6.6%	14.5%
2010	100.0	18.7	7.6	16.2	17.8	15.6	7.6	16.5
2008	100.0	23.9	8.0	17.6	18.7	12.6	7.1	12.2
2006	100.0	20.0	9.1	17.3	21.8	13.3	7.1	11.4
2004	100.0	20.3	8.2	18.5	18.8	12.4	7.5	14.4
2002	100.0	19.4	9.3	17.8	19.3	14.7	6.7	12.7
2000	100.0	15.7	11.2	16.1	20.0	14.3	9.0	13.7
1998	100.0	14.7	9.6	18.0	20.9	11.9	8.7	16.1
1996	100.0	17.5	10.8	15.9	21.9	12.5	8.8	12.7
1994	100.0	14.2	9.6	16.6	21.1	14.8	8.3	15.5
1993	100.0	17.2	12.0	19.1	18.1	13.4	8.0	12.1
1991	100.0	20.1	13.2	17.6	19.9	12.3	8.1	8.9
1990	100.0	22.6	12.3	17.1	22.2	8.9	6.4	10.6
1989	100.0	17.9	13.1	18.9	20.9	11.5	7.4	10.5
1988	100.0	19.4	8.9	18.8	20.7	12.4	8.1	11.7
1987	100.0	19.7	8.9	17.4	20.5	13.7	6.4	13.5
1986	100.0	22.7	8.7	17.0	21.6	10.8	6.2	12.9
1984	100.0	21.1	13.2	15.0	17.8	13.2	8.6	11.2
1983	100.0	21.9	10.5	15.9	18.6	11.1	8.4	13.6
1980	100.0	17.0	10.0	16.2	21.1	12.1	7.5	16.1
1978	100.0	19.0	12.4	19.1	20.8	10.2	7.3	11.2

Source: Survey Documentation and Analysis, Computer-assisted Survey Methods Program, University of California, Berkeley, General Social Survey, 1972–2012 Cumulative Data Files, Internet site http://sda.berkeley.edu/cgi-bin/hsda?harcsda+gss12; calculations by New Strategist

Table 2.38 Spending on Education, 1973 to 2012

"We are faced with many problems in this country, none of which can be solved easily or inexpensively. Are we spending too much, too little money, or about the right amount on improving the nation's education system?"

(percent distribution of people aged 18 or older by response for selected years)

	total	too little	about right	too much
2012	100.0%	74.9%	17.4%	7.7%
2010	100.0	72.1	22.9	5.0
2008	100.0	70.8	23.3	5.8
2006	100.0	73.7	21.6	4.7
2004	100.0	73.6	21.8	4.6
2002	100.0	73.7	20.6	5.7
2000	100.0	71.5	23.5	5.0
1998	100.0	71.3	21.8	6.9
1996	100.0	70.6	23.1	6.3
1994	100.0	72.4	21.6	6.1
1993	100.0	69.8	24.2	6.0
1991	100.0	70.8	24.4	4.8
1990	100.0	74.4	22.7	2.9
1989	100.0	69.4	27.8	2.8
1988	100.0	66.3	30.4	3.3
1987	100.0	62.9	30.5	6.5
1986	100.0	61.4	34.0	4.6
1985	100.0	65.1	30.6	4.3
1984	100.0	63.5	33.5	3.0
1983	100.0	61.5	32.2	6.3
1982	100.0	57.6	33.2	9.2
1980	100.0	56.0	33.8	10.2
1978	100.0	53.9	33.7	12.4
1977	100.0	50.4	39.8	9.8
1976	100.0	52.6	38.1	9.3
1975	100.0	51.8	36.5	11.7
1974	100.0	53.5	38.3	8.2
1973	100.0	51.3	39.4	9.3

Source: Survey Documentation and Analysis, Computer-assisted Survey Methods Program, University of California, Berkeley, General Social Survey, 1972–2012 Cumulative Data Files, Internet site http://sda.berkeley.edu/cgi-bin/hsda?harcsda+gss12; calculations by New Strategist

Table 2.39 Spending on the Environment, 1973 to 2012

"We are faced with many problems in this country, none of which can be solved easily or inexpensively. Are we spending too much, too little money, or about the right amount on improving and protecting the environment?"

(percent distribution of people aged 18 or older by response for selected years)

	total	too little	about right	too much
2012	100.0%	57.1%	31.2%	11.7%
2010	100.0	57.5	29.6	12.9
2008	100.0	67.6	24.5	7.9
2006	100.0	69.1	24.7	6.3
2004	100.0	64.3	29.4	6.3
2002	100.0	59.6	33.1	7.3
2000	100.0	63.0	28.5	8.5
1998	100.0	63.4	28.8	7.7
1996	100.0	60.9	27.9	11.2
1994	100.0	61.1	30.2	8.7
1993	100.0	59.4	31.2	9.4
1991	100.0	71.3	23.6	5.1
1990	100.0	76.0	19.7	4.4
1989	100.0	76.1	20.2	3.7
1988	100.0	67.7	27.9	4.5
1987	100.0	68.6	25.8	5.6
1986	100.0	64.1	30.7	5.2
1985	100.0	59.1	32.8	8.1
1984	100.0	62.8	33.3	3.9
1983	100.0	57.6	32.5	9.9
1982	100.0	54.5	33.4	12.1
1980	100.0	51.8	31.7	16.5
1978	100.0	57.1	33.3	9.6
1977	100.0	52.1	36.3	11.6
1976	100.0	58.6	32.0	9.4
1975	100.0	57.9	32.2	9.9
1974	100.0	63.7	28.0	8.3
1973	100.0	64.6	27.6	7.7

Source: Survey Documentation and Analysis, Computer-assisted Survey Methods Program, University of California, Berkeley, General Social Survey, 1972–2012 Cumulative Data Files, Internet site http://sda.berkeley.edu/cgi-bin/hsda?harcsda+gss12; calculations by New Strategist

Table 2.40 Spending on Drug Addiction, 1973 to 2012

"We are faced with many problems in this country, none of which can be solved easily or inexpensively. Are we spending too much, too little money, or about the right amount on dealing with drug addiction?"

(percent distribution of people aged 18 or older by response for selected years)

	total	too little	about right	too much
2012	100.0%	55.8%	31.9%	12.3%
2010	100.0	56.4	33.2	10.4
2008	100.0	57.3	32.6	10.1
2006	100.0	62.1	30.6	7.3
2004	100.0	55.3	35.0	9.7
2002	100.0	57.8	31.8	10.4
2000	100.0	62.2	28.8	9.1
1998	100.0	60.9	29.5	9.7
1996	100.0	60.4	27.8	11.7
1994	100.0	63.2	27.7	9.2
1993	100.0	63.3	28.7	8.1
1991	100.0	60.3	31.8	7.9
1990	100.0	64.6	28.6	6.9
1989	100.0	73.0	20.7	6.3
1988	100.0	70.9	25.0	4.1
1987	100.0	67.8	27.3	4.9
1986	100.0	60.1	33.8	6.1
1985	100.0	66.8	28.5	4.7
1984	100.0	64.4	30.0	5.6
1983	100.0	62.1	32.4	5.5
1982	100.0	61.6	28.7	9.7
1980	100.0	64.7	27.8	7.5
1978	100.0	57.2	33.0	9.8
1977	100.0	59.5	31.9	8.7
1976	100.0	63.6	28.6	7.9
1975	100.0	59.3	32.2	8.5
1974	100.0	63.6	29.4	7.0
1973	100.0	70.3	23.1	6.6

Source: Survey Documentation and Analysis, Computer-assisted Survey Methods Program, University of California, Berkeley, General Social Survey, 1972–2012 Cumulative Data Files, Internet site http://sda.berkeley.edu/cgi-bin/hsda?harcsda+gss12; calculations by New Strategist

Table 2.41 Spending on Halting the Rising Crime Rate, 1973 to 2012

"We are faced with many problems in this country, none of which can be solved easily or inexpensively. Are we spending too much, too little money, or about the right amount on halting the rising crime rate?"

(percent distribution of people aged 18 or older by response for selected years)

	total	too little	about right	too much
2012	100.0%	59.0%	33.9%	7.1%
2010	100.0	59.5	32.2	8.3
2008	100.0	61.7	31.5	6.8
2006	100.0	61.2	32.1	6.6
2004	100.0	57.7	37.0	5.3
2002	100.0	57.5	35.6	6.9
2000	100.0	60.8	33.6	5.6
1998	100.0	63.7	28.9	7.4
1996	100.0	69.3	23.1	7.6
1994	100.0	77.6	16.3	6.2
1993	100.0	73.7	21.2	5.1
1991	100.0	68.1	26.7	5.3
1990	100.0	70.9	24.8	4.3
1989	100.0	75.0	20.1	4.9
1988	100.0	72.4	23.4	4.2
1987	100.0	73.0	22.2	4.9
1986	100.0	66.4	29.1	4.5
1985	100.0	67.2	28.3	4.4
1984	100.0	70.2	25.2	4.6
1983	100.0	68.7	25.2	6.1
1982	100.0	75.9	18.9	5.2
1980	100.0	71.9	22.1	6.0
1978	100.0	67.8	26.1	6.1
1977	100.0	70.6	23.4	6.1
1976	100.0	70.0	21.8	8.2
1975	100.0	69.2	25.1	5.7
1974	100.0	70.6	24.4	5.1
1973	100.0	68.3	26.9	4.8

Source: Survey Documentation and Analysis, Computer-assisted Survey Methods Program, University of California, Berkeley, General Social Survey, 1972–2012 Cumulative Data Files, Internet site http://sda.berkeley.edu/cgi-bin/hsda?harcsda+gss12; calculations by New Strategist

Table 2.42 Spending on Solving the Problems of Big Cities, 1973 to 2012

"We are faced with many problems in this country, none of which can be solved easily or inexpensively. Are we spending too much, too little money, or about the right amount on solving the problems of big cities?"

(percent distribution of people aged 18 or older by response for selected years)

	total	too little	about right	too much
2012	100.0%	42.3%	39.4%	18.2%
2010	100.0	42.8	37.3	19.9
2008	100.0	48.5	38.6	12.9
2006	100.0	48.1	39.1	12.9
2004	100.0	43.3	42.5	14.2
2002	100.0	44.7	40.6	14.7
2000	100.0	51.9	35.8	12.3
1998	100.0	51.6	34.5	13.9
1996	100.0	59.1	25.9	14.9
1994	100.0	60.8	25.0	14.1
1993	100.0	62.1	25.3	12.6
1991	100.0	52.5	33.5	13.9
1990	100.0	59.0	30.4	10.7
1989	100.0	53.1	34.0	12.9
1988	100.0	54.7	34.4	10.9
1987	100.0	44.9	38.9	16.3
1986	100.0	49.2	33.3	17.5
1985	100.0	44.6	38.1	17.3
1984	100.0	53.8	33.0	13.3
1983	100.0	45.8	35.2	18.9
1982	100.0	50.8	26.3	23.0
1980	100.0	46.9	28.7	24.4
1978	100.0	44.2	34.9	20.9
1977	100.0	47.7	29.6	22.7
1976	100.0	48.0	29.9	22.0
1975	100.0	56.5	29.5	14.0
1974	100.0	58.6	29.0	12.3
1973	100.0	55.4	31.0	13.7

Source: Survey Documentation and Analysis, Computer-assisted Survey Methods Program, University of California, Berkeley, General Social Survey, 1972–2012 Cumulative Data Files, Internet site http://sda.berkeley.edu/cgi-bin/hsda?harcsda+gss12; calculations by New Strategist

Table 2.43 Spending on Improving the Nation's Health, 1973 to 2012

"We are faced with many problems in this country, none of which can be solved easily or inexpensively. Are we spending too much, too little money, or about the right amount on improving and protecting the nation's health?"

(percent distribution of people aged 18 or older by response for selected years)

	total	too little	about right	too much
2012	100.0%	61.7%	26.3%	12.0%
2010	100.0	59.7	24.5	15.8
2008	100.0	77.1	18.1	4.8
2006	100.0	73.9	21.1	5.0
2004	100.0	78.6	17.2	4.2
2002	100.0	74.2	21.7	4.1
2000	100.0	72.7	23.6	3.7
1998	100.0	68.5	25.3	6.3
1996	100.0	67.8	24.4	7.8
1994	100.0	67.3	24.1	8.6
1993	100.0	74.1	18.3	7.6
1991	100.0	71.4	26.0	2.6
1990	100.0	74.4	23.2	2.5
1989	100.0	70.0	26.8	3.2
1988	100.0	69.6	27.3	3.1
1987	100.0	70.5	25.1	4.4
1986	100.0	60.2	35.7	4.1
1985	100.0	63.1	31.3	5.6
1984	100.0	59.4	34.5	6.2
1983	100.0	59.9	33.7	6.4
1982	100.0	59.4	33.1	7.4
1980	100.0	58.4	33.9	7.8
1978	100.0	57.4	35.7	6.9
1977	100.0	59.2	34.0	6.8
1976	100.0	63.0	32.4	4.7
1975	100.0	65.5	29.2	5.4
1974	100.0	66.9	28.8	4.3
1973	100.0	63.4	31.8	4.8

Source: Survey Documentation and Analysis, Computer-assisted Survey Methods Program, University of California, Berkeley, General Social Survey, 1972–2012 Cumulative Data Files, Internet site http://sda.berkeley.edu/cgi-bin/hsda?harcsda+gss12; calculations by New Strategist

Table 2.44 Spending on Improving the Condition of Blacks, 1973 to 2012

"We are faced with many problems in this country, none of which can be solved easily or inexpensively. Are we spending too much, too little money, or about the right amount on improving the condition of blacks?"

(percent distribution of people aged 18 or older by response for selected years)

	total	too little	about right	too much
2012	100.0%	36.0%	49.0%	15.0%
2010	100.0	32.7	50.2	17.1
2008	100.0	38.2	47.8	14.0
2006	100.0	37.0	47.1	15.9
2004	100.0	34.7	50.1	15.2
2002	100.0	33.0	48.8	18.3
2000	100.0	38.0	45.4	16.7
1998	100.0	36.9	45.2	17.9
1996	100.0	35.4	43.2	21.4
1994	100.0	34.0	43.9	22.1
1993	100.0	39.4	43.6	17.0
1991	100.0	39.0	45.5	15.6
1990	100.0	41.4	42.7	15.9
1989	100.0	37.3	46.1	16.6
1988	100.0	38.0	45.4	16.6
1987	100.0	39.0	45.0	15.9
1986	100.0	37.2	46.2	16.6
1985	100.0	32.7	45.9	21.5
1984	100.0	38.5	45.8	15.7
1983	100.0	32.2	46.9	20.9
1982	100.0	29.9	47.7	22.4
1980	100.0	28.4	45.9	25.7
1978	100.0	26.4	47.2	26.5
1977	100.0	27.5	46.2	26.3
1976	100.0	29.6	42.7	27.6
1975	100.0	29.4	44.4	26.2
1974	100.0	33.4	44.5	22.0
1973	100.0	35.3	41.9	22.8

Source: Survey Documentation and Analysis, Computer-assisted Survey Methods Program, University of California, Berkeley, General Social Survey, 1972–2012 Cumulative Data Files, Internet site http://sda.berkeley.edu/cgi-bin/hsda?harcsda+gss12; calculations by New Strategist

Table 2.45 Spending on the Military, 1973 to 2012

"We are faced with many problems in this country, none of which can be solved easily or inexpensively. Are we spending too much, too little money, or about the right amount on military, armaments, and defense?"

(percent distribution of people aged 18 or older by response for selected years)

	total	too little	about right	too much
2012	100.0%	24.7%	42.9%	32.4%
2010	100.0	26.9	38.3	34.8
2008	100.0	24.1	33.3	42.6
2006	100.0	25.4	33.4	41.2
2004	100.0	34.8	39.2	26.0
2002	100.0	31.7	46.4	22.0
2000	100.0	24.6	49.7	25.7
1998	100.0	18.7	48.7	32.6
1996	100.0	18.1	48.7	33.1
1994	100.0	17.1	49.4	33.5
1993	100.0	10.4	46.5	43.1
1991	100.0	14.6	58.1	27.3
1990	100.0	11.7	45.5	42.8
1989	100.0	15.5	42.8	41.7
1988	100.0	16.5	42.4	41.1
1987	100.0	16.6	40.6	42.8
1986	100.0	16.4	41.1	42.5
1985	100.0	14.8	44.7	40.5
1984	100.0	16.0	43.3	40.7
1983	100.0	24.4	40.7	35.0
1982	100.0	31.2	37.0	31.8
1980	100.0	61.5	26.2	12.3
1978	100.0	28.9	46.8	24.3
1977	100.0	25.7	49.4	24.8
1976	100.0	26.2	45.0	28.9
1975	100.0	17.8	49.4	32.9
1974	100.0	17.9	48.5	33.6
1973	100.0	12.1	47.4	40.5

Source: Survey Documentation and Analysis, Computer-assisted Survey Methods Program, University of California, Berkeley, General Social Survey, 1972–2012 Cumulative Data Files, Internet site http://sda.berkeley.edu/cgi-bin/hsda?harcsda+gss12; calculations by New Strategist

Table 2.46 Spending on Foreign Aid, 1973 to 2012

"We are faced with many problems in this country, none of which can be solved easily or inexpensively. Are we spending too much, too little money, or about the right amount on foreign aid?"

(percent distribution of people aged 18 or older by response for selected years)

	total	too little	about right	too much
2012	100.0%	9.3%	26.9%	63.8%
2010	100.0	8.8	31.5	59.7
2008	100.0	12.1	28.8	59.1
2006	100.0	11.4	26.7	61.9
2004	100.0	10.2	26.5	63.3
2002	100.0	6.8	27.9	65.4
2000	100.0	9.3	31.0	59.7
1998	100.0	7.1	28.9	64.0
1996	100.0	4.3	22.6	73.1
1994	100.0	4.7	20.6	74.7
1993	100.0	5.7	22.1	72.2
1991	100.0	4.4	19.5	76.1
1990	100.0	6.2	25.9	67.8
1989	100.0	4.6	23.0	72.3
1988	100.0	5.0	24.4	70.6
1987	100.0	7.5	20.3	72.2
1986	100.0	6.2	21.4	72.4
1985	100.0	6.8	26.9	66.3
1984	100.0	6.5	22.8	70.7
1983	100.0	5.0	17.7	77.4
1982	100.0	5.3	18.7	75.9
1980	100.0	5.3	21.1	73.6
1978	100.0	3.8	25.3	70.9
1977	100.0	3.7	25.5	70.8
1976	100.0	2.9	18.5	78.6
1975	100.0	5.6	17.8	76.7
1974	100.0	3.2	18.3	78.5
1973	100.0	4.9	21.9	73.2

Source: Survey Documentation and Analysis, Computer-assisted Survey Methods Program, University of California, Berkeley, General Social Survey, 1972–2012 Cumulative Data Files, Internet site http://sda.berkeley.edu/cgi-bin/hsda?harcsda+gss12; calculations by New Strategist

Table 2.47 Spending on Welfare, 1973 to 2012

"We are faced with many problems in this country, none of which can
be solved easily or inexpensively. Are we spending too much,
too little money, or about the right amount on welfare?"

(percent distribution of people aged 18 or older by response for selected years)

	total	too little	about right	too much
2012	100.0%	19.1%	33.3%	47.6%
2010	100.0	23.1	34.5	42.4
2008	100.0	25.4	36.4	38.2
2006	100.0	25.1	36.5	38.4
2004	100.0	23.6	35.0	41.4
2002	100.0	20.9	37.8	41.3
2000	100.0	20.8	39.9	39.4
1998	100.0	16.0	37.7	46.3
1996	100.0	15.3	26.6	58.1
1994	100.0	13.1	24.6	62.4
1993	100.0	17.1	25.6	57.3
1991	100.0	24.0	36.7	39.3
1990	100.0	24.5	37.1	38.4
1989	100.0	24.2	32.7	43.1
1988	100.0	24.7	32.5	42.8
1987	100.0	23.3	31.4	45.3
1986	100.0	23.4	34.5	42.1
1985	100.0	19.3	35.5	45.2
1984	100.0	25.2	36.7	38.2
1983	100.0	23.9	28.4	47.7
1982	100.0	21.3	28.6	50.1
1980	100.0	14.6	26.8	58.6
1978	100.0	13.6	24.1	62.3
1977	100.0	13.1	24.2	62.7
1976	100.0	14.1	22.7	63.2
1975	100.0	24.6	30.1	45.4
1974	100.0	23.8	32.8	43.4
1973	100.0	20.9	25.0	54.1

*Source: Survey Documentation and Analysis, Computer-assisted Survey Methods Program, University of California, Berkeley,
General Social Survey, 1972–2012 Cumulative Data Files, Internet site http://sda.berkeley.edu/cgi-bin/hsda?harcsda+gss12;
calculations by New Strategist*

Table 2.48 Spending on Space Exploration, 1973 to 2012

"We are faced with many problems in this country, none of which can be solved easily or inexpensively. Are we spending too much, too little money, or about the right amount on space exploration?"

(percent distribution of people aged 18 or older by response for selected years)

	total	too little	about right	too much
2012	100.0%	21.7%	45.9%	32.5%
2010	100.0	17.2	45.1	37.7
2008	100.0	13.6	50.9	35.5
2006	100.0	13.9	49.2	36.8
2004	100.0	14.9	46.0	39.0
2002	100.0	12.5	49.9	37.6
2000	100.0	14.9	41.8	43.3
1998	100.0	10.3	47.4	42.3
1996	100.0	12.0	43.8	44.2
1994	100.0	10.2	40.2	49.6
1993	100.0	8.8	41.1	50.1
1991	100.0	12.6	47.2	40.3
1990	100.0	11.8	47.1	41.1
1989	100.0	16.9	46.9	36.2
1988	100.0	18.4	45.0	36.6
1987	100.0	16.8	41.3	41.9
1986	100.0	12.0	47.4	40.6
1985	100.0	11.2	45.2	43.7
1984	100.0	11.4	47.2	41.5
1983	100.0	14.3	42.0	43.7
1982	100.0	14.1	43.1	42.9
1980	100.0	19.7	35.6	44.7
1978	100.0	12.9	37.5	49.6
1977	100.0	10.8	37.3	51.9
1976	100.0	9.8	29.4	60.8
1975	100.0	8.0	32.2	59.8
1974	100.0	7.9	29.2	62.9
1973	100.0	7.5	31.1	61.4

Source: Survey Documentation and Analysis, Computer-assisted Survey Methods Program, University of California, Berkeley, General Social Survey, 1972–2012 Cumulative Data Files, Internet site http://sda.berkeley.edu/cgi-bin/hsda?harcsda+gss12; calculations by New Strategist

Table 2.49 Spending on Mass Transportation, 1984 to 2012

"We are faced with many problems in this country, none of which can be solved easily or inexpensively. Are we spending too much, too little money, or about the right amount on mass transportation?"

(percent distribution of people aged 18 or older by response for selected years)

	total	too little	about right	too much
2012	100.0%	39.9%	50.1%	10.0%
2010	100.0	42.7	46.5	10.8
2008	100.0	48.7	43.4	7.9
2006	100.0	41.0	50.0	9.1
2004	100.0	36.4	53.0	10.6
2002	100.0	36.0	53.3	10.7
2000	100.0	39.8	51.8	8.4
1998	100.0	35.0	54.6	10.4
1996	100.0	35.0	53.4	11.6
1994	100.0	38.2	53.1	8.7
1993	100.0	38.1	50.9	11.0
1991	100.0	37.2	53.0	9.8
1990	100.0	37.1	53.2	9.8
1989	100.0	33.3	56.3	10.3
1988	100.0	31.7	57.2	11.1
1987	100.0	32.6	52.8	14.6
1986	100.0	30.6	55.3	14.1
1985	100.0	32.7	53.9	13.4
1984	100.0	36.9	51.8	11.4

Source: Survey Documentation and Analysis, Computer-assisted Survey Methods Program, University of California, Berkeley, General Social Survey, 1972–2012 Cumulative Data Files, Internet site http://sda.berkeley.edu/cgi-bin/hsda?harcsda+gss12; calculations by New Strategist

Table 2.50 Spending on Highways and Bridges, 1984 to 2012

"We are faced with many problems in this country, none of which can be solved easily or inexpensively. Are we spending too much, too little money, or about the right amount on highways and bridges?"

(percent distribution of people aged 18 or older by response for selected years)

	total	too little	about right	too much
2012	100.0%	43.0%	43.9%	13.1%
2010	100.0	44.1	44.7	11.2
2008	100.0	45.2	44.9	9.8
2006	100.0	35.5	53.0	11.5
2004	100.0	30.1	56.7	13.2
2002	100.0	35.7	51.7	12.6
2000	100.0	35.2	52.5	12.4
1998	100.0	40.4	49.5	10.1
1996	100.0	38.1	52.3	9.6
1994	100.0	40.1	51.9	7.9
1993	100.0	38.5	52.4	9.1
1991	100.0	36.4	52.2	11.4
1990	100.0	47.0	46.7	6.3
1989	100.0	40.1	52.4	7.5
1988	100.0	37.4	54.7	7.9
1987	100.0	36.2	54.0	9.7
1986	100.0	36.5	54.9	8.6
1985	100.0	43.7	48.4	7.9
1984	100.0	47.9	44.3	7.8

Source: Survey Documentation and Analysis, Computer-assisted Survey Methods Program, University of California, Berkeley, General Social Survey, 1972–2012 Cumulative Data Files, Internet site http://sda.berkeley.edu/cgi-bin/hsda?harcsda+gss12; calculations by New Strategist

Table 2.51 Spending on Social Security, 1984 to 2012

"We are faced with many problems in this country, none of which can be solved easily or inexpensively. Are we spending too much, too little money, or about the right amount on Social Security?"

(percent distribution of people aged 18 or older by response for selected years)

	total	too little	about right	too much
2012	100.0%	55.9%	35.8%	8.3%
2010	100.0	57.3	34.3	8.4
2008	100.0	61.7	32.6	5.8
2006	100.0	63.9	31.4	4.7
2004	100.0	66.0	28.5	5.5
2002	100.0	61.0	34.3	4.7
2000	100.0	60.3	34.6	5.1
1998	100.0	59.9	33.2	6.9
1996	100.0	51.8	39.6	8.7
1994	100.0	49.1	43.6	7.3
1993	100.0	46.0	46.2	7.8
1991	100.0	55.8	40.2	4.0
1990	100.0	52.1	42.2	5.8
1989	100.0	57.1	37.9	5.0
1988	100.0	55.5	39.4	5.2
1987	100.0	57.0	35.8	7.2
1986	100.0	57.3	36.2	6.5
1985	100.0	54.0	39.0	7.1
1984	100.0	53.4	36.5	10.1

Source: Survey Documentation and Analysis, Computer-assisted Survey Methods Program, University of California, Berkeley, General Social Survey, 1972–2012 Cumulative Data Files, Internet site http://sda.berkeley.edu/cgi-bin/hsda?harcsda+gss12; calculations by New Strategist

Table 2.52 Spending on Parks and Recreation, 1984 to 2012

"We are faced with many problems in this country, none of which can be solved easily or inexpensively. Are we spending too much, too little money, or about the right amount on parks and recreation?"

(percent distribution of people aged 18 or older by response for selected years)

	total	too little	about right	too much
2012	100.0%	32.6%	61.3%	6.1%
2010	100.0	33.9	59.7	6.4
2008	100.0	31.3	63.3	5.4
2006	100.0	33.5	60.1	6.5
2004	100.0	31.9	61.1	7.0
2002	100.0	34.5	59.9	5.6
2000	100.0	36.7	57.6	5.7
1998	100.0	36.4	57.3	6.3
1996	100.0	33.5	60.2	6.2
1994	100.0	31.4	62.2	6.4
1993	100.0	32.5	60.6	6.9
1991	100.0	32.1	63.1	4.8
1990	100.0	32.7	61.3	6.0
1989	100.0	35.0	59.7	5.3
1988	100.0	31.3	63.2	5.5
1987	100.0	30.8	62.5	6.8
1986	100.0	30.5	63.1	6.4
1985	100.0	31.7	59.9	8.4
1984	100.0	33.5	61.3	5.2

Source: Survey Documentation and Analysis, Computer-assisted Survey Methods Program, University of California, Berkeley, General Social Survey, 1972–2012 Cumulative Data Files, Internet site http://sda.berkeley.edu/cgi-bin/hsda?harcsda+gss12; calculations by New Strategist

Table 2.53 Spending on Scientific Research, 2002 to 2012

"We are faced with many problems in this country, none of which can be solved
easily or inexpensively. Are we spending too much, too little money,
or about the right amount on supporting scientific research?"

(percent distribution of people aged 18 or older by response for selected years)

	total	too little	about right	too much
2012	100.0%	39.9%	45.9%	14.2%
2010	100.0	40.7	46.6	12.7
2008	100.0	40.6	48.2	11.2
2006	100.0	43.6	44.3	12.1
2004	100.0	40.2	47.3	12.5
2002	100.0	36.7	48.9	14.4

Source: Survey Documentation and Analysis, Computer-assisted Survey Methods Program, University of California, Berkeley, General Social Survey, 1972–2012 Cumulative Data Files, Internet site http://sda.berkeley.edu/cgi-bin/hsda?harcsda+gss12; calculations by New Strategist

Table 2.54 Spending on Assistance for Child Care, 2000 to 2012

"We are faced with many problems in this country, none of which can be solved easily or inexpensively. Are we spending too much, too little money, or about the right amount on assistance for child care?"

(percent distribution of people aged 18 or older by response for selected years)

	total	too little	about right	too much
2012	100.0%	48.1%	41.9%	10.1%
2010	100.0	51.7	40.4	7.9
2008	100.0	54.4	39.2	6.5
2006	100.0	55.0	37.4	7.6
2004	100.0	57.6	35.6	6.8
2002	100.0	60.0	32.5	7.5
2000	100.0	64.8	29.5	5.7

Source: Survey Documentation and Analysis, Computer-assisted Survey Methods Program, University of California, Berkeley, General Social Survey, 1972–2012 Cumulative Data Files, Internet site http://sda.berkeley.edu/cgi-bin/hsda?harcsda+gss12; calculations by New Strategist

3

Science and Information

Although Americans are most likely to get information about general news from television, the Internet is the most popular source of science and technology news. Most Americans think science and technology create opportunity, disagree with the notion that science makes our life change too fast, and support scientific research. Most can answer basic questions about science correctly. But there are differences in attitudes and knowledge by demographic characteristic. (Note: The science questions on the General Social Survey were first asked less than a decade ago, so historical tables are not included in this chapter.)

Generational Differences

• **Younger generations depend on the Internet.** The majority of Millennials and Generation Xers get most of their information about science and technology from the Internet, while television is number one for Boomers and older Americans. Only the oldest generation would turn to television before the Internet when seeking information about science issues, however.

• **Interest in issues often reflects self-interest.** When asked how interested they are in local school issues, those most likely to have school-aged children (Generation X) are most interested (66 percent are "very interested"). When asked how interested they are in medical discoveries, those most likely to have health concerns (older Americans) are most interested (69 percent are "very interested").

Educational Differences

• **College graduates have more interest in science.** The 57 percent majority of people with a bachelor's degree are "very interested" in science compared with just 35 percent of people without a bachelor's degree. College graduates are also much more interested than the less educated in environmental issues, economics, and international affairs.

• **Most Americans understand basic scientific concepts.** But college graduates are much more likely than the less educated to answer questions about science correctly. When asked whether antibiotics kill viruses as well as bacteria—true or false—77 percent of college graduates correctly answered "false" versus only 43 percent of those without a college degree.

Table 3.1 Internet Access at Home, 2012

"Do you have access to the Internet in your home?"

(percent of people aged 18 or older responding by selected characteristics, 2012)

	total	yes	no
Total people	**100.0%**	**79.9%**	**20.1%**
Men	100.0	80.7	19.3
Women	100.0	79.1	20.9
Millennials	100.0	86.7	13.3
Generation Xers	100.0	84.4	15.6
Baby Boomers	100.0	78.3	21.7
Older Americans	100.0	64.8	35.2
Black	100.0	63.9	36.1
Hispanic	100.0	72.6	27.4
Non-Hispanic white	100.0	85.1	14.9
Northeast	100.0	85.2	14.8
Midwest	100.0	85.4	14.6
South	100.0	74.6	25.4
West	100.0	78.7	21.3
Not a college graduate	100.0	73.2	26.8
Bachelor's degree or more	100.0	96.9	3.1

Note: Millennials are aged 18 to 35; Generation Xers are aged 36 to 47; Baby Boomers are aged 48 to 66; Older Americans are aged 67 or older.
Source: Survey Documentation and Analysis, Computer-assisted Survey Methods Program, University of California, Berkeley, General Social Survey, 1972–2012 Cumulative Data Files, Internet site http://sda.berkeley.edu/cgi-bin/hsda?harcsda+gss12; calculations by New Strategist

Table 3.2 Main Source of Information about Events in the News, 2012

"We are interested in how people get information about events in the news. Where do you get most of your information about current news events?"

(percent of people aged 18 or older responding by selected characteristics, 2012)

	total	television	Internet	newspapers	radio	family, friends, or colleagues	magazines, books, other
Total people	**100.0%**	**47.9%**	**30.0%**	**12.4%**	**4.7%**	**3.6%**	**1.4%**
Men	100.0	45.3	29.5	14.3	6.7	3.4	0.8
Women	100.0	50.3	30.5	10.7	2.8	3.9	1.8
Millennials	100.0	40.5	45.8	5.9	1.2	6.4	0.2
Generation Xers	100.0	38.5	39.8	8.1	9.2	2.1	2.3
Baby Boomers	100.0	54.1	22.1	14.7	4.3	3.2	1.6
Older Americans	100.0	58.9	7.7	24.8	5.9	1.4	1.3
Black	100.0	60.0	15.8	20.5	1.8	0.6	1.3
Hispanic	100.0	59.3	24.7	7.2	2.6	5.6	0.6
Non-Hispanic white	100.0	44.4	31.7	12.1	6.0	4.2	1.6
Northeast	100.0	50.0	23.6	15.7	5.6	3.6	1.5
Midwest	100.0	49.3	30.2	12.0	5.2	2.3	1.0
South	100.0	50.9	27.5	13.3	3.0	3.5	1.9
West	100.0	40.4	39.0	8.7	6.0	5.3	0.6
Not a college graduate	100.0	56.7	24.0	10.8	4.1	4.3	0.1
Bachelor's degree or more	100.0	25.5	45.7	16.6	6.2	2.0	4.0

Note: Millennials are aged 18 to 35; Generation Xers are aged 36 to 47; Baby Boomers are aged 48 to 66; Older Americans are aged 67 or older.
Source: Survey Documentation and Analysis, Computer-assisted Survey Methods Program, University of California, Berkeley, General Social Survey, 1972–2012 Cumulative Data Files, Internet site http://sda.berkeley.edu/cgi-bin/hsda?harcsda+gss12; calculations by New Strategist

Table 3.3 Main Source of Information about Science and Technology, 2012

"We are interested in how people get information about science and technology. Where do you get most of your information about science and technology?"

(percent of people aged 18 or older responding by selected characteristics, 2012)

	total	Internet	television	magazines	newspapers	family, friends, and colleagues	radio	books and other printed material	other
Total people	**100.0%**	**41.5%**	**35.9%**	**7.0%**	**5.5%**	**4.0%**	**2.8%**	**2.7%**	**0.6%**
Men	100.0	41.5	34.8	8.5	6.4	3.4	3.3	2.0	0.2
Women	100.0	41.5	36.9	5.7	4.7	4.5	2.3	3.4	0.8
Millennials	100.0	59.8	25.8	1.5	3.2	4.8	1.0	2.7	1.2
Generation Xers	100.0	51.6	25.4	8.7	4.5	4.4	2.9	2.5	0.0
Baby Boomers	100.0	33.4	41.9	7.7	5.8	4.5	4.1	2.4	0.2
Older Americans	100.0	14.7	54.8	12.7	9.9	0.6	2.9	3.9	0.6
Black	100.0	26.5	49.8	6.7	7.7	4.3	2.8	2.2	0.0
Hispanic	100.0	38.4	41.5	4.4	4.5	5.4	3.0	2.8	0.0
Non-Hispanic white	100.0	43.6	32.6	8.3	5.1	3.6	2.9	3.1	0.8
Northeast	100.0	36.2	35.0	10.8	8.9	3.5	2.1	3.6	0.0
Midwest	100.0	40.0	38.0	6.2	4.1	1.7	4.6	4.7	0.8
South	100.0	39.9	39.4	7.0	5.9	4.5	1.2	2.1	0.0
West	100.0	49.4	29.2	5.1	3.7	5.8	4.0	1.3	1.5
Not a college graduate	100.0	34.4	44.5	5.8	4.8	4.7	2.5	2.7	0.6
Bachelor's degree or more	100.0	59.5	14.1	10.2	7.4	2.1	3.6	2.7	0.3

Note: Millennials are aged 18 to 35; Generation Xers are aged 36 to 47; Baby Boomers are aged 48 to 66; Older Americans are aged 67 or older.
Source: Survey Documentation and Analysis, Computer-assisted Survey Methods Program, University of California, Berkeley, General Social Survey, 1972–2012 Cumulative Data Files, Internet site http://sda.berkeley.edu/cgi-bin/hsda?harcsda+gss12; calculations by New Strategist

Table 3.4 Where You Look for Information about Science and Technology, 2012

"If you wanted to learn about scientific issues such as global warming or biotechnology, where would you get information?"

(percent of people aged 18 or older responding by selected characteristics, 2012)

	total	Internet	television	books and other printed material	magazines	newspapers	family, friends, and colleagues	radio	other
Total people	**100.0%**	**63.2%**	**19.7%**	**6.4%**	**4.0%**	**3.1%**	**1.4%**	**1.1%**	**1.0%**
Men	100.0	63.2	16.8	6.3	6.4	4.2	0.8	1.5	0.9
Women	100.0	63.2	22.3	6.6	1.7	2.2	2.1	0.7	1.2
Millennials	100.0	78.4	11.2	3.8	2.8	2.0	0.9	0.3	0.6
Generation Xers	100.0	76.3	12.3	5.0	1.9	1.3	1.9	0.8	0.4
Baby Boomers	100.0	57.3	23.5	7.8	4.7	2.2	1.7	1.3	1.5
Older Americans	100.0	30.4	36.6	9.9	7.4	10.1	1.4	2.4	1.8
Black	100.0	49.4	31.8	8.6	4.0	3.4	0.6	0.0	2.2
Hispanic	100.0	61.4	24.6	3.5	2.2	2.6	3.4	1.4	0.8
Non-Hispanic white	100.0	66.0	16.6	7.2	4.0	2.9	1.3	1.2	0.8
Northeast	100.0	55.7	24.9	7.1	6.0	4.4	0.5	0.5	1.0
Midwest	100.0	65.9	15.4	6.9	4.3	1.8	1.8	1.8	2.2
South	100.0	60.0	22.3	7.4	3.5	3.6	1.5	0.9	0.7
West	100.0	71.4	15.6	3.9	2.8	2.8	1.9	1.1	0.6
Not a college graduate	100.0	56.8	25.2	6.7	3.7	3.4	1.8	1.0	1.3
Bachelor's degree or more	100.0	79.2	5.8	5.6	4.6	2.4	0.7	1.4	0.3

Note: Millennials are aged 18 to 35; Generation Xers are aged 36 to 47; Baby Boomers are aged 48 to 66; Older Americans are aged 67 or older.
Source: Survey Documentation and Analysis, Computer-assisted Survey Methods Program, University of California, Berkeley, General Social Survey, 1972–2012 Cumulative Data Files, Internet site http://sda.berkeley.edu/cgi-bin/hsda?harcsda+gss12; calculations by New Strategist

Table 3.5 Science and Technology Create Opportunity, 2012

"Because of science and technology, there will be
more opportunities for the next generation."

(percent of people aged 18 or older responding by selected characteristics, 2012)

	total	strongly agree	agree	disagree	strongly disagree
Total people	**100.0%**	**29.5%**	**60.4%**	**8.9%**	**1.2%**
Men	100.0	31.1	58.1	8.9	1.9
Women	100.0	28.0	62.6	8.9	0.5
Millennials	100.0	30.1	60.3	7.9	1.7
Generation Xers	100.0	25.2	64.9	8.2	1.7
Baby Boomers	100.0	30.3	57.8	11.2	0.7
Older Americans	100.0	32.0	61.1	6.3	0.6
Black	100.0	39.0	51.5	7.3	2.1
Hispanic	100.0	30.1	62.3	6.5	1.1
Non-Hispanic white	100.0	24.5	64.5	10.1	0.9
Northeast	100.0	37.9	50.9	9.9	1.2
Midwest	100.0	27.4	63.3	8.0	1.3
South	100.0	26.8	62.2	10.0	0.9
West	100.0	29.4	61.9	7.4	1.3
Not a college graduate	100.0	29.1	60.5	9.3	1.1
Bachelor's degree or more	100.0	30.6	60.1	7.9	1.4

Note: Millennials are aged 18 to 35; Generation Xers are aged 36 to 47; Baby Boomers are aged 48 to 66; Older Americans are aged 67 or older.
Source: Survey Documentation and Analysis, Computer-assisted Survey Methods Program, University of California, Berkeley, General Social Survey, 1972–2012 Cumulative Data Files, Internet site http://sda.berkeley.edu/cgi-bin/hsda?harcsda+gss12; calculations by New Strategist

Table 3.6 Benefits of Science Outweigh Harmful Results, 2012

"People have frequently noted that scientific research has produced benefits and harmful results. Would you say that, on balance, the benefits of scientific research have outweighed the harmful results, or have the harmful results of scientific research been greater than its benefits?"

(percent of people aged 18 or older responding by selected characteristics, 2012)

	total	benefits greater	about equal (volunteered)	harmful results greater
Total people	**100.0%**	**78.3%**	**12.5%**	**9.2%**
Men	100.0	80.1	11.6	8.3
Women	100.0	76.6	13.3	10.1
Millennials	100.0	73.6	16.1	10.3
Generation Xers	100.0	79.5	10.9	9.6
Baby Boomers	100.0	77.1	12.2	10.7
Older Americans	100.0	88.6	8.3	3.1
Black	100.0	67.5	14.1	18.4
Hispanic	100.0	75.4	20.1	4.4
Non-Hispanic white	100.0	82.2	10.4	7.4
Northeast	100.0	79.5	11.3	9.3
Midwest	100.0	83.5	7.7	8.8
South	100.0	73.9	14.5	11.6
West	100.0	79.1	15.0	5.9
Not a college graduate	100.0	73.2	15.4	11.4
Bachelor's degree or more	100.0	90.0	5.7	4.3

Note: Millennials are aged 18 to 35; Generation Xers are aged 36 to 47; Baby Boomers are aged 48 to 66; Older Americans are aged 67 or older.
Source: Survey Documentation and Analysis, Computer-assisted Survey Methods Program, University of California, Berkeley, General Social Survey, 1972–2012 Cumulative Data Files, Internet site http://sda.berkeley.edu/cgi-bin/hsda?harcsda+gss12; calculations by New Strategist

Table 3.7 Science Makes Our Way of Life Change Too Fast, 2012

"Science makes our way of life change too fast."

(percent of people aged 18 or older responding by selected characteristics, 2012)

	total	strongly agree	agree	disagree	strongly disagree
Total people	**100.0%**	**9.8%**	**33.7%**	**52.5%**	**4.0%**
Men	100.0	9.8	34.7	51.0	4.5
Women	100.0	9.7	32.9	53.8	3.6
Millennials	100.0	5.0	34.9	54.2	5.9
Generation Xers	100.0	13.1	29.5	54.0	3.4
Baby Boomers	100.0	12.1	33.2	50.7	4.0
Older Americans	100.0	8.1	39.1	51.4	1.3
Black	100.0	15.8	28.6	50.1	5.5
Hispanic	100.0	17.8	48.7	30.5	3.0
Non-Hispanic white	100.0	6.3	30.2	59.3	4.3
Northeast	100.0	11.5	39.4	44.2	4.9
Midwest	100.0	10.5	25.1	59.6	4.9
South	100.0	8.2	36.4	52.4	3.0
West	100.0	10.2	33.5	52.3	4.0
Not a college graduate	100.0	10.6	36.8	49.0	3.7
Bachelor's degree or more	100.0	7.7	26.2	61.3	4.7

Note: Millennials are aged 18 to 35; Generation Xers are aged 36 to 47; Baby Boomers are aged 48 to 66; Older Americans are aged 67 or older.
Source: Survey Documentation and Analysis, Computer-assisted Survey Methods Program, University of California, Berkeley, General Social Survey, 1972–2012 Cumulative Data Files, Internet site http://sda.berkeley.edu/cgi-bin/hsda?harcsda+gss12; calculations by New Strategist

Table 3.8 Science Research Should Be Supported by Federal Government, 2012

"Even if it brings no immediate benefits, scientific research that advances
the frontiers of knowledge is necessary and should be
supported by the federal government."

(percent of people aged 18 or older responding by selected characteristics, 2012)

	total	strongly agree	agree	disagree	strongly disagree
Total people	**100.0%**	**23.3%**	**62.7%**	**12.0%**	**2.0%**
Men	100.0	24.4	61.9	10.9	2.8
Women	100.0	22.3	63.4	13.0	1.3
Millennials	100.0	21.7	66.5	9.7	2.0
Generation Xers	100.0	28.8	63.0	7.6	0.6
Baby Boomers	100.0	23.4	59.9	13.6	3.0
Older Americans	100.0	17.5	62.5	18.5	1.5
Black	100.0	20.3	66.4	9.0	4.2
Hispanic	100.0	28.4	63.4	7.0	1.1
Non-Hispanic white	100.0	22.6	61.3	14.1	1.9
Northeast	100.0	35.4	55.0	8.6	1.0
Midwest	100.0	22.0	61.2	13.9	2.9
South	100.0	17.9	66.0	13.4	2.8
West	100.0	23.9	64.8	10.5	0.8
Not a college graduate	100.0	20.8	63.0	14.3	1.8
Bachelor's degree or more	100.0	29.5	61.8	6.2	2.5

Note: Millennials are aged 18 to 35; Generation Xers are aged 36 to 47; Baby Boomers are aged 48 to 66; Older Americans are aged 67 or older.
Source: Survey Documentation and Analysis, Computer-assisted Survey Methods Program, University of California, Berkeley, General Social Survey, 1972–2012 Cumulative Data Files, Internet site http://sda.berkeley.edu/cgi-bin/hsda?harcsda+gss12; calculations by New Strategist

Table 3.9 Interest in Science, 2012

"There are a lot of issues in the news, and it is hard to keep up with every area. Are you very interested, moderately interested, or not at all interested in new scientific discoveries?"

(percent of people aged 18 or older responding by selected characteristics, 2012)

	total	very interested	moderately interested	not at all interested
Total people	**100.0%**	**41.0%**	**43.6%**	**15.4%**
Men	100.0	44.8	43.3	11.9
Women	100.0	37.6	43.9	18.5
Millennials	100.0	41.7	41.5	16.8
Generation Xers	100.0	45.3	37.4	17.3
Baby Boomers	100.0	37.9	48.3	13.9
Older Americans	100.0	41.0	45.3	13.7
Black	100.0	38.0	40.4	21.6
Hispanic	100.0	37.5	40.3	22.2
Non-Hispanic white	100.0	40.5	46.5	13.1
Northeast	100.0	47.2	38.0	14.8
Midwest	100.0	38.2	47.3	14.5
South	100.0	38.2	44.4	17.5
West	100.0	43.5	43.2	13.3
Not a college graduate	100.0	34.9	46.2	18.9
Bachelor's degree or more	100.0	56.6	36.9	6.5

Note: Millennials are aged 18 to 35; Generation Xers are aged 36 to 47; Baby Boomers are aged 48 to 66; Older Americans are aged 67 or older.
Source: Survey Documentation and Analysis, Computer-assisted Survey Methods Program, University of California, Berkeley, General Social Survey, 1972–2012 Cumulative Data Files, Internet site http://sda.berkeley.edu/cgi-bin/hsda?harcsda+gss12; calculations by New Strategist

Table 3.10 Interest in Technology, 2012

"There are a lot of issues in the news, and it is hard to keep up with every area.
Are you very interested, moderately interested, or not at all interested in
issues about the use of new inventions and technologies?"

(percent of people aged 18 or older responding by selected characteristics, 2012)

	total	very interested	moderately interested	not at all interested
Total people	**100.0%**	**42.4%**	**47.3%**	**10.3%**
Men	100.0	50.9	40.4	8.7
Women	100.0	34.5	53.7	11.8
Millennials	100.0	44.1	44.5	11.5
Generation Xers	100.0	44.1	46.4	9.6
Baby Boomers	100.0	41.1	49.3	9.6
Older Americans	100.0	40.6	48.4	11.0
Black	100.0	45.2	43.5	11.3
Hispanic	100.0	40.0	40.1	19.9
Non-Hispanic white	100.0	42.0	49.9	8.2
Northeast	100.0	48.4	43.5	8.1
Midwest	100.0	39.3	50.6	10.1
South	100.0	42.2	47.0	10.8
West	100.0	40.7	47.7	11.6
Not a college graduate	100.0	40.8	46.9	12.3
Bachelor's degree or more	100.0	46.2	48.4	5.4

Note: Millennials are aged 18 to 35; Generation Xers are aged 36 to 47; Baby Boomers are aged 48 to 66; Older Americans are aged 67 or older.
Source: Survey Documentation and Analysis, Computer-assisted Survey Methods Program, University of California, Berkeley, General Social Survey, 1972–2012 Cumulative Data Files, Internet site http://sda.berkeley.edu/cgi-bin/hsda?harcsda+gss12; calculations by New Strategist

Table 3.11 Interest in Local School Issues, 2012

"There are a lot of issues in the news, and it is hard to keep up with every area. Are you very interested, moderately interested, or not at all interested in local school issues?"

(percent of people aged 18 or older responding by selected characteristics, 2012)

	total	very interested	moderately interested	not at all interested
Total people	**100.0%**	**54.8%**	**35.8%**	**9.4%**
Men	100.0	45.0	42.8	12.2
Women	100.0	63.7	29.4	6.9
Millennials	100.0	57.2	35.1	7.8
Generation Xers	100.0	66.4	30.1	3.5
Baby Boomers	100.0	53.8	34.8	11.4
Older Americans	100.0	36.5	47.7	15.8
Black	100.0	73.2	22.0	4.8
Hispanic	100.0	60.0	33.4	6.6
Non-Hispanic white	100.0	49.8	39.0	11.2
Northeast	100.0	55.5	35.8	8.7
Midwest	100.0	54.6	36.9	8.5
South	100.0	57.0	32.3	10.7
West	100.0	50.9	40.2	8.9
Not a college graduate	100.0	55.3	34.8	9.9
Bachelor's degree or more	100.0	53.5	38.3	8.2

Note: Millennials are aged 18 to 35; Generation Xers are aged 36 to 47; Baby Boomers are aged 48 to 66; Older Americans are aged 67 or older.
Source: Survey Documentation and Analysis, Computer-assisted Survey Methods Program, University of California, Berkeley, General Social Survey, 1972–2012 Cumulative Data Files, Internet site http://sda.berkeley.edu/cgi-bin/hsda?harcsda+gss12; calculations by New Strategist

Table 3.12 Interest in Medical Discoveries, 2012

"There are a lot of issues in the news, and it is hard to keep up with every area. Are you very interested, moderately interested, or not at all interested in issues about new medical discoveries?"

(percent of people aged 18 or older responding by selected characteristics, 2012)

	total	very interested	moderately interested	not at all interested
Total people	**100.0%**	**59.8%**	**35.4%**	**4.8%**
Men	100.0	57.1	36.4	6.6
Women	100.0	62.3	34.6	3.2
Millennials	100.0	52.1	41.4	6.5
Generation Xers	100.0	59.0	32.7	8.2
Baby Boomers	100.0	62.1	35.0	2.9
Older Americans	100.0	69.0	29.3	1.6
Black	100.0	71.3	23.7	4.9
Hispanic	100.0	54.3	38.6	7.2
Non-Hispanic white	100.0	57.9	38.8	3.3
Northeast	100.0	58.2	36.5	5.3
Midwest	100.0	57.4	35.9	6.6
South	100.0	63.0	32.3	4.7
West	100.0	58.2	39.1	2.8
Not a college graduate	100.0	59.0	35.5	5.5
Bachelor's degree or more	100.0	61.9	35.2	2.9

Note: Millennials are aged 18 to 35; Generation Xers are aged 36 to 47; Baby Boomers are aged 48 to 66; Older Americans are aged 67 or older.
Source: Survey Documentation and Analysis, Computer-assisted Survey Methods Program, University of California, Berkeley, General Social Survey, 1972–2012 Cumulative Data Files, Internet site http://sda.berkeley.edu/cgi-bin/hsda?harcsda+gss12; calculations by New Strategist

Table 3.13 Interest in Space Exploration, 2012

"There are a lot of issues in the news, and it is hard to keep up with every area. Are you very interested, moderately interested, or not at all interested in issues about space exploration?"

(percent of people aged 18 or older responding by selected characteristics, 2012)

	total	very interested	moderately interested	not at all interested
Total people	100.0%	22.4%	44.0%	33.6%
Men	100.0	32.3	41.8	26.0
Women	100.0	13.4	46.0	40.6
Millennials	100.0	23.0	45.3	31.7
Generation Xers	100.0	24.0	41.7	34.3
Baby Boomers	100.0	21.3	42.2	36.5
Older Americans	100.0	22.2	48.0	29.7
Black	100.0	19.1	42.8	38.1
Hispanic	100.0	21.1	34.8	44.1
Non-Hispanic white	100.0	23.0	46.9	30.1
Northeast	100.0	22.4	43.1	34.5
Midwest	100.0	22.2	43.1	34.7
South	100.0	20.4	44.7	34.9
West	100.0	26.0	44.3	29.7
Not a college graduate	100.0	21.3	40.7	38.0
Bachelor's degree or more	100.0	25.3	52.2	22.5

Note: Millennials are aged 18 to 35; Generation Xers are aged 36 to 47; Baby Boomers are aged 48 to 66; Older Americans are aged 67 or older.
Source: Survey Documentation and Analysis, Computer-assisted Survey Methods Program, University of California, Berkeley, General Social Survey, 1972–2012 Cumulative Data Files, Internet site http://sda.berkeley.edu/cgi-bin/hsda?harcsda+gss12; calculations by New Strategist

Table 3.14 Interest in Environmental Issues, 2012

"There are a lot of issues in the news, and it is hard to keep up with every area. Are you very interested, moderately interested, or not at all interested in issues about environmental pollution?"

(percent of people aged 18 or older responding by selected characteristics, 2012)

	total	very interested	moderately interested	not at all interested
Total people	**100.0%**	**46.8%**	**43.9%**	**9.4%**
Men	100.0	47.8	42.7	9.6
Women	100.0	45.8	45.0	9.2
Millennials	100.0	41.7	48.2	10.1
Generation Xers	100.0	50.0	38.4	11.6
Baby Boomers	100.0	49.4	42.7	8.0
Older Americans	100.0	44.9	46.6	8.4
Black	100.0	53.5	35.8	10.8
Hispanic	100.0	45.2	44.1	10.6
Non-Hispanic white	100.0	44.6	47.0	8.4
Northeast	100.0	51.6	41.5	6.9
Midwest	100.0	43.0	47.2	9.8
South	100.0	46.4	44.7	8.9
West	100.0	47.1	41.2	11.6
Not a college graduate	100.0	44.4	44.8	10.8
Bachelor's degree or more	100.0	52.8	41.5	5.7

Note: Millennials are aged 18 to 35; Generation Xers are aged 36 to 47; Baby Boomers are aged 48 to 66; Older Americans are aged 67 or older.

Source: Survey Documentation and Analysis, Computer-assisted Survey Methods Program, University of California, Berkeley, General Social Survey, 1972–2012 Cumulative Data Files, Internet site http://sda.berkeley.edu/cgi-bin/hsda?harcsda+gss12; calculations by New Strategist

Table 3.15 Interest in Economic Issues, 2012

"There are a lot of issues in the news, and it is hard to keep up with every area. Are you very interested, moderately interested, or not at all interested in economic issues and business conditions?"

(percent of people aged 18 or older responding by selected characteristics, 2012)

	total	very interested	moderately interested	not at all interested
Total people	**100.0%**	**52.0%**	**37.2%**	**10.8%**
Men	100.0	57.1	34.3	8.6
Women	100.0	47.4	39.9	12.7
Millennials	100.0	45.3	43.0	11.7
Generation Xers	100.0	53.1	37.2	9.7
Baby Boomers	100.0	58.4	33.3	8.3
Older Americans	100.0	48.0	35.4	16.6
Black	100.0	60.9	30.9	8.2
Hispanic	100.0	43.3	36.6	20.1
Non-Hispanic white	100.0	51.2	39.8	9.1
Northeast	100.0	50.0	40.6	9.4
Midwest	100.0	52.7	36.5	10.9
South	100.0	54.9	33.3	11.8
West	100.0	48.6	41.4	10.1
Not a college graduate	100.0	47.0	39.4	13.6
Bachelor's degree or more	100.0	64.8	31.7	3.5

Note: Millennials are aged 18 to 35; Generation Xers are aged 36 to 47; Baby Boomers are aged 48 to 66; Older Americans are aged 67 or older.
Source: Survey Documentation and Analysis, Computer-assisted Survey Methods Program, University of California, Berkeley, General Social Survey, 1972–2012 Cumulative Data Files, Internet site http://sda.berkeley.edu/cgi-bin/hsda?harcsda+gss12; calculations by New Strategist

Table 3.16 Interest in Farm Issues, 2012

"There are a lot of issues in the news, and it is hard to keep up with every area.
Are you very interested, moderately interested, or not at all
interested in agricultural and farm issues?"

(percent of people aged 18 or older responding by selected characteristics, 2012)

	total	very interested	moderately interested	not at all interested
Total people	**100.0%**	**24.6%**	**49.1%**	**26.3%**
Men	100.0	24.1	51.8	24.1
Women	100.0	25.2	46.6	28.2
Millennials	100.0	18.8	50.6	30.6
Generation Xers	100.0	22.2	48.3	29.6
Baby Boomers	100.0	29.5	47.2	23.3
Older Americans	100.0	27.4	51.0	21.6
Black	100.0	30.2	38.3	31.5
Hispanic	100.0	20.6	48.3	31.1
Non-Hispanic white	100.0	23.2	52.7	24.1
Northeast	100.0	18.5	55.7	25.8
Midwest	100.0	24.9	47.3	27.8
South	100.0	28.9	43.0	28.1
West	100.0	22.4	55.3	22.3
Not a college graduate	100.0	25.8	49.2	25.1
Bachelor's degree or more	100.0	21.7	48.9	29.4

Note: Millennials are aged 18 to 35; Generation Xers are aged 36 to 47; Baby Boomers are aged 48 to 66; Older Americans are aged 67 or older.
Source: Survey Documentation and Analysis, Computer-assisted Survey Methods Program, University of California, Berkeley, General Social Survey, 1972–2012 Cumulative Data Files, Internet site http://sda.berkeley.edu/cgi-bin/hsda?harcsda+gss12; calculations by New Strategist

Table 3.17 Interest in Military Policy, 2012

"There are a lot of issues in the news, and it is hard to keep up with
every area. Are you very interested, moderately interested, or
not at all interested in issues about military and defense policy?"

(percent of people aged 18 or older responding by selected characteristics, 2012)

	total	very interested	moderately interested	not at all interested
Total people	100.0%	40.4%	45.9%	13.7%
Men	100.0	48.9	42.4	8.7
Women	100.0	32.5	49.2	18.3
Millennials	100.0	30.7	49.9	19.5
Generation Xers	100.0	37.0	47.3	15.8
Baby Boomers	100.0	46.1	44.2	9.7
Older Americans	100.0	49.4	40.7	9.9
Black	100.0	43.7	41.3	15.0
Hispanic	100.0	30.2	50.3	19.5
Non-Hispanic white	100.0	42.0	47.0	11.0
Northeast	100.0	37.1	48.0	14.9
Midwest	100.0	37.8	46.2	16.1
South	100.0	46.4	42.6	11.0
West	100.0	36.0	49.3	14.8
Not a college graduate	100.0	39.2	46.3	14.4
Bachelor's degree or more	100.0	43.3	44.8	11.9

Note: Millennials are aged 18 to 35; Generation Xers are aged 36 to 47; Baby Boomers are aged 48 to 66; Older Americans are aged 67 or older.
Source: Survey Documentation and Analysis, Computer-assisted Survey Methods Program, University of California, Berkeley, General Social Survey, 1972–2012 Cumulative Data Files, Internet site http://sda.berkeley.edu/cgi-bin/hsda?harcsda+gss12; calculations by New Strategist

Table 3.18 Interest in International Issues, 2012

"There are a lot of issues in the news, and it is hard to keep up with every area. Are you very interested, moderately interested, or not at all interested in international and foreign policy issues?"

(percent of people aged 18 or older responding by selected characteristics, 2012)

	total	very interested	moderately interested	not at all interested
Total people	**100.0%**	**22.3%**	**46.8%**	**30.9%**
Men	100.0	27.7	47.4	24.9
Women	100.0	17.4	46.3	36.4
Millennials	100.0	12.5	45.3	42.3
Generation Xers	100.0	23.9	43.0	33.0
Baby Boomers	100.0	26.2	49.3	24.6
Older Americans	100.0	29.2	47.8	23.0
Black	100.0	16.2	46.0	37.8
Hispanic	100.0	19.4	40.7	39.8
Non-Hispanic white	100.0	23.6	48.7	27.8
Northeast	100.0	29.5	44.0	26.5
Midwest	100.0	18.4	44.8	36.8
South	100.0	22.0	47.0	31.0
West	100.0	20.9	50.6	28.5
Not a college graduate	100.0	16.0	46.4	37.6
Bachelor's degree or more	100.0	38.5	47.7	13.8

Note: Millennials are aged 18 to 35; Generation Xers are aged 36 to 47; Baby Boomers are aged 48 to 66; Older Americans are aged 67 or older.
Source: Survey Documentation and Analysis, Computer-assisted Survey Methods Program, University of California, Berkeley, General Social Survey, 1972–2012 Cumulative Data Files, Internet site http://sda.berkeley.edu/cgi-bin/hsda?harcsda+gss12; calculations by New Strategist

Table 3.19 **Astrology Is Scientific, 2012**

"Would you say that astrology is very scientific,
sort of scientific, or not at all scientific?"

(percent of people aged 18 or older responding by selected characteristics, 2012)

	total	very scientific	sort of scientific	not at all scientific
Total people	**100.0%**	**9.2%**	**35.8%**	**55.0%**
Men	100.0	9.0	32.6	58.4
Women	100.0	9.4	38.7	51.9
Millennials	100.0	11.6	41.4	47.0
Generation Xers	100.0	11.3	39.9	48.9
Baby Boomers	100.0	6.1	30.9	63.0
Older Americans	100.0	9.5	31.4	59.1
Black	100.0	16.8	47.7	35.5
Hispanic	100.0	9.1	43.4	47.5
Non-Hispanic white	100.0	7.9	31.6	60.5
Northeast	100.0	6.0	39.1	54.9
Midwest	100.0	10.9	33.2	55.9
South	100.0	9.8	38.3	51.8
West	100.0	9.0	31.7	59.3
Not a college graduate	100.0	11.8	39.6	48.7
Bachelor's degree or more	100.0	2.9	26.5	70.6

Note: Millennials are aged 18 to 35; Generation Xers are aged 36 to 47; Baby Boomers are aged 48 to 66; Older Americans are aged 67 or older.
Source: Survey Documentation and Analysis, Computer-assisted Survey Methods Program, University of California, Berkeley, General Social Survey, 1972–2012 Cumulative Data Files, Internet site http://sda.berkeley.edu/cgi-bin/hsda?harcsda+gss12; calculations by New Strategist

Table 3.20 Understanding of Scientific Study, 2012

"When you read or hear the term 'scientific study,' do you have a clear understanding of what it means, a general sense of what it means, or little understanding of what it means?"

(percent of people aged 18 or older responding by selected characteristics, 2012)

	total	clear understanding	general sense	little understanding
Total people	**100.0%**	**24.5%**	**51.4%**	**24.1%**
Men	100.0	25.1	52.0	22.9
Women	100.0	23.8	50.9	25.2
Millennials	100.0	30.9	44.9	24.2
Generation Xers	100.0	29.5	47.9	22.6
Baby Boomers	100.0	20.0	57.9	22.1
Older Americans	100.0	15.9	52.9	31.2
Black	100.0	19.4	49.0	31.5
Hispanic	100.0	20.9	42.3	36.8
Non-Hispanic white	100.0	26.3	54.4	19.3
Northeast	100.0	30.0	45.4	24.5
Midwest	100.0	19.2	59.7	21.1
South	100.0	23.2	50.0	26.8
West	100.0	27.2	50.3	22.5
Not a college graduate	100.0	18.8	52.3	28.9
Bachelor's degree or more	100.0	38.5	49.2	12.3

Note: Millennials are aged 18 to 35; Generation Xers are aged 36 to 47; Baby Boomers are aged 48 to 66; Older Americans are aged 67 or older.
Source: Survey Documentation and Analysis, Computer-assisted Survey Methods Program, University of California, Berkeley, General Social Survey, 1972–2012 Cumulative Data Files, Internet site http://sda.berkeley.edu/cgi-bin/hsda?harcsda+gss12; calculations by New Strategist

Table 3.21 Scientific Knowledge: The Center of Earth Is Very Hot, 2012

"The center of the earth is very hot. Is that true or false?"

(percent of people aged 18 or older responding by selected characteristics, 2012)

	total	true	false
Total people	**100.0%**	**93.9%**	**6.1%**
Men	100.0	95.0	5.0
Women	100.0	92.8	7.2
Millennials	100.0	95.4	4.6
Generation Xers	100.0	94.1	5.9
Baby Boomers	100.0	92.4	7.5
Older Americans	100.0	94.2	5.8
Black	100.0	92.4	7.6
Hispanic	100.0	87.6	12.4
Non-Hispanic white	100.0	95.5	4.5
Northeast	100.0	94.5	5.5
Midwest	100.0	96.7	3.3
South	100.0	93.7	6.3
West	100.0	91.2	8.8
Not a college graduate	100.0	93.4	6.6
Bachelor's degree or more	100.0	95.0	5.0

Note: Millennials are aged 18 to 35; Generation Xers are aged 36 to 47; Baby Boomers are aged 48 to 66; Older Americans are aged 67 or older.
Source: Survey Documentation and Analysis, Computer-assisted Survey Methods Program, University of California, Berkeley, General Social Survey, 1972–2012 Cumulative Data Files, Internet site http://sda.berkeley.edu/cgi-bin/hsda?harcsda+gss12; calculations by New Strategist

Table 3.22 Scientific Knowledge: All Radioactivity Is Man-Made, 2012

"All radioactivity is man-made. Is that true or false?"

(percent of people aged 18 or older responding by selected characteristics, 2012)

	total	true	false
Total people	**100.0%**	**20.7%**	**79.3%**
Men	100.0	17.6	82.4
Women	100.0	23.7	76.3
Millennials	100.0	28.4	71.6
Generation Xers	100.0	21.5	78.5
Baby Boomers	100.0	16.7	83.3
Older Americans	100.0	14.0	86.0
Black	100.0	30.4	69.6
Hispanic	100.0	45.0	55.0
Non-Hispanic white	100.0	11.5	88.5
Northeast	100.0	17.4	82.6
Midwest	100.0	15.9	84.1
South	100.0	22.8	77.2
West	100.0	24.4	75.6
Not a college graduate	100.0	27.3	72.7
Bachelor's degree or more	100.0	5.1	94.9

Note: Millennials are aged 18 to 35; Generation Xers are aged 36 to 47; Baby Boomers are aged 48 to 66; Older Americans are aged 67 or older.
Source: Survey Documentation and Analysis, Computer-assisted Survey Methods Program, University of California, Berkeley, General Social Survey, 1972–2012 Cumulative Data Files, Internet site http://sda.berkeley.edu/cgi-bin/hsda?harcsda+gss12; calculations by New Strategist

Table 3.23 Scientific Knowledge: Father's Gene Decides Sex of Baby, 2012

"It is the father's gene that decides whether the baby
is a boy or a girl. Is that true or false?"

(percent of people aged 18 or older responding by selected characteristics, 2012)

	total	true	false
Total people	**100.0%**	**70.6%**	**29.4%**
Men	100.0	63.9	36.1
Women	100.0	76.2	23.8
Millennials	100.0	73.0	27.0
Generation Xers	100.0	68.0	32.0
Baby Boomers	100.0	71.8	28.2
Older Americans	100.0	66.4	33.6
Black	100.0	66.8	33.2
Hispanic	100.0	64.4	35.6
Non-Hispanic white	100.0	73.8	26.2
Northeast	100.0	66.6	33.4
Midwest	100.0	72.7	27.3
South	100.0	71.4	28.6
West	100.0	70.3	29.7
Not a college graduate	100.0	68.3	31.7
Bachelor's degree or more	100.0	75.9	24.1

Note: Millennials are aged 18 to 35; Generation Xers are aged 36 to 47; Baby Boomers are aged 48 to 66; Older Americans are aged 67 or older.
Source: Survey Documentation and Analysis, Computer-assisted Survey Methods Program, University of California, Berkeley, General Social Survey, 1972–2012 Cumulative Data Files, Internet site http://sda.berkeley.edu/cgi-bin/hsda?harcsda+gss12; calculations by New Strategist

Table 3.24 Scientific Knowledge: Lasers Work by Focusing Sound Waves, 2012

"Lasers work by focusing sound waves. Is that true or false?"

(percent of people aged 18 or older responding by selected characteristics, 2012)

	total	true	false
Total people	**100.0%**	**34.7%**	**65.3%**
Men	100.0	23.3	76.7
Women	100.0	48.0	52.0
Millennials	100.0	33.8	66.2
Generation Xers	100.0	33.1	66.9
Baby Boomers	100.0	32.6	67.4
Older Americans	100.0	42.6	57.4
Black	100.0	47.2	52.8
Hispanic	100.0	44.4	55.6
Non-Hispanic white	100.0	29.5	70.5
Northeast	100.0	32.1	67.9
Midwest	100.0	34.3	65.7
South	100.0	38.8	61.2
West	100.0	30.5	69.5
Not a college graduate	100.0	41.4	58.6
Bachelor's degree or more	100.0	20.9	79.1

Note: Millennials are aged 18 to 35; Generation Xers are aged 36 to 47; Baby Boomers are aged 48 to 66; Older Americans are aged 67 or older.
Source: Survey Documentation and Analysis, Computer-assisted Survey Methods Program, University of California, Berkeley, General Social Survey, 1972–2012 Cumulative Data Files, Internet site http://sda.berkeley.edu/cgi-bin/hsda?harcsda+gss12; calculations by New Strategist

Table 3.25 Scientific Knowledge: The Earth Goes around the Sun, 2012

"Does the earth go around the sun, or does the sun go around the earth?"

(percent of people aged 18 or older responding by selected characteristics, 2012)

	total	earth around sun	sun around earth
Total people	**100.0%**	**77.4%**	**22.6%**
Men	100.0	83.6	16.4
Women	100.0	71.3	28.7
Millennials	100.0	79.3	20.7
Generation Xers	100.0	86.6	13.4
Baby Boomers	100.0	71.5	28.5
Older Americans	100.0	76.4	23.6
Black	100.0	54.9	45.1
Hispanic	100.0	77.8	22.2
Non-Hispanic white	100.0	80.5	19.5
Northeast	100.0	82.5	17.5
Midwest	100.0	78.5	21.5
South	100.0	71.7	28.3
West	100.0	81.4	18.6
Not a college graduate	100.0	72.3	27.7
Bachelor's degree or more	100.0	89.5	10.5

Note: Millennials are aged 18 to 35; Generation Xers are aged 36 to 47; Baby Boomers are aged 48 to 66; Older Americans are aged 67 or older.
Source: Survey Documentation and Analysis, Computer-assisted Survey Methods Program, University of California, Berkeley, General Social Survey, 1972–2012 Cumulative Data Files, Internet site http://sda.berkeley.edu/cgi-bin/hsda?harcsda+gss12; calculations by New Strategist

Table 3.26 Scientific Knowledge: Electrons Are Smaller than Atoms, 2012

"Electrons are smaller than atoms. Is that true or false?"

(percent of people aged 18 or older responding by selected characteristics, 2012)

	total	true	false
Total people	**100.0%**	**72.8%**	**27.2%**
Men	100.0	74.5	25.5
Women	100.0	71.1	28.9
Millennials	100.0	73.3	26.7
Generation Xers	100.0	76.2	23.8
Baby Boomers	100.0	72.1	27.9
Older Americans	100.0	68.6	31.4
Black	100.0	62.2	37.8
Hispanic	100.0	76.4	23.6
Non-Hispanic white	100.0	75.1	24.9
Northeast	100.0	76.2	23.8
Midwest	100.0	73.5	26.5
South	100.0	68.7	31.3
West	100.0	76.0	24.0
Not a college graduate	100.0	71.2	28.8
Bachelor's degree or more	100.0	75.9	24.1

Note: Millennials are aged 18 to 35; Generation Xers are aged 36 to 47; Baby Boomers are aged 48 to 66; Older Americans are aged 67 or older.
Source: Survey Documentation and Analysis, Computer-assisted Survey Methods Program, University of California, Berkeley, General Social Survey, 1972–2012 Cumulative Data Files, Internet site http://sda.berkeley.edu/cgi-bin/hsda?harcsda+gss12; calculations by New Strategist

Table 3.27 Scientific Knowledge: How Long the Earth Goes around the Sun, 2012

"How long does it take for the earth to go around
the sun: one day, one month, or one year?"

(percent of people aged 18 or older responding by selected characteristics, 2012)

	total	one day	one month	one year
Total people	**100.0%**	**17.1%**	**1.2%**	**81.7%**
Men	100.0	13.4	1.1	85.4
Women	100.0	21.4	1.3	77.4
Millennials	100.0	11.2	0.0	88.8
Generation Xers	100.0	16.3	2.3	81.4
Baby Boomers	100.0	21.6	1.3	77.1
Older Americans	100.0	20.1	1.5	77.9
Black	100.0	35.6	0.6	63.7
Hispanic	100.0	16.5	0.8	82.3
Non-Hispanic white	100.0	14.5	1.3	84.2
Northeast	100.0	16.3	1.1	82.6
Midwest	100.0	14.2	2.3	83.5
South	100.0	21.0	0.4	78.7
West	100.0	15.0	1.2	83.5
Not a college graduate	100.0	21.0	1.5	77.4
Bachelor's degree or more	100.0	10.0	0.5	89.5

Note: Millennials are aged 18 to 35; Generation Xers are aged 36 to 47; Baby Boomers are aged 48 to 66; Older Americans are aged 67 or older.
Source: Survey Documentation and Analysis, Computer-assisted Survey Methods Program, University of California, Berkeley, General Social Survey, 1972–2012 Cumulative Data Files, Internet site http://sda.berkeley.edu/cgi-bin/hsda?harcsda+gss12; calculations by New Strategist

Table 3.28 Scientific Knowledge: Antibiotics Kill Viruses as Well as Bacteria, 2012

"Antibiotics kill viruses, as well as bacteria. Is that true or false?"

(percent of people aged 18 or older responding by selected characteristics, 2012)

	total	true	false
Total people	**100.0%**	**47.3%**	**52.7%**
Men	100.0	49.2	50.8
Women	100.0	45.6	54.4
Millennials	100.0	51.7	48.3
Generation Xers	100.0	47.2	52.8
Baby Boomers	100.0	43.6	56.4
Older Americans	100.0	48.1	51.9
Black	100.0	67.0	33.0
Hispanic	100.0	69.3	30.7
Non-Hispanic white	100.0	36.7	63.3
Northeast	100.0	47.6	52.4
Midwest	100.0	41.2	59.8
South	100.0	50.2	49.8
West	100.0	49.2	50.8
Not a college graduate	100.0	57.2	42.8
Bachelor's degree or more	100.0	22.9	77.1

Note: Millennials are aged 18 to 35; Generation Xers are aged 36 to 47; Baby Boomers are aged 48 to 66; Older Americans are aged 67 or older.
Source: Survey Documentation and Analysis, Computer-assisted Survey Methods Program, University of California, Berkeley, General Social Survey, 1972–2012 Cumulative Data Files, Internet site http://sda.berkeley.edu/cgi-bin/hsda?harcsda+gss12; calculations by New Strategist

Table 3.29 Scientific Knowledge: The Universe Began with a Big Explosion, 2012

"The universe began with a huge explosion. Is that true or false?"

(percent of people aged 18 or older responding by selected characteristics, 2012)

	total	true	false
Total people	**100.0%**	**54.8%**	**45.2%**
Men	100.0	59.9	40.1
Women	100.0	50.4	49.6
Millennials	100.0	64.5	35.5
Generation Xers	100.0	55.8	44.2
Baby Boomers	100.0	47.7	52.3
Older Americans	100.0	51.4	48.6
Black	100.0	33.0	67.0
Hispanic	100.0	56.6	43.4
Non-Hispanic white	100.0	57.0	43.0
Northeast	100.0	73.8	26.2
Midwest	100.0	52.3	47.8
South	100.0	40.8	59.2
West	100.0	59.6	40.4
Not a college graduate	100.0	53.2	46.8
Bachelor's degree or more	100.0	59.5	40.5

Note: Millennials are aged 18 to 35; Generation Xers are aged 36 to 47; Baby Boomers are aged 48 to 66; Older Americans are aged 67 or older.
Source: Survey Documentation and Analysis, Computer-assisted Survey Methods Program, University of California, Berkeley, General Social Survey, 1972–2012 Cumulative Data Files, Internet site http://sda.berkeley.edu/cgi-bin/hsda?harcsda+gss12; calculations by New Strategist

Table 3.30 Scientific Knowledge: The Continents Have Been Moving, 2012

"The continents on which we live have been moving their locations
for millions of years and will continue to move
in the future. Is that true or false?"

(percent of people aged 18 or older responding by selected characteristics, 2012)

	total	true	false
Total people	**100.0%**	**92.1%**	**7.9%**
Men	100.0	94.1	5.9
Women	100.0	90.0	10.0
Millennials	100.0	95.6	4.4
Generation Xers	100.0	92.3	7.7
Baby Boomers	100.0	88.3	11.7
Older Americans	100.0	93.6	6.4
Black	100.0	83.9	16.1
Hispanic	100.0	94.0	6.0
Non-Hispanic white	100.0	92.7	7.3
Northeast	100.0	93.3	6.7
Midwest	100.0	91.6	8.4
South	100.0	89.6	10.4
West	100.0	95.3	4.7
Not a college graduate	100.0	90.6	9.4
Bachelor's degree or more	100.0	95.4	4.6

Note: Millennials are aged 18 to 35; Generation Xers are aged 36 to 47; Baby Boomers are aged 48 to 66; Older Americans are aged 67 or older.
Source: Survey Documentation and Analysis, Computer-assisted Survey Methods Program, University of California, Berkeley, General Social Survey, 1972–2012 Cumulative Data Files, Internet site http://sda.berkeley.edu/cgi-bin/hsda?harcsda+gss12; calculations by New Strategist

Table 3.31 Scientific Knowledge: Human Beings Developed from Animals, 2012

"Human beings, as we know them today, developed from
earlier species of animals. Is that true or false?"

(percent of people aged 18 or older responding by selected characteristics, 2012)

	total	true	false
Total people	**100.0%**	**55.8%**	**44.2%**
Men	100.0	63.6	36.4
Women	100.0	48.7	51.3
Millennials	100.0	61.0	39.0
Generation Xers	100.0	58.7	41.3
Baby Boomers	100.0	55.7	44.3
Older Americans	100.0	38.0	62.0
Black	100.0	46.9	53.1
Hispanic	100.0	53.3	46.7
Non-Hispanic white	100.0	57.4	42.6
Northeast	100.0	72.6	27.4
Midwest	100.0	57.2	42.8
South	100.0	47.4	52.6
West	100.0	51.1	48.9
Not a college graduate	100.0	53.0	47.0
Bachelor's degree or more	100.0	63.1	36.9

Note: Millennials are aged 18 to 35; Generation Xers are aged 36 to 47; Baby Boomers are aged 48 to 66; Older Americans are aged 67 or older.
Source: Survey Documentation and Analysis, Computer-assisted Survey Methods Program, University of California, Berkeley, General Social Survey, 1972–2012 Cumulative Data Files, Internet site http://sda.berkeley.edu/cgi-bin/hsda?harcsda+gss12; calculations by New Strategist

4

Religion

Religion is of central importance to most Americans. In recent decades, however, there has been a trend away from organized religion and traditional denominations. The Millennial generation, in particular, is shunning religious affiliation. Nevertheless, most Americans believe in God and life after death, and most also pray at least once a day.

Little or No Change

• **Belief in God.** Fifty-nine percent of people aged 18 or older say they know God exists and have no doubt about it. Although this figure is down from the 66 percent who felt this way two decades ago, it remains firmly the majority opinion. Among Millennials, however, fewer than half have no doubt about God's existence.

• **Frequent prayer.** In 2012, the 59 percent majority of Americans said they prayed at least once a day, up slightly from the 54 percent of 1983. More than 80 percent of the public believes in life after death.

• **Bible is inspired word of God.** The largest share of Americans continues to believe that the Bible is the inspired word of God and not to be taken literally—a percentage that has not changed much in the past three decades.

Big Changes

• **Attendance is down at religious services.** The 43 percent of Americans who attend religious services once a year or less often are now almost as numerous as the 46 percent who attend nearly once a week or more often. Most Millennials attend religious services infrequently.

• **Fewer Protestants.** Protestants no longer dominate the religious landscape. The percentage of Americans who identify themselves as Protestant fell to 44 percent in 2012. Only 32 percent of Millennials identify themselves as Protestant and 30 percent say they have no religious affiliation.

Religion: 2012 Profiles

Table 4.1 Religious Background, 2012

"In what religion were you raised?"

(percent of people aged 18 or older responding by selected characteristics, 2012)

	total	Protestant	Catholic	none	Jewish	Moslem/ Islam	Hinduism	Buddhism	other
Total people	100.0%	49.0%	35.0%	8.1%	1.5%	1.1%	0.9%	0.3%	4.1%
Men	100.0	46.3	36.3	8.2	1.5	2.1	0.6	0.4	4.6
Women	100.0	51.3	33.9	8.0	1.5	0.3	1.1	0.2	3.7
Millennials	100.0	41.9	37.3	10.3	0.9	1.1	1.4	0.7	6.4
Generation Xers	100.0	46.1	35.5	7.6	2.7	1.5	1.3	0.2	5.1
Baby Boomers	100.0	52.9	34.7	7.3	0.9	1.0	0.4	0.0	2.8
Older Americans	100.0	62.0	29.1	5.4	2.1	0.3	0.0	0.0	1.1
Black	100.0	77.2	12.2	3.7	0.3	0.9	0.3	0.0	5.4
Hispanic	100.0	11.8	77.7	4.9	0.0	0.6	0.0	0.0	5.0
Non-Hispanic white	100.0	54.2	30.9	9.4	2.0	0.6	0.0	0.0	2.9
Northeast	100.0	31.4	48.9	7.9	3.5	3.7	1.6	0.4	2.6
Midwest	100.0	53.9	34.9	7.3	0.3	0.5	0.2	0.0	2.9
South	100.0	61.9	25.1	6.4	1.2	0.8	0.8	0.0	3.8
West	100.0	36.4	40.9	11.7	1.6	0.4	1.1	1.0	6.9
Not a college graduate	100.0	48.8	36.0	8.5	0.6	1.0	0.4	0.2	4.5
Bachelor's degree or more	100.0	49.6	32.5	6.9	3.7	1.5	2.2	0.4	3.2

Note: Millennials are aged 18 to 35; Generation Xers are aged 36 to 47; Baby Boomers are aged 48 to 66; Older Americans are aged 67 or older.

Source: Survey Documentation and Analysis, Computer-assisted Survey Methods Program, University of California, Berkeley, General Social Survey, 1972–2012 Cumulative Data Files, Internet site http://sda.berkeley.edu/cgi-bin/hsda?harcsda+gss12; calculations by New Strategist

Table 4.2 Religious Preference, 2012

"What is your religious preference?"

(percent of people aged 18 or older responding by selected characteristics, 2012)

	total	Protestant	Catholic	none	Jewish	Moslem/ Islam	Hinduism	Buddhism	other
Total people	100.0%	44.3%	24.2%	19.7%	1.5%	1.1%	0.5%	0.4%	8.3%
Men	100.0	39.4	24.9	23.6	1.3	2.0	0.5	0.6	7.7
Women	100.0	48.5	23.7	16.4	1.6	0.2	0.6	0.2	8.8
Millennials	100.0	31.9	24.4	29.5	0.8	0.7	0.9	0.9	10.9
Generation Xers	100.0	42.5	24.7	18.4	2.7	2.2	0.7	0.2	8.6
Baby Boomers	100.0	50.5	24.7	15.1	0.9	1.0	0.3	0.1	7.4
Older Americans	100.0	62.9	21.5	9.7	2.6	0.3	0.0	0.0	3.0
Black	100.0	65.9	6.8	17.1	0.6	2.0	0.0	0.1	7.5
Hispanic	100.0	21.0	56.9	15.7	0.0	0.0	0.0	0.0	6.4
Non-Hispanic white	100.0	47.3	20.9	21.2	2.0	0.5	0.0	0.2	7.9
Northeast	100.0	29.5	33.3	23.9	3.6	2.9	0.9	0.4	5.5
Midwest	100.0	48.2	23.8	18.7	0.3	0.5	0.2	0.3	8.0
South	100.0	58.1	16.8	14.6	1.2	1.0	0.6	0.1	7.6
West	100.0	29.3	29.9	25.8	1.5	0.4	0.4	1.0	11.7
Not a college graduate	100.0	44.4	25.8	18.3	0.8	0.9	0.2	0.3	9.3
Bachelor's degree or more	100.0	44.1	20.1	23.4	3.1	1.5	1.4	0.4	6.0

Note: Millennials are aged 18 to 35; Generation Xers are aged 36 to 47; Baby Boomers are aged 48 to 66; Older Americans are aged 67 or older.
Source: Survey Documentation and Analysis, Computer-assisted Survey Methods Program, University of California, Berkeley, General Social Survey, 1972–2012 Cumulative Data Files, Internet site http://sda.berkeley.edu/cgi-bin/hsda?harcsda+gss12; calculations by New Strategit

Table 4.3 Attendance at Religious Services, 2012

"How often do you attend religious services?"

(percent of people aged 18 or older responding by selected characteristics, 2012)

	total	once a week or more	one to three times a month	several times a year	once a year	less than once a year	never
Total people	**100.0%**	**26.2%**	**19.7%**	**10.8%**	**13.0%**	**5.0%**	**25.3%**
Men	100.0	23.8	16.9	11.8	13.7	5.1	28.7
Women	100.0	28.3	22.1	10.0	12.4	4.8	22.3
Millennials	100.0	18.1	19.3	10.4	16.4	5.7	30.1
Generation Xers	100.0	27.8	20.2	12.1	13.0	3.8	23.2
Baby Boomers	100.0	28.6	20.9	10.1	12.2	5.0	23.3
Older Americans	100.0	37.7	16.8	11.6	7.2	4.7	22.0
Black	100.0	31.7	31.2	11.9	9.4	2.5	13.2
Hispanic	100.0	27.7	25.7	12.9	9.8	4.2	19.7
Non-Hispanic white	100.0	24.2	16.3	10.2	14.0	5.8	29.5
Northeast	100.0	18.4	15.6	10.7	18.1	5.6	31.7
Midwest	100.0	23.9	20.9	11.1	14.0	5.8	24.2
South	100.0	32.0	23.3	11.9	9.3	3.8	19.7
West	100.0	25.0	15.7	8.9	14.3	5.5	30.6
Not a college graduate	100.0	24.7	19.4	11.2	12.8	5.4	26.4
Bachelor's degree or more	100.0	30.1	20.3	9.8	13.6	3.8	22.4

Note: Millennials are aged 18 to 35; Generation Xers are aged 36 to 47; Baby Boomers are aged 48 to 66; Older Americans are aged 67 or older.
Source: Survey Documentation and Analysis, Computer-assisted Survey Methods Program, University of California, Berkeley, General Social Survey, 1972–2012 Cumulative Data Files, Internet site http://sda.berkeley.edu/cgi-bin/hsda?harcsda+gss12; calculations by New Strategist

Table 4.4 Frequency of Prayer, 2012

"About how often do you pray?"

(percent of people aged 18 or older responding by selected characteristics, 2012)

	total	several times a day	once a day	several times a week	once a week	less than once a week	never
Total people	**100.0%**	**29.0%**	**30.4%**	**10.0%**	**6.8%**	**10.1%**	**13.8%**
Men	100.0	23.3	26.7	11.6	7.2	12.3	18.8
Women	100.0	33.8	33.5	8.6	6.4	8.1	9.6
Millennials	100.0	19.4	26.2	12.3	8.3	12.7	21.2
Generation Xers	100.0	32.8	33.0	8.9	5.3	7.6	12.5
Baby Boomers	100.0	32.5	32.6	9.4	7.3	8.0	10.1
Older Americans	100.0	37.6	30.9	7.6	4.1	12.6	7.2
Black	100.0	45.5	34.6	8.3	4.6	3.2	3.9
Hispanic	100.0	26.5	37.6	10.4	7.2	9.5	8.8
Non-Hispanic white	100.0	25.8	28.0	10.3	7.2	12.0	16.7
Northeast	100.0	22.6	22.3	10.4	10.7	12.5	21.4
Midwest	100.0	21.8	31.9	15.2	7.3	12.6	11.3
South	100.0	39.0	34.3	7.6	4.4	6.6	8.1
West	100.0	24.4	28.4	8.3	7.3	11.4	20.1
Not a college graduate	100.0	28.6	31.3	10.3	7.1	9.5	13.2
Bachelor's degree or more	100.0	30.1	28.0	8.9	6.1	11.6	15.4

Note: Millennials are aged 18 to 35; Generation Xers are aged 36 to 47; Baby Boomers are aged 48 to 66; Older Americans are aged 67 or older.
Source: Survey Documentation and Analysis, Computer-assisted Survey Methods Program, University of California, Berkeley, General Social Survey, 1972–2012 Cumulative Data Files, Internet site http://sda.berkeley.edu/cgi-bin/hsda?harcsda+gss12; calculations by New Strategist

Table 4.5 Belief in God, 2012

"Which statement comes closest to expressing what you believe about God? 1) I don't believe in God; 2) I don't know whether there is a God and I don't believe there is any way to find out; 3) I don't believe in a personal God, but I do believe in a Higher Power of some kind; 4) I find myself believing in God some of the time, but not at others; 5) While I have doubts, I feel that I do believe in God; 6) I know God really exists and I have no doubts about it."

(percent of people aged 18 or older responding by selected characteristics, 2012)

	total	1 don't believe	2 no way to find out	3 higher power	4 believe sometimes	5 believe but have doubts	6 know God exists
Total people	100.0%	3.1%	5.6%	11.6%	4.2%	16.5%	59.1%
Men	100.0	4.8	7.3	11.9	4.4	18.0	53.6
Women	100.0	1.6	4.2	11.4	4.0	15.2	63.7
Millennials	100.0	3.1	7.2	17.7	4.7	19.4	47.9
Generation Xers	100.0	4.1	5.7	9.5	4.1	13.4	63.2
Baby Boomers	100.0	2.7	4.4	9.0	3.6	17.1	63.3
Older Americans	100.0	2.2	4.5	6.5	4.4	13.3	69.1
Black	100.0	0.7	2.2	3.2	1.2	10.8	81.8
Hispanic	100.0	2.2	5.3	7.8	2.1	15.6	67.0
Non-Hispanic white	100.0	3.8	6.4	14.0	5.1	18.3	52.4
Northeast	100.0	5.5	7.0	15.4	4.4	19.8	47.9
Midwest	100.0	3.1	4.5	12.6	4.7	20.7	54.4
South	100.0	1.6	4.2	7.8	2.4	11.8	72.2
West	100.0	3.6	7.9	14.1	6.4	17.5	50.5
Not a college graduate	100.0	2.7	4.4	10.8	4.2	16.0	62.0
Bachelor's degree or more	100.0	4.1	8.7	13.8	4.1	17.7	51.6

Note: Millennials are aged 18 to 35; Generation Xers are aged 36 to 47; Baby Boomers are aged 48 to 66; Older Americans are aged 67 or older.
Source: Survey Documentation and Analysis, Computer-assisted Survey Methods Program, University of California, Berkeley, General Social Survey, 1972–2012 Cumulative Data Files, Internet site http://sda.berkeley.edu/cgi-bin/hsda?harcsda+gss12; calculations by New Strategist

Table 4.6 Belief in Life after Death, 2012

"Do you believe there is life after death?"

(percent of people aged 18 or older responding by selected characteristics, 2012)

	total	yes	no
Total people	**100.0%**	**81.1%**	**18.9%**
Men	100.0	77.7	22.3
Women	100.0	84.1	15.9
Millennials	100.0	82.2	17.8
Generation Xers	100.0	78.6	21.4
Baby Boomers	100.0	81.6	18.4
Older Americans	100.0	81.0	19.0
Black	100.0	87.2	12.8
Hispanic	100.0	77.3	22.7
Non-Hispanic white	100.0	80.8	19.2
Northeast	100.0	80.1	19.9
Midwest	100.0	83.4	16.6
South	100.0	84.0	16.0
West	100.0	74.5	25.5
Not a college graduate	100.0	80.7	19.3
Bachelor's degree or more	100.0	82.2	17.8

Note: Millennials are aged 18 to 35; Generation Xers are aged 36 to 47; Baby Boomers are aged 48 to 66; Older Americans are aged 67 or older.
Source: Survey Documentation and Analysis, Computer-assisted Survey Methods Program, University of California, Berkeley, General Social Survey, 1972–2012 Cumulative Data Files, Internet site http://sda.berkeley.edu/cgi-bin/hsda?harcsda+gss12; calculations by New Strategist

Table 4.7 Belief in the Bible, 2012

"Which of these statements comes closest to describing your feelings about the Bible? a) The Bible is the actual word of God and is to be taken literally, word for word; b) The Bible is the inspired word of God but not everything in it should be taken literally, word for word; c) The Bible is an ancient book of fables, legends, history, and moral precepts recorded by men."

(percent of people aged 18 or older responding by selected characteristics, 2012)

	total	word of God	inspired word	book of fables	other
Total people	**100.0%**	**32.1%**	**44.6%**	**21.8%**	**1.5%**
Men	100.0	28.3	44.1	25.5	2.0
Women	100.0	35.3	45.1	18.6	1.0
Millennials	100.0	25.9	45.1	27.8	1.3
Generation Xers	100.0	33.5	44.7	21.4	0.4
Baby Boomers	100.0	33.8	45.1	18.3	2.8
Older Americans	100.0	41.2	41.4	16.6	0.8
Black	100.0	55.8	35.1	8.6	0.5
Hispanic	100.0	34.5	45.5	18.6	1.4
Non-Hispanic white	100.0	26.4	47.3	24.7	1.5
Northeast	100.0	23.8	43.2	31.0	2.0
Midwest	100.0	27.9	48.2	23.0	0.9
South	100.0	42.3	42.9	13.0	1.8
West	100.0	25.8	45.0	27.9	1.3
Not a college graduate	100.0	37.0	42.5	19.3	1.2
Bachelor's degree or more	100.0	19.6	50.2	28.0	2.2

Note: Millennials are aged 18 to 35; Generation Xers are aged 36 to 47; Baby Boomers are aged 48 to 66; Older Americans are aged 67 or older.
Source: Survey Documentation and Analysis, Computer-assisted Survey Methods Program, University of California, Berkeley, General Social Survey, 1972–2012 Cumulative Data Files, Internet site http://sda.berkeley.edu/cgi-bin/hsda?harcsda+gss12; calculations by New Strategist

Table 4.8 Prayer in the Public Schools, 2012

"The United States Supreme Court has ruled that no state or local government may require the reading of the Lord's Prayer or Bible verses in public schools. Do you approve or disapprove of the court's ruling?"

(percent of people aged 18 or older responding by selected characteristics, 2012)

	total	approve	disapprove
Total people	**100.0%**	**40.8%**	**59.2%**
Men	100.0	43.4	56.6
Women	100.0	38.5	61.5
Millennials	100.0	50.4	49.6
Generation Xers	100.0	40.6	59.4
Baby Boomers	100.0	33.9	66.1
Older Americans	100.0	31.5	68.5
Black	100.0	26.5	73.5
Hispanic	100.0	40.8	59.2
Non-Hispanic white	100.0	44.3	55.7
Northeast	100.0	55.9	44.1
Midwest	100.0	43.2	56.8
South	100.0	24.5	75.5
West	100.0	53.7	46.3
Not a college graduate	100.0	34.7	65.3
Bachelor's degree or more	100.0	57.4	42.6

Note: Millennials are aged 18 to 35; Generation Xers are aged 36 to 47; Baby Boomers are aged 48 to 66; Older Americans are aged 67 or older.
Source: Survey Documentation and Analysis, Computer-assisted Survey Methods Program, University of California, Berkeley, General Social Survey, 1972–2012 Cumulative Data Files, Internet site http://sda.berkeley.edu/cgi-bin/hsda?harcsda+gss12; calculations by New Strategist

Table 4.9 Degree of Religiosity, 2012

"To what extent do you consider yourself a religious person?"

(percent of people aged 18 or older responding by selected characteristics, 2012)

	total	very religious	moderately religious	slightly religious	not religious
Total people	**100.0%**	**18.8%**	**39.5%**	**21.6%**	**20.1%**
Men	100.0	16.1	37.1	24.1	22.7
Women	100.0	21.2	41.5	19.5	17.8
Millennials	100.0	11.2	34.5	26.2	28.1
Generation Xers	100.0	20.3	38.3	20.1	21.3
Baby Boomers	100.0	25.0	40.7	18.6	15.7
Older Americans	100.0	20.0	50.1	20.5	9.4
Black	100.0	30.1	47.4	13.7	8.8
Hispanic	100.0	12.6	42.4	30.8	14.2
Non-Hispanic white	100.0	17.0	38.1	21.2	23.8
Northeast	100.0	14.1	34.9	22.5	28.5
Midwest	100.0	13.8	44.7	25.0	16.6
South	100.0	27.1	41.9	17.0	14.0
West	100.0	14.1	33.8	25.1	27.0
Not a college graduate	100.0	18.5	39.8	23.6	18.1
Bachelor's degree or more	100.0	19.6	38.6	16.6	25.2

Note: Millennials are aged 18 to 35; Generation Xers are aged 36 to 47; Baby Boomers are aged 48 to 66; Older Americans are aged 67 or older.
Source: Survey Documentation and Analysis, Computer-assisted Survey Methods Program, University of California, Berkeley, General Social Survey, 1972–2012 Cumulative Data Files, Internet site http://sda.berkeley.edu/cgi-bin/hsda?harcsda+gss12; calculations by New Strategist

Table 4.10 Degree of Spirituality, 2012

"To what extent do you consider yourself a spiritual person?"

(percent of people aged 18 or older responding by selected characteristics, 2012)

	total	very spiritual	moderately spiritual	slightly spiritual	not spiritual
Total people	**100.0%**	**29.2%**	**37.2%**	**22.6%**	**11.0%**
Men	100.0	22.6	37.7	27.3	12.4
Women	100.0	34.7	36.9	18.5	9.9
Millennials	100.0	20.2	32.7	31.2	15.8
Generation Xers	100.0	30.5	38.7	19.1	11.7
Baby Boomers	100.0	37.1	39.3	16.7	6.8
Older Americans	100.0	29.8	40.8	21.2	8.2
Black	100.0	42.1	39.8	12.7	5.4
Hispanic	100.0	25.2	38.2	31.7	5.0
Non-Hispanic white	100.0	27.2	36.0	23.3	13.6
Northeast	100.0	25.9	32.9	26.2	15.0
Midwest	100.0	21.8	40.1	28.2	9.9
South	100.0	38.4	36.9	16.9	7.7
West	100.0	23.8	38.2	23.5	14.4
Not a college graduate	100.0	27.9	35.1	25.1	11.9
Bachelor's degree or more	100.0	32.5	42.7	16.1	8.7

Note: Millennials are aged 18 to 35; Generation Xers are aged 36 to 47; Baby Boomers are aged 48 to 66; Older Americans are aged 67 or older.
Source: Survey Documentation and Analysis, Computer-assisted Survey Methods Program, University of California, Berkeley, General Social Survey, 1972–2012 Cumulative Data Files, Internet site http://sda.berkeley.edu/cgi-bin/hsda?harcsda+gss12; calculations by New Strategist

Table 4.11 Ever Been Born Again, 2012

"Would you say you have been 'born again' or have had a 'born again' experience—that is, a turning point in your life when you committed yourself to Christ?"

(percent of people aged 18 or older responding by selected characteristics, 2012)

	total	yes	no
Total people	**100.0%**	**41.7%**	**58.3%**
Men	100.0	37.6	62.4
Women	100.0	45.1	54.9
Millennials	100.0	37.4	62.6
Generation Xers	100.0	43.7	56.3
Baby Boomers	100.0	43.3	56.7
Older Americans	100.0	45.1	54.9
Black	100.0	66.2	33.8
Hispanic	100.0	44.0	56.0
Non-Hispanic white	100.0	37.6	62.4
Northeast	100.0	19.6	80.4
Midwest	100.0	37.0	63.0
South	100.0	60.8	39.2
West	100.0	31.9	68.1
Not a college graduate	100.0	44.5	55.5
Bachelor's degree or more	100.0	34.3	65.7

Note: Millennials are aged 18 to 35; Generation Xers are aged 36 to 47; Baby Boomers are aged 48 to 66; Older Americans are aged 67 or older.
Source: Survey Documentation and Analysis, Computer-assisted Survey Methods Program, University of California, Berkeley, General Social Survey, 1972–2012 Cumulative Data Files, Internet site http://sda.berkeley.edu/cgi-bin/hsda?harcsda+gss12; calculations by New Strategist

Table 4.12 Ever Tried to Convince Others to Accept Jesus, 2012

"Have you ever tried to encourage someone to believe in Jesus Christ
or to accept Jesus Christ as his or her savior?"

(percent of people aged 18 or older responding by selected characteristics, 2012)

	total	yes	no
Total people	**100.0%**	**43.0%**	**57.0%**
Men	100.0	38.7	61.3
Women	100.0	46.7	53.3
Millennials	100.0	36.1	63.9
Generation Xers	100.0	42.5	57.5
Baby Boomers	100.0	48.4	51.6
Older Americans	100.0	47.4	52.6
Black	100.0	63.4	36.6
Hispanic	100.0	44.8	55.2
Non-Hispanic white	100.0	40.0	60.0
Northeast	100.0	25.4	74.6
Midwest	100.0	41.4	58.6
South	100.0	57.4	42.6
West	100.0	34.4	65.6
Not a college graduate	100.0	44.6	55.4
Bachelor's degree or more	100.0	39.0	61.0

Note: Millennials are aged 18 to 35; Generation Xers are aged 36 to 47; Baby Boomers are aged 48 to 66; Older Americans are aged 67 or older.
Source: Survey Documentation and Analysis, Computer-assisted Survey Methods Program, University of California, Berkeley, General Social Survey, 1972–2012 Cumulative Data Files, Internet site http://sda.berkeley.edu/cgi-bin/hsda?harcsda+gss12; calculations by New Strategist

Religion: Historical Trends

Table 4.13 Religious Background, 1973 to 2012

"In what religion were you raised?"

(percent distribution of people aged 18 or older by response for selected years)

	total	Protestant	Catholic	none	Jewish	other
2012	100.0%	49.0%	35.0%	8.1%	1.5%	6.4%
2010	100.0	51.1	33.4	6.9	1.5	7.2
2008	100.0	52.9	33.2	8.7	1.8	3.3
2006	100.0	51.4	34.0	8.2	2.2	4.2
2004	100.0	54.0	31.0	8.3	2.2	4.6
2002	100.0	55.7	30.7	7.2	1.9	4.5
2000	100.0	56.4	31.0	6.8	2.3	3.5
1998	100.0	57.9	31.2	5.9	1.8	3.2
1996	100.0	58.7	29.8	5.7	2.1	3.7
1994	100.0	60.6	30.8	4.3	1.7	2.6
1993	100.0	64.0	27.4	4.4	2.2	2.1
1991	100.0	63.2	29.8	3.5	2.1	1.3
1990	100.0	64.3	26.9	5.1	1.9	1.9
1989	100.0	62.3	29.8	3.8	1.8	2.3
1988	100.0	62.9	29.4	3.6	2.1	2.1
1987	100.0	67.3	26.8	3.0	1.4	1.5
1986	100.0	63.9	29.0	2.9	2.3	1.9
1985	100.0	65.7	28.0	3.5	2.3	0.5
1984	100.0	64.2	29.0	2.9	2.1	1.9
1983	100.0	63.5	29.2	3.1	3.2	1.0
1982	100.0	65.4	27.5	3.2	2.5	1.5
1980	100.0	66.7	26.8	3.4	2.0	1.0
1978	100.0	66.0	28.2	3.2	1.8	0.8
1977	100.0	67.7	26.7	2.4	2.2	1.0
1976	100.0	63.8	29.8	3.0	2.2	1.2
1975	100.0	68.3	26.5	2.8	1.7	0.8
1974	100.0	65.3	28.1	2.7	3.4	0.5
1973	100.0	64.3	29.1	2.3	2.8	1.6

Source: Survey Documentation and Analysis, Computer-assisted Survey Methods Program, University of California, Berkeley, General Social Survey, 1972–2012 Cumulative Data Files, Internet site http://sda.berkeley.edu/cgi-bin/hsda?harcsda+gss12; calculations by New Strategist

Table 4.14 Religious Preference, 1972 to 2012

"What is your religious preference? Is it Protestant, Catholic,
Jewish, some other religion, or no religion?"

(percent distribution of people aged 18 or older by response for selected years)

	total	Protestant	Catholic	none	Jewish	other
2012	100.0%	44.3%	24.2%	19.7%	1.5%	10.3%
2010	100.0	46.7	25.2	18.0	1.6	8.4
2008	100.0	49.8	25.1	16.8	1.7	6.6
2006	100.0	50.3	26.8	15.9	1.9	5.2
2004	100.0	51.6	24.7	14.1	2.1	7.6
2002	100.0	52.4	25.5	13.8	1.5	6.9
2000	100.0	52.7	25.4	14.1	2.2	5.5
1998	100.0	53.7	26.2	13.7	1.8	4.6
1996	100.0	56.5	24.2	11.9	2.1	5.3
1994	100.0	58.4	26.9	9.0	1.9	3.8
1993	100.0	63.1	23.0	9.0	2.1	2.8
1991	100.0	63.3	26.8	6.3	1.9	1.7
1990	100.0	62.6	24.5	7.7	1.9	3.3
1989	100.0	62.3	26.2	7.8	1.5	2.1
1988	100.0	60.4	27.1	7.7	2.0	2.8
1987	100.0	64.9	24.6	7.1	1.3	2.1
1986	100.0	61.2	27.4	6.9	2.5	2.0
1985	100.0	62.9	26.8	6.9	2.0	1.3
1984	100.0	62.8	26.7	7.1	1.9	1.5
1983	100.0	61.8	27.0	6.9	2.7	1.6
1982	100.0	64.8	25.3	6.8	1.9	1.2
1980	100.0	64.6	24.8	6.7	2.0	1.9
1978	100.0	63.0	25.8	8.4	1.6	1.1
1977	100.0	64.9	26.0	5.9	2.1	1.1
1976	100.0	62.6	27.4	7.4	1.7	0.9
1975	100.0	64.7	25.3	7.3	1.5	1.1
1974	100.0	63.3	26.1	7.0	3.0	0.6
1973	100.0	61.8	26.4	6.6	2.7	2.4
1972	100.0	62.5	27.4	5.1	3.0	1.9

Source: Survey Documentation and Analysis, Computer-assisted Survey Methods Program, University of California, Berkeley, General Social Survey, 1972–2012 Cumulative Data Files, Internet site http://sda.berkeley.edu/cgi-bin/hsda?harcsda+gss12; calculations by New Strategist

Table 4.15 Attendance at Religious Services, 1972 to 2012

"How often do you attend religious services?"

(percent distribution of people aged 18 or older by response for selected years)

	total	once a week or more	one to three times a month	several times a year	once a year	less than once a year	never
2012	100.0%	26.2%	19.7%	10.8%	13.0%	5.0%	25.3%
2010	100.0	25.8	20.4	10.3	14.2	6.7	22.6
2008	100.0	25.5	21.2	11.1	13.5	6.9	21.8
2006	100.0	26.2	20.3	11.6	12.7	6.8	22.4
2004	100.0	27.5	22.3	13.3	14.2	7.3	15.4
2002	100.0	24.8	23.1	12.6	14.4	6.9	18.3
2000	100.0	25.2	20.2	13.7	12.6	7.7	20.6
1998	100.0	26.6	22.4	11.1	10.4	10.6	18.9
1996	100.0	24.2	22.0	14.7	14.6	9.2	15.3
1994	100.0	27.9	21.5	13.2	14.0	7.6	15.7
1993	100.0	29.8	21.9	10.9	12.4	9.0	16.1
1991	100.0	29.2	23.5	12.4	14.1	9.2	11.7
1990	100.0	29.6	23.3	13.4	11.9	8.5	13.3
1989	100.0	30.1	21.3	12.0	13.4	7.2	15.9
1988	100.0	26.9	25.0	12.4	12.1	6.9	16.6
1987	100.0	28.6	23.2	15.4	14.2	6.5	12.1
1986	100.0	32.5	22.1	11.3	12.6	7.3	14.3
1985	100.0	33.6	18.8	11.9	14.9	6.8	14.1
1984	100.0	33.6	20.6	13.2	13.1	7.3	12.2
1983	100.0	32.3	21.0	11.7	13.0	9.3	12.8
1982	100.0	28.8	19.8	15.1	14.6	7.8	14.0
1980	100.0	29.2	21.1	14.8	16.2	6.9	11.8
1978	100.0	28.6	22.5	12.7	13.7	8.1	14.5
1977	100.0	30.3	21.9	12.5	13.5	8.5	13.3
1976	100.0	29.1	19.7	15.6	14.0	9.5	12.2
1975	100.0	29.9	22.6	14.1	12.2	7.1	14.1
1974	100.0	31.1	22.7	12.6	15.1	6.5	12.0
1973	100.0	28.1	22.0	15.1	13.5	7.8	13.5
1972	100.0	35.3	21.8	14.5	10.9	8.3	9.3

Source: Survey Documentation and Analysis, Computer-assisted Survey Methods Program, University of California, Berkeley, General Social Survey, 1972–2012 Cumulative Data Files, Internet site http://sda.berkeley.edu/cgi-bin/hsda?harcsda+gss12; calculations by New Strategist

Table 4.16 Frequency of Prayer, 1983 to 2012

"About how often do you pray?"

(percent distribution of people aged 18 or older by response for selected years)

	total	several times a day	once a day	several times a week	once a week	less than once a week	never
2012	100.0%	29.0%	30.4%	10.0%	6.8%	10.1%	13.8%
2010	100.0	28.2	29.0	12.9	6.0	10.7	13.2
2008	100.0	27.4	29.9	11.0	6.2	13.5	11.9
2006	100.0	29.9	29.3	11.6	6.6	11.5	11.1
2004	100.0	31.4	27.8	14.4	5.6	10.4	10.3
2002	100.0	25.4	31.7	11.0	8.1	23.1	0.6
2000	100.0	25.7	29.6	14.3	6.6	23.0	1.0
1998	100.0	24.0	29.5	14.9	7.4	22.6	1.6
1996	100.0	26.0	30.8	13.9	8.1	18.9	2.3
1994	100.0	22.2	32.4	11.8	9.5	22.9	1.1
1993	100.0	25.2	29.8	13.6	7.9	21.9	1.6
1990	100.0	22.6	28.9	14.3	8.8	25.4	0.0
1989	100.0	22.6	29.1	15.9	6.6	25.2	0.6
1988	100.0	22.0	30.8	16.1	8.5	22.4	0.3
1987	100.0	24.5	31.4	13.8	8.8	21.0	0.6
1985	100.0	26.3	31.5	13.7	7.1	20.4	1.0
1984	100.0	27.3	29.4	13.7	7.4	21.0	1.2
1983	100.0	24.7	29.2	14.3	7.1	20.9	3.8

Source: Survey Documentation and Analysis, Computer-assisted Survey Methods Program, University of California, Berkeley, General Social Survey, 1972–2012 Cumulative Data Files, Internet site http://sda.berkeley.edu/cgi-bin/hsda?harcsda+gss12; calculations by New Strategist

Table 4.17 Belief in God, 1988 to 2012

"Which statement comes closest to expressing what you believe about God?
1) I don't believe in God; 2) I don't know whether there is a God and I don't
believe there is any way to find out; 3) I don't believe in a personal God, but I do
believe in a Higher Power of some kind; 4) I find myself believing in God some
of the time, but not at others; 5) While I have doubts, I feel that I do believe in
God; 6) I know God really exists and I have no doubts about it."

(percent distribution of people aged 18 or older by response for selected years)

	total	1 don't believe	2 no way to find out	3 higher power	4 believe sometimes	5 believe but have doubts	6 know God exists
2012	100.0%	3.1%	5.6%	11.6%	4.2%	16.5%	59.1%
2010	100.0	3.3	5.7	10.7	4.8	16.9	58.6
2008	100.0	3.1	4.9	10.1	3.4	16.9	61.6
2006	100.0	2.1	4.3	9.6	4.2	16.7	63.1
2000	100.0	2.9	4.3	7.5	3.9	16.6	64.8
1998	100.0	3.2	5.1	10.0	4.6	13.8	63.3
1994	100.0	2.6	2.8	9.7	3.7	16.0	65.1
1993	100.0	3.0	4.4	8.2	3.4	15.1	66.0
1991	100.0	2.2	4.1	6.6	5.3	18.0	63.9
1988	100.0	1.5	3.6	7.4	5.1	19.0	63.3

*Source: Survey Documentation and Analysis, Computer-assisted Survey Methods Program, University of California, Berkeley,
General Social Survey, 1972–2012 Cumulative Data Files, Internet site http://sda.berkeley.edu/cgi-bin/hsda?harcsda+gss12;
calculations by New Strategist*

Table 4.18 Belief in Life after Death, 1973 to 2012

"Do you believe there is life after death?"

(percent distribution of people aged 18 or older by response for selected years)

	total	yes	no
2012	100.0%	81.1%	18.9%
2010	100.0	81.1	18.9
2008	100.0	81.3	18.7
2006	100.0	82.8	17.2
2004	100.0	82.9	17.1
2002	100.0	81.1	18.9
2000	100.0	82.0	18.0
1998	100.0	81.8	18.2
1996	100.0	82.3	17.7
1994	100.0	81.6	18.4
1993	100.0	80.9	19.1
1991	100.0	80.3	19.7
1990	100.0	79.0	21.0
1989	100.0	77.3	22.7
1988	100.0	78.9	21.2
1987	100.0	79.4	20.6
1986	100.0	82.1	17.9
1984	100.0	81.7	18.3
1983	100.0	73.6	26.4
1980	100.0	82.3	17.7
1978	100.0	77.5	22.5
1976	100.0	78.4	21.6
1975	100.0	74.3	25.7
1973	100.0	76.3	23.7

Source: Survey Documentation and Analysis, Computer-assisted Survey Methods Program, University of California, Berkeley, General Social Survey, 1972–2012 Cumulative Data Files, Internet site http://sda.berkeley.edu/cgi-bin/hsda?harcsda+gss12; calculations by New Strategist

Table 4.19 Belief in the Bible, 1984 to 2012

"Which of these statements comes closest to describing your feelings about the Bible? a) The Bible is the actual word of God and is to be taken literally, word for word; b) The Bible is the inspired word of God but not everything in it should be taken literally, word for word; c) The Bible is an ancient book of fables, legends, history, and moral precepts recorded by men."

(percent distribution of people aged 18 or older by response for selected years)

	total	word of God	inspired word	book of fables	other
2012	100.0%	32.1%	44.6%	21.8%	1.5%
2010	100.0	34.1	43.6	20.6	1.7
2008	100.0	32.0	47.0	19.6	1.4
2006	100.0	33.8	47.2	16.7	2.3
2004	100.0	34.2	47.9	15.7	2.2
2002	100.0	29.3	54.2	13.7	2.7
2000	100.0	33.8	49.4	15.9	0.9
1998	100.0	32.0	50.9	16.0	1.1
1996	100.0	30.6	51.5	17.4	0.5
1994	100.0	32.5	51.9	14.6	0.9
1993	100.0	34.1	49.5	15.5	1.0
1991	100.0	35.9	49.0	14.5	0.6
1990	100.0	33.4	50.7	15.3	0.6
1989	100.0	32.2	52.0	15.3	0.5
1988	100.0	34.7	48.3	16.3	0.7
1987	100.0	36.1	47.9	15.5	0.6
1985	100.0	39.1	48.6	12.1	0.1
1984	100.0	38.4	46.2	14.6	0.7

Source: Survey Documentation and Analysis, Computer-assisted Survey Methods Program, University of California, Berkeley, General Social Survey, 1972–2012 Cumulative Data Files, Internet site http://sda.berkeley.edu/cgi-bin/hsda?harcsda+gss12; calculations by New Strategist

Table 4.20 Prayer in the Public Schools, 1974 to 2012

"The United States Supreme Court has ruled that no state or local government
may require the reading of the Lord's Prayer or Bible verses in public schools.
Do you approve or disapprove of the court's ruling?"

(percent distribution of people aged 18 or older by response for selected years)

	total	approve	disapprove
2012	100.0%	40.8%	59.2%
2010	100.0	44.1	55.9
2008	100.0	41.8	58.3
2006	100.0	43.9	56.2
2004	100.0	36.3	63.7
2002	100.0	40.6	59.4
2000	100.0	39.0	61.0
1998	100.0	44.7	55.3
1996	100.0	41.4	58.6
1994	100.0	38.8	61.2
1993	100.0	41.2	58.8
1991	100.0	39.8	60.2
1990	100.0	42.4	57.6
1989	100.0	42.2	57.8
1988	100.0	39.4	60.6
1986	100.0	37.8	62.2
1985	100.0	44.7	55.3
1983	100.0	40.3	59.7
1982	100.0	38.1	61.9
1977	100.0	33.2	66.8
1975	100.0	37.4	62.6
1974	100.0	31.7	68.3

Source: Survey Documentation and Analysis, Computer-assisted Survey Methods Program, University of California, Berkeley, General Social Survey, 1972–2012 Cumulative Data Files, Internet site http://sda.berkeley.edu/cgi-bin/hsda?harcsda+gss12; calculations by New Strategist

Table 4.21 Degree of Religiosity, 1998 to 2012

"To what extent do you consider yourself a religious person?"

(percent distribution of people aged 18 or older by response for selected years)

	total	very religious	moderately religious	slightly religious	not religious
2012	100.0%	18.8%	39.5%	21.6%	20.1%
2010	100.0	16.8	41.5	23.6	18.1
2008	100.0	18.2	42.2	23.4	16.2
2006	100.0	19.0	43.7	23.1	14.2
1998	100.0	18.7	42.9	23.5	14.9

Source: Survey Documentation and Analysis, Computer-assisted Survey Methods Program, University of California, Berkeley, General Social Survey, 1972–2012 Cumulative Data Files, Internet site http://sda.berkeley.edu/cgi-bin/hsda?harcsda+gss12; calculations by New Strategist

Table 4.22 Degree of Spirituality, 1998 to 2012

"To what extent do you consider yourself a spiritual person?"

(percent distribution of people aged 18 or older by response for selected years)

	total	very spiritual	moderately spiritual	slightly spiritual	not spiritual
2012	100.0%	29.2%	37.2%	22.6%	11.0%
2010	100.0	27.9	39.0	22.2	10.9
2008	100.0	26.2	41.4	22.7	9.8
2006	100.0	28.4	41.2	21.3	9.0
1998	100.0	21.7	40.1	26.6	11.7

Source: Survey Documentation and Analysis, Computer-assisted Survey Methods Program, University of California, Berkeley, General Social Survey, 1972–2012 Cumulative Data Files, Internet site http://sda.berkeley.edu/cgi-bin/hsda?harcsda+gss12; calculations by New Strategist

Table 4.23 Ever Been Born Again, 1988 to 2012

"Would you say you have been 'born again' or have had a 'born
again' experience—that is, a turning point in your life
when you committed yourself to Christ?"

(percent distribution of people aged 18 or older by response for selected years)

	total	yes	no
2012	100.0%	41.7%	58.3%
2010	100.0	37.6	62.4
2008	100.0	37.4	62.6
2006	100.0	36.3	63.7
2004	100.0	33.6	66.4
1998	100.0	37.5	62.5
1991	100.0	35.9	64.1
1988	100.0	36.6	63.4

Source: Survey Documentation and Analysis, Computer-assisted Survey Methods Program, University of California, Berkeley, General Social Survey, 1972–2012 Cumulative Data Files, Internet site http://sda.berkeley.edu/cgi-bin/hsda?harcsda+gss12; calculations by New Strategist

Table 4.24 Ever Tried to Convince Others to Accept Jesus, 1988 to 2012

"Have you ever tried to encourage someone to believe in Jesus Christ
or to accept Jesus Christ as his or her savior?"

(percent distribution of people aged 18 or older by response for selected years)

	total	yes	no
2012	100.0%	43.0%	57.0%
2010	100.0	43.9	56.1
2008	100.0	44.2	55.8
2006	100.0	43.0	57.0
1998	100.0	43.6	56.4
1988	100.0	46.5	53.5

Source: Survey Documentation and Analysis, Computer-assisted Survey Methods Program, University of California, Berkeley, General Social Survey, 1972–2012 Cumulative Data Files, Internet site http://sda.berkeley.edu/cgi-bin/hsda?harcsda+gss12; calculations by New Strategist

5

Work and Money

Most Americans are "very" satisfied with their work and are at least "more or less" satisfied with their financial situation—despite the Great Recession and its aftermath. But the slow economic recovery and partisan bickering has taken its toll. Barely half the population still believes in the American Dream.

Little or No Change

• **Job satisfaction.** If anything, Americans today are even more satisfied with their work than they were three or four decades ago. In 2012, the share that was "very satisfied" topped 50 percent, up from a low of 43 percent in 1993.

• **Satisfaction with finances.** The plurality of Americans is more or less satisfied with their present financial situation, a figure that has not changed much despite the economic turmoil of the past decade. Only 28 percent were "not at all" satisfied with their finances in 2012, somewhat higher than the low of 21 percent in 1977.

• **Class identification.** Americans strongly identify with the working (44 percent) or middle (44 percent) class. The proportions have barely changed over the decades.

Big Changes

• **Family income compared with others.** When asked how their family income ranks relative to others, the share of Americans who say it is average fell from a high of 59 percent in 1973 to 46 percent in 2012. Thirty-three percent say their family income is below average, up from the low of 21 percent who felt that way in 1973.

• **Belief in the American Dream.** Belief in the American Dream has slipped. Only 55 percent agree that the United States provides opportunities for people like them to improve their standard of living, down sharply from the 77 percent who felt that way in 2000. Only 43 percent of older Americans think their family can get ahead versus 64 percent of Millennials.

Work and Money: 2012 Profiles

Table 5.1 Satisfaction with Work, 2012

"On the whole, how satisfied are you with the work you do?"

(percent of people aged 18 or older responding by selected characteristics, 2012)

	total	very satisfied	moderately satisfied	a little dissatisfied	very dissatisfied
Total people	**100.0%**	**50.5%**	**37.1%**	**8.9%**	**3.4%**
Men	100.0	49.1	38.1	9.3	3.5
Women	100.0	51.7	36.3	8.6	3.3
Millennials	100.0	44.7	40.8	8.6	5.9
Generation Xers	100.0	51.7	37.0	9.3	1.9
Baby Boomers	100.0	54.7	33.9	9.2	2.3
Older Americans	100.0	58.6	32.7	8.6	0.0
Black	100.0	41.8	43.2	10.3	4.6
Hispanic	100.0	36.3	47.4	11.8	4.5
Non-Hispanic white	100.0	56.4	33.0	8.0	2.6
Northeast	100.0	46.2	43.7	6.7	3.4
Midwest	100.0	57.8	30.7	10.0	1.5
South	100.0	51.1	36.6	8.4	3.9
West	100.0	46.0	39.1	10.5	4.4
Not a college graduate	100.0	49.9	35.4	10.6	4.0
Bachelor's degree or more	100.0	51.8	41.2	5.1	2.0

Note: Includes job or housework. Millennials are aged 18 to 35; Generation Xers are aged 36 to 47; Baby Boomers are aged 48 to 66; Older Americans are aged 67 or older.
Source: Survey Documentation and Analysis, Computer-assisted Survey Methods Program, University of California, Berkeley, General Social Survey, 1972–2012 Cumulative Data Files, Internet site http://sda.berkeley.edu/cgi-bin/hsda?harcsda+gss12; calculations by New Strategist

Table 5.2 Likely to Lose Job, 2012

"Thinking about the next 12 months, how likely do you think it is that you will lose your job or be laid off?" (Note: Asked only of those with jobs.)

(percent of people aged 18 or older responding by selected characteristics, 2012)

	total	very likely	fairly likely	not too likely	unlikely
Total people	**100.0%**	**5.7%**	**5.4%**	**27.0%**	**61.8%**
Men	100.0	4.8	5.2	23.1	67.0
Women	100.0	6.8	5.6	31.4	56.1
Millennials	100.0	5.4	5.7	27.1	61.8
Generation Xers	100.0	5.8	6.0	30.1	58.0
Baby Boomers	100.0	6.4	5.0	24.0	64.6
Older Americans	100.0	3.0	1.5	28.7	66.8
Black	100.0	6.8	10.9	23.7	58.6
Hispanic	100.0	13.0	9.5	27.8	49.7
Non-Hispanic white	100.0	3.7	2.6	28.4	65.2
Northeast	100.0	4.0	3.0	30.5	62.5
Midwest	100.0	5.6	2.2	25.3	66.9
South	100.0	6.2	6.4	24.2	63.2
West	100.0	6.4	8.7	30.5	54.4
Not a college graduate	100.0	7.2	6.9	25.4	60.5
Bachelor's degree or more	100.0	2.6	2.1	30.5	64.8

Note: Millennials are aged 18 to 35; Generation Xers are aged 36 to 47; Baby Boomers are aged 48 to 66; Older Americans are aged 67 or older.
Source: Survey Documentation and Analysis, Computer-assisted Survey Methods Program, University of California, Berkeley, General Social Survey, 1972–2012 Cumulative Data Files, Internet site http://sda.berkeley.edu/cgi-bin/hsda?harcsda+gss12; calculations by New Strategist

Table 5.3 Could Find Equally Good Job, 2012

"About how easy would it be for you to find a job with another employer with approximately the same income and fringe benefits you now have?"
(Note: Asked only of those with jobs.)

(percent of people aged 18 or older responding by selected characteristics, 2012)

	total	very easy	somewhat easy	not easy
Total people	**100.0%**	**16.0%**	**38.1%**	**45.9%**
Men	100.0	18.5	35.7	45.9
Women	100.0	13.2	40.7	46.1
Millennials	100.0	19.4	47.8	32.8
Generation Xers	100.0	12.8	34.5	52.6
Baby Boomers	100.0	14.9	32.4	52.7
Older Americans	100.0	12.4	6.2	81.4
Black	100.0	10.4	36.2	53.5
Hispanic	100.0	17.3	30.4	52.3
Non-Hispanic white	100.0	18.0	38.3	43.6
Northeast	100.0	11.2	45.4	43.4
Midwest	100.0	18.7	31.8	49.4
South	100.0	19.1	36.7	44.3
West	100.0	12.0	41.2	46.8
Not a college graduate	100.0	16.2	34.0	49.8
Bachelor's degree or more	100.0	15.6	47.0	37.4

Note: Millennials are aged 18 to 35; Generation Xers are aged 36 to 47; Baby Boomers are aged 48 to 66; Older Americans are aged 67 or older.
Source: Survey Documentation and Analysis, Computer-assisted Survey Methods Program, University of California, Berkeley, General Social Survey, 1972–2012 Cumulative Data Files, Internet site http://sda.berkeley.edu/cgi-bin/hsda?harcsda+gss12; calculations by New Strategist

Table 5.4 Unemployed in Last 10 Years, 2012

"At any time during the last 10 years, have you been unemployed
and looking for work for as long as a month?"

(percent of people aged 18 or older responding by selected characteristics, 2012)

	total	yes	no
Total people	**100.0%**	**36.6%**	**63.4%**
Men	100.0	38.2	61.8
Women	100.0	35.3	64.7
Millennials	100.0	58.3	41.7
Generation Xers	100.0	31.3	68.7
Baby Boomers	100.0	30.7	69.4
Older Americans	100.0	11.2	88.8
Black	100.0	34.6	65.4
Hispanic	100.0	48.7	51.3
Non-Hispanic white	100.0	33.4	66.6
Northeast	100.0	38.7	61.3
Midwest	100.0	31.1	68.9
South	100.0	33.1	66.9
West	100.0	46.1	53.9
Not a college graduate	100.0	39.7	60.3
Bachelor's degree or more	100.0	29.1	70.9

Note: Millennials are aged 18 to 35; Generation Xers are aged 36 to 47; Baby Boomers are aged 48 to 66; Older Americans are aged 67 or older.
Source: Survey Documentation and Analysis, Computer-assisted Survey Methods Program, University of California, Berkeley, General Social Survey, 1972–2012 Cumulative Data Files, Internet site http://sda.berkeley.edu/cgi-bin/hsda?harcsda+gss12; calculations by New Strategist

Table 5.5 Affirmative Action for Women, 2012

"Tell me whether you strongly agree, agree, neither agree nor disagree, disagree,
or strongly disagree: Because of past discrimination, employers should
make special efforts to hire and promote qualified women."

(percent of people aged 18 or older responding by selected characteristics, 2012)

	total	strongly agree	agree	neither agree nor disagree	disagree	strongly disagree
Total people	**100.0%**	**14.5%**	**48.1%**	**11.4%**	**23.3%**	**2.7%**
Men	100.0	11.1	45.8	10.7	29.6	2.8
Women	100.0	18.3	50.7	12.2	16.1	2.6
Millennials	100.0	9.2	43.0	18.1	26.8	3.0
Generation Xers	100.0	13.7	46.8	14.1	20.5	4.8
Baby Boomers	100.0	16.6	48.3	6.6	26.0	2.5
Older Americans	100.0	21.9	59.1	5.2	13.8	0.0
Black	100.0	23.3	52.0	10.1	13.3	1.3
Hispanic	100.0	12.8	63.8	8.6	14.0	0.8
Non-Hispanic white	100.0	13.1	45.6	12.2	25.9	3.3
Northeast	100.0	14.7	45.9	9.5	26.3	3.7
Midwest	100.0	11.8	48.0	13.9	22.8	3.4
South	100.0	15.2	54.4	7.5	20.6	2.3
West	100.0	16.0	41.5	15.2	25.4	2.0
Not a college graduate	100.0	14.6	50.4	10.9	21.5	2.6
Bachelor's degree or more	100.0	14.2	41.4	12.8	28.5	3.1

Note: Millennials are aged 18 to 35; Generation Xers are aged 36 to 47; Baby Boomers are aged 48 to 66; Older Americans are aged 67 or older.
Source: Survey Documentation and Analysis, Computer-assisted Survey Methods Program, University of California, Berkeley, General Social Survey, 1972–2012 Cumulative Data Files, Internet site http://sda.berkeley.edu/cgi-bin/hsda?harcsda+gss12; calculations by New Strategist

Table 5.6 Man Won't Get Job or Promotion, 2012

"What do you think the chances are these days that a man won't get a job or a promotion while an equally or less qualified woman gets one instead?"

(percent of people aged 18 or older responding by selected characteristics, 2012)

	total	very likely	somewhat likely	somewhat unlikely	very unlikely
Total people	**100.0%**	**11.5%**	**39.3%**	**33.3%**	**16.0%**
Men	100.0	17.3	37.9	32.8	12.0
Women	100.0	7.5	40.2	33.6	18.7
Millennials	100.0	12.5	42.0	31.6	13.9
Generation Xers	100.0	7.4	39.1	37.6	16.0
Baby Boomers	100.0	16.5	34.6	30.4	18.5
Older Americans	100.0	6.0	40.5	36.7	16.8
Black	100.0	13.4	34.2	28.1	24.4
Hispanic	100.0	20.1	39.8	23.4	16.7
Non-Hispanic white	100.0	8.5	39.7	37.4	14.4
Northeast	100.0	6.8	36.4	41.3	15.5
Midwest	100.0	13.2	42.7	33.0	11.1
South	100.0	13.8	36.8	27.5	21.8
West	100.0	9.0	42.4	37.8	10.8
Not a college graduate	100.0	13.7	41.2	28.6	16.4
Bachelor's degree or more	100.0	5.8	34.2	45.2	14.9

Note: Millennials are aged 18 to 35; Generation Xers are aged 36 to 47; Baby Boomers are aged 48 to 66; Older Americans are aged 67 or older.
Source: Survey Documentation and Analysis, Computer-assisted Survey Methods Program, University of California, Berkeley, General Social Survey, 1972–2012 Cumulative Data Files, Internet site http://sda.berkeley.edu/cgi-bin/hsda?harcsda+gss12; calculations by New Strategist

Table 5.7 Woman Won't Get Job or Promotion, 2012

"What do you think the chances are these days that a woman won't get a job or a promotion while an equally or less qualified man gets one instead?"

(percent of people aged 18 or older responding by selected characteristics, 2012)

	total	very likely	somewhat likely	somewhat unlikely	very unlikely
Total people	**100.0%**	**21.1%**	**46.8%**	**22.7%**	**9.4%**
Men	100.0	18.8	45.3	26.2	9.7
Women	100.0	23.5	48.5	18.9	9.1
Millennials	100.0	13.6	56.3	22.3	7.7
Generation Xers	100.0	19.4	47.6	22.7	10.4
Baby Boomers	100.0	26.7	38.7	24.6	10.0
Older Americans	100.0	25.7	44.5	19.6	10.2
Black	100.0	28.2	34.9	24.5	12.4
Hispanic	100.0	29.0	41.8	21.5	7.6
Non-Hispanic white	100.0	18.0	52.8	21.7	7.4
Northeast	100.0	15.8	56.0	18.3	9.9
Midwest	100.0	14.5	53.3	24.9	7.3
South	100.0	25.6	41.6	23.9	8.8
West	100.0	24.7	41.6	21.8	11.9
Not a college graduate	100.0	22.5	46.8	20.4	10.4
Bachelor's degree or more	100.0	17.1	47.0	29.1	6.8

Note: Millennials are aged 18 to 35; Generation Xers are aged 36 to 47; Baby Boomers are aged 48 to 66; Older Americans are aged 67 or older.
Source: Survey Documentation and Analysis, Computer-assisted Survey Methods Program, University of California, Berkeley, General Social Survey, 1972–2012 Cumulative Data Files, Internet site http://sda.berkeley.edu/cgi-bin/hsda?harcsda+gss12; calculations by New Strategist

Table 5.8 Satisfaction with Financial Situation, 2012

"We are interested in how people are getting along financially these days.
As far as you and your family are concerned, would you say that you
are pretty well satisfied with your present financial situation,
more or less satisfied, or not satisfied at all?"

(percent of people aged 18 or older responding by selected characteristics, 2012)

	total	satisfied	more or less satisfied	not at all satisfied
Total people	**100.0%**	**27.0%**	**45.0%**	**28.0%**
Men	100.0	27.8	45.8	26.4
Women	100.0	26.2	44.3	29.5
Millennials	100.0	22.4	48.7	28.9
Generation Xers	100.0	25.2	46.3	28.5
Baby Boomers	100.0	27.2	41.9	30.9
Older Americans	100.0	39.9	41.2	18.9
Black	100.0	22.0	39.0	39.0
Hispanic	100.0	18.3	52.2	29.5
Non-Hispanic white	100.0	30.3	43.5	26.2
Northeast	100.0	30.3	41.3	28.4
Midwest	100.0	29.5	42.9	27.5
South	100.0	26.5	45.4	28.1
West	100.0	22.7	49.3	28.0
Not a college graduate	100.0	21.8	46.3	32.0
Bachelor's degree or more	100.0	40.4	41.9	17.8

Note: Millennials are aged 18 to 35; Generation Xers are aged 36 to 47; Baby Boomers are aged 48 to 66; Older Americans are aged 67 or older.
Source: Survey Documentation and Analysis, Computer-assisted Survey Methods Program, University of California, Berkeley, General Social Survey, 1972–2012 Cumulative Data Files, Internet site http://sda.berkeley.edu/cgi-bin/hsda?harcsda+gss12; calculations by New Strategist

Table 5.9 Change in Financial Situation, 2012

"During the last few years, has your financial situation been getting better, worse, or has it stayed the same?"

(percent of people aged 18 or older responding by selected characteristics, 2012)

	total	better	worse	stayed same
Total people	**100.0%**	**28.2%**	**30.2%**	**41.6%**
Men	100.0	27.6	28.6	43.8
Women	100.0	28.7	31.5	39.8
Millennials	100.0	39.1	22.7	38.1
Generation Xers	100.0	29.3	28.9	41.8
Baby Boomers	100.0	23.2	38.0	38.8
Older Americans	100.0	12.5	32.0	55.5
Black	100.0	29.1	27.5	43.4
Hispanic	100.0	29.6	30.0	40.4
Non-Hispanic white	100.0	28.0	31.5	40.5
Northeast	100.0	25.3	32.9	41.9
Midwest	100.0	31.3	28.8	39.9
South	100.0	28.5	30.0	41.5
West	100.0	26.8	29.8	43.4
Not a college graduate	100.0	27.3	32.4	40.3
Bachelor's degree or more	100.0	30.5	24.5	45.0

Note: Millennials are aged 18 to 35; Generation Xers are aged 36 to 47; Baby Boomers are aged 48 to 66; Older Americans are aged 67 or older.
Source: Survey Documentation and Analysis, Computer-assisted Survey Methods Program, University of California, Berkeley, General Social Survey, 1972–2012 Cumulative Data Files, Internet site http://sda.berkeley.edu/cgi-bin/hsda?harcsda+gss12; calculations by New Strategist

Table 5.10 Continue to Work if Rich, 2012

"If you were to get enough money to live as comfortably as you would like for the rest of your life, would you continue to work or would you stop working?"

(percent of people aged 18 or older responding by selected characteristics, 2012)

	total	continue working	stop working
Total people	**100.0%**	**72.9%**	**27.1%**
Men	100.0	71.0	29.0
Women	100.0	74.9	25.1
Millennials	100.0	81.3	18.7
Generation Xers	100.0	77.3	22.7
Baby Boomers	100.0	61.5	38.5
Older Americans	100.0	63.3	36.7
Black	100.0	71.1	28.9
Hispanic	100.0	81.4	18.6
Non-Hispanic white	100.0	71.8	28.2
Northeast	100.0	79.0	21.0
Midwest	100.0	70.1	29.9
South	100.0	73.8	26.2
West	100.0	68.5	31.5
Not a college graduate	100.0	73.0	27.0
Bachelor's degree or more	100.0	72.5	27.5

Note: Millennials are aged 18 to 35; Generation Xers are aged 36 to 47; Baby Boomers are aged 48 to 66; Older Americans are aged 67 or older.
Source: Survey Documentation and Analysis, Computer-assisted Survey Methods Program, University of California, Berkeley, General Social Survey, 1972–2012 Cumulative Data Files, Internet site http://sda.berkeley.edu/cgi-bin/hsda?harcsda+gss12; calculations by New Strategist

Table 5.11 How People Get Ahead, 2012

"Some people say that people get ahead by their own hard work; others say that lucky breaks or help from other people are more important. Which do you think is most important?"

(percent of people aged 18 or older responding by selected characteristics, 2012)

	total	hard work	both equally	luck or help
Total people	**100.0%**	**69.9%**	**20.1%**	**10.0%**
Men	100.0	66.0	20.5	13.5
Women	100.0	73.1	19.8	7.1
Millennials	100.0	73.9	16.5	9.6
Generation Xers	100.0	69.6	20.1	10.2
Baby Boomers	100.0	66.6	23.4	9.9
Older Americans	100.0	69.2	19.8	11.0
Black	100.0	70.3	19.5	10.2
Hispanic	100.0	76.4	11.3	12.4
Non-Hispanic white	100.0	68.9	21.7	9.4
Northeast	100.0	61.3	26.0	12.6
Midwest	100.0	75.6	13.9	10.5
South	100.0	70.4	21.0	8.5
West	100.0	70.0	20.0	10.0
Not a college graduate	100.0	72.7	16.7	10.6
Bachelor's degree or more	100.0	62.5	29.0	8.5

Note: Millennials are aged 18 to 35; Generation Xers are aged 36 to 47; Baby Boomers are aged 48 to 66; Older Americans are aged 67 or older.
Source: Survey Documentation and Analysis, Computer-assisted Survey Methods Program, University of California, Berkeley, General Social Survey, 1972–2012 Cumulative Data Files, Internet site http://sda.berkeley.edu/cgi-bin/hsda?harcsda+gss12; calculations by New Strategist

Table 5.12 Class Identification, 2012

"If you were asked to use one of four names for your social class, which would you say you belong in: the lower class, the working class, the middle class, or the upper class?"

(percent of people aged 18 or older responding by selected characteristics, 2012)

	total	lower class	working class	middle class	upper class
Total people	**100.0%**	**8.4%**	**44.3%**	**43.7%**	**3.6%**
Men	100.0	8.3	43.1	44.1	4.5
Women	100.0	8.5	45.3	43.3	2.8
Millennials	100.0	9.3	52.3	35.7	2.7
Generation Xers	100.0	5.6	48.4	42.0	4.1
Baby Boomers	100.0	9.0	40.6	46.2	4.2
Older Americans	100.0	9.7	27.6	59.6	3.1
Black	100.0	12.4	51.0	33.7	3.0
Hispanic	100.0	7.7	64.3	26.1	1.9
Non-Hispanic white	100.0	7.9	38.2	49.5	4.4
Northeast	100.0	7.7	38.8	48.0	5.4
Midwest	100.0	7.4	47.8	41.4	3.4
South	100.0	8.6	45.5	43.3	2.6
West	100.0	9.7	43.0	43.3	4.0
Not a college graduate	100.0	10.9	52.5	34.6	2.0
Bachelor's degree or more	100.0	2.1	23.1	67.1	7.7

Note: Millennials are aged 18 to 35; Generation Xers are aged 36 to 47; Baby Boomers are aged 48 to 66; Older Americans are aged 67 or older.
Source: Survey Documentation and Analysis, Computer-assisted Survey Methods Program, University of California, Berkeley, General Social Survey, 1972–2012 Cumulative Data Files, Internet site http://sda.berkeley.edu/cgi-bin/hsda?harcsda+gss12; calculations by New Strategist

Table 5.13 Family Income Relative to Others, 2012

"Compared with American families in general, would you say your family income is far below average, below average, average, above average, or far above average?"

(percent of people aged 18 or older responding by selected characteristics, 2012)

	total	far below average	below average	average	above average	far above average
Total people	**100.0%**	**6.8%**	**25.9%**	**45.5%**	**19.0%**	**2.7%**
Men	100.0	6.2	25.7	43.7	21.5	2.9
Women	100.0	7.4	26.1	47.1	16.8	2.6
Millennials	100.0	5.7	27.7	49.9	15.3	1.4
Generation Xers	100.0	7.7	22.3	40.5	25.3	4.3
Baby Boomers	100.0	8.3	24.9	:43.6	19.9	3.2
Older Americans	100.0	4.6	29.8	48.1	15.0	2.4
Black	100.0	9.0	29.9	45.5	12.5	3.1
Hispanic	100.0	8.6	35.6	43.3	10.9	1.7
Non-Hispanic white	100.0	6.1	23.6	44.4	23.0	3.0
Northeast	100.0	5.5	21.4	48.8	22.2	2.1
Midwest	100.0	4.6	27.4	48.0	16.8	3.3
South	100.0	7.9	26.7	43.1	19.2	3.0
West	100.0	8.2	26.6	44.6	18.3	2.3
Not a college graduate	100.0	8.1	31.6	46.9	11.8	1.6
Bachelor's degree or more	100.0	3.4	11.4	42.0	37.4	5.8

Note: Millennials are aged 18 to 35; Generation Xers are aged 36 to 47; Baby Boomers are aged 48 to 66; Older Americans are aged 67 or older.
Source: Survey Documentation and Analysis, Computer-assisted Survey Methods Program, University of California, Berkeley, General Social Survey, 1972–2012 Cumulative Data Files, Internet site http://sda.berkeley.edu/cgi-bin/hsda?harcsda+gss12; calculations by New Strategist

Table 5.14 Parents' Standard of Living, 2012

"Compared to your parents when they were the age you are now, do you think your own standard of living now is much better, somewhat better, about the same, somewhat worse, or much worse than theirs was?"

(percent of people aged 18 or older responding by selected characteristics, 2012)

	total	much better	somewhat better	about the same	somewhat worse	much worse
Total people	**100.0%**	**33.5%**	**28.6%**	**21.2%**	**12.0%**	**4.6%**
Men	100.0	34.9	30.5	20.8	10.3	3.7
Women	100.0	32.3	27.0	21.6	13.6	5.5
Millennials	100.0	33.0	30.5	22.2	10.2	4.1
Generation Xers	100.0	32.1	25.6	21.5	14.6	6.3
Baby Boomers	100.0	33.1	27.2	20.5	13.6	5.7
Older Americans	100.0	37.7	32.1	20.5	8.6	1.1
Black	100.0	35.7	33.2	19.0	8.9	3.3
Hispanic	100.0	45.1	27.0	14.3	10.9	2.8
Non-Hispanic white	100.0	28.9	27.8	24.5	13.7	5.1
Northeast	100.0	36.0	25.1	22.5	11.6	4.8
Midwest	100.0	26.5	34.0	22.1	13.3	4.1
South	100.0	35.2	29.1	20.0	11.4	4.4
West	100.0	35.5	25.3	21.4	12.3	5.5
Not a college graduate	100.0	33.3	29.6	18.9	12.7	5.4
Bachelor's degree or more	100.0	33.9	26.1	26.8	10.4	2.7

Note: Millennials are aged 18 to 35; Generation Xers are aged 36 to 47; Baby Boomers are aged 48 to 66; Older Americans are aged 67 or older.
Source: Survey Documentation and Analysis, Computer-assisted Survey Methods Program, University of California, Berkeley, General Social Survey, 1972–2012 Cumulative Data Files, Internet site http://sda.berkeley.edu/cgi-bin/hsda?harcsda+gss12; calculations by New Strategist

Table 5.15 Children's Standard of Living, 2012

"When your children are at the age you are now, do you think their standard of living will be much better, somewhat better, about the same, somewhat worse, or much worse than yours is now?"

(percent of people aged 18 or older responding by selected characteristics, 2012)

	total	much better	somewhat better	about the same	somewhat worse	much worse	no children
Total people	**100.0%**	**27.9%**	**22.7%**	**18.2%**	**14.5%**	**5.5%**	**11.2%**
Men	100.0	26.4	19.2	17.6	17.0	6.0	13.8
Women	100.0	29.1	25.7	18.7	12.4	5.1	9.0
Millennials	100.0	36.8	23.9	16.6	7.7	2.1	12.8
Generation Xers	100.0	30.3	25.4	17.0	11.0	6.8	9.5
Baby Boomers	100.0	21.8	19.9	20.0	19.8	6.3	12.3
Older Americans	100.0	19.2	22.5	19.7	22.6	8.6	7.5
Black	100.0	44.3	20.1	7.8	9.4	6.0	12.4
Hispanic	100.0	45.0	24.1	14.1	9.0	2.9	5.0
Non-Hispanic white	100.0	19.0	22.8	22.6	17.6	6.0	12.0
Northeast	100.0	23.0	20.1	23.3	11.9	6.4	15.3
Midwest	100.0	21.8	27.9	17.8	18.5	4.2	9.8
South	100.0	33.8	18.7	15.4	15.1	6.6	10.4
West	100.0	28.2	26.2	19.2	11.5	4.2	10.7
Not a college graduate	100.0	32.3	23.4	15.5	13.8	6.4	8.7
Bachelor's degree or more	100.0	17.2	21.2	24.9	16.3	3.1	17.4

Note: Millennials are aged 18 to 35; Generation Xers are aged 36 to 47; Baby Boomers are aged 48 to 66; Older Americans are aged 67 or older.
Source: Survey Documentation and Analysis, Computer-assisted Survey Methods Program, University of California, Berkeley, General Social Survey, 1972–2012 Cumulative Data Files, Internet site http://sda.berkeley.edu/cgi-bin/hsda?harcsda+gss12; calculations by New Strategist

Table 5.16 Standard of Living Will Improve, 2012

"The way things are in America, people like me and my family have a good chance of improving our standard of living. Do you agree or disagree?"

(percent of people aged 18 or older responding by selected characteristics, 2012)

	total	strongly agree	agree	neither	disagree	strongly disagree
Total people	100.0%	14.1%	40.7%	17.9%	23.4%	4.0%
Men	100.0	15.2	43.1	17.5	21.6	2.5
Women	100.0	13.1	38.6	18.2	24.9	5.2
Millennials	100.0	19.6	44.3	17.7	16.1	2.4
Generation Xers	100.0	16.2	39.4	18.9	21.1	4.4
Baby Boomers	100.0	9.7	41.1	17.5	26.0	5.6
Older Americans	100.0	8.7	34.5	17.8	35.9	3.0
Black	100.0	19.1	52.1	9.7	17.1	2.0
Hispanic	100.0	25.6	47.5	17.7	5.7	3.4
Non-Hispanic white	100.0	9.2	36.5	19.9	29.6	4.8
Northeast	100.0	13.6	38.9	21.5	22.6	3.4
Midwest	100.0	10.1	37.6	20.0	29.5	2.8
South	100.0	14.2	42.8	14.9	23.8	4.2
West	100.0	18.1	41.7	17.9	17.3	5.0
Not a college graduate	100.0	15.7	40.3	17.8	22.5	3.8
Bachelor's degree or more	100.0	10.1	41.8	18.2	25.5	4.4

Note: Millennials are aged 18 to 35; Generation Xers are aged 36 to 47; Baby Boomers are aged 48 to 66; Older Americans are aged 67 or older.
Source: Survey Documentation and Analysis, Computer-assisted Survey Methods Program, University of California, Berkeley, General Social Survey, 1972–2012 Cumulative Data Files, Internet site http://sda.berkeley.edu/cgi-bin/hsda?harcsda+gss12; calculations by New Strategist

Work and Money: Historical Trends

Table 5.17 Satisfaction with Work, 1972 to 2012

"On the whole, how satisfied are you with the work you do?"

(percent distribution of people aged 18 or older by response for selected years)

	total	very satisfied	moderately satisfied	a little dissatisfied	very dissatisfied
2012	100.0%	50.5%	37.1%	8.9%	3.4%
2010	100.0	49.8	36.2	10.3	3.7
2008	100.0	51.5	36.3	9.1	3.1
2006	100.0	49.4	38.3	8.2	4.0
2004	100.0	50.9	36.1	8.6	4.4
2002	100.0	50.8	36.5	9.2	3.5
2000	100.0	45.5	43.2	8.2	3.1
1998	100.0	48.4	38.7	9.7	3.2
1996	100.0	44.9	40.4	10.6	4.1
1994	100.0	45.6	40.5	10.6	3.3
1993	100.0	43.4	40.8	10.8	5.0
1991	100.0	44.8	41.7	9.5	4.0
1990	100.0	46.2	39.8	10.4	3.7
1989	100.0	46.3	39.3	10.4	4.0
1988	100.0	46.1	39.6	10.3	4.0
1987	100.0	44.3	39.0	12.2	4.5
1986	100.0	49.2	39.2	8.9	2.7
1985	100.0	47.7	38.7	9.2	4.4
1984	100.0	46.9	33.5	12.7	6.8
1983	100.0	48.2	37.5	9.2	5.1
1982	100.0	46.5	38.5	10.2	4.9
1980	100.0	47.1	36.0	12.4	4.4
1978	100.0	49.1	36.0	10.3	4.6
1977	100.0	47.0	39.7	10.5	2.8
1976	100.0	50.7	35.4	9.6	4.4
1975	100.0	53.8	33.1	9.2	3.9
1974	100.0	47.6	38.1	9.7	4.6
1973	100.0	49.2	39.0	7.5	4.3
1972	100.0	48.3	36.5	11.8	3.4

Note: Includes job or housework.
Source: Survey Documentation and Analysis, Computer-assisted Survey Methods Program, University of California, Berkeley, General Social Survey, 1972–2012 Cumulative Data Files, Internet site http://sda.berkeley.edu/cgi-bin/hsda?harcsda+gss12; calculations by New Strategist

Table 5.18 Likely to Lose Job, 1977 to 2012

"Thinking about the next 12 months, how likely do you think it is that you will lose your job or be laid off?" (Note: Asked only of those with jobs.)

(percent distribution of people aged 18 or older by response for selected years)

	total	very likely	fairly likely	not too likely	unlikely
2012	100.0%	5.7%	5.4%	27.0%	61.8%
2010	100.0	7.7	8.8	31.4	52.2
2008	100.0	5.5	5.8	29.3	59.4
2006	100.0	4.8	5.4	26.3	63.6
2004	100.0	5.3	4.8	26.1	63.9
2002	100.0	6.0	6.9	24.2	62.9
2000	100.0	3.5	4.1	21.5	70.9
1998	100.0	3.3	4.3	26.7	65.7
1996	100.0	4.1	6.3	28.6	61.0
1994	100.0	5.6	4.7	26.5	63.3
1993	100.0	4.4	7.6	27.0	60.9
1991	100.0	6.6	6.5	25.0	61.9
1990	100.0	3.3	4.8	23.0	68.9
1989	100.0	4.5	3.5	21.4	70.6
1988	100.0	4.2	4.4	25.7	65.7
1986	100.0	3.7	6.8	21.3	68.2
1985	100.0	6.3	4.7	22.9	66.1
1983	100.0	5.0	9.0	25.4	60.6
1982	100.0	7.1	6.6	27.1	59.2
1978	100.0	3.7	2.7	19.2	74.4
1977	100.0	4.0	6.1	23.9	65.4

Source: Survey Documentation and Analysis, Computer-assisted Survey Methods Program, University of California, Berkeley, General Social Survey, 1972–2012 Cumulative Data Files, Internet site http://sda.berkeley.edu/cgi-bin/hsda?harcsda+gss12; calculations by New Strategist

Table 5.19 Could Find Equally Good Job, 1977 to 2012

"About how easy would it be for you to find a job with another employer with
approximately the same income and fringe benefits you now have?"
(Note: Asked only of those with jobs.)

(percent distribution of people aged 18 or older by response for selected years)

	total	very easy	somewhat easy	not easy
2012	100.0%	16.0%	38.1%	45.9%
2010	100.0	12.6	34.3	53.1
2008	100.0	22.0	34.0	44.0
2006	100.0	31.8	36.5	31.6
2004	100.0	24.8	33.4	41.9
2002	100.0	26.8	36.8	36.4
2000	100.0	38.3	32.9	28.7
1998	100.0	31.9	36.2	31.9
1996	100.0	27.8	32.7	39.6
1994	100.0	21.8	32.5	45.8
1993	100.0	21.7	33.7	44.7
1991	100.0	24.5	35.9	39.6
1990	100.0	33.6	29.4	37.0
1989	100.0	32.2	28.6	39.2
1988	100.0	28.2	36.9	34.9
1986	100.0	29.0	32.7	38.4
1985	100.0	24.9	31.7	43.5
1983	100.0	19.1	28.4	52.4
1982	100.0	22.7	24.9	52.4
1978	100.0	28.8	32.8	38.4
1977	100.0	25.8	31.4	42.9

*Source: Survey Documentation and Analysis, Computer-assisted Survey Methods Program, University of California, Berkeley,
General Social Survey, 1972–2012 Cumulative Data Files, Internet site http://sda.berkeley.edu/cgi-bin/hsda?harcsda+gss12;
calculations by New Strategist*

Table 5.20 Unemployed in Last 10 Years, 1973 to 2012

"At any time during the last 10 years, have you been unemployed and looking for work for as long as a month?"

(percent distribution of people aged 18 or older by response for selected years)

	total	yes	no
2012	100.0%	36.6%	63.4%
2010	100.0	38.8	61.2
2008	100.0	34.0	66.0
2006	100.0	32.2	67.8
2004	100.0	30.3	69.7
2002	100.0	30.1	69.9
2000	100.0	31.2	68.8
1998	100.0	30.3	69.7
1996	100.0	34.3	65.7
1994	100.0	31.6	68.4
1993	100.0	32.6	67.4
1991	100.0	30.2	69.8
1990	100.0	29.2	70.8
1989	100.0	29.1	70.9
1988	100.0	32.0	68.0
1986	100.0	31.5	68.5
1984	100.0	33.9	66.1
1983	100.0	35.0	65.0
1980	100.0	27.6	72.4
1978	100.0	28.6	71.4
1977	100.0	28.5	71.5
1976	100.0	28.6	71.4
1975	100.0	27.4	72.6
1974	100.0	25.9	74.1
1973	100.0	29.0	71.0

Source: Survey Documentation and Analysis, Computer-assisted Survey Methods Program, University of California, Berkeley, General Social Survey, 1972–2012 Cumulative Data Files, Internet site http://sda.berkeley.edu/cgi-bin/hsda?harcsda+gss12; calculations by New Strategist

Table 5.21 Affirmative Action for Women, 1996 to 2012

"Tell me whether you strongly agree, agree, neither agree nor disagree, disagree, or strongly disagree: Because of past discrimination, employers should make special efforts to hire and promote qualified women."

(percent distribution of people aged 18 or older by response for selected years)

	total	strongly agree	agree	neither agree nor disagree	disagree	strongly disagree
2012	100.0%	14.5%	48.1%	11.4%	23.3%	2.7%
2010	100.0	18.2	47.5	10.6	19.1	4.6
2008	100.0	16.9	48.6	8.7	22.6	3.3
2006	100.0	16.9	46.2	13.9	19.2	3.7
2004	100.0	13.2	48.6	13.1	20.9	4.2
2002	100.0	19.7	47.4	8.9	19.7	4.2
2000	100.0	19.5	45.3	10.6	19.9	4.7
1996	100.0	16.6	38.5	13.7	24.4	6.8

Source: Survey Documentation and Analysis, Computer-assisted Survey Methods Program, University of California, Berkeley, General Social Survey, 1972–2012 Cumulative Data Files, Internet site http://sda.berkeley.edu/cgi-bin/hsda?harcsda+gss12; calculations by New Strategist

Table 5.22 Man Won't Get Job or Promotion, 1996 to 2012

"What do you think the chances are these days that a man won't get a job or a promotion while an equally or less qualified woman gets one instead?"

(percent distribution of people aged 18 or older by response for selected years)

	total	very likely	somewhat likely	somewhat unlikely	very unlikely
2012	100.0%	11.5%	39.3%	33.3%	16.0%
2010	100.0	12.4	40.3	32.9	14.4
2008	100.0	13.3	44.7	28.9	13.1
2006	100.0	11.7	39.4	31.4	17.5
2004	100.0	13.9	38.5	31.6	16.0
2002	100.0	16.1	39.3	28.6	16.1
2000	100.0	13.4	36.4	32.3	17.9
1996	100.0	15.0	40.7	28.9	15.5

Source: Survey Documentation and Analysis, Computer-assisted Survey Methods Program, University of California, Berkeley, General Social Survey, 1972–2012 Cumulative Data Files, Internet site http://sda.berkeley.edu/cgi-bin/hsda?harcsda+gss12; calculations by New Strategist

Table 5.23 Woman Won't Get Job or Promotion, 1996 to 2012

"What do you think the chances are these days that a woman won't get a job or a promotion while an equally or less qualified man gets one instead?"

(percent distribution of people aged 18 or older by response for selected years)

	total	very likely	somewhat likely	somewhat unlikely	very unlikely
2012	100.0%	21.1%	46.8%	22.7%	9.4%
2010	100.0	24.3	47.7	18.9	9.2
2008	100.0	22.8	51.2	18.2	7.8
2006	100.0	22.2	46.3	21.6	10.0
2004	100.0	24.5	50.1	16.9	8.5
2002	100.0	25.9	52.4	15.4	6.4
2000	100.0	24.9	47.1	19.9	8.1
1996	100.0	17.7	50.0	21.6	10.8

Source: Survey Documentation and Analysis, Computer-assisted Survey Methods Program, University of California, Berkeley, General Social Survey, 1972–2012 Cumulative Data Files, Internet site http://sda.berkeley.edu/cgi-bin/hsda?harcsda+gss12; calculations by New Strategist

Table 5.24 Satisfaction with Financial Situation, 1972 to 2012

"We are interested in how people are getting along financially these days.
As far as you and your family are concerned, would you say that you
are pretty well satisfied with your present financial situation,
more or less satisfied, or not satisfied at all?"

(percent distribution of people aged 18 or older by response for selected years)

	total	satisfied	more or less satisfied	not at all satisfied
2012	100.0%	27.0%	45.0%	28.0%
2010	100.0	23.3	45.2	31.5
2008	100.0	28.9	41.7	29.4
2006	100.0	30.1	45.5	24.5
2004	100.0	33.1	42.3	24.5
2002	100.0	30.7	42.2	27.1
2000	100.0	30.6	45.4	24.0
1998	100.0	30.6	44.3	25.1
1996	100.0	27.9	44.6	27.5
1994	100.0	28.6	46.4	24.9
1993	100.0	27.3	45.5	27.2
1991	100.0	28.1	46.9	25.0
1990	100.0	30.3	42.7	26.9
1989	100.0	30.7	44.7	24.6
1988	100.0	30.7	46.3	23.0
1987	100.0	30.1	48.6	21.3
1986	100.0	31.4	42.7	25.9
1985	100.0	30.7	43.4	25.9
1984	100.0	27.9	46.5	25.6
1983	100.0	29.4	41.3	29.4
1982	100.0	27.3	45.4	27.3
1980	100.0	27.6	44.0	28.4
1978	100.0	34.4	41.8	23.8
1977	100.0	34.9	44.4	20.7
1976	100.0	30.9	45.7	23.4
1975	100.0	31.4	42.8	25.8
1974	100.0	31.1	45.9	23.0
1973	100.0	31.7	45.3	23.0
1972	100.0	32.2	45.2	22.6

Source: Survey Documentation and Analysis, Computer-assisted Survey Methods Program, University of California, Berkeley, General Social Survey, 1972–2012 Cumulative Data Files, Internet site http://sda.berkeley.edu/cgi-bin/hsda?harcsda+gss12; calculations by New Strategist

Table 5.25 Change in Financial Situation, 1972 to 2012

"During the last few years, has your financial situation been getting better, worse, or has it stayed the same?"

(percent distribution of people aged 18 or older by response for selected years)

	total	better	worse	stayed same
2012	100.0%	28.2%	30.2%	41.6%
2010	100.0	24.9	37.4	37.7
2008	100.0	31.7	28.3	40.0
2006	100.0	40.2	20.7	39.0
2004	100.0	38.7	23.7	37.6
2002	100.0	42.3	21.7	36.1
2000	100.0	46.1	15.7	38.3
1998	100.0	46.0	15.5	38.5
1996	100.0	39.8	20.9	39.4
1994	100.0	36.6	22.3	41.1
1993	100.0	35.3	25.0	39.7
1991	100.0	36.7	21.0	42.3
1990	100.0	39.9	20.0	40.1
1989	100.0	44.7	17.8	37.5
1988	100.0	41.5	18.3	40.2
1987	100.0	40.3	19.2	40.5
1986	100.0	42.1	20.5	37.4
1985	100.0	39.2	21.8	39.0
1984	100.0	38.4	22.3	39.3
1983	100.0	34.0	28.0	38.0
1982	100.0	31.3	29.8	38.9
1980	100.0	34.0	26.2	39.8
1978	100.0	41.9	19.0	39.1
1977	100.0	38.8	21.9	39.3
1976	100.0	36.5	22.6	40.9
1975	100.0	36.1	28.2	35.7
1974	100.0	40.0	21.8	38.2
1973	100.0	42.6	16.5	40.9
1972	100.0	43.2	18.0	38.8

Source: Survey Documentation and Analysis, Computer-assisted Survey Methods Program, University of California, Berkeley, General Social Survey, 1972–2012 Cumulative Data Files, Internet site http://sda.berkeley.edu/cgi-bin/hsda?harcsda+gss12; calculations by New Strategist

Table 5.26 Continue to Work if Rich, 1973 to 2012

"If you were to get enough money to live as comfortably as you
would like for the rest of your life, would you continue
to work or would you stop working?"

(percent distribution of people aged 18 or older by response for selected years)

	total	continue working	stop working
2012	100.0%	72.9%	27.1%
2010	100.0	68.7	31.3
2008	100.0	72.0	28.0
2006	100.0	70.3	29.7
2004	100.0	69.2	30.8
2002	100.0	69.3	30.7
2000	100.0	67.5	32.5
1998	100.0	68.8	31.2
1996	100.0	68.3	31.7
1994	100.0	66.1	33.9
1993	100.0	70.3	29.7
1991	100.0	67.5	32.5
1990	100.0	71.4	28.6
1989	100.0	73.7	26.3
1988	100.0	70.9	29.1
1987	100.0	74.6	25.4
1985	100.0	69.5	30.5
1984	100.0	76.2	23.8
1982	100.0	72.1	27.9
1980	100.0	76.6	23.4
1977	100.0	69.5	30.5
1976	100.0	68.0	32.0
1974	100.0	64.8	35.2
1973	100.0	70.0	30.0

Source: Survey Documentation and Analysis, Computer-assisted Survey Methods Program, University of California, Berkeley, General Social Survey, 1972–2012 Cumulative Data Files, Internet site http://sda.berkeley.edu/cgi-bin/hsda?harcsda+gss12; calculations by New Strategist

Table 5.27 How People Get Ahead, 1973 to 2012

"Some people say that people get ahead by their own hard work; others say
that lucky breaks or help from other people are more important.
Which do you think is most important?"

(percent distribution of people aged 18 or older by response for selected years)

	total	hard work	both equally	luck or help
2012	100.0%	69.9%	20.1%	10.0%
2010	100.0	69.6	20.4	10.0
2008	100.0	67.1	20.8	12.1
2006	100.0	68.8	19.9	11.3
2004	100.0	66.4	24.3	9.3
2002	100.0	64.7	25.8	9.5
2000	100.0	65.8	23.9	10.2
1998	100.0	67.9	21.7	10.4
1996	100.0	69.3	18.8	11.9
1994	100.0	70.2	19.6	10.2
1993	100.0	66.9	20.8	12.4
1991	100.0	66.9	21.0	12.1
1990	100.0	65.8	21.1	13.1
1989	100.0	66.9	18.7	14.4
1988	100.0	67.6	20.4	12.0
1987	100.0	66.1	18.4	15.6
1985	100.0	66.7	18.1	15.2
1984	100.0	66.8	17.4	15.8
1982	100.0	61.1	25.7	13.1
1980	100.0	64.3	27.8	7.9
1977	100.0	60.6	28.8	10.6
1976	100.0	62.1	24.7	13.2
1974	100.0	60.6	29.2	8.8
1973	100.0	64.5	24.4	10.0

*Source: Survey Documentation and Analysis, Computer-assisted Survey Methods Program, University of California, Berkeley,
General Social Survey, 1972–2012 Cumulative Data Files, Internet site http://sda.berkeley.edu/cgi-bin/hsda?harcsda+gss12;
calculations by New Strategist*

Table 5.28 Class Identification, 1972 to 2012

"If you were asked to use one of four names for your social class, which would you say you belong in: the lower class, the working class, the middle class, or the upper class?"

(percent distribution of people aged 18 or older by response for selected years)

	total	lower class	working class	middle class	upper class
2012	100.0%	8.4%	44.3%	43.7%	3.6%
2010	100.0	8.2	46.8	42.4	2.5
2008	100.0	7.3	45.7	43.4	3.6
2006	100.0	5.4	45.6	46.2	2.8
2004	100.0	5.5	42.7	48.6	3.2
2002	100.0	5.4	44.9	46.2	3.5
2000	100.0	4.5	45.6	46.0	3.9
1998	100.0	5.0	45.5	45.7	3.8
1996	100.0	5.4	46.3	44.3	4.0
1994	100.0	4.2	46.1	46.6	3.2
1993	100.0	5.4	44.9	46.6	3.1
1991	100.0	4.4	44.3	49.1	2.3
1990	100.0	3.8	47.0	46.1	3.1
1989	100.0	4.2	43.3	48.7	3.7
1988	100.0	4.4	45.5	47.4	2.7
1987	100.0	4.9	43.7	47.5	3.9
1986	100.0	5.9	43.2	48.0	2.9
1985	100.0	3.7	45.8	45.3	5.2
1984	100.0	4.8	47.4	44.9	3.0
1983	100.0	4.6	48.8	43.2	3.5
1982	100.0	4.3	49.6	43.4	2.8
1980	100.0	4.2	45.8	46.6	3.4
1978	100.0	4.7	47.2	45.9	2.2
1977	100.0	4.0	48.6	43.5	3.9
1976	100.0	4.1	47.3	47.1	1.5
1975	100.0	4.5	48.3	44.5	2.7
1974	100.0	4.1	47.4	45.4	3.1
1973	100.0	3.7	47.0	46.5	2.7
1972	100.0	5.8	48.1	43.8	2.3

Source: Survey Documentation and Analysis, Computer-assisted Survey Methods Program, University of California, Berkeley, General Social Survey, 1972–2012 Cumulative Data Files, Internet site http://sda.berkeley.edu/cgi-bin/hsda?harcsda+gss12; calculations by New Strategist

Table 5.29 Family Income Relative to Others, 1972 to 2012

"Compared with American families in general, would you say your family
income is far below average, below average, average,
above average, or far above average?"

(percent distribution of people aged 18 or older by response for selected years)

	total	far below average	below average	average	above average	far above average
2012	100.0%	6.8%	25.9%	45.5%	19.0%	2.7%
2010	100.0	6.9	28.8	43.5	18.4	2.5
2008	100.0	6.3	25.2	46.7	19.8	2.0
2006	100.0	5.2	23.1	50.2	19.8	1.6
2004	100.0	4.0	22.6	48.5	22.3	2.6
2002	100.0	5.5	23.3	49.0	19.4	2.7
2000	100.0	5.3	20.9	49.3	21.4	3.1
1998	100.0	5.5	22.0	48.5	21.6	2.3
1996	100.0	5.6	23.2	49.4	19.4	2.5
1994	100.0	3.8	23.2	50.0	20.7	2.3
1993	100.0	5.8	22.4	50.1	19.9	1.8
1991	100.0	4.7	21.4	52.2	20.0	1.7
1990	100.0	4.4	21.3	52.2	20.1	2.0
1989	100.0	4.0	20.9	51.9	21.7	1.5
1988	100.0	4.1	22.3	52.0	19.3	2.4
1987	100.0	4.1	23.4	50.3	20.8	1.3
1986	100.0	5.2	21.9	51.6	19.3	2.0
1985	100.0	5.0	22.3	53.2	17.5	2.0
1984	100.0	4.9	21.8	52.6	19.5	1.2
1983	100.0	6.7	21.5	50.4	19.2	2.1
1982	100.0	5.0	24.7	53.2	15.9	1.3
1980	100.0	3.9	23.5	53.5	17.0	2.1
1978	100.0	3.9	20.9	52.8	20.0	2.4
1977	100.0	4.6	21.9	52.6	19.0	2.0
1976	100.0	3.9	24.2	55.9	15.2	0.9
1975	100.0	3.7	22.3	53.3	19.4	1.3
1974	100.0	3.7	19.9	56.1	19.1	1.2
1973	100.0	3.4	18.1	59.1	17.9	1.6
1972	100.0	3.1	21.3	58.0	16.7	1.0

*Source: Survey Documentation and Analysis, Computer-assisted Survey Methods Program, University of California, Berkeley,
General Social Survey, 1972–2012 Cumulative Data Files, Internet site http://sda.berkeley.edu/cgi-bin/hsda?harcsda+gss12;
calculations by New Strategist*

Table 5.30 Parents' Standard of Living, 1994 to 2012

"Compared to your parents when they were the age you are now, do you think your own standard of living now is much better, somewhat better, about the same, somewhat worse, or much worse than theirs was?"

(percent distribution of people aged 18 or older by response for selected years)

	total	much better	somewhat better	about the same	somewhat worse	much worse
2012	100.0%	33.5%	28.6%	21.2%	12.0%	4.6%
2010	100.0	29.2	29.7	24.8	12.1	4.2
2008	100.0	31.6	31.1	21.1	11.5	4.6
2006	100.0	35.4	31.7	20.9	9.3	2.6
2004	100.0	39.6	30.9	17.8	8.4	3.3
2002	100.0	34.9	33.8	19.0	10.1	2.2
2000	100.0	35.7	31.3	21.0	8.9	3.2
1998	100.0	33.7	32.5	21.5	9.7	2.6
1996	100.0	33.9	29.3	21.4	12.2	3.3
1994	100.0	32.6	33.0	21.0	10.5	2.8

Source: Survey Documentation and Analysis, Computer-assisted Survey Methods Program, University of California, Berkeley, General Social Survey, 1972–2012 Cumulative Data Files, Internet site http://sda.berkeley.edu/cgi-bin/hsda?harcsda+gss12; calculations by New Strategist

Table 5.31 Children's Standard of Living, 1994 to 2012

"When your children are at the age you are now, do you think their standard of living will be much better, somewhat better, about the same, somewhat worse, or much worse than yours is now?"

(percent distribution of people aged 18 or older by response for selected years)

	total	much better	somewhat better	about the same	somewhat worse	much worse	no children
2012	100.0%	27.9%	22.7%	18.2%	14.5%	5.5%	11.2%
2010	100.0	25.1	29.3	18.9	13.7	4.7	8.4
2008	100.0	27.9	26.6	18.2	13.0	5.2	9.1
2006	100.0	28.3	29.2	18.5	10.9	2.7	10.4
2004	100.0	23.3	30.5	22.4	11.5	3.5	8.7
2002	100.0	26.8	34.9	18.2	8.5	2.3	9.4
2000	100.0	29.1	31.5	17.0	7.6	3.2	11.5
1998	100.0	22.4	34.8	20.5	9.7	3.3	9.4
1996	100.0	20.4	28.4	21.3	18.1	4.9	7.0
1994	100.0	17.1	29.8	23.1	16.2	4.8	9.0

Source: Survey Documentation and Analysis, Computer-assisted Survey Methods Program, University of California, Berkeley, General Social Survey, 1972–2012 Cumulative Data Files, Internet site http://sda.berkeley.edu/cgi-bin/hsda?harcsda+gss12; calculations by New Strategist

Table 5.32 Standard of Living Will Improve, 1987 to 2012

"The way things are in America, people like me and my family have a good chance of improving our standard of living. Do you agree or disagree?"

(percent distribution of people aged 18 or older by response for selected years)

	total	strongly agree	agree	neither	disagree	strongly disagree
2012	100.0%	14.1%	40.7%	17.9%	23.4%	4.0%
2010	100.0	13.1	44.9	16.2	21.6	4.2
2008	100.0	14.7	44.7	13.9	22.9	3.8
2006	100.0	21.6	48.2	14.9	12.8	2.4
2004	100.0	18.5	50.2	13.2	15.1	3.0
2002	100.0	26.6	48.2	10.9	12.3	1.9
2000	100.0	23.7	53.7	9.4	11.1	2.2
1998	100.0	18.5	56.0	11.0	11.9	2.5
1996	100.0	13.5	51.2	11.3	20.0	4.0
1994	100.0	10.5	52.1	11.9	21.9	3.5
1987	100.0	19.8	53.4	16.9	8.6	1.3

Source: Survey Documentation and Analysis, Computer-assisted Survey Methods Program, University of California, Berkeley, General Social Survey, 1972–2012 Cumulative Data Files, Internet site http://sda.berkeley.edu/cgi-bin/hsda?harcsda+gss12; calculations by New Strategist

6

Family and Friends

Some pundits worry that Americans are becoming increasingly isolated from one another, geographically separated from their families and playing with their smartphones rather than socializing. Those stories may make interesting headlines, but the facts contradict them. Most Americans live close to where they grew up, and they socialize with relatives more frequently than with anyone else. Some things have changed, however. Here is a look at trends in relationships over the past decade.

Little or No Change

• **Geographic mobility.** Although many believe otherwise, most Americans do not move far from home when they grow up—a pattern that has been fairly stable for decades. Forty percent of the population lives in the same city they lived in at age 16, and most still live in the same state.

• **Marital happiness.** Marital happiness has been relatively stable for the past three decades. More than six out of 10 married people say their marriage is "very happy."

• **Socializing with family.** Americans are most likely to socialize with family members, a fact that has not changed over the years. More than one-third socialize with family members at least several times a week.

Big Changes

• **Sex roles.** Attitudes toward sex roles have changed profoundly over the decades as younger generations replaced older ones. Most Americans no longer believe traditional sex roles are best, nor do they believe working mothers harm children.

• **Ideal number of children.** Two is still the ideal number of children for the largest share of Americans, but the share has declined over the past few decades from a high of 58 percent in 1993 to the 47 percent of 2012. Behind the decline is the rise of the Hispanic population, with many Hispanics favoring larger families.

• **Multigeneration households.** The percentage of people who think it is a good idea for older Americans to share a home with grown children has increased from 33 percent in 1973 to 53 percent in 2012. Interestingly, this living arrangement is favored by 55 to 56 percent of people under age 67, but only 36 percent of older Americans.

Family and Friends: 2012 Profiles

Table 6.1 Geographic Mobility since Age 16, 2012

"When you were 16 years old, were you living in
this same (city/town/county)?"

(percent of people aged 18 or older responding by selected characteristics, 2012)

	total	same city, town, or county	same state, different city, town, or county	different state
Total people	**100.0%**	**39.5%**	**23.8%**	**36.6%**
Men	100.0	40.9	22.1	37.0
Women	100.0	38.3	25.3	36.4
Millennials	100.0	50.9	24.1	25.0
Generation Xers	100.0	31.3	25.4	43.3
Baby Boomers	100.0	35.2	23.2	41.7
Older Americans	100.0	35.9	21.8	42.3
Black	100.0	51.4	18.2	30.4
Hispanic	100.0	34.0	17.0	48.9
Non-Hispanic white	100.0	38.5	28.2	33.4
Northeast	100.0	43.3	24.7	32.0
Midwest	100.0	44.8	29.1	26.1
South	100.0	39.8	21.0	39.1
West	100.0	31.1	22.6	46.3
Not a college graduate	100.0	45.0	22.4	32.5
Bachelor's degree or more	100.0	25.4	27.4	47.2

Note: Millennials are aged 18 to 35; Generation Xers are aged 36 to 47; Baby Boomers are aged 48 to 66; Older Americans are aged 67 or older.
Source: Survey Documentation and Analysis, Computer-assisted Survey Methods Program, University of California, Berkeley, General Social Survey, 1972–2012 Cumulative Data Files, Internet site http://sda.berkeley.edu/cgi-bin/hsda?harcsda+gss12; calculations by New Strategist

Table 6.2 Type of Place Lived In at Age 16, 2012

"Which comes closest to the type of place you were living
in when you were 16 years old?"

(percent of people aged 18 or older responding by selected characteristics, 2012)

	total	city, greater than 250,000 population	big-city suburb	city, 50,000 to 250,000 population	town, less than 50,000 population	farm	country, nonfarm
Total people	**100.0%**	**15.2%**	**14.9%**	**18.7%**	**30.8%**	**9.5%**	**10.9%**
Men	100.0	15.6	16.3	18.7	28.0	11.1	10.2
Women	100.0	14.9	13.6	18.8	33.1	8.1	11.5
Millennials	100.0	15.8	16.5	17.9	33.0	5.8	11.0
Generation Xers	100.0	14.4	17.9	22.6	25.5	6.5	13.1
Baby Boomers	100.0	15.5	15.2	19.7	30.2	9.7	9.7
Older Americans	100.0	14.6	5.3	12.8	35.2	22.5	9.6
Black	100.0	25.2	11.4	20.0	28.2	8.5	6.6
Hispanic	100.0	21.6	8.5	23.5	31.9	4.0	10.4
Non-Hispanic white	100.0	10.9	17.7	17.3	30.6	11.3	12.2
Northeast	100.0	18.2	19.1	13.8	32.8	5.7	10.4
Midwest	100.0	14.8	13.4	19.4	28.4	14.9	9.0
South	100.0	12.9	13.7	18.8	30.8	9.8	14.0
West	100.0	17.2	14.9	21.6	31.6	6.6	8.1
Not a college graduate	100.0	14.2	12.0	18.9	33.9	10.1	11.0
Bachelor's degree or more	100.0	18.0	22.4	18.4	22.6	7.9	10.7

Note: Millennials are aged 18 to 35; Generation Xers are aged 36 to 47; Baby Boomers are aged 48 to 66; Older Americans are aged 67 or older.
Source: Survey Documentation and Analysis, Computer-assisted Survey Methods Program, University of California, Berkeley, General Social Survey, 1972–2012 Cumulative Data Files, Internet site http://sda.berkeley.edu/cgi-bin/hsda?harcsda+gss12; calculations by New Strategist

Table 6.3 Family Type at Age 16, 2012

"Were you living with both your own mother and father around the time you were 16? If not, with whom were you living around that time?"

(percent of people aged 18 or older responding by selected characteristics, 2012)

	total	mother and father	mother	mother and stepfather	father	father and stepmother	other relatives	other
Total people	100.0%	67.8%	14.9%	6.1%	2.3%	1.8%	4.5%	2.6%
Men	100.0	71.7	12.8	4.3	2.5	2.2	4.5	1.9
Women	100.0	64.4	16.6	7.6	2.1	1.5	4.4	3.3
Millennials	100.0	60.6	18.1	8.5	3.2	1.3	6.1	2.1
Generation Xers	100.0	61.8	18.2	7.1	2.6	4.2	4.0	2.1
Baby Boomers	100.0	75.1	11.8	4.6	1.1	1.1	3.0	3.3
Older Americans	100.0	76.6	9.1	2.4	2.6	1.3	4.8	3.2
Black	100.0	50.5	27.3	7.1	2.3	1.8	8.4	2.7
Hispanic	100.0	68.9	15.9	4.2	0.4	0.8	7.6	2.3
Non-Hispanic white	100.0	70.9	12.7	6.9	2.6	2.1	2.1	2.6
Northeast	100.0	66.7	16.0	4.8	3.3	1.1	4.6	3.6
Midwest	100.0	68.8	12.2	7.2	2.7	2.1	4.6	2.5
South	100.0	66.3	16.6	6.5	1.8	1.2	4.9	2.8
West	100.0	70.0	13.7	5.4	2.2	3.3	3.7	1.7
Not a college graduate	100.0	63.3	17.4	6.2	2.8	1.8	5.3	3.2
Bachelor's degree or more	100.0	79.3	8.3	6.0	1.1	1.9	2.3	1.2

Note: Millennials are aged 18 to 35; Generation Xers are aged 36 to 47; Baby Boomers are aged 48 to 66; Older Americans are aged 67 or older.
Source: Survey Documentation and Analysis, Computer-assisted Survey Methods Program, University of California, Berkeley, General Social Survey, 1972–2012 Cumulative Data Files, Internet site http://sda.berkeley.edu/cgi-bin/hsda?harcsda+gss12; calculations by New Strategist

Table 6.4 Why Not Living with Both Parents at Age 16, 2012

"If you were not living with both your own mother
and father at age 16, what happened?"

(percent of people aged 18 or older responding by selected characteristics, 2012)

	total	parent died	parents were divorced or separated	other
Total people	**100.0%**	**16.9%**	**59.2%**	**23.8%**
Men	100.0	18.5	57.5	24.0
Women	100.0	15.9	60.4	23.7
Millennials	100.0	7.0	64.7	28.3
Generation Xers	100.0	13.0	69.3	17.7
Baby Boomers	100.0	28.9	49.1	22.0
Older Americans	100.0	37.7	36.3	26.0
Black	100.0	19.1	48.7	32.2
Hispanic	100.0	16.2	57.5	26.3
Non-Hispanic white	100.0	16.1	66.2	17.7
Northeast	100.0	17.8	64.7	17.5
Midwest	100.0	14.5	62.0	23.5
South	100.0	20.5	52.8	26.7
West	100.0	12.0	63.6	24.4
Not a college graduate	100.0	15.8	58.8	25.4
Bachelor's degree or more	100.0	21.8	61.1	17.1

Note: Millennials are aged 18 to 35; Generation Xers are aged 36 to 47; Baby Boomers are aged 48 to 66; Older Americans are aged 67 or older.
Source: Survey Documentation and Analysis, Computer-assisted Survey Methods Program, University of California, Berkeley, General Social Survey, 1972–2012 Cumulative Data Files, Internet site http://sda.berkeley.edu/cgi-bin/hsda?harcsda+gss12; calculations by New Strategist

Table 6.5 Family Income at Age 16, 2012

"Thinking about the time when you were 16 years old, compared with American families in general then, would you say your family income was far below average, below average, average, above average, or far above average?"

(percent of people aged 18 or older responding by selected characteristics, 2012)

	total	far below average	below average	average	above average	far above average
Total people	**100.0%**	**9.3%**	**26.9%**	**45.8%**	**15.7%**	**2.3%**
Men	100.0	9.6	26.7	44.0	16.6	3.1
Women	100.0	9.1	27.1	47.3	15.0	1.6
Millennials	100.0	8.0	22.2	48.8	18.1	3.0
Generation Xers	100.0	8.4	28.2	42.7	17.8	2.9
Baby Boomers	100.0	10.3	28.1	46.3	14.3	1.0
Older Americans	100.0	12.0	33.1	42.8	9.7	2.4
Black	100.0	12.0	30.0	42.6	13.9	1.5
Hispanic	100.0	19.6	32.0	37.1	9.0	2.3
Non-Hispanic white	100.0	6.4	24.7	48.3	18.3	2.3
Northeast	100.0	9.1	23.3	45.7	19.6	2.3
Midwest	100.0	8.4	25.6	47.0	15.9	3.1
South	100.0	10.3	29.0	45.4	14.0	1.4
West	100.0	8.8	27.6	45.3	15.5	2.8
Not a college graduate	100.0	11.1	29.3	45.6	12.3	1.7
Bachelor's degree or more	100.0	4.7	20.8	46.3	24.5	3.7

Note: Millennials are aged 18 to 35; Generation Xers are aged 36 to 47; Baby Boomers are aged 48 to 66; Older Americans are aged 67 or older.
Source: Survey Documentation and Analysis, Computer-assisted Survey Methods Program, University of California, Berkeley, General Social Survey, 1972–2012 Cumulative Data Files, Internet site http://sda.berkeley.edu/cgi-bin/hsda?harcsda+gss12; calculations by New Strategist

Table 6.6 Born in the United States, 2012

"Were you born in this country?"

(percent of people aged 18 or older responding by selected characteristics, 2012)

	total	yes	no
Total people	**100.0%**	**85.3%**	**14.7%**
Men	100.0	85.7	14.3
Women	100.0	84.9	15.1
Millennials	100.0	86.3	13.7
Generation Xers	100.0	82.4	17.6
Baby Boomers	100.0	85.3	14.7
Older Americans	100.0	87.6	12.4
Black	100.0	89.8	10.2
Hispanic	100.0	52.8	47.2
Non-Hispanic white	100.0	95.4	4.6
Northeast	100.0	81.8	18.2
Midwest	100.0	92.7	7.3
South	100.0	87.4	12.6
West	100.0	77.2	22.8
Not a college graduate	100.0	85.4	14.6
Bachelor's degree or more	100.0	85.1	14.9

Note: Millennials are aged 18 to 35; Generation Xers are aged 36 to 47; Baby Boomers are aged 48 to 66; Older Americans are aged 67 or older.
Source: Survey Documentation and Analysis, Computer-assisted Survey Methods Program, University of California, Berkeley, General Social Survey, 1972–2012 Cumulative Data Files, Internet site http://sda.berkeley.edu/cgi-bin/hsda?harcsda+gss12; calculations by New Strategist

Table 6.7 Were Your Parents Born in the United States, 2012

"Were both your parents born in this country?"

(percent of people aged 18 or older responding by selected characteristics, 2012)

	total	born in United States			neither born in United States	don't know
		both	mother only	father only		
Total people	**100.0%**	**74.8%**	**3.0%**	**2.9%**	**18.8%**	**0.5%**
Men	100.0	73.5	3.6	3.3	19.1	0.5
Women	100.0	75.9	2.5	2.6	18.7	0.3
Millennials	100.0	69.7	4.6	4.0	21.3	0.4
Generation Xers	100.0	73.6	1.1	1.6	23.3	0.4
Baby Boomers	100.0	81.0	1.8	2.2	14.8	0.2
Older Americans	100.0	74.3	5.1	4.0	15.2	1.4
Black	100.0	87.6	0.3	0.4	10.8	0.9
Hispanic	100.0	25.1	8.1	1.2	64.8	0.8
Non-Hispanic white	100.0	87.8	2.4	3.5	5.9	0.4
Northeast	100.0	66.5	2.5	3.3	27.5	0.2
Midwest	100.0	84.8	1.5	3.3	9.6	0.8
South	100.0	80.9	2.4	1.6	14.3	0.8
West	100.0	61.2	5.7	4.2	28.9	0.0
Not a college graduate	100.0	75.1	2.8	2.3	19.1	0.7
Bachelor's degree or more	100.0	73.9	3.5	4.4	18.1	0.1

Note: Millennials are aged 18 to 35; Generation Xers are aged 36 to 47; Baby Boomers are aged 48 to 66; Older Americans are aged 67 or older.
Source: Survey Documentation and Analysis, Computer-assisted Survey Methods Program, University of California, Berkeley, General Social Survey, 1972–2012 Cumulative Data Files, Internet site http://sda.berkeley.edu/cgi-bin/hsda?harcsda+gss12; calculations by New Strategist

Table 6.8 How Many Grandparents Were Born outside the United States, 2012

"How many of your grandparents were born outside the United States?"

(percent of people aged 18 or older responding by selected characteristics, 2012)

	total	all born in United States	grandparents born outside United States			
			one	two	three	four
Total people	**100.0%**	**56.2%**	**7.2%**	**10.7%**	**1.9%**	**24.0%**
Men	100.0	53.1	8.3	10.3	2.2	26.1
Women	100.0	58.9	6.2	11.0	1.7	22.2
Millennials	100.0	55.8	8.9	10.2	1.5	23.6
Generation Xers	100.0	59.2	6.1	8.5	1.6	24.6
Baby Boomers	100.0	57.9	6.0	10.9	3.1	22.1
Older Americans	100.0	49.3	6.8	15.4	0.8	27.7
Black	100.0	83.9	2.4	3.0	0.3	10.4
Hispanic	100.0	15.0	4.2	11.4	4.4	65.1
Non-Hispanic white	100.0	63.6	9.1	12.9	1.8	12.6
Northeast	100.0	39.1	8.6	12.6	2.9	36.7
Midwest	100.0	63.4	9.9	11.1	1.6	14.1
South	100.0	68.2	5.4	8.5	1.5	16.5
West	100.0	42.7	6.4	12.4	2.2	36.3
vNot a college graduate	100.0	58.6	6.8	9.0	1.6	24.0
Bachelor's degree or more	100.0	50.2	8.2	14.9	2.7	23.9

Note: Millennials are aged 18 to 35; Generation Xers are aged 36 to 47; Baby Boomers are aged 48 to 66; Older Americans are aged 67 or older.
Source: Survey Documentation and Analysis, Computer-assisted Survey Methods Program, University of California, Berkeley, General Social Survey, 1972–2012 Cumulative Data Files, Internet site http://sda.berkeley.edu/cgi-bin/hsda?harcsda+gss12; calculations by New Strategist

Table 6.9 Happiness of Marriage, 2012

"Taking things all together, how would you describe your marriage? Would you say that your marriage is very happy, pretty happy, or not too happy?"

(percent of married people aged 18 or older responding by selected characteristics, 2012)

	total	very happy	pretty happy	not too happy
Total people	**100.0%**	**65.4%**	**32.2%**	**2.3%**
Men	100.0	66.4	32.7	0.9
Women	100.0	64.6	31.8	3.6
Millennials	100.0	74.5	24.0	1.4
Generation Xers	100.0	65.5	32.4	2.1
Baby Boomers	100.0	61.2	35.1	3.8
Older Americans	100.0	63.2	36.2	0.5
Black	100.0	49.0	44.6	6.4
Hispanic	100.0	60.7	36.2	3.1
Non-Hispanic white	100.0	67.6	30.6	1.8
Northeast	100.0	70.7	25.2	4.1
Midwest	100.0	66.5	32.8	0.7
South	100.0	60.6	35.9	3.4
West	100.0	69.2	29.8	1.0
Not a college graduate	100.0	65.0	32.7	2.3
Bachelor's degree or more	100.0	66.3	31.2	2.4

Note: Millennials are aged 18 to 35; Generation Xers are aged 36 to 47; Baby Boomers are aged 48 to 66; Older Americans are aged 67 or older.

Source: Survey Documentation and Analysis, Computer-assisted Survey Methods Program, University of California, Berkeley, General Social Survey, 1972–2012 Cumulative Data Files, Internet site http://sda.berkeley.edu/cgi-bin/hsda?harcsda+gss12; calculations by New Strategist

Table 6.10 Ever Been Divorced, 2012

"Have you ever been divorced or legally separated?"

(percent of people aged 18 or older responding by selected characteristics, 2012)

	total	yes	no
Total people	**100.0%**	**24.2%**	**75.8%**
Men	100.0	24.6	75.4
Women	100.0	23.9	76.1
Millennials	100.0	14.0	86.0
Generation Xers	100.0	19.0	81.0
Baby Boomers	100.0	33.0	67.0
Older Americans	100.0	24.7	75.3
Black	100.0	30.2	69.8
Hispanic	100.0	17.9	82.1
Non-Hispanic white	100.0	26.9	73.1
Northeast	100.0	20.0	80.0
Midwest	100.0	22.4	77.6
South	100.0	29.6	70.4
West	100.0	19.5	80.5
Not a college graduate	100.0	28.0	72.0
Bachelor's degree or more	100.0	16.5	83.5

Note: Millennials are aged 18 to 35; Generation Xers are aged 36 to 47; Baby Boomers are aged 48 to 66; Older Americans are aged 67 or older.
Source: Survey Documentation and Analysis, Computer-assisted Survey Methods Program, University of California, Berkeley, General Social Survey, 1972–2012 Cumulative Data Files, Internet site http://sda.berkeley.edu/cgi-bin/hsda?harcsda+gss12; calculations by New Strategist

Table 6.11 Divorce Laws, 2012

"Should divorce in this country be easier or more difficult to obtain than it is now?"

(percent of people aged 18 or older responding by selected characteristics, 2012)

	total	easier	more difficult	stay same
Total people	**100.0%**	**35.6%**	**40.9%**	**23.5%**
Men	100.0	33.7	40.0	26.3
Women	100.0	37.3	41.6	21.0
Millennials	100.0	42.9	33.1	24.0
Generation Xers	100.0	35.9	40.7	23.4
Baby Boomers	100.0	32.0	44.2	23.8
Older Americans	100.0	24.3	54.1	21.6
Black	100.0	52.1	33.1	14.7
Hispanic	100.0	51.9	33.1	15.0
Non-Hispanic white	100.0	28.8	44.1	27.1
Northeast	100.0	33.9	32.1	33.9
Midwest	100.0	30.3	47.1	22.6
South	100.0	37.3	45.0	17.6
West	100.0	39.2	33.8	26.9
Not a college graduate	100.0	40.1	40.2	19.7
Bachelor's degree or more	100.0	23.4	42.8	33.8

Note: Millennials are aged 18 to 35; Generation Xers are aged 36 to 47; Baby Boomers are aged 48 to 66; Older Americans are aged 67 or older.
Source: Survey Documentation and Analysis, Computer-assisted Survey Methods Program, University of California, Berkeley, General Social Survey, 1972–2012 Cumulative Data Files, Internet site http://sda.berkeley.edu/cgi-bin/hsda?harcsda+gss12; calculations by New Strategist

Table 6.12 Better for Man to Work and Woman to Stay Home, 2012

"It is much better for everyone involved if the man is the achiever
outside the home and the woman takes care of the home
and family. Do you agree or disagree?"

(percent of people aged 18 or older responding by selected characteristics, 2012)

	total	strongly agree	agree	disagree	strongly disagree
Total people	**100.0%**	**6.5%**	**25.2%**	**48.3%**	**20.0%**
Men	100.0	9.0	28.7	48.3	13.9
Women	100.0	4.2	22.1	48.2	25.4
Millennials	100.0	6.0	18.9	51.9	23.2
Generation Xers	100.0	7.5	19.1	51.9	21.5
Baby Boomers	100.0	6.0	30.9	43.6	19.4
Older Americans	100.0	7.0	39.9	41.9	11.1
Black	100.0	5.2	24.7	46.9	23.2
Hispanic	100.0	7.3	31.4	47.7	13.5
Non-Hispanic white	100.0	5.8	23.8	48.5	21.8
Northeast	100.0	7.0	15.5	51.7	25.9
Midwest	100.0	6.8	20.9	47.5	24.8
South	100.0	6.7	30.8	46.1	16.4
West	100.0	5.5	27.3	50.0	17.2
Not a college graduate	100.0	7.1	29.3	47.2	16.5
Bachelor's degree or more	100.0	4.9	14.2	51.3	29.6

Note: Millennials are aged 18 to 35; Generation Xers are aged 36 to 47; Baby Boomers are aged 48 to 66; Older Americans are aged 67 or older.
Source: Survey Documentation and Analysis, Computer-assisted Survey Methods Program, University of California, Berkeley, General Social Survey, 1972–2012 Cumulative Data Files, Internet site http://sda.berkeley.edu/cgi-bin/hsda?harcsda+gss12; calculations by New Strategist

Table 6.13 A Working Mother's Relationship with Children, 2012

"A working mother can establish just as warm and secure a relationship with her children as a mother who does not work. Do you agree or disagree?"

(percent of people aged 18 or older responding by selected characteristics, 2012)

	total	strongly agree	agree	disagree	strongly disagree
Total people	**100.0%**	**25.0%**	**46.7%**	**23.1%**	**5.2%**
Men	100.0	17.7	47.0	29.0	6.3
Women	100.0	31.5	46.4	17.9	4.2
Millennials	100.0	25.7	48.0	22.0	4.4
Generation Xers	100.0	29.7	44.2	19.9	6.1
Baby Boomers	100.0	24.3	45.2	25.3	5.2
Older Americans	100.0	17.6	50.0	26.8	5.6
Black	100.0	30.8	42.0	23.1	4.1
Hispanic	100.0	14.0	42.5	34.8	8.8
Non-Hispanic white	100.0	27.0	49.2	19.8	4.0
Northeast	100.0	29.4	49.9	19.7	1.0
Midwest	100.0	30.0	45.4	18.7	5.9
South	100.0	22.2	44.9	27.7	5.2
West	100.0	21.7	48.5	22.5	7.2
Not a college graduate	100.0	22.9	47.3	24.4	5.4
Bachelor's degree or more	100.0	30.8	45.3	19.4	4.5

Note: Millennials are aged 18 to 35; Generation Xers are aged 36 to 47; Baby Boomers are aged 48 to 66; Older Americans are aged 67 or older.
Source: Survey Documentation and Analysis, Computer-assisted Survey Methods Program, University of California, Berkeley, General Social Survey, 1972–2012 Cumulative Data Files, Internet site http://sda.berkeley.edu/cgi-bin/hsda?harcsda+gss12; calculations by New Strategist

Table 6.14 Preschool Children Suffer when Mother Works, 2012

"A preschool child is likely to suffer if his or her mother works.
Do you agree or disagree?"

(percent of people aged 18 or older responding by selected characteristics, 2012)

	total	strongly agree	agree	disagree	strongly disagree
Total people	**100.0%**	**6.4%**	**28.8%**	**50.3%**	**14.5%**
Men	100.0	9.2	35.0	46.9	8.8
Women	100.0	3.9	23.3	53.2	19.5
Millennials	100.0	6.6	23.4	53.5	16.4
Generation Xers	100.0	4.7	23.6	48.9	22.9
Baby Boomers	100.0	7.1	35.4	48.4	9.0
Older Americans	100.0	7.3	36.9	48.4	7.5
Black	100.0	3.8	21.1	54.5	20.6
Hispanic	100.0	12.9	38.5	43.5	5.1
Non-Hispanic white	100.0	5.2	26.7	52.8	15.4
Northeast	100.0	8.0	22.7	51.7	17.6
Midwest	100.0	2.6	30.8	48.6	18.0
South	100.0	7.9	29.2	51.3	11.5
West	100.0	6.6	30.4	49.4	13.6
Not a college graduate	100.0	6.6	31.7	50.0	11.8
Bachelor's degree or more	100.0	5.9	20.9	51.2	22.0

Note: Millennials are aged 18 to 35; Generation Xers are aged 36 to 47; Baby Boomers are aged 48 to 66; Older Americans are aged 67 or older.
Source: Survey Documentation and Analysis, Computer-assisted Survey Methods Program, University of California, Berkeley, General Social Survey, 1972–2012 Cumulative Data Files, Internet site http://sda.berkeley.edu/cgi-bin/hsda?harcsda+gss12; calculations by New Strategist

Table 6.15 Mother Worked while You Were Growing Up, 2012

"Did your mother ever work for pay for as long
as a year while you were growing up?"

(percent of people aged 18 or older responding by selected characteristics, 2012)

	total	yes	no
Total people	**100.0%**	**72.5%**	**27.5%**
Men	100.0	71.7	28.3
Women	100.0	73.2	26.8
Millennials	100.0	82.6	17.4
Generation Xers	100.0	80.1	19.9
Baby Boomers	100.0	67.9	32.1
Older Americans	100.0	47.7	52.3
Black	100.0	81.2	18.8
Hispanic	100.0	64.5	35.5
Non-Hispanic white	100.0	73.3	26.7
Northeast	100.0	77.5	22.5
Midwest	100.0	73.1	26.9
South	100.0	72.4	27.6
West	100.0	68.5	31.5
Not a college graduate	100.0	71.1	28.9
Bachelor's degree or more	100.0	76.0	24.0

Note: Millennials are aged 18 to 35; Generation Xers are aged 36 to 47; Baby Boomers are aged 48 to 66; Older Americans are aged 67 or older.
Source: Survey Documentation and Analysis, Computer-assisted Survey Methods Program, University of California, Berkeley, General Social Survey, 1972–2012 Cumulative Data Files, Internet site http://sda.berkeley.edu/cgi-bin/hsda?harcsda+gss12; calculations by New Strategist

Table 6.16 Work outside Home when Child Was a Preschooler, 2012

"Did you work outside the home full-time, part-time, or
not at all when a child was under school age?"

(percent of people aged 18 or older responding by selected characteristics, 2012)

	total	full-time	part-time	stayed home
Total people	**100.0%**	**69.9%**	**13.9%**	**16.2%**
Men	100.0	94.7	3.5	1.8
Women	100.0	51.0	21.9	27.1
Millennials	100.0	73.6	15.6	10.8
Generation Xers	100.0	75.6	12.8	11.5
Baby Boomers	100.0	67.5	15.4	17.1
Older Americans	100.0	62.6	11.0	26.4
Black	100.0	70.5	15.7	13.8
Hispanic	100.0	71.2	12.8	16.1
Non-Hispanic white	100.0	68.6	14.1	17.3
Northeast	100.0	69.8	13.4	16.8
Midwest	100.0	72.1	14.8	13.1
South	100.0	69.6	13.6	16.8
West	100.0	68.1	13.9	18.0
Not a college graduate	100.0	69.1	12.8	18.1
Bachelor's degree or more	100.0	72.2	17.4	10.4

Note: Millennials are aged 18 to 35; Generation Xers are aged 36 to 47; Baby Boomers are aged 48 to 66; Older Americans are aged 67 or older.
Source: Survey Documentation and Analysis, Computer-assisted Survey Methods Program, University of California, Berkeley, General Social Survey, 1972–2012 Cumulative Data Files, Internet site http://sda.berkeley.edu/cgi-bin/hsda?harcsda+gss12; calculations by New Strategist

Table 6.17 Work outside Home after Youngest Child Started School, 2012

"Did you work outside the home full-time, part-time, or
not at all after the youngest child started school?"

(percent of people aged 18 or older responding by selected characteristics, 2012)

	total	full-time	part-time	stayed home
Total people	**100.0%**	**76.1%**	**12.1%**	**11.8%**
Men	100.0	96.6	2.0	1.4
Women	100.0	60.3	19.8	19.9
Millennials	100.0	74.4	10.8	14.7
Generation Xers	100.0	76.0	10.9	13.1
Baby Boomers	100.0	80.2	13.2	6.6
Older Americans	100.0	70.2	12.8	17.0
Black	100.0	78.1	12.5	9.4
Hispanic	100.0	75.6	13.7	10.7
Non-Hispanic white	100.0	75.8	12.1	12.1
Northeast	100.0	75.5	13.7	10.8
Midwest	100.0	78.1	10.8	11.1
South	100.0	78.2	11.6	10.2
West	100.0	70.6	13.3	16.1
Not a college graduate	100.0	74.6	12.0	13.4
Bachelor's degree or more	100.0	80.6	12.3	7.1

Note: Millennials are aged 18 to 35; Generation Xers are aged 36 to 47; Baby Boomers are aged 48 to 66; Older Americans are aged 67 or older.
Source: Survey Documentation and Analysis, Computer-assisted Survey Methods Program, University of California, Berkeley, General Social Survey, 1972–2012 Cumulative Data Files, Internet site http://sda.berkeley.edu/cgi-bin/hsda?harcsda+gss12; calculations by New Strategist

Table 6.18 Best Way to Organize Family Life, 2012

"Consder a family with a child under school age. What, in your opinion, is the best way for them to organize their family and work life?"

(percent of people aged 18 or older responding by selected characteristics, 2012)

	total	mother stays home, father works full-time	mother works part-time, father works full-time	both work full-time	both work part-time	father works part-time, mother works full-time	father stays home, mother works full-time
Total people	**100.0%**	**39.7%**	**41.6%**	**11.3%**	**6.8%**	**0.2%**	**0.5%**
Men	100.0	46.4	37.0	10.9	4.9	0.2	0.7
Women	100.0	33.6	45.7	11.7	8.5	0.2	0.3
Millennials	100.0	30.3	46.7	11.4	10.8	0.2	0.6
Generation Xers	100.0	35.0	41.8	15.7	7.4	0.0	0.0
Baby Boomers	100.0	48.1	36.6	10.7	3.7	0.3	0.6
Older Americans	100.0	55.2	37.9	5.0	1.3	0.0	0.7
Black	100.0	34.7	43.2	17.3	4.7	0.0	0.0
Hispanic	100.0	46.5	33.5	9.3	10.0	0.0	0.7
Non-Hispanic white	100.0	39.6	43.2	10.7	5.6	0.3	0.6
Northeast	100.0	32.6	44.5	9.4	12.9	0.0	0.6
Midwest	100.0	35.4	46.0	15.4	2.7	0.0	0.5
South	100.0	43.9	38.3	10.7	6.4	0.2	0.4
West	100.0	41.5	40.6	9.3	7.7	0.3	0.5
Not a college graduate	100.0	41.4	41.0	10.3	6.5	0.2	0.6
Bachelor's degree or more	100.0	33.9	43.5	14.6	7.9	0.0	0.0

Note: Millennials are aged 18 to 35; Generation Xers are aged 36 to 47; Baby Boomers are aged 48 to 66; Older Americans are aged 67 or older.
Source: Survey Documentation and Analysis, Computer-assisted Survey Methods Program, University of California, Berkeley, General Social Survey, 1972–2012 Cumulative Data Files, Internet site http://sda.berkeley.edu/cgi-bin/hsda?harcsda+gss12; calculations by New Strategist

Table 6.19 Worst Way to Organize Family Life, 2012

"Consider a family with a child under school age. What, in your opinion, is the least desirable way for them to organize their family and work life?"

(percent of people aged 18 or older responding by selected characteristics, 2012)

	total	mother stays home, father works full-time	mother works part-time, father works full-time	both work full-time	both work part-time	father works part-time, mother works full-time	father stays home, mother works full-time
Total people	**100.0%**	**5.4%**	**1.7%**	**36.3%**	**12.9%**	**4.9%**	**38.8%**
Men	100.0	3.5	1.5	37.7	14.0	5.2	38.1
Women	100.0	7.2	1.9	35.0	11.9	4.6	39.4
Millennials	100.0	5.4	1.1	40.6	12.6	3.6	36.7
Generation Xers	100.0	4.2	2.4	33.6	13.4	6.4	40.0
Baby Boomers	100.0	5.0	1.6	33.6	13.8	5.1	40.9
Older Americans	100.0	8.5	2.6	33.7	11.2	5.6	38.4
Black	100.0	9.6	2.4	15.0	10.6	6.9	55.4
Hispanic	100.0	9.1	1.4	27.5	9.5	5.5	47.0
Non-Hispanic white	100.0	4.0	1.7	43.6	15.1	4.5	31.1
Northeast	100.0	8.3	0.8	35.6	12.5	4.9	37.8
Midwest	100.0	3.9	1.4	37.0	18.1	3.4	36.2
South	100.0	4.2	2.1	33.3	10.9	7.0	42.4
West	100.0	7.0	2.1	40.8	11.1	2.9	36.1
Not a college graduate	100.0	6.1	2.1	32.6	11.9	5.4	42.0
Bachelor's degree or more	100.0	3.4	0.8	47.7	16.0	3.1	29.0

Note: Millennials are aged 18 to 35; Generation Xers are aged 36 to 47; Baby Boomers are aged 48 to 66; Older Americans are aged 67 or older.
Source: Survey Documentation and Analysis, Computer-assisted Survey Methods Program, University of California, Berkeley, General Social Survey, 1972–2012 Cumulative Data Files, Internet site http://sda.berkeley.edu/cgi-bin/hsda?harcsda+gss12; calculations by New Strategist

Table 6.20 Ideal Number of Children, 2012

"What do you think is the ideal number of children for a family to have?"

(percent of people aged 18 or older responding by selected characteristics, 2012)

	total	none	one	two	three	four or more	as many as want
Total people	**100.0%**	**0.8%**	**2.6%**	**46.8%**	**27.8%**	**11.3%**	**10.7%**
Men	100.0	1.0	3.4	45.5	29.3	12.5	8.3
Women	100.0	0.6	1.9	47.9	26.5	10.3	12.8
Millennials	100.0	0.7	3.1	42.7	36.0	9.4	8.1
Generation Xers	100.0	0.9	3.6	50.2	24.2	9.9	11.2
Baby Boomers	100.0	0.9	1.9	50.6	23.5	9.6	13.5
Older Americans	100.0	0.5	1.5	43.2	21.3	22.6	10.9
Black	100.0	1.1	0.7	35.7	34.3	20.9	7.3
Hispanic	100.0	0.0	5.0	35.7	43.2	11.5	4.6
Non-Hispanic white	100.0	0.9	2.6	50.6	24.6	8.7	12.6
Northeast	100.0	1.2	4.6	48.5	23.2	9.2	13.3
Midwest	100.0	1.1	1.8	45.3	30.2	11.2	10.4
South	100.0	0.4	1.8	45.1	28.3	13.5	10.9
West	100.0	0.6	3.4	49.6	27.9	9.6	8.9
Not a college graduate	100.0	0.6	2.3	44.3	30.0	13.9	8.9
Bachelor's degree or more	100.0	1.1	3.5	53.6	21.9	4.1	15.8

Note: Millennials are aged 18 to 35; Generation Xers are aged 36 to 47; Baby Boomers are aged 48 to 66; Older Americans are aged 67 or older.
Source: Survey Documentation and Analysis, Computer-assisted Survey Methods Program, University of California, Berkeley, General Social Survey, 1972–2012 Cumulative Data Files, Internet site http://sda.berkeley.edu/cgi-bin/hsda?harcsda+gss12; calculations by New Strategist

Table 6.21 Child Should Learn to Obey, 2012

"How important is it for a child to learn to obey to prepare him or her for life?"

(percent of people aged 18 or older responding by selected characteristics, 2012)

| | total | importance of learning to obey | | | | |
		most important	second most important	third most important	fourth most important	least important
Total people	**100.0%**	**14.4%**	**11.4%**	**17.7%**	**40.5%**	**15.9%**
Men	100.0	13.0	12.7	21.5	34.2	18.5
Women	100.0	15.6	10.4	14.4	45.8	13.8
Millennials	100.0	11.7	11.5	19.8	43.6	13.3
Generation Xers	100.0	12.9	11.6	14.7	43.0	17.8
Baby Boomers	100.0	13.7	10.6	17.3	40.3	18.1
Older Americans	100.0	23.6	13.1	18.5	31.0	13.8
Black	100.0	23.9	17.2	22.7	27.8	8.5
Hispanic	100.0	24.4	12.5	17.0	36.1	10.0
Non-Hispanic white	100.0	10.1	9.7	16.8	45.6	17.8
Northeast	100.0	12.3	12.2	20.4	36.7	18.5
Midwest	100.0	9.6	13.7	19.6	41.0	16.1
South	100.0	20.8	11.0	17.8	38.6	11.9
West	100.0	10.4	9.5	13.7	46.2	20.3
Not a college graduate	100.0	18.4	12.9	19.3	38.0	11.4
Bachelor's degree or more	100.0	4.7	7.8	13.7	46.7	27.0

Note: Millennials are aged 18 to 35; Generation Xers are aged 36 to 47; Baby Boomers are aged 48 to 66; Older Americans are aged 67 or older.
Source: Survey Documentation and Analysis, Computer-assisted Survey Methods Program, University of California, Berkeley, General Social Survey, 1972–2012 Cumulative Data Files, Internet site http://sda.berkeley.edu/cgi-bin/hsda?harcsda+gss12; calculations by New Strategist

Table 6.22 Child Should Learn to Think for Self, 2012

"How important is it for a child to learn to think for himself
or herself to prepare him or her for life?"

(percent of people aged 18 or older responding by selected characteristics, 2012)

	total	most important	second most important	third most important	fourth most important	least important
		importance of thinking for self				
Total people	**100.0%**	**44.0%**	**19.2%**	**17.4%**	**15.1%**	**4.4%**
Men	100.0	40.5	19.2	17.4	16.4	6.5
Women	100.0	47.0	19.1	17.3	14.0	2.6
Millennials	100.0	39.1	25.3	17.7	13.8	4.2
Generation Xers	100.0	40.2	22.8	18.8	13.6	4.5
Baby Boomers	100.0	52.2	13.8	15.6	16.0	2.3
Older Americans	100.0	41.4	12.7	18.8	17.7	9.4
Black	100.0	44.0	18.6	15.3	18.7	3.4
Hispanic	100.0	30.2	25.6	17.9	18.9	7.4
Non-Hispanic white	100.0	49.2	17.4	17.0	13.2	3.2
Northeast	100.0	39.0	23.2	17.5	15.0	5.3
Midwest	100.0	47.6	18.2	16.3	13.7	4.2
South	100.0	42.9	17.8	18.3	17.6	3.4
West	100.0	46.2	19.2	16.8	12.5	5.4
Not a college graduate	100.0	37.8	20.1	18.7	17.9	5.5
Bachelor's degree or more	100.0	59.0	17.0	14.2	8.3	1.5

Note: Millennials are aged 18 to 35; Generation Xers are aged 36 to 47; Baby Boomers are aged 48 to 66; Older Americans are aged 67 or older.
Source: Survey Documentation and Analysis, Computer-assisted Survey Methods Program, University of California, Berkeley, General Social Survey, 1972–2012 Cumulative Data Files, Internet site http://sda.berkeley.edu/cgi-bin/hsda?harcsda+gss12; calculations by New Strategist

Table 6.23 Child Should Learn to Be Popular, 2012

"How important is it for a child to learn to be well-liked or popular to prepare him or her for life?"

(percent of people aged 18 or older responding by selected characteristics, 2012)

	total	importance of popularity				
		most important	second most important	third most important	fourth most important	least important
Total people	**100.0%**	**0.5%**	**1.7%**	**2.7%**	**18.7%**	**76.3%**
Men	100.0	0.8	1.4	4.2	23.0	70.7
Women	100.0	0.4	1.9	1.5	15.1	81.2
Millennials	100.0	0.4	0.9	2.3	15.7	80.7
Generation Xers	100.0	0.6	0.9	3.8	19.6	75.1
Baby Boomers	100.0	0.0	1.5	1.9	20.3	76.3
Older Americans	100.0	2.0	5.0	4.0	20.2	68.8
Black	100.0	0.0	1.2	0.9	15.2	82.7
Hispanic	100.0	1.7	3.7	3.6	13.8	77.2
Non-Hispanic white	100.0	0.3	1.2	2.8	19.4	76.4
Northeast	100.0	0.9	2.4	4.5	19.6	72.5
Midwest	100.0	0.3	1.4	1.3	20.6	76.4
South	100.0	0.3	1.6	2.1	14.1	81.8
West	100.0	0.8	1.5	3.7	23.5	70.4
Not a college graduate	100.0	0.7	1.9	1.6	16.5	79.2
Bachelor's degree or more	100.0	0.2	1.1	5.3	24.0	69.3

Note: Millennials are aged 18 to 35; Generation Xers are aged 36 to 47; Baby Boomers are aged 48 to 66; Older Americans are aged 67 or older.
Source: Survey Documentation and Analysis, Computer-assisted Survey Methods Program, University of California, Berkeley, General Social Survey, 1972–2012 Cumulative Data Files, Internet site http://sda.berkeley.edu/cgi-bin/hsda?harcsda+gss12; calculations by New Strategist

Table 6.24 Child Should Learn to Work Hard, 2012

"How important is it for a child to learn to work hard
to prepare him or her for life?"

(percent of people aged 18 or older responding by selected characteristics, 2012)

	total	importance of working hard				
		most important	second most important	third most important	fourth most important	least important
Total people	**100.0%**	**25.1%**	**35.2%**	**28.8%**	**9.6%**	**1.3%**
Men	100.0	28.8	33.7	26.2	10.1	1.3
Women	100.0	22.1	36.4	31.0	9.1	1.4
Millennials	100.0	33.8	31.3	29.2	5.5	0.2
Generation Xers	100.0	29.1	29.2	31.4	8.8	1.5
Baby Boomers	100.0	19.0	41.5	28.3	9.6	1.5
Older Americans	100.0	14.7	37.6	25.0	19.6	3.2
Black	100.0	19.9	38.1	28.2	11.3	2.5
Hispanic	100.0	20.8	26.9	34.3	16.4	1.6
Non-Hispanic white	100.0	26.0	37.4	27.4	8.1	1.1
Northeast	100.0	29.4	31.3	27.3	9.7	2.2
Midwest	100.0	27.7	35.7	25.4	10.2	1.0
South	100.0	22.6	36.1	29.5	10.4	1.3
West	100.0	23.5	36.0	32.0	7.4	1.1
Not a college graduate	100.0	25.8	33.3	28.8	10.4	1.7
Bachelor's degree or more	100.0	23.5	39.7	28.9	7.4	0.5

Note: Millennials are aged 18 to 35; Generation Xers are aged 36 to 47; Baby Boomers are aged 48 to 66; Older Americans are aged 67 or older.
Source: Survey Documentation and Analysis, Computer-assisted Survey Methods Program, University of California, Berkeley, General Social Survey, 1972–2012 Cumulative Data Files, Internet site http://sda.berkeley.edu/cgi-bin/hsda?harcsda+gss12; calculations by New Strategist

Table 6.25 Child Should Learn to Help Others, 2012

"How important is it for a child to learn to help others
to prepare him or her for life?"

(percent of people aged 18 or older responding by selected characteristics, 2012)

	total	importance of helping others				
		most important	second most important	third most important	fourth most important	least important
Total people	**100.0%**	**15.9%**	**32.6%**	**33.4%**	**16.1%**	**2.0%**
Men	100.0	17.0	33.1	30.7	16.2	3.1
Women	100.0	15.0	32.2	35.7	16.0	1.1
Millennials	100.0	15.0	31.0	30.9	21.4	1.6
Generation Xers	100.0	17.1	35.4	31.4	15.1	1.1
Baby Boomers	100.0	15.1	32.6	36.8	13.8	1.7
Older Americans	100.0	18.3	31.6	33.8	11.4	4.8
Black	100.0	12.2	25.0	32.9	27.0	2.8
Hispanic	100.0	22.9	31.2	27.2	14.8	3.9
Non-Hispanic white	100.0	14.4	34.3	36.1	13.7	1.5
Northeast	100.0	18.3	31.0	30.2	19.0	1.5
Midwest	100.0	14.8	30.9	37.4	14.5	2.4
South	100.0	13.4	33.5	32.3	19.2	1.5
West	100.0	19.1	33.9	33.8	10.4	2.8
Not a college graduate	100.0	17.3	31.8	31.6	17.1	2.2
Bachelor's degree or more	100.0	12.5	34.4	37.9	13.6	1.6

Note: Millennials are aged 18 to 35; Generation Xers are aged 36 to 47; Baby Boomers are aged 48 to 66; Older Americans are aged 67 or older.
Source: Survey Documentation and Analysis, Computer-assisted Survey Methods Program, University of California, Berkeley, General Social Survey, 1972–2012 Cumulative Data Files, Internet site http://sda.berkeley.edu/cgi-bin/hsda?harcsda+gss12; calculations by New Strategist

Table 6.26 Favor Spanking to Discipline Child, 2012

"Do you strongly agree, agree, disagree, or strongly disagree that it is sometimes necessary to discipline a child with a good, hard spanking?"

(percent of people aged 18 or older responding by selected characteristics, 2012)

	total	strongly agree	agree	disagree	strongly disagree
Total people	100.0%	23.4%	47.4%	21.0%	8.1%
Men	100.0	26.6	50.6	17.3	5.4
Women	100.0	20.7	44.6	24.3	10.5
Millennials	100.0	22.6	48.4	20.8	8.2
Generation Xers	100.0	23.4	48.2	19.4	8.9
Baby Boomers	100.0	24.4	46.0	20.7	8.9
Older Americans	100.0	23.9	47.0	23.9	5.2
Black	100.0	34.7	46.1	13.7	5.5
Hispanic	100.0	21.4	51.6	18.2	8.8
Non-Hispanic white	100.0	21.5	48.9	22.1	7.5
Northeast	100.0	16.9	46.0	25.3	11.7
Midwest	100.0	24.7	47.6	22.4	5.2
South	100.0	30.3	47.5	15.3	7.0
West	100.0	15.8	48.1	25.8	10.4
Not a college graduate	100.0	24.6	47.8	19.6	8.0
Bachelor's degree or more	100.0	20.2	46.3	25.1	8.4

Note: Millennials are aged 18 to 35; Generation Xers are aged 36 to 47; Baby Boomers are aged 48 to 66; Older Americans are aged 67 or older.
Source: Survey Documentation and Analysis, Computer-assisted Survey Methods Program, University of California, Berkeley, General Social Survey, 1972–2012 Cumulative Data Files, Internet site http://sda.berkeley.edu/cgi-bin/hsda?harcsda+gss12; calculations by New Strategist

Table 6.27 Children Are a Financial Burden, 2012

"To what extent do you agree or disagree with the following statement?
Children are a financial burden on their parents."

(percent of people aged 18 or older responding by selected characteristics, 2012)

	total	strongly agree	agree	neither agree nor disagree	disagree	strongly disagree
Total people	**100.0%**	**3.8%**	**22.1%**	**15.1%**	**42.9%**	**16.1%**
Men	100.0	4.4	26.0	15.6	39.8	14.2
Women	100.0	3.3	18.7	14.6	45.7	17.7
Millennials	100.0	3.1	23.2	17.6	42.3	13.9
Generation Xers	100.0	3.3	22.9	11.5	42.9	19.5
Baby Boomers	100.0	4.3	19.3	14.7	44.5	17.2
Older Americans	100.0	5.9	24.4	15.5	41.3	12.8
Black	100.0	4.3	25.5	9.7	49.7	10.8
Hispanic	100.0	2.9	18.1	13.0	45.5	20.6
Non-Hispanic white	100.0	4.3	22.2	16.4	40.3	16.8
Northeast	100.0	5.0	25.8	15.1	36.6	17.5
Midwest	100.0	3.4	21.1	13.6	46.3	15.6
South	100.0	3.9	21.5	14.0	45.1	15.6
West	100.0	3.4	21.5	18.2	40.8	16.2
Not a college graduate	100.0	3.2	19.0	14.1	46.8	16.9
Bachelor's degree or more	100.0	5.4	30.4	17.6	32.8	13.8

Note: Millennials are aged 18 to 35; Generation Xers are aged 36 to 47; Baby Boomers are aged 48 to 66; Older Americans are aged 67 or older.
Source: Survey Documentation and Analysis, Computer-assisted Survey Methods Program, University of California, Berkeley, General Social Survey, 1972–2012 Cumulative Data Files, Internet site http://sda.berkeley.edu/cgi-bin/hsda?harcsda+gss12; calculations by New Strategist

Table 6.28 Adult Children Help Elderly Parents, 2012

"To what extent do you agree or disagree with the following statement?
Adult children are an important source of help for elderly parents."

(percent of people aged 18 or older responding by selected characteristics, 2012)

	total	strongly agree	agree	neither agree nor disagree	disagree	strongly disagree
Total people	100.0%	21.4%	64.9%	7.2%	5.7%	0.8%
Men	100.0	18.5	68.4	6.5	6.2	0.3
Women	100.0	24.0	61.7	7.8	5.2	1.2
Millennials	100.0	19.5	69.1	8.2	3.1	0.1
Generation Xers	100.0	24.1	64.7	4.0	6.6	0.6
Baby Boomers	100.0	23.5	62.5	5.1	7.3	1.6
Older Americans	100.0	17.0	59.6	14.6	7.5	1.3
Black	100.0	28.1	61.8	5.0	4.1	1.0
Hispanic	100.0	19.8	62.9	7.0	8.1	2.2
Non-Hispanic white	100.0	20.2	65.4	8.2	5.8	0.5
Northeast	100.0	24.9	59.4	7.4	8.1	0.2
Midwest	100.0	19.9	65.9	6.9	6.1	1.2
South	100.0	21.5	67.2	6.5	4.1	0.7
West	100.0	20.6	64.0	8.5	6.0	1.0
Not a college graduate	100.0	21.0	65.3	7.2	5.5	1.1
Bachelor's degree or more	100.0	22.7	63.8	7.2	6.2	0.1

Note: Millennials are aged 18 to 35; Generation Xers are aged 36 to 47; Baby Boomers are aged 48 to 66; Older Americans are aged 67 or older.
Source: Survey Documentation and Analysis, Computer-assisted Survey Methods Program, University of California, Berkeley, General Social Survey, 1972–2012 Cumulative Data Files, Internet site http://sda.berkeley.edu/cgi-bin/hsda?harcsda+gss12; calculations by New Strategist

Table 6.29 Who Should Help Elderly Parents, 2012

"Thinking about elderly people who need some help in their everyday lives, such as help with grocery shopping, cleaning the house, doing the laundry, etc., who do you think should primarily provide this help?"

(percent of people aged 18 or older responding by selected characteristics, 2012)

	total	family members	government agencies	nonprofit organizations	private providers
Total people	**100.0%**	**68.6%**	**15.5%**	**7.5%**	**8.4%**
Men	100.0	69.7	14.5	9.1	6.7
Women	100.0	67.6	16.4	6.0	10.0
Millennials	100.0	68.1	15.9	5.7	10.3
Generation Xers	100.0	71.7	15.1	6.5	6.8
Baby Boomers	100.0	70.5	15.3	7.1	7.1
Older Americans	100.0	59.9	16.1	15.1	8.9
Black	100.0	53.0	27.0	9.2	10.9
Hispanic	100.0	68.6	17.4	3.6	10.4
Non-Hispanic white	100.0	72.4	11.6	8.2	7.9
Northeast	100.0	61.8	17.4	12.8	8.0
Midwest	100.0	74.6	11.8	5.6	7.9
South	100.0	66.2	15.3	8.7	9.8
West	100.0	70.8	18.3	3.9	7.0
Not a college graduate	100.0	65.5	18.6	7.2	8.7
Bachelor's degree or more	100.0	77.8	6.2	8.3	7.7

Note: Millennials are aged 18 to 35; Generation Xers are aged 36 to 47; Baby Boomers are aged 48 to 66; Older Americans are aged 67 or older.
Source: Survey Documentation and Analysis, Computer-assisted Survey Methods Program, University of California, Berkeley, General Social Survey, 1972–2012 Cumulative Data Files, Internet site http://sda.berkeley.edu/cgi-bin/hsda?harcsda+gss12; calculations by New Strategist

Table 6.30 Who Should Pay the Cost of Help for Elderly, 2012

"Thinking about elderly people who need some help in their everyday lives, such as help with grocery shopping, cleaning the house, doing the laundry, etc., who do you think should primarily cover the cost of this help to these elderly people?"

(percent of people aged 18 or older responding by selected characteristics, 2012)

	total	elderly themselves or their family	government or public funds
Total people	**100.0%**	**53.6%**	**46.4%**
Men	100.0	55.3	44.7
Women	100.0	51.9	48.1
Millennials	100.0	48.7	51.3
Generation Xers	100.0	55.2	44.8
Baby Boomers	100.0	54.1	45.9
Older Americans	100.0	62.4	37.6
Black	100.0	23.8	76.2
Hispanic	100.0	46.0	54.0
Non-Hispanic white	100.0	62.0	38.0
Northeast	100.0	49.4	50.6
Midwest	100.0	62.0	38.0
South	100.0	48.4	51.6
West	100.0	56.1	43.9
Not a college graduate	100.0	47.3	52.7
Bachelor's degree or more	100.0	71.7	28.3

Note: Millennials are aged 18 to 35; Generation Xers are aged 36 to 47; Baby Boomers are aged 48 to 66; Older Americans are aged 67 or older.
Source: Survey Documentation and Analysis, Computer-assisted Survey Methods Program, University of California, Berkeley, General Social Survey, 1972–2012 Cumulative Data Files, Internet site http://sda.berkeley.edu/cgi-bin/hsda?harcsda+gss12; calculations by New Strategist

Table 6.31 Should Aged Share Home with Grown Children, 2012

"As you know, many older people share a home with their grown children.
Do you think this is generally a good idea or a bad idea?"

(percent of people aged 18 or older responding by selected characteristics, 2012)

	total	good idea	bad idea	depends
Total people	**100.0%**	**52.5%**	**32.4%**	**15.1%**
Men	100.0	52.7	32.8	14.5
Women	100.0	52.4	32.0	15.6
Millennials	100.0	55.3	29.3	15.4
Generation Xers	100.0	55.8	30.9	13.3
Baby Boomers	100.0	54.7	32.7	12.6
Older Americans	100.0	36.1	41.0	22.9
Black	100.0	51.6	30.4	18.0
Hispanic	100.0	64.4	29.3	6.2
Non-Hispanic white	100.0	48.4	34.7	16.9
Northeast	100.0	58.3	26.2	15.5
Midwest	100.0	54.3	30.4	15.3
South	100.0	49.8	33.8	16.5
West	100.0	50.8	36.8	12.5
Not a college graduate	100.0	53.1	33.4	13.5
Bachelor's degree or more	100.0	51.1	29.8	19.1

Note: Millennials are aged 18 to 35; Generation Xers are aged 36 to 47; Baby Boomers are aged 48 to 66; Older Americans are aged 67 or older.
Source: Survey Documentation and Analysis, Computer-assisted Survey Methods Program, University of California, Berkeley, General Social Survey, 1972–2012 Cumulative Data Files, Internet site http://sda.berkeley.edu/cgi-bin/hsda?harcsda+gss12; calculations by New Strategist

Table 6.32 Spend Evening with Relatives, 2012

"How often do you spend a social evening with relatives?"

(percent of people aged 18 or older responding by selected characteristics, 2012)

	total	almost daily	several times a week	several times a month	once a month	several times a year	once a year	never
Total people	**100.0%**	**13.6%**	**23.5%**	**22.4%**	**13.6%**	**15.8%**	**6.7%**	**4.4%**
Men	100.0	11.8	22.5	22.3	13.5	18.3	7.0	4.6
Women	100.0	15.2	24.5	22.5	13.7	13.6	6.4	4.2
Millennials	100.0	21.0	25.2	25.3	9.5	11.8	3.5	3.6
Generation Xers	100.0	12.0	22.1	18.3	18.2	16.2	8.0	5.1
Baby Boomers	100.0	9.1	23.4	22.2	14.0	17.9	9.8	3.7
Older Americans	100.0	7.0	21.5	21.2	16.0	21.5	5.9	6.9
Black	100.0	19.0	28.9	16.8	11.1	12.1	4.7	7.3
Hispanic	100.0	16.4	20.6	19.8	15.8	9.4	12.7	5.3
Non-Hispanic white	100.0	10.2	23.4	24.3	13.8	18.6	6.0	3.7
Northeast	100.0	17.2	17.6	25.8	11.3	20.3	4.9	2.9
Midwest	100.0	9.5	18.5	25.0	18.0	19.5	6.7	2.8
South	100.0	14.5	28.3	20.1	11.9	13.5	6.2	5.6
West	100.0	13.8	25.1	21.1	13.4	12.8	8.6	5.1
Not a college graduate	100.0	15.6	24.5	22.2	13.2	13.0	6.8	4.8
Bachelor's degree or more	100.0	8.3	20.8	23.0	14.7	23.6	6.4	3.3

Note: Millennials are aged 18 to 35; Generation Xers are aged 36 to 47; Baby Boomers are aged 48 to 66; Older Americans are aged 67 or older.
Source: Survey Documentation and Analysis, Computer-assisted Survey Methods Program, University of California, Berkeley, General Social Survey, 1972–2012 Cumulative Data Files, Internet site http://sda.berkeley.edu/cgi-bin/hsda?harcsda+gss12; calculations by New Strategist

Table 6.33 Spend Evening with Neighbors, 2012

"How often do you spend a social evening with neighbors?"

(percent of people aged 18 or older responding by selected characteristics, 2012)

	total	almost daily	several times a week	several times a month	once a month	several times a year	once a year	never
Total people	**100.0%**	**5.8%**	**13.5%**	**11.1%**	**15.9%**	**11.2%**	**9.4%**	**33.1%**
Men	100.0	5.4	13.9	13.0	16.6	11.0	11.3	28.8
Women	100.0	6.1	13.2	9.5	15.3	11.4	7.8	36.7
Millennials	100.0	8.8	16.1	12.5	14.4	8.1	6.9	33.2
Generation Xers	100.0	4.0	11.8	11.4	16.9	10.6	8.9	36.4
Baby Boomers	100.0	4.9	13.3	9.4	15.8	14.9	11.6	30.1
Older Americans	100.0	2.9	10.4	10.8	17.9	12.4	12.1	33.6
Black	100.0	9.0	11.8	8.4	16.8	6.5	8.2	39.2
Hispanic	100.0	3.2	12.0	6.2	12.9	16.2	10.3	39.0
Non-Hispanic white	100.0	5.6	14.3	13.3	15.5	11.5	9.9	30.0
Northeast	100.0	5.5	14.6	11.0	16.2	13.1	8.2	31.4
Midwest	100.0	3.5	13.8	14.8	16.1	10.3	10.4	31.3
South	100.0	7.3	12.7	11.2	14.7	13.0	7.4	33.7
West	100.0	5.9	13.9	7.5	17.4	8.0	12.5	34.8
Not a college graduate	100.0	6.8	14.9	8.5	15.3	9.8	8.9	35.8
Bachelor's degree or more	100.0	3.1	9.9	18.1	17.6	15.0	10.7	25.6

Note: Millennials are aged 18 to 35; Generation Xers are aged 36 to 47; Baby Boomers are aged 48 to 66; Older Americans are aged 67 or older.
Source: Survey Documentation and Analysis, Computer-assisted Survey Methods Program, University of California, Berkeley, General Social Survey, 1972–2012 Cumulative Data Files, Internet site http://sda.berkeley.edu/cgi-bin/hsda?harcsda+gss12; calculations by New Strategist

Table 6.34 Spend Evening with Friends, 2012

"How often do you spend a social evening with friends?"

(percent of people aged 18 or older responding by selected characteristics, 2012)

	total	almost daily	several times a week	several times a month	once a month	several times a year	once a year	never
Total people	**100.0%**	**4.5%**	**19.6%**	**21.0%**	**21.0%**	**16.2%**	**8.3%**	**9.5%**
Men	100.0	5.7	18.9	18.9	22.8	17.1	8.2	8.4
Women	100.0	3.4	20.2	22.8	19.4	15.4	8.3	10.5
Millennials	100.0	9.1	26.6	27.7	13.9	12.1	5.7	5.0
Generation Xers	100.0	2.6	14.7	21.9	27.0	17.2	7.1	9.5
Baby Boomers	100.0	2.2	17.3	16.6	25.9	18.4	10.7	8.9
Older Americans	100.0	0.7	14.4	11.1	18.4	20.7	12.0	22.8
Black	100.0	5.3	18.7	27.0	20.0	10.0	5.5	13.6
Hispanic	100.0	5.6	22.2	13.0	15.7	14.0	12.7	16.8
Non-Hispanic white	100.0	4.3	19.5	21.3	21.6	18.5	7.7	7.0
Northeast	100.0	5.6	21.8	21.0	21.3	16.3	7.7	6.4
Midwest	100.0	2.9	17.6	22.8	19.5	18.2	7.9	11.1
South	100.0	5.5	18.8	18.9	23.1	15.4	8.0	10.3
West	100.0	3.8	21.2	22.4	18.9	15.4	9.5	8.9
Not a college graduate	100.0	5.2	19.7	20.4	19.5	15.3	8.2	11.6
Bachelor's degree or more	100.0	2.5	19.3	22.4	25.0	18.5	8.4	3.9

Note: Millennials are aged 18 to 35; Generation Xers are aged 36 to 47; Baby Boomers are aged 48 to 66; Older Americans are aged 67 or older.
Source: Survey Documentation and Analysis, Computer-assisted Survey Methods Program, University of California, Berkeley, General Social Survey, 1972–2012 Cumulative Data Files, Internet site http://sda.berkeley.edu/cgi-bin/hsda?harcsda+gss12; calculations by New Strategist

Table 6.35 Spend Evening at Bar, 2012

"How often do you spend the evening at a bar?"

(percent of people aged 18 or older responding by selected characteristics, 2012)

	total	almost daily	several times a week	several times a month	once a month	several times a year	once a year	never
Total people	**100.0%**	**0.6%**	**6.6%**	**8.4%**	**11.0%**	**11.2%**	**13.2%**	**49.0%**
Men	100.0	1.3	8.1	11.3	11.2	11.5	13.7	43.0
Women	100.0	0.1	5.2	5.9	10.9	10.9	12.7	54.3
Millennials	100.0	0.9	10.2	13.3	15.0	10.0	8.8	41.8
Generation Xers	100.0	0.3	5.4	7.3	15.1	15.2	17.4	39.4
Baby Boomers	100.0	0.2	5.9	6.2	7.0	12.0	17.5	51.2
Older Americans	100.0	1.4	0.7	2.7	2.1	6.0	8.4	78.7
Black	100.0	0.0	6.4	10.5	7.8	9.0	8.1	58.1
Hispanic	100.0	0.8	5.0	6.2	10.6	9.3	11.6	56.6
Non-Hispanic white	100.0	0.8	6.7	8.4	12.4	12.6	14.1	45.0
Northeast	100.0	0.6	11.8	10.8	9.1	17.0	10.8	39.8
Midwest	100.0	0.1	6.9	9.6	15.7	12.5	12.9	42.1
South	100.0	0.9	4.7	7.2	10.2	9.4	13.3	54.4
West	100.0	0.8	5.6	7.5	9.0	8.7	14.9	53.5
Not a college graduate	100.0	0.8	5.4	7.3	9.7	10.3	12.8	53.7
Bachelor's degree or more	100.0	0.2	9.6	11.5	14.7	13.6	14.1	36.2

Note: Millennials are aged 18 to 35; Generation Xers are aged 36 to 47; Baby Boomers are aged 48 to 66; Older Americans are aged 67 or older.
Source: Survey Documentation and Analysis, Computer-assisted Survey Methods Program, University of California, Berkeley, General Social Survey, 1972–2012 Cumulative Data Files, Internet site http://sda.berkeley.edu/cgi-bin/hsda?harcsda+gss12; calculations by New Strategist

Family and Friends: Historical Trends

Table 6.36 Geographic Mobility since Age 16, 1972 to 2012

"When you were 16 years old, were you living in this same (city/town/county)?"

(percent distribution of people aged 18 or older by response for selected years)

	total	same city, town, or county	same state, different city, town, or county	different state
2012	100.0%	39.5%	23.8%	36.6%
2010	100.0	39.4	25.7	34.9
2008	100.0	40.0	23.2	36.8
2006	100.0	38.1	24.2	37.6
2004	100.0	40.4	26.2	33.4
2002	100.0	42.3	25.0	32.6
2000	100.0	39.9	26.0	34.1
1998	100.0	40.1	25.4	34.6
1996	100.0	38.0	23.9	38.1
1994	100.0	40.4	24.9	34.7
1993	100.0	42.1	26.1	31.8
1991	100.0	42.2	26.0	31.8
1990	100.0	40.8	28.6	30.7
1989	100.0	42.0	26.3	31.7
1988	100.0	41.8	25.4	32.8
1987	100.0	43.3	24.1	32.7
1986	100.0	44.1	25.3	30.7
1985	100.0	41.0	25.2	33.8
1984	100.0	39.5	26.8	33.8
1983	100.0	47.2	24.3	28.5
1982	100.0	46.8	24.7	28.4
1980	100.0	46.5	25.1	28.4
1978	100.0	41.4	28.6	30.0
1977	100.0	45.0	25.1	29.9
1976	100.0	45.9	24.6	29.5
1975	100.0	44.7	24.3	30.9
1974	100.0	44.7	26.5	28.9
1973	100.0	44.1	22.6	33.4
1972	100.0	48.7	19.8	31.6

Source: Survey Documentation and Analysis, Computer-assisted Survey Methods Program, University of California, Berkeley, General Social Survey, 1972–2012 Cumulative Data Files, Internet site http://sda.berkeley.edu/cgi-bin/hsda?harcsda+gss12; calculations by New Strategist

Table 6.37 Type of Place Lived In at Age 16, 1972 to 2012

"Which comes closest to the type of place you were living
in when you were 16 years old?"

(percent distribution of people aged 18 or older by response for selected years)

	total	city greater than 250,000 population	big-city suburb	city, 50,000 to 250,000 population	town less than 50,000 population	farm	country, nonfarm
2012	100.0%	15.2%	14.9%	18.7%	30.8%	9.5%	10.9%
2010	100.0	16.4	13.5	18.2	32.4	10.7	8.8
2008	100.0	16.9	12.6	16.8	32.0	11.1	10.5
2006	100.0	13.8	14.0	19.5	32.4	12.4	7.9
2004	100.0	15.4	13.6	15.2	35.6	11.3	8.9
2002	100.0	16.2	14.6	15.8	30.8	11.5	11.2
2000	100.0	15.4	12.1	16.8	30.9	11.6	13.2
1998	100.0	15.7	12.7	16.4	30.3	12.1	12.8
1996	100.0	13.3	12.9	17.4	31.9	11.9	12.6
1994	100.0	15.1	12.9	15.5	31.6	11.9	13.1
1993	100.0	13.5	13.8	14.2	28.7	12.3	17.5
1991	100.0	13.9	11.1	13.9	33.1	11.8	16.2
1990	100.0	17.8	10.4	14.0	30.7	10.2	16.9
1989	100.0	12.8	11.8	15.5	31.8	12.2	16.0
1988	100.0	14.3	10.4	14.6	32.1	12.0	16.7
1987	100.0	14.7	11.0	15.1	28.2	12.1	18.9
1986	100.0	15.8	9.4	16.3	30.7	10.1	17.6
1985	100.0	12.4	10.3	14.8	34.5	9.5	18.6
1984	100.0	14.9	9.1	13.9	32.1	9.3	20.8
1983	100.0	15.7	10.4	15.1	31.5	11.7	15.6
1982	100.0	14.8	9.5	12.0	33.7	10.0	20.0
1980	100.0	15.0	8.0	13.6	31.4	10.5	21.6
1978	100.0	12.9	9.9	14.9	30.8	11.0	20.5
1977	100.0	13.7	5.9	12.1	34.3	11.6	22.3
1976	100.0	15.4	7.8	12.3	30.8	11.4	22.3
1975	100.0	16.6	7.2	11.6	29.3	12.9	22.5
1974	100.0	15.3	8.8	12.9	29.7	9.6	23.7
1973	100.0	17.3	7.1	12.6	31.4	9.1	22.6
1972	100.0	21.1	6.2	12.8	30.4	9.4	20.2

Source: Survey Documentation and Analysis, Computer-assisted Survey Methods Program, University of California, Berkeley, General Social Survey, 1972–2012 Cumulative Data Files, Internet site http://sda.berkeley.edu/cgi-bin/hsda?harcsda+gss12; calculations by New Strategist

Table 6.38 Family Type at Age 16, 1972 to 2012

"Were you living with both your own mother and father around the time you were 16? If not, with whom were you living around that time?"

(percent distribution of people aged 18 or older by response for selected years)

	total	mother and father	mother	mother and stepfather	father	father and stepmother	other relatives	other
2012	100.0%	67.8%	14.9%	6.1%	2.3%	1.8%	4.5%	2.6%
2010	100.0	67.4	15.1	6.6	2.9	1.5	3.4	3.1
2008	100.0	69.1	13.9	5.9	2.9	1.2	3.8	3.1
2006	100.0	70.8	13.6	5.8	2.7	1.6	3.0	2.6
2004	100.0	71.9	12.7	5.2	2.4	1.6	3.2	3.0
2002	100.0	68.0	13.6	6.6	2.6	1.8	4.7	2.8
2000	100.0	70.0	14.0	5.4	2.2	2.1	3.6	2.6
1998	100.0	69.9	13.2	5.5	1.8	3.4	3.3	2.9
1996	100.0	70.4	13.2	4.8	2.3	2.9	3.8	2.8
1994	100.0	71.6	12.6	5.5	2.3	2.6	3.4	2.0
1993	100.0	75.1	10.0	4.3	2.0	2.0	4.4	2.1
1991	100.0	73.9	11.6	4.4	1.9	2.3	3.8	2.1
1990	100.0	72.8	12.1	5.5	1.7	1.6	3.8	2.3
1989	100.0	75.9	11.2	3.8	2.1	1.1	3.2	2.9
1988	100.0	73.1	11.3	6.1	2.2	1.9	3.7	1.7
1987	100.0	77.1	10.1	3.5	2.0	2.0	4.0	1.2
1986	100.0	74.6	11.7	5.2	1.5	1.2	3.9	1.9
1985	100.0	75.2	10.6	3.4	2.0	2.6	4.3	1.9
1984	100.0	75.6	10.5	4.4	1.9	1.7	3.9	1.9
1983	100.0	77.6	9.7	3.6	2.2	2.0	3.1	1.7
1982	100.0	76.3	10.4	3.6	2.3	1.7	4.0	1.6
1980	100.0	73.1	11.9	5.1	2.1	1.7	3.4	2.6
1978	100.0	76.8	10.6	3.6	1.6	1.5	4.2	1.7
1977	100.0	75.5	10.7	4.8	2.6	1.6	3.4	1.5
1976	100.0	77.5	10.7	2.8	2.5	1.6	3.2	1.8
1975	100.0	77.1	8.0	5.3	1.9	2.1	4.0	1.6
1974	100.0	76.9	10.2	3.0	2.4	1.5	3.5	2.5
1973	100.0	78.9	7.5	3.0	3.1	2.0	4.0	1.4
1972	100.0	75.1	10.6	3.1	2.0	1.5	7.7	0.0

Source: Survey Documentation and Analysis, Computer-assisted Survey Methods Program, University of California, Berkeley, General Social Survey, 1972–2012 Cumulative Data Files, Internet site http://sda.berkeley.edu/cgi-bin/hsda?harcsda+gss12; calculations by New Strategist

Table 6.39 Why Not Living with Both Parents at Age 16, 1973 to 2012

"If you were not living with both your own mother
and father at age 16, what happened?"

(percent distribution of people aged 18 or older by response for selected years)

	total	parent died	parents were divorced or separated	other
2012	100.0%	16.9%	59.2%	23.8%
2010	100.0	21.3	59.0	19.7
2008	100.0	26.1	55.2	18.7
2006	100.0	22.9	59.3	17.8
2004	100.0	22.1	57.8	20.2
2002	100.0	25.2	54.7	20.1
2000	100.0	29.3	51.3	19.4
1998	100.0	27.8	53.6	18.6
1996	100.0	30.3	51.7	18.0
1994	100.0	34.3	51.4	14.4
1993	100.0	32.5	49.1	18.4
1991	100.0	39.9	49.3	10.8
1990	100.0	38.3	47.3	14.4
1989	100.0	38.4	46.2	15.3
1988	100.0	38.8	48.6	12.6
1987	100.0	42.9	41.8	15.3
1986	100.0	44.5	44.4	11.1
1985	100.0	48.5	40.9	10.6
1984	100.0	50.5	38.9	10.6
1983	100.0	50.0	44.0	6.0
1982	100.0	45.9	45.4	8.6
1980	100.0	54.2	35.0	10.8
1978	100.0	55.3	36.8	7.8
1977	100.0	55.6	36.7	7.7
1976	100.0	60.8	34.8	4.4
1975	100.0	53.5	39.4	7.2
1974	100.0	57.7	34.4	7.9
1973	100.0	61.8	30.6	7.6

Source: Survey Documentation and Analysis, Computer-assisted Survey Methods Program, University of California, Berkeley, General Social Survey, 1972–2012 Cumulative Data Files, Internet site http://sda.berkeley.edu/cgi-bin/hsda?harcsda+gss12; calculations by New Strategist

Table 6.40 Family Income at Age 16, 1972 to 2012

"Thinking about the time when you were 16 years old, compared with American families in general then, would you say your family income was far below average, below average, average, above average, or far above average?"

(percent distribution of people aged 18 or older by response for selected years)

	total	far below average	below average	average	above average	far above average
2012	100.0%	9.3%	26.9%	45.8%	15.7%	2.3%
2010	100.0	10.2	27.3	43.1	17.0	2.4
2008	100.0	9.6	26.0	45.2	16.9	2.2
2006	100.0	11.0	25.6	45.3	16.4	1.8
2004	100.0	9.5	26.2	46.7	15.2	2.4
2002	100.0	8.0	21.6	50.4	18.2	1.8
1994	100.0	7.9	21.3	53.1	16.2	1.5
1993	100.0	6.8	24.7	50.1	16.4	2.1
1991	100.0	8.5	23.8	49.2	17.0	1.5
1990	100.0	8.6	25.6	48.7	15.6	1.5
1989	100.0	9.1	22.6	52.7	14.3	1.3
1988	100.0	7.4	23.3	52.2	15.3	1.8
1987	100.0	6.3	23.4	51.7	16.1	2.5
1986	100.0	6.6	22.3	51.8	17.2	1.9
1985	100.0	7.6	24.0	50.5	15.4	2.4
1984	100.0	8.4	24.8	52.7	13.9	0.3
1983	100.0	7.4	23.8	52.0	15.7	1.1
1982	100.0	7.7	21.7	54.1	14.5	1.9
1980	100.0	8.7	22.4	53.0	14.8	1.1
1978	100.0	6.7	23.4	56.6	11.7	1.6
1977	100.0	7.9	24.3	52.7	13.3	1.8
1976	100.0	7.1	27.6	51.5	12.4	1.4
1975	100.0	6.9	25.1	53.5	13.2	1.4
1974	100.0	7.0	24.7	53.2	13.3	1.8
1973	100.0	5.9	20.6	58.6	13.5	1.4
1972	100.0	7.2	24.1	57.0	10.6	1.1

Source: Survey Documentation and Analysis, Computer-assisted Survey Methods Program, University of California, Berkeley, General Social Survey, 1972–2012 Cumulative Data Files, Internet site http://sda.berkeley.edu/cgi-bin/hsda?harcsda+gss12; calculations by New Strategist

Table 6.41 Born in the United States, 1977 to 2012

"Were you born in this country?"

(percent distribution of people aged 18 or older by response for selected years)

	total	yes	no
2012	100.0%	85.3%	14.7%
2010	100.0	86.8	13.2
2008	100.0	86.1	13.9
2006	100.0	84.1	15.9
2004	100.0	89.3	10.7
2002	100.0	89.7	10.3
2000	100.0	89.4	10.6
1998	100.0	90.8	9.2
1996	100.0	90.9	9.1
1994	100.0	92.1	7.9
1993	100.0	92.0	8.0
1991	100.0	93.2	6.8
1990	100.0	93.2	6.8
1989	100.0	92.9	7.1
1988	100.0	93.6	6.4
1987	100.0	94.0	6.0
1986	100.0	92.5	7.5
1985	100.0	94.3	5.7
1984	100.0	93.3	6.7
1983	100.0	92.6	7.4
1982	100.0	94.1	5.9
1980	100.0	93.7	6.3
1978	100.0	93.5	6.5
1977	100.0	93.4	6.6

Source: Survey Documentation and Analysis, Computer-assisted Survey Methods Program, University of California, Berkeley, General Social Survey, 1972–2012 Cumulative Data Files, Internet site http://sda.berkeley.edu/cgi-bin/hsda?harcsda+gss12; calculations by New Strategist

Table 6.42 Were Your Parents Born in the United States, 1977 to 2012

"Were both your parents born in this country?"

(percent distribution of people aged 18 or older by response for selected years)

	total	born in United States			neither born in United States	don't know
		both	mother only	father only		
2012	100.0%	74.8%	3.0%	2.9%	18.8%	0.5%
2010	100.0	78.4	1.9	2.0	17.4	0.3
2008	100.0	78.3	3.1	1.8	16.6	0.3
2006	100.0	77.0	3.1	2.0	17.5	0.4
2004	100.0	80.7	2.8	2.3	14.1	0.1
2002	100.0	81.8	3.1	2.6	12.2	0.3
2000	100.0	81.9	3.0	2.5	12.3	0.4
1998	100.0	82.4	3.1	1.6	12.4	0.6
1996	100.0	83.7	3.1	2.0	11.0	0.2
1994	100.0	82.6	3.0	2.5	11.4	0.5
1993	100.0	84.2	2.3	2.1	11.0	0.4
1991	100.0	83.1	4.0	2.7	9.8	0.4
1990	100.0	83.3	4.0	2.0	10.5	0.3
1989	100.0	82.9	3.2	2.5	11.2	0.3
1988	100.0	83.6	3.2	1.9	10.8	0.5
1987	100.0	84.1	2.8	2.7	10.2	0.2
1986	100.0	82.5	2.9	2.2	12.0	0.4
1985	100.0	84.4	3.6	2.1	9.6	0.2
1984	100.0	84.6	4.2	1.1	9.9	0.1
1983	100.0	78.5	4.2	3.1	14.1	0.1
1982	100.0	80.8	3.6	2.6	12.8	0.3
1980	100.0	82.3	3.9	1.6	11.8	0.4
1978	100.0	81.8	4.1	2.4	11.2	0.6
1977	100.0	78.6	4.3	2.3	14.5	0.3

Source: Survey Documentation and Analysis, Computer-assisted Survey Methods Program, University of California, Berkeley, General Social Survey, 1972–2012 Cumulative Data Files, Internet site http://sda.berkeley.edu/cgi-bin/hsda?harcsda+gss12; calculations by New Strategist

Table 6.43 How Many Grandparents Were Born outside the United States, 1977 to 2012

"How many of your grandparents were born outside the United States?"

(percent distribution of people aged 18 or older by response for selected years)

	total	all born in United States	grandparents born outside United States			
			one	two	three	four
2012	100.0%	56.2%	7.2%	10.7%	1.9%	24.0%
2010	100.0	59.3	5.9	10.0	2.0	22.9
2008	100.0	58.6	6.6	10.9	2.1	21.8
2006	100.0	56.9	6.5	9.9	2.7	24.1
2004	100.0	61.0	5.9	10.0	1.9	21.2
2002	100.0	61.6	5.9	10.6	2.1	19.8
2000	100.0	61.0	5.8	11.9	2.5	18.9
1998	100.0	60.8	6.5	11.6	2.3	18.7
1996	100.0	61.4	6.7	11.8	2.4	17.7
1994	100.0	61.7	6.6	10.9	2.0	18.9
1993	100.0	61.7	6.5	11.1	2.4	18.4
1991	100.0	60.6	6.7	10.9	2.9	18.9
1990	100.0	59.6	6.5	12.1	2.9	18.9
1989	100.0	60.2	6.6	11.2	2.6	19.5
1988	100.0	59.5	6.9	11.5	3.4	18.7
1987	100.0	61.3	6.4	12.6	2.0	17.6
1986	100.0	56.6	7.1	10.9	3.1	22.3
1985	100.0	60.3	7.4	11.6	2.0	18.8
1984	100.0	59.2	6.1	11.2	3.1	20.5
1983	100.0	52.1	7.1	13.4	3.5	23.8
1982	100.0	54.9	5.9	13.8	3.7	21.7
1980	100.0	58.2	6.7	11.8	2.7	20.5
1978	100.0	58.7	7.0	10.4	3.4	20.4
1977	100.0	57.4	5.2	12.9	2.0	22.6

Source: Survey Documentation and Analysis, Computer-assisted Survey Methods Program, University of California, Berkeley, General Social Survey, 1972–2012 Cumulative Data Files, Internet site http://sda.berkeley.edu/cgi-bin/hsda?harcsda+gss12; calculations by New Strategist

Table 6.44 Happiness of Marriage, 1973 to 2012

"Taking things all together, how would you describe your marriage? Would you say that your marriage is very happy, pretty happy, or not too happy?"

(percent of married people aged 18 or older responding by selected characteristics, 2012)

	total	very happy	pretty happy	not too happy
2012	100.0%	65.4%	32.2%	2.3%
2010	100.0	63.0	34.3	2.6
2008	100.0	62.1	35.3	2.6
2006	100.0	60.7	37.1	2.3
2004	100.0	61.8	35.0	3.1
2002	100.0	60.2	37.2	2.7
2000	100.0	62.4	34.4	3.2
1998	100.0	63.6	33.7	2.7
1996	100.0	61.9	36.0	2.0
1994	100.0	60.4	36.8	2.7
1993	100.0	61.3	36.0	2.7
1991	100.0	63.6	33.2	3.2
1990	100.0	64.6	33.3	2.1
1989	100.0	60.3	37.4	2.3
1988	100.0	62.0	34.5	3.5
1987	100.0	64.8	33.1	2.2
1986	100.0	63.2	33.3	3.5
1985	100.0	56.6	40.2	3.2
1984	100.0	65.4	31.8	2.8
1983	100.0	62.0	35.4	2.7
1982	100.0	64.8	32.5	2.8
1980	100.0	68.4	28.8	2.8
1978	100.0	64.8	32.0	3.2
1977	100.0	65.3	31.1	3.6
1976	100.0	66.1	31.3	2.7
1975	100.0	67.4	29.7	2.9
1974	100.0	68.8	27.2	4.0
1973	100.0	67.2	30.0	2.9

Source: Survey Documentation and Analysis, Computer-assisted Survey Methods Program, University of California, Berkeley, General Social Survey, 1972–2012 Cumulative Data Files, Internet site http://sda.berkeley.edu/cgi-bin/hsda?harcsda+gss12; calculations by New Strategist

Table 6.45 Ever Been Divorced, 1972 to 2012

"Have you ever been divorced or legally separated?"

(percent distribution of people aged 18 or older by response for selected years)

	total	yes	no
2012	100.0%	24.2%	75.8%
2010	100.0	23.3	76.7
2008	100.0	25.0	75.0
2006	100.0	26.3	73.7
2004	100.0	23.9	76.1
2002	100.0	23.6	76.4
2000	100.0	23.0	77.0
1998	100.0	22.5	77.5
1996	100.0	23.3	76.7
1994	100.0	22.6	77.4
1993	100.0	20.8	79.2
1991	100.0	20.9	79.1
1990	100.0	22.4	77.6
1989	100.0	18.6	81.4
1988	100.0	19.2	80.8
1987	100.0	18.0	82.0
1986	100.0	18.5	81.5
1985	100.0	20.1	79.9
1984	100.0	16.3	83.7
1983	100.0	17.6	82.4
1982	100.0	17.9	82.1
1980	100.0	15.6	84.4
1978	100.0	16.5	83.5
1977	100.0	15.3	84.7
1976	100.0	13.6	86.4
1975	100.0	14.9	85.1
1974	100.0	13.6	86.4
1973	100.0	13.3	86.7
1972	100.0	14.5	85.5

Source: Survey Documentation and Analysis, Computer-assisted Survey Methods Program, University of California, Berkeley, General Social Survey, 1972–2012 Cumulative Data Files, Internet site http://sda.berkeley.edu/cgi-bin/hsda?harcsda+gss12; calculations by New Strategist

Table 6.46 Divorce Laws, 1974 to 2012

"Should divorce in this country be easier or more difficult to obtain than it is now?"

(percent distribution of people aged 18 or older by response for selected years)

	total	easier	more difficult	stay same
2012	100.0%	35.6%	40.9%	23.5%
2010	100.0	33.3	42.0	24.7
2008	100.0	27.4	48.7	23.9
2006	100.0	24.6	46.9	28.5
2004	100.0	25.7	55.3	19.1
2002	100.0	25.9	52.8	21.3
2000	100.0	24.9	52.6	22.5
1998	100.0	24.6	56.3	19.1
1996	100.0	27.6	53.6	18.8
1994	100.0	27.0	49.8	23.2
1993	100.0	27.4	51.6	21.0
1991	100.0	29.5	50.2	20.3
1990	100.0	24.6	51.8	23.6
1989	100.0	27.3	54.5	18.2
1988	100.0	25.2	52.2	22.6
1986	100.0	27.7	53.8	18.5
1985	100.0	24.1	55.7	20.2
1983	100.0	25.1	55.3	19.6
1982	100.0	23.7	55.6	20.7
1978	100.0	28.0	44.6	27.4
1977	100.0	29.3	52.5	18.2
1976	100.0	29.2	52.8	17.9
1975	100.0	29.0	49.5	21.5
1974	100.0	33.5	44.6	22.0

Source: Survey Documentation and Analysis, Computer-assisted Survey Methods Program, University of California, Berkeley, General Social Survey, 1972–2012 Cumulative Data Files, Internet site http://sda.berkeley.edu/cgi-bin/hsda?harcsda+gss12; calculations by New Strategist

Table 6.47 Better for Man to Work and Woman to Stay Home, 1977 to 2012

"It is much better for everyone involved if the man is the achiever
outside the home and the woman takes care of the home
and family. Do you agree or disagree?"

(percent distribution of people aged 18 or older by response for selected years)

	total	strongly agree	agree	disagree	strongly disagree
2012	100.0%	6.5%	25.2%	48.3%	20.0%
2010	100.0	6.8	28.6	43.5	21.2
2008	100.0	8.3	27.0	47.2	17.5
2006	100.0	9.1	26.2	47.4	17.3
2004	100.0	8.7	28.0	45.9	17.5
2002	100.0	10.3	28.8	42.9	18.0
2000	100.0	11.1	28.9	40.7	19.3
1998	100.0	6.8	27.2	47.2	18.7
1996	100.0	7.4	30.5	44.6	17.4
1994	100.0	6.4	27.7	47.9	18.1
1993	100.0	5.5	29.4	47.5	17.6
1991	100.0	7.6	33.3	42.0	17.1
1990	100.0	6.6	32.5	46.5	14.4
1989	100.0	9.6	30.6	43.1	16.7
1988	100.0	9.0	32.0	43.3	15.8
1986	100.0	8.8	38.3	40.1	12.8
1985	100.0	9.7	38.7	39.3	12.3
1977	100.0	19.0	47.0	28.2	5.9

Source: Survey Documentation and Analysis, Computer-assisted Survey Methods Program, University of California, Berkeley, General Social Survey, 1972–2012 Cumulative Data Files, Internet site http://sda.berkeley.edu/cgi-bin/hsda?harcsda+gss12; calculations by New Strategist

Table 6.48 A Working Mother's Relationship with Children, 1977 to 2012

"A working mother can establish just as warm and secure a relationship with her children as a mother who does not work. Do you agree or disagree?"

(percent distribution of people aged 18 or older by response for selected years)

	total	strongly agree	agree	disagree	strongly disagree
2012	100.0%	25.0%	46.7%	23.1%	5.2%
2010	100.0	28.8	45.9	20.1	5.1
2008	100.0	26.3	46.0	22.2	5.4
2006	100.0	23.4	43.5	27.3	5.8
2004	100.0	21.9	42.7	28.3	7.1
2002	100.0	23.4	39.9	26.5	10.3
2000	100.0	20.3	41.4	29.4	8.9
1998	100.0	22.1	45.8	25.2	7.0
1996	100.0	24.0	42.2	26.1	7.7
1994	100.0	23.4	46.9	25.0	4.7
1993	100.0	20.8	46.9	25.9	6.4
1991	100.0	19.9	46.1	27.9	6.1
1990	100.0	22.0	41.5	29.3	7.2
1989	100.0	20.7	43.8	28.1	7.4
1988	100.0	22.4	40.1	28.4	9.1
1986	100.0	22.4	40.1	29.6	7.9
1985	100.0	20.5	39.0	30.3	10.2
1977	100.0	15.4	33.5	33.8	17.3

Source: Survey Documentation and Analysis, Computer-assisted Survey Methods Program, University of California, Berkeley, General Social Survey, 1972–2012 Cumulative Data Files, Internet site http://sda.berkeley.edu/cgi-bin/hsda?harcsda+gss12; calculations by New Strategist

Table 6.49 Preschool Children Suffer when Mother Works, 1977 to 2012

"A preschool child is likely to suffer if his or her mother works.
Do you agree or disagree?"

(percent distribution of people aged 18 or older by response for selected years)

	total	strongly agree	agree	disagree	strongly disagree
2012	100.0%	6.4%	28.8%	50.3%	14.5%
2010	100.0	5.7	29.5	50.8	14.1
2008	100.0	7.2	27.8	52.8	12.2
2006	100.0	8.7	32.1	48.7	10.5
2004	100.0	6.0	36.6	45.7	11.6
2002	100.0	10.5	35.9	43.0	10.7
2000	100.0	10.0	36.6	42.8	10.6
1998	100.0	8.7	33.6	47.6	10.1
1996	100.0	9.0	37.6	42.4	11.0
1994	100.0	7.3	34.0	47.7	11.0
1993	100.0	7.5	35.3	47.4	9.8
1991	100.0	9.5	38.7	41.4	10.4
1990	100.0	7.9	41.3	42.9	7.9
1989	100.0	9.3	38.4	42.6	9.8
1988	100.0	10.5	37.9	41.1	10.5
1986	100.0	10.7	41.0	39.1	9.3
1985	100.0	12.4	42.3	36.0	9.3
1977	100.0	21.3	46.9	27.4	4.4

Source: Survey Documentation and Analysis, Computer-assisted Survey Methods Program, University of California, Berkeley, General Social Survey, 1972–2012 Cumulative Data Files, Internet site http://sda.berkeley.edu/cgi-bin/hsda?harcsda+gss12; calculations by New Strategist

Table 6.50 Mother Worked while You Were Growing Up, 1994 to 2012

"Did your mother ever work for pay for as long
as a year while you were growing up?"

(percent distribution of people aged 18 or older by response for selected years)

	total	yes	no
2012	100.0%	72.5%	27.5%
2010	100.0	71.2	28.8
2008	100.0	68.8	31.2
2006	100.0	67.0	33.0
2004	100.0	66.4	33.6
2002	100.0	65.2	34.8
2000	100.0	62.7	37.3
1998	100.0	62.9	37.1
1996	100.0	64.8	35.2
1994	100.0	60.1	39.9

Source: Survey Documentation and Analysis, Computer-assisted Survey Methods Program, University of California, Berkeley, General Social Survey, 1972–2012 Cumulative Data Files, Internet site http://sda.berkeley.edu/cgi-bin/hsda?harcsda+gss12; calculations by New Strategist

Table 6.51 Ideal Number of Children, 1972 to 2012

"What do you think is the ideal number of children for a family to have?"

(percent distribution of people aged 18 or older by response for selected years)

	total	none	one	two	three	four or more	as many as want
2012	100.0%	0.8%	2.6%	46.8%	27.8%	11.3%	10.7%
2010	100.0	0.3	2.5	48.4	26.3	12.0	10.5
2008	100.0	1.0	2.5	47.7	26.6	10.1	12.1
2006	100.0	0.9	2.2	49.5	26.1	10.0	11.4
2004	100.0	1.0	1.6	49.8	25.5	12.6	9.5
2002	100.0	1.1	2.8	49.9	26.1	11.4	8.8
2000	100.0	1.2	3.5	52.3	25.8	10.0	7.2
1998	100.0	1.5	2.4	56.8	20.2	10.6	8.6
1996	100.0	1.2	3.0	57.4	21.5	10.8	6.1
1994	100.0	1.3	2.8	54.3	23.2	12.2	6.2
1993	100.0	1.1	3.2	57.8	21.7	10.8	5.5
1991	100.0	1.0	3.1	53.8	23.0	13.6	5.5
1990	100.0	1.2	1.6	55.4	24.4	12.6	4.7
1989	100.0	1.2	2.5	53.9	23.8	13.6	5.0
1988	100.0	1.6	1.7	51.3	26.6	13.9	4.9
1986	100.0	0.9	1.7	51.5	25.0	16.4	4.5
1985	100.0	1.0	3.2	56.6	21.3	14.1	3.9
1983	100.0	1.0	1.7	50.5	24.0	16.4	6.4
1982	100.0	1.0	2.4	54.7	20.6	16.7	4.5
1978	100.0	1.4	2.0	51.0	24.1	16.8	4.8
1977	100.0	1.1	1.8	48.9	23.3	19.3	5.6
1976	100.0	2.4	3.0	51.0	20.3	16.6	6.5
1975	100.0	1.2	1.9	48.8	23.9	18.1	6.0
1974	100.0	1.2	1.9	44.7	23.9	19.9	8.3
1972	100.0	1.5	1.3	40.6	24.1	26.6	6.0

Source: Survey Documentation and Analysis, Computer-assisted Survey Methods Program, University of California, Berkeley, General Social Survey, 1972–2012 Cumulative Data Files, Internet site http://sda.berkeley.edu/cgi-bin/hsda?harcsda+gss12; calculations by New Strategist

Table 6.52 Child Should Learn to Obey, 1986 to 2012

"How important is it for a child to learn to obey to prepare him or her for life?"

(percent distribution of people aged 18 or older by response for selected years)

		importance of learning to obey				
	total	most important	second most important	third most important	fourth most important	least important
2012	100.0%	14.4%	11.4%	17.7%	40.5%	15.9%
2010	100.0	14.2	12.6	18.7	40.2	14.4
2008	100.0	15.5	11.4	16.6	41.7	14.8
2006	100.0	17.0	12.1	18.4	39.3	13.2
2004	100.0	12.4	15.4	16.2	41.5	14.5
2002	100.0	14.4	12.4	17.2	41.0	15.0
2000	100.0	21.0	12.4	15.5	36.1	14.9
1998	100.0	18.5	12.8	17.0	37.0	14.7
1996	100.0	18.5	13.1	18.3	35.7	14.4
1994	100.0	17.7	13.3	17.5	38.2	13.3
1993	100.0	18.1	15.6	16.7	34.8	14.8
1991	100.0	20.0	13.8	14.7	34.3	17.2
1990	100.0	18.1	12.8	19.6	32.1	17.4
1989	100.0	19.2	14.0	16.1	33.5	17.2
1988	100.0	22.6	11.8	19.6	30.3	15.7
1987	100.0	20.4	13.6	15.5	30.7	19.8
1986	100.0	23.4	16.2	16.3	30.7	13.3

Source: Survey Documentation and Analysis, Computer-assisted Survey Methods Program, University of California, Berkeley, General Social Survey, 1972–2012 Cumulative Data Files, Internet site http://sda.berkeley.edu/cgi-bin/hsda?harcsda+gss12; calculations by New Strategist

Table 6.53 Child Should Learn to Think for Self, 1986 to 2012

"How important is it for a child to learn to think for himself
or herself to prepare him or her for life?"

(percent distribution of people aged 18 or older by response for selected years)

| | | importance of thinking for self | | | | |
	total	most important	second most important	third most important	fourth most important	least important
2012	100.0%	44.0%	19.2%	17.4%	15.1%	4.4%
2010	100.0	41.5	18.3	17.1	17.7	5.3
2008	100.0	45.0	21.6	14.2	14.8	4.4
2006	100.0	46.5	17.9	15.5	17.0	3.1
2004	100.0	47.2	18.9	12.7	15.1	6.0
2002	100.0	47.7	20.7	13.2	13.2	5.2
2000	100.0	47.3	19.7	14.7	14.0	4.3
1998	100.0	49.4	18.1	13.9	14.1	4.6
1996	100.0	50.6	17.6	12.1	14.4	5.4
1994	100.0	53.0	17.3	11.9	12.9	4.9
1993	100.0	52.9	14.3	13.3	13.9	5.5
1991	100.0	50.8	16.5	13.0	14.8	4.9
1990	100.0	51.3	19.5	9.9	12.8	6.6
1989	100.0	53.0	18.3	10.4	12.8	5.6
1988	100.0	50.1	17.1	12.8	13.1	6.8
1987	100.0	53.9	17.8	10.1	10.8	7.4
1986	100.0	51.2	18.1	14.9	10.6	5.3

Source: Survey Documentation and Analysis, Computer-assisted Survey Methods Program, University of California, Berkeley, General Social Survey, 1972–2012 Cumulative Data Files, Internet site http://sda.berkeley.edu/cgi-bin/hsda?harcsda+gss12; calculations by New Strategist

Table 6.54 Child Should Learn to Be Popular, 1986 to 2012

"How important is it for a child to learn to be well-liked
or popular to prepare him or her for life?"

(percent distribution of people aged 18 or older by response for selected years)

	total	importance of popularity				
		most important	second most important	third most important	fourth most important	least important
2012	100.0%	0.5%	1.7%	2.7%	18.7%	76.3%
2010	100.0	0.2	1.5	3.9	17.2	77.1
2008	100.0	0.9	0.9	3.0	18.1	77.1
2006	100.0	0.7	1.1	2.3	15.7	80.2
2004	100.0	1.0	1.3	3.9	17.8	76.0
2002	100.0	0.3	1.1	3.5	19.8	75.3
2000	100.0	0.6	1.1	3.8	18.0	76.4
1998	100.0	1.0	2.0	3.3	16.7	77.0
1996	100.0	0.6	1.6	3.5	18.3	76.0
1994	100.0	0.4	1.9	3.9	16.4	77.4
1993	100.0	1.1	2.3	4.6	17.4	74.5
1991	100.0	0.4	2.7	5.0	19.1	72.7
1990	100.0	0.9	1.9	5.6	21.1	70.6
1989	100.0	1.0	2.8	5.1	19.3	71.8
1988	100.0	0.7	4.7	5.0	19.8	69.8
1987	100.0	0.8	3.7	5.7	23.8	66.1
1986	100.0	0.5	3.5	4.4	18.5	73.1

Source: Survey Documentation and Analysis, Computer-assisted Survey Methods Program, University of California, Berkeley, General Social Survey, 1972–2012 Cumulative Data Files, Internet site http://sda.berkeley.edu/cgi-bin/hsda?harcsda+gss12; calculations by New Strategist

Table 6.55 Child Should Learn to Work Hard, 1986 to 2012

"How important is it for a child to learn to work hard
to prepare him or her for life?"

(percent distribution of people aged 18 or older by response for selected years)

		importance of working hard				
	total	most important	second most important	third most important	fourth most important	least important
2012	100.0%	25.1%	35.2%	28.8%	9.6%	1.3%
2010	100.0	26.2	34.6	28.5	8.7	2.0
2008	100.0	22.9	34.7	28.7	11.8	1.8
2006	100.0	19.7	37.1	29.5	12.1	1.6
2004	100.0	22.1	32.3	33.8	10.5	1.4
2002	100.0	22.5	34.8	31.2	9.4	2.0
2000	100.0	17.6	34.8	32.5	13.4	1.7
1998	100.0	17.8	36.6	31.8	12.4	1.4
1996	100.0	17.6	36.6	32.1	12.1	1.6
1994	100.0	16.0	39.2	30.7	12.8	1.2
1993	100.0	14.4	35.6	35.5	12.8	1.8
1991	100.0	15.0	35.2	34.0	14.1	1.8
1990	100.0	16.0	34.5	34.0	12.8	2.7
1989	100.0	14.4	32.7	35.8	15.4	1.8
1988	100.0	14.5	32.6	32.7	16.8	3.4
1987	100.0	12.3	35.3	32.7	16.3	3.3
1986	100.0	11.2	34.2	31.0	19.1	4.6

Source: Survey Documentation and Analysis, Computer-assisted Survey Methods Program, University of California, Berkeley, General Social Survey, 1972–2012 Cumulative Data Files, Internet site http://sda.berkeley.edu/cgi-bin/hsda?harcsda+gss12; calculations by New Strategist

Table 6.56 Child Should Learn to Help Others, 1986 to 2012

"How important is it for a child to learn to help others
to prepare him or her for life?"

(percent distribution of people aged 18 or older by response for selected years)

	total	importance of helping others				
		most important	second most important	third most important	fourth most important	least important
2012	100.0%	15.9%	32.6%	33.4%	16.1%	2.0%
2010	100.0	17.8	33.0	31.8	16.1	1.2
2008	100.0	15.7	31.4	37.6	13.6	1.8
2006	100.0	16.0	31.7	34.4	16.0	2.0
2004	100.0	17.3	32.1	33.4	15.1	2.0
2002	100.0	15.1	30.9	34.9	16.6	2.5
2000	100.0	13.5	31.9	33.5	18.5	2.7
1998	100.0	13.3	30.5	34.0	19.9	2.3
1996	100.0	12.7	31.1	34.1	19.4	2.7
1994	100.0	12.9	28.3	35.9	19.7	3.2
1993	100.0	13.4	32.2	29.9	21.1	3.4
1991	100.0	13.8	31.9	33.3	17.6	3.4
1990	100.0	13.7	31.3	31.0	21.3	2.8
1989	100.0	12.4	32.1	32.7	19.1	3.7
1988	100.0	12.4	33.3	29.7	20.1	4.5
1987	100.0	12.6	29.6	36.0	18.4	3.4
1986	100.0	13.7	28.0	33.5	21.1	3.7

Source: Survey Documentation and Analysis, Computer-assisted Survey Methods Program, University of California, Berkeley, General Social Survey, 1972–2012 Cumulative Data Files, Internet site http://sda.berkeley.edu/cgi-bin/hsda?harcsda+gss12; calculations by New Strategist

Table 6.57 Favor Spanking to Discipline Child, 1986 to 2012

"Do you strongly agree, agree, disagree, or strongly disagree that it is sometimes necessary to discipline a child with a good, hard spanking?"

(percent distribution of people aged 18 or older by response for selected years)

	total	strongly agree	agree	disagree	strongly disagree
2012	100.0%	23.4%	47.4%	21.0%	8.1%
2010	100.0	23.6	45.4	23.5	7.5
2008	100.0	24.7	46.2	23.1	6.0
2006	100.0	26.0	45.6	20.3	8.0
2004	100.0	22.8	49.2	21.2	6.9
2002	100.0	31.1	43.1	18.5	7.3
2000	100.0	31.9	42.5	18.1	7.6
1998	100.0	26.7	48.6	17.9	6.8
1996	100.0	26.9	46.5	18.5	8.1
1994	100.0	27.1	46.6	18.5	7.8
1993	100.0	22.5	51.4	19.2	6.9
1991	100.0	25.8	49.1	19.6	5.5
1990	100.0	27.6	51.2	17.4	3.8
1989	100.0	31.4	45.3	17.5	5.9
1988	100.0	30.7	49.1	15.2	5.0
1986	100.0	27.0	56.5	13.2	3.3

Source: Survey Documentation and Analysis, Computer-assisted Survey Methods Program, University of California, Berkeley, General Social Survey, 1972–2012 Cumulative Data Files, Internet site http://sda.berkeley.edu/cgi-bin/hsda?harcsda+gss12; calculations by New Strategist

Table 6.58 Should Aged Share Home with Grown Children, 1973 to 2012

"As you know, many older people share a home with their grown children.
Do you think this is generally a good idea or a bad idea?"

(percent distribution of people aged 18 or older by response for selected years)

	total	good idea	bad idea	depends
2012	100.0%	52.5%	32.4%	15.1%
2010	100.0	54.7	27.3	18.1
2008	100.0	50.9	31.8	17.3
2006	100.0	49.3	29.6	21.1
2004	100.0	49.4	28.9	21.6
2002	100.0	48.8	32.4	18.8
2000	100.0	53.2	30.9	15.9
1998	100.0	46.7	34.1	19.3
1996	100.0	47.8	32.6	19.5
1994	100.0	48.8	34.6	16.5
1993	100.0	46.3	33.3	20.4
1991	100.0	46.3	37.1	16.6
1990	100.0	47.4	36.1	16.5
1989	100.0	43.6	38.8	17.5
1988	100.0	46.0	40.1	13.9
1987	100.0	52.0	34.0	13.9
1986	100.0	41.9	45.5	12.6
1984	100.0	50.5	35.8	13.7
1983	100.0	44.1	41.6	14.2
1980	100.0	41.6	42.2	16.2
1978	100.0	36.3	46.7	16.9
1976	100.0	38.7	47.0	14.3
1975	100.0	33.9	51.2	14.9
1973	100.0	32.8	56.5	10.7

Source: Survey Documentation and Analysis, Computer-assisted Survey Methods Program, University of California, Berkeley, General Social Survey, 1972–2012 Cumulative Data Files, Internet site http://sda.berkeley.edu/cgi-bin/hsda?harcsda+gss12; calculations by New Strategist

Table 6.59 Spend Evening with Relatives, 1974 to 2012

"How often do you spend a social evening with relatives?"

(percent distribution of people aged 18 or older by response for selected years)

	total	almost daily	several times a week	several times a month	once a month	several times a year	once a year	never
2012	100.0%	13.6%	23.5%	22.4%	13.6%	15.8%	6.7%	4.4%
2010	100.0	15.5	25.4	17.3	17.2	15.8	5.8	3.1
2008	100.0	13.8	24.3	19.7	15.1	16.6	6.5	4.0
2006	100.0	11.7	28.8	17.5	15.9	17.2	5.8	3.2
2004	100.0	13.4	27.1	18.9	16.2	17.6	4.3	2.6
2002	100.0	13.2	24.3	18.8	16.4	17.0	5.8	4.4
2000	100.0	11.0	26.5	19.6	16.0	17.0	5.6	4.3
1998	100.0	8.9	28.0	16.6	17.6	18.3	7.0	3.6
1996	100.0	10.3	26.2	16.1	17.9	18.5	6.6	4.4
1994	100.0	8.4	26.0	18.5	17.9	18.9	6.5	3.7
1993	100.0	8.5	24.7	19.2	19.8	16.7	7.9	3.2
1991	100.0	10.6	25.0	21.0	15.0	18.3	6.4	3.7
1990	100.0	8.5	26.5	19.7	15.4	19.3	7.4	3.2
1989	100.0	7.5	26.7	16.5	16.9	20.3	6.5	5.6
1988	100.0	10.9	25.9	18.6	15.1	18.2	7.7	3.6
1986	100.0	11.0	26.2	15.5	16.7	18.3	7.0	5.2
1985	100.0	9.0	27.6	18.6	16.0	18.3	7.1	3.3
1983	100.0	6.6	24.5	20.9	16.5	18.4	8.7	4.5
1982	100.0	7.7	26.9	18.6	16.5	18.1	8.4	3.8
1978	100.0	7.0	27.3	19.2	14.4	19.7	7.7	4.6
1977	100.0	8.9	28.6	17.7	17.3	16.9	6.0	4.6
1975	100.0	7.3	31.5	16.4	16.8	17.2	6.6	4.3
1974	100.0	9.5	28.9	19.5	15.5	16.2	7.6	2.8

Source: Survey Documentation and Analysis, Computer-assisted Survey Methods Program, University of California, Berkeley, General Social Survey, 1972–2012 Cumulative Data Files, Internet site http://sda.berkeley.edu/cgi-bin/hsda?harcsda+gss12; calculations by New Strategist

Table 6.60 Spend Evening with Neighbors, 1974 to 2012

"How often do you spend a social evening with neighbors?"

(percent distribution of people aged 18 or older by response for selected years)

	total	almost daily	several times a week	several times a month	once a month	several times a year	once a year	never
2012	100.0%	5.8%	13.5%	11.1%	15.9%	11.2%	9.4%	33.1%
2010	100.0	7.2	17.1	11.0	13.9	13.5	10.1	27.3
2008	100.0	5.1	14.3	10.8	14.9	13.2	11.6	30.1
2006	100.0	4.6	16.8	10.7	14.4	13.9	10.8	28.7
2004	100.0	5.9	14.9	11.1	15.8	15.3	9.4	27.6
2002	100.0	8.7	14.3	11.8	11.5	12.9	10.9	29.8
2000	100.0	5.3	16.7	10.7	13.4	12.3	11.4	30.3
1998	100.0	5.0	15.4	10.5	16.3	14.6	10.6	27.6
1996	100.0	4.8	15.6	11.4	15.9	12.9	10.1	29.3
1994	100.0	5.0	15.7	11.7	14.7	12.8	10.1	30.1
1993	100.0	4.9	15.6	12.7	14.7	13.2	10.2	28.8
1991	100.0	4.8	18.0	11.6	14.4	12.8	7.8	30.5
1990	100.0	5.2	16.4	11.5	15.4	12.0	9.8	29.7
1989	100.0	5.4	17.0	8.2	15.5	13.5	10.8	29.6
1988	100.0	4.4	20.5	11.1	15.1	13.5	7.4	27.9
1986	100.0	6.4	21.2	11.1	15.4	10.7	9.8	25.4
1985	100.0	5.3	17.7	14.3	14.1	13.3	10.7	24.6
1983	100.0	5.5	18.2	12.7	14.9	13.1	9.5	26.0
1982	100.0	5.4	17.5	12.6	18.3	14.0	11.0	21.2
1978	100.0	4.9	23.5	10.7	11.9	13.9	8.9	26.2
1977	100.0	5.1	21.4	12.2	15.9	13.0	8.5	23.9
1975	100.0	5.7	20.9	13.6	14.8	12.9	8.5	23.7
1974	100.0	6.9	23.0	13.6	17.3	11.6	6.3	21.3

Source: Survey Documentation and Analysis, Computer-assisted Survey Methods Program, University of California, Berkeley, General Social Survey, 1972–2012 Cumulative Data Files, Internet site http://sda.berkeley.edu/cgi-bin/hsda?harcsda+gss12; calculations by New Strategist

Table 6.61 Spend Evening with Friends, 1974 to 2012

"How often do you spend a social evening with friends?"

(percent distribution of people aged 18 or older by response for selected years)

	total	almost daily	several times a week	several times a month	once a month	several times a year	once a year	never
2012	100.0%	4.5%	19.6%	21.0%	21.0%	16.2%	8.3%	9.5%
2010	100.0	3.0	21.1	21.8	21.5	17.4	6.3	8.9
2008	100.0	4.5	17.6	20.4	21.2	18.7	7.8	9.8
2006	100.0	3.6	19.9	18.8	23.9	16.6	8.0	9.3
2004	100.0	4.1	17.2	20.1	25.3	18.6	5.5	9.2
2002	100.0	5.7	19.2	23.1	22.8	15.7	6.7	6.8
2000	100.0	4.0	19.0	20.8	21.3	18.3	7.7	8.7
1998	100.0	3.6	18.0	21.1	21.4	21.1	6.7	8.0
1996	100.0	4.1	20.2	20.4	23.1	17.1	7.3	7.7
1994	100.0	2.7	20.1	20.2	22.6	18.6	7.1	8.7
1993	100.0	3.4	20.7	19.9	20.0	21.4	6.2	8.4
1991	100.0	4.1	20.2	18.6	23.7	15.7	7.5	10.2
1990	100.0	2.7	17.5	20.5	22.9	19.4	6.6	10.5
1989	100.0	4.4	18.0	17.0	22.8	19.0	7.9	10.9
1988	100.0	3.2	17.2	20.9	24.3	18.0	6.4	10.0
1986	100.0	1.9	19.5	18.4	23.8	20.7	5.4	10.4
1985	100.0	2.9	19.4	19.2	22.2	18.4	9.3	8.5
1983	100.0	2.2	18.8	20.6	22.2	18.9	6.7	10.6
1982	100.0	4.2	17.2	21.1	21.5	18.6	8.7	8.7
1978	100.0	1.7	20.3	20.4	16.6	21.3	8.6	11.2
1977	100.0	3.1	18.7	19.8	22.3	18.8	7.4	9.8
1975	100.0	3.9	17.3	17.0	23.1	19.1	7.8	11.8
1974	100.0	2.7	19.5	18.1	22.2	18.7	8.3	10.5

Source: Survey Documentation and Analysis, Computer-assisted Survey Methods Program, University of California, Berkeley, General Social Survey, 1972–2012 Cumulative Data Files, Internet site http://sda.berkeley.edu/cgi-bin/hsda?harcsda+gss12; calculations by New Strategist

Table 6.62 Spend Evening at Bar, 1974 to 2012

"How often do you spend the evening at a bar?"

(percent distribution of people aged 18 or older by response for selected years)

	total	almost daily	several times a week	several times a month	once a month	several times a year	once a year	never
2012	100.0%	0.6%	6.6%	8.4%	11.0%	11.2%	13.2%	49.0%
2010	100.0	0.9	6.4	9.2	11.3	13.7	12.4	46.2
2008	100.0	0.6	7.2	5.6	11.7	14.0	11.9	49.0
2006	100.0	0.6	6.0	5.9	10.6	12.7	13.3	50.9
2004	100.0	0.6	7.2	6.4	10.9	11.3	15.2	48.4
2002	100.0	1.1	8.9	8.4	12.4	11.7	13.1	44.5
2000	100.0	1.1	7.8	7.3	10.2	11.9	12.7	49.1
1998	100.0	1.5	6.3	6.4	10.4	12.6	13.1	49.7
1996	100.0	1.2	7.3	6.8	10.1	12.5	13.4	48.6
1994	100.0	1.1	7.2	7.2	9.2	13.1	12.5	49.7
1993	100.0	0.7	7.3	7.3	10.3	11.4	11.4	51.7
1991	100.0	1.8	6.9	5.7	10.5	10.3	11.6	53.2
1990	100.0	0.6	7.7	6.6	9.8	11.1	12.3	52.0
1989	100.0	1.2	7.2	5.2	8.5	10.4	11.0	56.6
1988	100.0	0.9	8.8	6.6	9.8	10.4	12.1	51.4
1986	100.0	1.1	8.4	5.7	9.7	11.2	10.1	53.8
1985	100.0	1.4	8.2	8.5	11.0	11.5	11.7	47.7
1983	100.0	1.5	10.1	8.9	7.5	11.0	10.9	50.1
1982	100.0	1.7	11.0	7.2	8.6	12.0	11.5	48.1
1978	100.0	1.6	8.8	8.9	7.7	13.2	9.7	50.0
1977	100.0	2.5	8.8	8.4	9.9	10.6	9.7	50.1
1975	100.0	1.6	7.6	6.7	9.1	9.1	9.7	56.3
1974	100.0	2.3	9.2	6.7	9.1	12.5	7.5	52.7

Source: Survey Documentation and Analysis, Computer-assisted Survey Methods Program, University of California, Berkeley, General Social Survey, 1972–2012 Cumulative Data Files, Internet site http://sda.berkeley.edu/cgi-bin/hsda?harcsda+gss12; calculations by New Strategist

7

Diversity

The election and reelection of the first black president in 2008 and 2012 held out the promise that America was becoming a "postracial" society. Unfortunately, becoming "postracial" is a slow process. Results from the General Social Survey show how much progress we have made, and how much farther we have to go. Integration is now the norm in neighborhoods and the workplace, but questions about hard work and intelligence reveal deep-seated prejudices against African Americans.

No Change

• **Most continue to oppose affirmative action.** More than 80 percent of the public is against affirmative action for blacks—a figure that has not changed over the past two decades. Even the majority of blacks are against it.

• **Most think blacks should work their way up.** More than 70 percent of Americans agree that blacks should overcome prejudice without favors, a figure that has fallen only slightly over the past two decades. The 58 percent majority of African Americans agree.

Big Changes

• **Fewer think discrimination explains the lower socioeconomic status of blacks.** The percentage who blame discrimination for the lower socioeconomic status of blacks has fallen from a high of 46 percent in 1985 to 35 percent in 2012.

• **More live in integrated neighborhoods.** The percentage of people who say blacks live in their neighborhood has grown from 30 to 72 percent during the past 40 years.

• **Fewer oppose interracial marriages.** The percentage of Americans who would oppose having a close relative marry an African American fell from 57 percent in 1990 to just 17 percent in 2012. Similarly, opposition to a close relative marrying a Hispanic or Asian has also declined.

Diversity: 2012 Profiles

Table 7.1 Reason for Racial Differences: Discrimination, 2012

"On the average (blacks/African Americans) have worse jobs, income, and housing than white people. Do you think these differences are mainly due to discrimination?"

(percent of people aged 18 or older responding by selected characteristics, 2012)

	total	yes	no
Total people	**100.0%**	**34.9%**	**65.1%**
Men	100.0	33.8	66.2
Women	100.0	35.9	64.1
Millennials	100.0	35.9	64.1
Generation Xers	100.0	29.3	70.7
Baby Boomers	100.0	35.0	65.0
Older Americans	100.0	41.7	58.3
Black	100.0	46.1	53.9
Hispanic	100.0	44.1	55.9
Non-Hispanic white	100.0	30.3	69.7
Northeast	100.0	38.4	61.6
Midwest	100.0	35.0	65.0
South	100.0	30.4	69.6
West	100.0	39.7	60.3
Not a college graduate	100.0	35.7	64.3
Bachelor's degree or more	100.0	32.8	67.2

Note: Millennials are aged 18 to 35; Generation Xers are aged 36 to 47; Baby Boomers are aged 48 to 66; Older Americans are aged 67 or older.

Source: Survey Documentation and Analysis, Computer-assisted Survey Methods Program, University of California, Berkeley, General Social Survey, 1972–2012 Cumulative Data Files, Internet site http://sda.berkeley.edu/cgi-bin/hsda?harcsda+gss12; calculations by New Strategist

Table 7.2 Reason for Racial Differences: Inborn Ability, 2012

"On the average (blacks/African Americans) have worse jobs, income,
and housing than white people. Do you think these differences
are because most have less inborn ability to learn?"

(percent of people aged 18 or older responding by selected characteristics, 2012)

	total	yes	no
Total people	**100.0%**	**9.8%**	**90.2%**
Men	100.0	9.4	90.6
Women	100.0	10.2	89.8
Millennials	100.0	9.1	90.9
Generation Xers	100.0	10.3	89.7
Baby Boomers	100.0	6.6	93.4
Older Americans	100.0	18.2	81.8
Black	100.0	12.5	87.5
Hispanic	100.0	12.8	87.2
Non-Hispanic white	100.0	7.5	92.5
Northeast	100.0	11.7	88.3
Midwest	100.0	6.9	93.1
South	100.0	11.7	88.3
West	100.0	8.5	91.5
Not a college graduate	100.0	11.9	88.1
Bachelor's degree or more	100.0	4.5	95.5

Note: Millennials are aged 18 to 35; Generation Xers are aged 36 to 47; Baby Boomers are aged 48 to 66; Older Americans are aged 67 or older.
Source: Survey Documentation and Analysis, Computer-assisted Survey Methods Program, University of California, Berkeley, General Social Survey, 1972–2012 Cumulative Data Files, Internet site http://sda.berkeley.edu/cgi-bin/hsda?harcsda+gss12; calculations by New Strategist

Table 7.3 Reason for Racial Differences: Education, 2012

"On the average (blacks/African Americans) have worse jobs, income, and housing than white people. Do you think these differences are because most don't have the chance for education that it takes to rise out of poverty?"

(percent of people aged 18 or older responding by selected characteristics, 2012)

	total	yes	no
Total people	**100.0%**	**42.0%**	**58.0%**
Men	100.0	39.3	60.7
Women	100.0	44.3	55.7
Millennials	100.0	38.0	62.0
Generation Xers	100.0	42.3	57.7
Baby Boomers	100.0	43.0	57.0
Older Americans	100.0	50.0	50.0
Black	100.0	46.1	53.9
Hispanic	100.0	38.0	62.0
Non-Hispanic white	100.0	41.4	58.6
Northeast	100.0	46.3	53.7
Midwest	100.0	41.5	58.5
South	100.0	36.6	63.4
West	100.0	47.7	52.3
Not a college graduate	100.0	37.5	62.5
Bachelor's degree or more	100.0	54.1	45.9

Note: Millennials are aged 18 to 35; Generation Xers are aged 36 to 47; Baby Boomers are aged 48 to 66; Older Americans are aged 67 or older.
Source: Survey Documentation and Analysis, Computer-assisted Survey Methods Program, University of California, Berkeley, General Social Survey, 1972–2012 Cumulative Data Files, Internet site http://sda.berkeley.edu/cgi-bin/hsda?harcsda+gss12; calculations by New Strategist

Table 7.4 Reason for Racial Differences: Lack of Will, 2012

"On the average (blacks/African Americans) have worse jobs, income, and housing than white people. Do you think these differences are because most just don't have the motivation or willpower to pull themselves up out of poverty?"

(percent of people aged 18 or older responding by selected characteristics, 2012)

	total	yes	no
Total people	**100.0%**	**50.2%**	**49.8%**
Men	100.0	52.9	47.1
Women	100.0	47.9	52.1
Millennials	100.0	46.0	54.0
Generation Xers	100.0	50.6	49.4
Baby Boomers	100.0	50.8	49.2
Older Americans	100.0	60.6	39.4
Black	100.0	50.7	49.3
Hispanic	100.0	64.2	35.8
Non-Hispanic white	100.0	46.3	53.7
Northeast	100.0	39.9	60.1
Midwest	100.0	52.5	47.5
South	100.0	55.8	44.2
West	100.0	46.6	53.4
Not a college graduate	100.0	57.3	42.7
Bachelor's degree or more	100.0	31.1	68.9

Note: Millennials are aged 18 to 35; Generation Xers are aged 36 to 47; Baby Boomers are aged 48 to 66; Older Americans are aged 67 or older.
Source: Survey Documentation and Analysis, Computer-assisted Survey Methods Program, University of California, Berkeley, General Social Survey, 1972–2012 Cumulative Data Files, Internet site http://sda.berkeley.edu/cgi-bin/hsda?harcsda+gss12; calculations by New Strategist

Table 7.5 Are Blacks Hardworking or Lazy, 2012

"On a seven-point scale on which the characteristics of people in a group
can be rated, a score of 1 means that you think almost all of the people in that
group are hardworking. A score of 7 means that you think almost everyone
in the group is lazy. A score of 4 means that you think that the group
is not towards one end or another, and you may choose any number in
between that comes closest to where you think people in that group
stand. Are blacks hardworking or do they tend to be lazy?"

(percent of people aged 18 or older responding by selected characteristics, 2012)

	total	1 hardworking	2	3	4 neither	5	6	7 lazy
Total people	**100.0%**	**1.8%**	**3.5%**	**12.0%**	**49.1%**	**21.1%**	**8.7%**	**3.9%**
Men	100.0	0.9	2.7	12.5	46.6	24.3	9.6	3.4
Women	100.0	2.5	4.2	11.5	51.2	18.3	7.9	4.3
Millennials	100.0	0.4	2.6	11.9	54.7	20.8	6.9	2.7
Generation Xers	100.0	2.2	5.9	12.2	47.7	19.5	8.7	3.8
Baby Boomers	100.0	2.4	3.2	12.2	49.1	20.7	7.7	4.8
Older Americans	100.0	3.5	2.5	11.4	35.8	25.8	15.9	5.1
Black	100.0	4.6	5.5	18.0	45.6	16.6	7.4	2.3
Hispanic	100.0	0.9	5.3	8.0	33.5	26.8	13.0	12.6
Non-Hispanic white	100.0	1.5	2.7	11.9	52.9	20.4	8.3	2.4
Northeast	100.0	1.8	3.1	12.5	52.8	18.6	7.5	3.7
Midwest	100.0	0.9	2.0	12.5	48.1	23.1	10.7	2.7
South	100.0	2.9	3.9	12.1	46.0	22.6	7.3	5.2
West	100.0	0.8	4.5	10.9	52.5	18.5	9.6	3.2
Not a college graduate	100.0	1.8	3.6	12.6	44.3	22.6	10.2	4.9
Bachelor's degree or more	100.0	1.7	3.2	10.1	62.0	17.2	4.6	1.1

Note: Millennials are aged 18 to 35; Generation Xers are aged 36 to 47; Baby Boomers are aged 48 to 66; Older Americans are aged 67 or older.
Source: Survey Documentation and Analysis, Computer-assisted Survey Methods Program, University of California, Berkeley, General Social Survey, 1972–2012 Cumulative Data Files, Internet site http://sda.berkeley.edu/cgi-bin/hsda?harcsda+gss12; calculations by New Strategist

Table 7.6 Are Whites Hardworking or Lazy, 2012

"On a seven-point scale on which the characteristics of people in a group can be rated, a score of 1 means that you think almost all of the people in that group are hardworking. A score of 7 means that you think almost everyone in the group is lazy. A score of 4 means that you think that the group is not towards one end or another, and you may choose any number in between that comes closest to where you think people in that group stand. Are whites hardworking or do they tend to be lazy?"

(percent of people aged 18 or older responding by selected characteristics, 2012)

	total	1 hardworking	2	3	4 neither	5	6	7 lazy
Total people	100.0%	6.4%	10.3%	21.0%	49.4%	9.7%	2.1%	1.1%
Men	100.0	6.1	8.9	22.6	48.0	10.9	2.1	1.4
Women	100.0	6.6	11.6	19.7	50.6	8.7	2.0	0.8
Millennials	100.0	2.1	11.3	22.0	51.1	10.7	1.8	1.0
Generation Xers	100.0	7.4	7.3	21.3	49.3	11.1	2.3	1.4
Baby Boomers	100.0	7.4	10.8	18.7	53.0	6.3	2.7	1.0
Older Americans	100.0	13.6	12.0	22.3	37.4	12.4	1.2	1.2
Black	100.0	7.3	8.6	13.8	53.7	13.4	2.5	0.7
Hispanic	100.0	8.1	14.9	22.0	41.4	9.3	2.2	2.2
Non-Hispanic white	100.0	6.0	9.7	22.5	49.9	9.7	1.9	0.4
Northeast	100.0	6.5	10.1	19.4	50.8	11.3	1.8	0.0
Midwest	100.0	6.0	11.2	22.6	47.8	10.7	1.7	0.0
South	100.0	8.8	9.1	19.5	48.2	9.5	2.5	2.4
West	100.0	2.8	11.5	23.1	51.8	8.0	2.0	0.9
Not a college graduate	100.0	7.8	11.4	21.6	44.9	10.7	2.3	1.3
Bachelor's degree or more	100.0	2.6	7.5	19.4	61.3	7.0	1.6	0.5

Note: Millennials are aged 18 to 35; Generation Xers are aged 36 to 47; Baby Boomers are aged 48 to 66; Older Americans are aged 67 or older.
Source: Survey Documentation and Analysis, Computer-assisted Survey Methods Program, University of California, Berkeley, General Social Survey, 1972–2012 Cumulative Data Files, Internet site http://sda.berkeley.edu/cgi-bin/hsda?harcsda+gss12; calculations by New Strategist

Table 7.7 Are Blacks Unintelligent or Intelligent, 2012

"On a seven-point scale on which the characteristics of people in a group can be rated, a score of 1 means that you think almost all of the people in that group are unintelligent. A score of 7 means that you think almost everyone in the group is intelligent. A score of 4 means that you think that the group is not towards one end or another, and you may choose any number in between that comes closest to where you think people in that group stand. Do blacks tend to be unintelligent or intelligent?"

(percent of people aged 18 or older responding by selected characteristics, 2012)

	total	1 unintelligent	2	3	4 neither	5	6	7 intelligent
Total people	**100.0%**	**0.0%**	**2.8%**	**10.6%**	**57.3%**	**18.8%**	**7.5%**	**2.9%**
Men	100.0	0.0	3.5	13.3	54.9	19.5	6.1	2.7
Women	100.0	0.1	2.2	8.2	59.4	18.3	8.8	3.1
Millennials	100.0	0.0	1.9	8.4	62.1	18.5	7.1	2.0
Generation Xers	100.0	0.0	1.7	9.9	58.6	18.4	7.9	3.6
Baby Boomers	100.0	0.1	3.6	8.9	55.1	20.0	8.9	3.5
Older Americans	100.0	0.0	5.6	21.6	46.1	18.3	5.2	3.2
Black	100.0	0.0	0.9	6.3	51.3	22.7	12.0	6.8
Hispanic	100.0	0.0	4.1	16.9	47.6	21.0	6.6	3.9
Non-Hispanic white	100.0	0.0	3.0	10.2	60.2	17.9	6.8	1.8
Northeast	100.0	0.0	3.2	8.2	58.5	19.9	6.9	3.3
Midwest	100.0	0.0	5.3	8.6	55.9	21.1	6.5	2.6
South	100.0	0.0	1.4	11.8	55.4	19.7	7.8	3.8
West	100.0	0.1	2.4	12.2	60.8	14.4	8.6	1.5
Not a college graduate	100.0	0.0	3.4	10.8	53.6	20.0	8.6	3.4
Bachelor's degree or more	100.0	0.0	1.2	10.0	67.0	15.6	4.6	1.7

Note: Millennials are aged 18 to 35; Generation Xers are aged 36 to 47; Baby Boomers are aged 48 to 66; Older Americans are aged 67 or older.
Source: Survey Documentation and Analysis, Computer-assisted Survey Methods Program, University of California, Berkeley, General Social Survey, 1972–2012 Cumulative Data Files, Internet site http://sda.berkeley.edu/cgi-bin/hsda?harcsda+gss12; calculations by New Strategist

Table 7.8 Are Whites Unintelligent or Intelligent, 2012

"On a seven-point scale on which the characteristics of people in a group can be rated, a score of 1 means that you think almost all of the people in that group are unintelligent. A score of 7 means that you think almost everyone in the group is intelligent. A score of 4 means that you think that the group is not towards one end or another, and you may choose any number in between that comes closest to where you think people in that group stand. Do whites tend to be unintelligent or intelligent?"

(percent of people aged 18 or older responding by selected characteristics, 2012)

	total	1 unintelligent	2	3	4 neither	5	6	7 intelligent
Total people	100.0%	0.5%	1.8%	5.3%	47.9%	25.1%	13.6%	5.8%
Men	100.0	0.2	2.2	5.2	46.8	25.8	13.2	6.6
Women	100.0	0.7	1.4	5.5	48.9	24.5	14.0	5.1
Millennials	100.0	0.0	0.4	5.1	49.7	25.9	15.8	3.1
Generation Xers	100.0	0.3	0.9	4.9	54.1	21.3	12.2	6.3
Baby Boomers	100.0	1.3	3.4	5.9	44.6	24.6	13.4	6.9
Older Americans	100.0	0.2	3.5	5.7	40.2	29.8	10.6	10.0
Black	100.0	0.2	0.9	7.0	44.3	23.2	15.6	8.8
Hispanic	100.0	1.8	4.8	7.8	36.2	24.5	14.5	10.5
Non-Hispanic white	100.0	0.1	1.4	4.0	51.9	26.2	12.4	4.0
Northeast	100.0	0.0	1.2	6.5	54.4	19.9	10.4	7.7
Midwest	100.0	0.0	1.4	5.3	42.3	32.8	12.9	5.2
South	100.0	0.9	2.2	4.3	45.5	25.0	16.0	6.1
West	100.0	0.5	1.8	6.3	52.9	21.0	12.7	4.7
Not a college graduate	100.0	0.5	2.3	5.4	42.9	25.8	16.1	7.1
Bachelor's degree or more	100.0	0.5	0.4	5.3	61.3	23.1	7.0	2.4

Note: Millennials are aged 18 to 35; Generation Xers are aged 36 to 47; Baby Boomers are aged 48 to 66; Older Americans are aged 67 or older.
Source: Survey Documentation and Analysis, Computer-assisted Survey Methods Program, University of California, Berkeley, General Social Survey, 1972–2012 Cumulative Data Files, Internet site http://sda.berkeley.edu/cgi-bin/hsda?harcsda+gss12; calculations by New Strategist

Table 7.9 Are Blacks Rich or Poor, 2012

"On a seven-point scale on which the characteristics of people in a group can be rated, a score of 1 means that you think almost all of the people in that group are rich. A score of 7 means that you think almost everyone in the group is poor. A score of 4 means that you think that the group is not towards one end or another, and you may choose any number in between that comes closest to where you think people in that group stand. Are blacks rich or poor?"

(percent of people aged 18 or older responding by selected characteristics, 2012)

	total	1 rich	2	3	4 neither	5	6	7 poor
Total people	**100.0%**	**0.3%**	**1.5%**	**6.3%**	**29.7%**	**40.3%**	**18.7%**	**3.3%**
Men	100.0	0.3	1.8	7.8	25.6	41.9	19.6	2.9
Women	100.0	0.3	1.2	5.0	33.2	38.8	17.9	3.6
Millennials	100.0	0.0	1.6	6.1	34.6	42.4	13.2	2.2
Generation Xers	100.0	1.2	0.7	9.0	29.7	38.9	18.0	2.4
Baby Boomers	100.0	0.0	1.9	6.2	26.5	38.2	22.9	4.3
Older Americans	100.0	0.0	1.7	2.7	23.8	40.2	26.0	5.6
Black	100.0	1.9	2.2	3.8	37.6	39.5	11.2	3.7
Hispanic	100.0	0.0	1.3	2.4	33.4	31.2	26.3	5.4
Non-Hispanic white	100.0	0.0	1.1	7.5	28.5	42.7	17.9	2.3
Northeast	100.0	0.0	2.0	7.3	31.2	38.0	17.8	3.8
Midwest	100.0	0.0	0.8	8.3	26.4	43.9	19.2	1.4
South	100.0	0.7	1.6	6.5	32.2	38.7	15.4	4.9
West	100.0	0.0	1.7	3.3	28.1	40.7	23.9	2.2
Not a college graduate	100.0	0.4	1.8	6.3	32.9	35.8	18.8	4.0
Bachelor's degree or more	100.0	0.0	0.8	6.3	21.3	51.9	18.2	1.4

Note: Millennials are aged 18 to 35; Generation Xers are aged 36 to 47; Baby Boomers are aged 48 to 66; Older Americans are aged 67 or older.
Source: Survey Documentation and Analysis, Computer-assisted Survey Methods Program, University of California, Berkeley, General Social Survey, 1972–2012 Cumulative Data Files, Internet site http://sda.berkeley.edu/cgi-bin/hsda?harcsda+gss12; calculations by New Strategist

Table 7.10 Are Whites Rich or Poor, 2012

"On a seven-point scale on which the characteristics of people in a group can be rated, a score of 1 means that you think almost all of the people in that group are rich. A score of 7 means that you think almost everyone in the group is poor. A score of 4 means that you think that the group is not towards one end or another, and you may choose any number in between that comes closest to where you think people in that group stand. Are whites rich or poor?"

(percent of people aged 18 or older responding by selected characteristics, 2012)

	total	1 rich	2	3	4 neither	5	6	7 poor
Total people	**100.0%**	**5.9%**	**7.6%**	**27.0%**	**51.8%**	**6.6%**	**0.9%**	**0.2%**
Men	100.0	6.5	8.3	29.9	47.2	6.7	1.0	0.3
Women	100.0	5.3	7.0	24.4	55.8	6.5	0.8	0.1
Millennials	100.0	6.5	11.0	34.2	44.1	3.7	0.6	0.0
Generation Xers	100.0	8.1	7.3	19.9	55.8	7.0	0.9	0.9
Baby Boomers	100.0	3.1	5.9	27.7	55.1	6.9	1.3	0.0
Older Americans	100.0	6.8	3.0	17.0	59.2	13.3	0.7	0.0
Black	100.0	12.4	8.9	21.8	50.8	5.4	0.7	0.0
Hispanic	100.0	9.6	13.4	33.2	38.1	4.4	0.0	1.3
Non-Hispanic white	100.0	2.3	6.1	26.9	56.1	7.6	1.1	0.0
Northeast	100.0	9.1	9.8	25.9	48.1	6.8	0.4	0.0
Midwest	100.0	2.7	6.4	32.7	48.0	9.2	1.0	0.0
South	100.0	8.5	6.9	21.7	55.9	5.9	1.1	0.0
West	100.0	2.8	8.5	30.4	51.9	5.0	0.6	0.9
Not a college graduate	100.0	6.8	7.3	25.6	51.8	7.2	1.0	0.1
Bachelor's degree or more	100.0	3.4	8.4	30.5	51.8	5.0	0.4	0.5

Note: Millennials are aged 18 to 35; Generation Xers are aged 36 to 47; Baby Boomers are aged 48 to 66; Older Americans are aged 67 or older.
Source: Survey Documentation and Analysis, Computer-assisted Survey Methods Program, University of California, Berkeley, General Social Survey, 1972–2012 Cumulative Data Files, Internet site http://sda.berkeley.edu/cgi-bin/hsda?harcsda+gss12; calculations by New Strategist

Table 7.11 Racial Makeup of Workplace, 2012

"Are the people who work where you work all white, mostly white,
about half and half, mostly black, or all black?"

(percent of people aged 18 or older responding by selected characteristics, 2012)

	total	all white	mostly white	half and half	mostly black	all black
Total people	**100.0%**	**22.3%**	**43.8%**	**26.9%**	**6.0%**	**1.0%**
Men	100.0	21.3	50.6	22.9	4.1	1.0
Women	100.0	23.4	36.7	31.2	7.9	0.9
Millennials	100.0	23.6	38.2	30.4	6.8	1.1
Generation Xers	100.0	18.1	44.7	30.8	5.8	0.6
Baby Boomers	100.0	22.6	50.2	20.8	5.1	1.3
Older Americans	100.0	41.0	33.0	18.8	7.3	0.0
Black	100.0	2.7	27.9	40.4	21.8	7.1
Hispanic	100.0	20.1	43.4	29.9	5.6	1.0
Non-Hispanic white	100.0	28.9	46.6	20.9	3.5	0.0
Northeast	100.0	27.4	46.9	22.3	3.4	0.0
Midwest	100.0	22.3	52.2	22.5	3.0	0.0
South	100.0	20.6	34.7	31.6	11.2	2.0
West	100.0	21.1	48.9	27.1	1.9	1.0
Not a college graduate	100.0	24.7	38.2	28.5	7.5	1.1
Bachelor's degree or more	100.0	17.4	55.5	23.7	2.8	0.7

Note: Millennials are aged 18 to 35; Generation Xers are aged 36 to 47; Baby Boomers are aged 48 to 66; Older Americans are aged 67 or older.
Source: Survey Documentation and Analysis, Computer-assisted Survey Methods Program, University of California, Berkeley, General Social Survey, 1972–2012 Cumulative Data Files, Internet site http://sda.berkeley.edu/cgi-bin/hsda?harcsda+gss12; calculations by New Strategist

Table 7.12 Blacks Should Overcome Prejudice without Favors, 2012

"Do you agree strongly, agree somewhat, neither agree nor disagree, disagree somewhat, or disagree strongly with the following statement? Irish, Italian, Jewish and many other minorities overcame prejudice and worked their way up; blacks should do the same without any special favors."

(percent of people aged 18 or older responding by selected characteristics, 2012)

	total	agree strongly	agree somewhat	neither agree nor disagree	disagree somewhat	disagree strongly
Total people	**100.0%**	**41.7%**	**29.1%**	**14.5%**	**9.1%**	**5.5%**
Men	100.0	40.4	31.5	14.2	9.8	4.1
Women	100.0	42.9	27.0	14.7	8.5	6.8
Millennials	100.0	38.8	33.2	16.7	7.3	4.0
Generation Xers	100.0	42.7	21.4	16.2	12.7	7.1
Baby Boomers	100.0	40.8	31.3	11.7	9.3	6.9
Older Americans	100.0	50.6	25.7	12.4	7.5	3.8
Black	100.0	35.9	21.8	9.5	15.4	17.4
Hispanic	100.0	38.9	34.3	16.9	5.6	4.2
Non-Hispanic white	100.0	45.2	28.1	15.0	8.5	3.2
Northeast	100.0	35.7	27.5	17.4	12.2	7.2
Midwest	100.0	47.9	27.2	12.2	9.0	3.7
South	100.0	44.9	29.7	12.1	8.1	5.2
West	100.0	35.1	31.2	18.4	8.7	6.6
Not a college graduate	100.0	46.6	31.3	11.7	6.5	3.9
Bachelor's degree or more	100.0	28.9	23.3	21.9	16.2	9.7

Note: Millennials are aged 18 to 35; Generation Xers are aged 36 to 47; Baby Boomers are aged 48 to 66; Older Americans are aged 67 or older.
Source: Survey Documentation and Analysis, Computer-assisted Survey Methods Program, University of California, Berkeley, General Social Survey, 1972–2012 Cumulative Data Files, Internet site http://sda.berkeley.edu/cgi-bin/hsda?harcsda+gss12; calculations by New Strategist

Table 7.13 Should Government Aid Blacks, 2012

"Some people think that (blacks/African Americans) have been discriminated against for so long that the government has a special obligation to help improve their living standards. Others believe that the government should not be giving special treatment to (blacks/African Americans). Where would you place yourself on this scale?"

(percent of people aged 18 or older responding by selected characteristics, 2012)

	total	1 government should help	2	3 agree with both	4	5 no special treatment
Total people	100.0%	7.7%	8.4%	29.6%	18.6%	35.6%
Men	100.0	8.0	8.0	26.9	17.7	39.4
Women	100.0	7.5	8.8	31.9	19.5	32.3
Millennials	100.0	7.0	10.4	32.1	20.0	30.5
Generation Xers	100.0	8.0	7.5	30.3	18.2	36.0
Baby Boomers	100.0	7.4	7.6	26.0	19.4	39.7
Older Americans	100.0	9.8	7.2	31.3	14.8	36.9
Black	100.0	21.7	14.9	41.9	12.5	9.0
Hispanic	100.0	13.0	7.0	37.4	10.1	32.5
Non-Hispanic white	100.0	2.7	7.5	25.2	22.0	42.6
Northeast	100.0	11.3	9.6	29.9	12.1	37.1
Midwest	100.0	7.5	5.5	26.4	24.4	36.3
South	100.0	7.1	6.7	31.3	16.9	38.0
West	100.0	6.2	13.1	29.9	21.1	29.8
Not a college graduate	100.0	8.3	7.0	30.7	16.7	37.3
Bachelor's degree or more	100.0	6.3	11.9	27.0	23.4	31.4

Note: Millennials are aged 18 to 35; Generation Xers are aged 36 to 47; Baby Boomers are aged 48 to 66; Older Americans are aged 67 or older.
Source: Survey Documentation and Analysis, Computer-assisted Survey Methods Program, University of California, Berkeley, General Social Survey, 1972–2012 Cumulative Data Files, Internet site http://sda.berkeley.edu/cgi-bin/hsda?harcsda+gss12; calculations by New Strategist

Table 7.14 Affirmative Action, 2012

"Some people say that because of past discrimination, blacks should be given preference in hiring and promotion. Others say that such preferences in hiring and promotion of blacks is wrong because it discriminates against whites. What about your opinion—are you for or against preferential hiring and promotion of blacks?"

(percent of people aged 18 or older responding by selected characteristics, 2012)

	total	strongly support	support	oppose	strongly oppose
Total people	**100.0%**	**10.6%**	**8.3%**	**27.6%**	**53.5%**
Men	100.0	9.7	8.4	24.4	57.4
Women	100.0	11.3	8.2	30.4	50.0
Millennials	100.0	8.3	10.7	29.2	51.8
Generation Xers	100.0	9.8	7.6	29.7	52.9
Baby Boomers	100.0	12.8	7.6	22.7	56.9
Older Americans	100.0	12.9	5.2	31.2	50.7
Black	100.0	30.4	11.5	28.1	30.0
Hispanic	100.0	9.0	10.3	34.5	46.1
Non-Hispanic white	100.0	6.7	6.9	26.3	60.2
Northeast	100.0	11.1	11.2	25.0	52.7
Midwest	100.0	8.7	6.3	26.4	58.6
South	100.0	12.6	10.0	26.2	51.2
West	100.0	8.9	5.8	32.7	52.5
Not a college graduate	100.0	11.3	7.1	26.9	54.7
Bachelor's degree or more	100.0	8.6	11.5	29.5	50.4

Note: Millennials are aged 18 to 35; Generation Xers are aged 36 to 47; Baby Boomers are aged 48 to 66; Older Americans are aged 67 or older.
Source: Survey Documentation and Analysis, Computer-assisted Survey Methods Program, University of California, Berkeley, General Social Survey, 1972–2012 Cumulative Data Files, Internet site http://sda.berkeley.edu/cgi-bin/hsda?harcsda+gss12; calculations by New Strategist

Table 7.15 Whites Hurt by Affirmative Action, 2012

"What do you think the chances are these days that a white person won't get a job or promotion while an equally qualified black person gets one instead?"

(percent of people aged 18 or older responding by selected characteristics, 2012)

	total	very likely	somewhat likely	not very likely
Total people	**100.0%**	**16.7%**	**41.9%**	**41.4%**
Men	100.0	16.7	39.8	43.5
Women	100.0	16.7	43.7	39.6
Millennials	100.0	11.1	44.4	44.4
Generation Xers	100.0	13.8	39.2	47.0
Baby Boomers	100.0	22.7	39.1	38.3
Older Americans	100.0	19.3	48.3	32.4
Black	100.0	15.0	33.3	51.7
Hispanic	100.0	18.4	35.4	46.2
Non-Hispanic white	100.0	16.7	45.4	37.9
Northeast	100.0	13.7	43.1	43.2
Midwest	100.0	16.4	47.7	35.9
South	100.0	21.6	37.7	40.7
West	100.0	10.6	42.5	46.9
Not a college graduate	100.0	19.5	44.1	36.4
Bachelor's degree or more	100.0	9.3	36.2	54.4

Note: Millennials are aged 18 to 35; Generation Xers are aged 36 to 47; Baby Boomers are aged 48 to 66; Older Americans are aged 67 or older.
Source: Survey Documentation and Analysis, Computer-assisted Survey Methods Program, University of California, Berkeley, General Social Survey, 1972–2012 Cumulative Data Files, Internet site http://sda.berkeley.edu/cgi-bin/hsda?harcsda+gss12; calculations by New Strategist

Table 7.16 Blacks Living in the Neighborhood, 2012

"Are there any (blacks/African Americans) living in this neighborhood now?"

(percent of people aged 18 or older responding by selected characteristics, 2012)

	total	yes	no
Total people	**100.0%**	**72.3%**	**27.7%**
Men	100.0	72.5	27.5
Women	100.0	72.1	27.9
Millennials	100.0	81.6	18.4
Generation Xers	100.0	72.2	27.8
Baby Boomers	100.0	69.4	30.6
Older Americans	100.0	56.8	43.2
Black	100.0	92.1	7.9
Hispanic	100.0	71.0	29.0
Non-Hispanic white	100.0	68.1	31.9
Northeast	100.0	73.5	26.5
Midwest	100.0	69.2	30.8
South	100.0	76.4	23.6
West	100.0	67.3	32.7
Not a college graduate	100.0	70.9	29.1
Bachelor's degree or more	100.0	76.0	24.0

Note: Millennials are aged 18 to 35; Generation Xers are aged 36 to 47; Baby Boomers are aged 48 to 66; Older Americans are aged 67 or older.
Source: Survey Documentation and Analysis, Computer-assisted Survey Methods Program, University of California, Berkeley, General Social Survey, 1972–2012 Cumulative Data Files, Internet site http://sda.berkeley.edu/cgi-bin/hsda?harcsda+gss12; calculations by New Strategist

Table 7.17 Open Housing Laws, 2012

"Suppose there is a community-wide vote on the general housing issue. There are two possible laws to vote on: One law says that a homeowner can decide for himself to whom he sells his house, even if he prefers not to sell to blacks/African Americans. The other law says a homeowner cannot refuse to sell to someone because of their race or color. Which law would you vote for?"

(percent of people aged 18 or older responding by selected characteristics, 2012)

	total	owner decides	can't discriminate	neither
Total people	**100.0%**	**25.0%**	**72.3%**	**2.7%**
Men	100.0	31.0	67.2	1.8
Women	100.0	20.0	76.5	3.5
Millennials	100.0	21.8	75.0	3.2
Generation Xers	100.0	28.7	67.6	3.7
Baby Boomers	100.0	23.0	75.6	1.4
Older Americans	100.0	32.0	65.8	2.3
Black	100.0	14.1	84.6	1.3
Hispanic	100.0	20.3	77.5	2.2
Non-Hispanic white	100.0	29.7	66.9	3.4
Northeast	100.0	24.6	72.8	2.6
Midwest	100.0	23.9	73.3	2.8
South	100.0	27.3	69.5	3.1
West	100.0	22.5	75.5	2.0
Not a college graduate	100.0	24.4	72.7	2.9
Bachelor's degree or more	100.0	26.6	71.3	2.1

Note: Millennials are aged 18 to 35; Generation Xers are aged 36 to 47; Baby Boomers are aged 48 to 66; Older Americans are aged 67 or older.
Source: Survey Documentation and Analysis, Computer-assisted Survey Methods Program, University of California, Berkeley, General Social Survey, 1972–2012 Cumulative Data Files, Internet site http://sda.berkeley.edu/cgi-bin/hsda?harcsda+gss12; calculations by New Strategist

Table 7.18 Favor Living in Neighborhood Half Black, 2012

"Please tell me whether you would very much favor, somewhat favor,
neither favor nor oppose, somewhat oppose, or very much oppose living
in a neighborhood where half of your neighbors were black?"

(percent of people aged 18 or older responding by selected characteristics, 2012)

	total	strongly favor	favor	neither favor nor oppose	oppose	strongly oppose
Total people	**100.0%**	**8.7%**	**18.4%**	**52.0%**	**14.1%**	**6.8%**
Men	100.0	6.4	17.0	53.0	15.3	8.3
Women	100.0	10.7	19.6	51.1	13.0	5.5
Millennials	100.0	9.9	14.4	56.1	14.3	5.2
Generation Xers	100.0	8.5	18.9	56.1	10.5	6.1
Baby Boomers	100.0	9.3	21.3	49.9	12.8	6.7
Older Americans	100.0	4.9	21.9	38.2	22.3	12.8
Black	100.0	18.2	27.9	41.4	8.9	3.6
Hispanic	100.0	6.5	15.1	50.1	17.3	10.9
Non-Hispanic white	100.0	7.4	17.3	54.4	14.7	6.1
Northeast	100.0	10.4	16.7	59.0	8.6	5.2
Midwest	100.0	9.8	15.9	51.3	16.2	6.8
South	100.0	8.8	22.5	46.7	15.1	6.8
West	100.0	6.4	15.6	56.0	14.1	7.9
Not a college graduate	100.0	8.7	20.2	47.3	16.1	7.8
Bachelor's degree or more	100.0	8.8	13.5	64.7	8.7	4.3

Note: Millennials are aged 18 to 35; Generation Xers are aged 36 to 47; Baby Boomers are aged 48 to 66; Older Americans are aged 67 or older.
Source: Survey Documentation and Analysis, Computer-assisted Survey Methods Program, University of California, Berkeley, General Social Survey, 1972–2012 Cumulative Data Files, Internet site http://sda.berkeley.edu/cgi-bin/hsda?harcsda+gss12; calculations by New Strategist

Table 7.19 Favor Living in Neighborhood Half White, 2012

"Please tell me whether you would very much favor, somewhat favor,
neither favor nor oppose, somewhat oppose, or very much oppose living
in a neighborhood where half of your neighbors were white?"

(percent of people aged 18 or older responding by selected characteristics, 2012)

	total	strongly favor	favor	neither favor nor oppose	oppose	strongly oppose
Total people	100.0%	21.1%	23.4%	51.4%	3.0%	1.1%
Men	100.0	17.9	24.0	54.0	2.8	1.4
Women	100.0	23.9	23.0	49.1	3.1	1.0
Millennials	100.0	24.0	19.0	55.5	1.5	0.0
Generation Xers	100.0	17.5	23.4	55.0	3.4	0.7
Baby Boomers	100.0	20.8	24.7	49.0	3.9	1.6
Older Americans	100.0	20.2	32.9	39.0	4.1	3.8
Black	100.0	23.2	28.6	42.4	3.6	2.2
Hispanic	100.0	14.0	25.4	55.5	3.8	1.3
Non-Hispanic white	100.0	22.7	21.9	51.4	2.8	1.1
Northeast	100.0	19.8	21.0	55.8	1.8	1.6
Midwest	100.0	21.2	25.7	48.1	3.7	1.4
South	100.0	23.9	24.8	46.6	3.5	1.1
West	100.0	17.5	20.8	58.7	2.3	0.7
Not a college graduate	100.0	21.9	25.0	48.4	3.5	1.2
Bachelor's degree or more	100.0	18.9	19.2	59.5	1.4	0.9

Note: Millennials are aged 18 to 35; Generation Xers are aged 36 to 47; Baby Boomers are aged 48 to 66; Older Americans are aged 67 or older.
Source: Survey Documentation and Analysis, Computer-assisted Survey Methods Program, University of California, Berkeley, General Social Survey, 1972–2012 Cumulative Data Files, Internet site http://sda.berkeley.edu/cgi-bin/hsda?harcsda+gss12; calculations by New Strategist

Table 7.20 Favor Relative Marrying an Asian American, 2012

"What about having a close relative marry an Asian American? Would you
be very much in favor of it, somewhat in favor, neither in favor
nor opposed, somewhat opposed, or very opposed to it?"

(percent of people aged 18 or older responding by selected characteristics, 2012)

	total	strongly favor	favor	neither favor nor oppose	oppose	strongly oppose
Total people	**100.0%**	**18.0%**	**14.1%**	**55.8%**	**8.2%**	**3.9%**
Men	100.0	14.2	14.9	56.9	10.6	3.3
Women	100.0	21.3	13.4	54.9	6.1	4.4
Millennials	100.0	21.3	10.4	62.5	4.1	1.7
Generation Xers	100.0	19.2	12.8	58.9	5.4	3.8
Baby Boomers	100.0	17.6	15.5	51.6	10.9	4.4
Older Americans	100.0	8.5	23.4	41.8	17.7	8.7
Black	100.0	35.6	11.9	44.6	4.8	3.0
Hispanic	100.0	23.3	8.4	58.3	5.6	4.4
Non-Hispanic white	100.0	14.4	15.2	56.5	10.2	3.8
Northeast	100.0	14.4	13.4	58.7	8.4	5.1
Midwest	100.0	17.9	15.2	52.3	11.0	3.6
South	100.0	21.1	15.8	48.7	10.1	4.4
West	100.0	15.8	10.8	68.3	2.4	2.6
Not a college graduate	100.0	19.1	14.2	52.5	9.2	5.1
Bachelor's degree or more	100.0	15.1	14.0	64.7	5.5	0.7

Note: Millennials are aged 18 to 35; Generation Xers are aged 36 to 47; Baby Boomers are aged 48 to 66; Older Americans are aged 67 or older.
Source: Survey Documentation and Analysis, Computer-assisted Survey Methods Program, University of California, Berkeley, General Social Survey, 1972–2012 Cumulative Data Files, Internet site http://sda.berkeley.edu/cgi-bin/hsda?harcsda+gss12; calculations by New Strategist

Table 7.21 Favor Relative Marrying a Black Person, 2012

"What about having a close relative marry a black person? Would you be very much in favor of it, somewhat in favor, neither in favor nor opposed, somewhat opposed, or very opposed to it?"

(percent of people aged 18 or older responding by selected characteristics, 2012)

	total	strongly favor	favor	neither favor nor oppose	oppose	strongly oppose
Total people	100.0%	17.9%	12.5%	52.8%	8.3%	8.6%
Men	100.0	13.0	13.7	53.3	10.1	9.9
Women	100.0	22.1	11.4	52.3	6.7	7.4
Millennials	100.0	21.0	11.4	58.9	4.7	4.0
Generation Xers	100.0	20.3	10.0	58.8	4.5	6.4
Baby Boomers	100.0	17.4	14.0	49.9	8.8	9.9
Older Americans	100.0	6.8	16.3	32.5	22.9	21.5
Black	100.0	46.7	11.1	39.9	1.6	0.7
Hispanic	100.0	19.5	13.6	53.5	4.8	8.6
Non-Hispanic white	100.0	12.6	12.5	53.3	11.0	10.6
Northeast	100.0	17.3	12.4	56.5	6.7	7.1
Midwest	100.0	16.5	12.6	48.3	13.3	9.3
South	100.0	20.5	14.8	45.8	8.1	10.7
West	100.0	15.5	8.9	65.2	4.8	5.7
Not a college graduate	100.0	18.6	13.4	49.1	8.2	10.7
Bachelor's degree or more	100.0	15.9	9.9	62.8	8.4	2.9

Note: Millennials are aged 18 to 35; Generation Xers are aged 36 to 47; Baby Boomers are aged 48 to 66; Older Americans are aged 67 or older.
Source: Survey Documentation and Analysis, Computer-assisted Survey Methods Program, University of California, Berkeley, General Social Survey, 1972–2012 Cumulative Data Files, Internet site http://sda.berkeley.edu/cgi-bin/hsda?harcsda+gss12; calculations by New Strategist

Table 7.22 Favor Relative Marrying a Hispanic American, 2012

"What about having a close relative marry a Hispanic American? Would you be very much in favor of it, somewhat in favor, neither in favor nor opposed, somewhat opposed, or very opposed to it?"

(percent of people aged 18 or older responding by selected characteristics, 2012)

	total	strongly favor	favor	neither favor nor oppose	oppose	strongly oppose
Total people	**100.0%**	**20.0%**	**14.3%**	**54.4%**	**7.0%**	**4.3%**
Men	100.0	17.7	15.6	54.4	8.0	4.3
Women	100.0	21.9	13.2	54.4	6.1	4.3
Millennials	100.0	23.7	9.9	59.5	5.5	1.5
Generation Xers	100.0	20.6	14.0	57.0	4.6	3.8
Baby Boomers	100.0	20.8	16.3	51.1	8.0	3.9
Older Americans	100.0	7.5	22.2	43.5	13.0	13.8
Black	100.0	35.6	13.8	45.4	3.0	2.3
Hispanic	100.0	38.5	11.7	48.6	0.8	0.4
Non-Hispanic white	100.0	13.9	14.6	56.4	9.5	5.6
Northeast	100.0	19.1	13.2	57.9	4.7	5.1
Midwest	100.0	17.9	14.6	52.6	8.8	6.2
South	100.0	22.8	16.9	46.9	9.3	4.2
West	100.0	18.2	10.8	65.4	3.3	2.3
Not a college graduate	100.0	21.2	14.7	51.3	7.1	5.7
Bachelor's degree or more	100.0	16.5	13.3	62.7	6.7	0.7

Note: Millennials are aged 18 to 35; Generation Xers are aged 36 to 47; Baby Boomers are aged 48 to 66; Older Americans are aged 67 or older.
Source: Survey Documentation and Analysis, Computer-assisted Survey Methods Program, University of California, Berkeley, General Social Survey, 1972–2012 Cumulative Data Files, Internet site http://sda.berkeley.edu/cgi-bin/hsda?harcsda+gss12; calculations by New Strategist

Table 7.23 Favor Relative Marrying a White Person, 2012

"What about having a close relative marry a white person? Would you
be very much in favor of it, somewhat in favor, neither in favor
nor opposed, somewhat opposed, or very opposed to it?"

(percent of people aged 18 or older responding by selected characteristics, 2012)

	total	strongly favor	favor	neither favor nor oppose	oppose	strongly oppose
Total people	**100.0%**	**37.7%**	**12.5%**	**47.4%**	**1.5%**	**0.9%**
Men	100.0	34.0	14.2	49.5	1.5	0.7
Women	100.0	41.0	11.0	45.4	1.5	1.1
Millennials	100.0	32.0	11.3	54.9	0.6	1.2
Generation Xers	100.0	32.2	12.2	54.1	0.9	0.6
Baby Boomers	100.0	44.5	12.0	42.2	1.2	0.1
Older Americans	100.0	47.5	17.5	27.2	5.4	2.4
Black	100.0	41.6	10.5	42.5	3.2	2.2
Hispanic	100.0	25.4	17.5	54.8	1.4	0.8
Non-Hispanic white	100.0	42.7	11.8	44.1	0.9	0.5
Northeast	100.0	35.2	16.5	47.3	0.8	0.2
Midwest	100.0	41.9	10.4	43.8	2.8	1.1
South	100.0	46.0	14.2	37.4	1.7	0.8
West	100.0	22.7	9.3	66.2	0.5	1.3
Not a college graduate	100.0	38.6	14.4	44.0	1.7	1.2
Bachelor's degree or more	100.0	35.3	7.5	56.3	1.0	0.0

Note: Millennials are aged 18 to 35; Generation Xers are aged 36 to 47; Baby Boomers are aged 48 to 66; Older Americans are aged 67 or older.
Source: Survey Documentation and Analysis, Computer-assisted Survey Methods Program, University of California, Berkeley, General Social Survey, 1972–2012 Cumulative Data Files, Internet site http://sda.berkeley.edu/cgi-bin/hsda?harcsda+gss12; calculations by New Strategist

Table 7.24 How Close to Blacks, 2012

"In general, how close do you feel to blacks?"

(percent of people aged 18 or older responding by selected characteristics, 2012)

	total	1 not at all close	2	3	4	5 neither	6	7	8	9 very close
Total people	**100.0%**	**3.8%**	**2.4%**	**3.5%**	**4.1%**	**40.8%**	**8.4%**	**11.6%**	**6.9%**	**18.6%**
Men	100.0	3.6	2.4	4.3	4.0	40.2	9.6	12.4	7.1	16.4
Women	100.0	4.0	2.4	2.9	4.2	41.2	7.4	10.8	6.7	20.4
Millennials	100.0	3.8	2.3	3.7	1.9	40.0	10.2	12.2	7.3	18.7
Generation Xers	100.0	4.6	2.6	6.1	4.8	36.1	9.8	12.0	6.0	18.2
Baby Boomers	100.0	3.2	1.9	2.1	5.4	41.0	6.0	12.3	8.4	19.6
Older Americans	100.0	4.2	3.0	2.7	4.8	49.5	8.1	7.1	3.7	16.9
Black	100.0	1.3	0.9	0.8	5.0	16.1	5.5	5.3	5.7	59.4
Hispanic	100.0	7.6	3.1	4.0	3.6	48.1	4.0	11.2	4.4	14.1
Non-Hispanic white	100.0	3.5	2.6	4.0	3.7	43.9	10.4	13.2	7.7	11.0
Northeast	100.0	1.5	4.4	3.9	3.1	46.1	9.1	11.8	7.8	12.2
Midwest	100.0	2.5	3.7	5.0	5.9	37.6	8.1	9.3	9.8	18.1
South	100.0	4.3	1.4	3.2	4.5	35.0	9.6	12.3	5.6	24.1
West	100.0	6.2	1.4	2.3	2.2	49.7	5.9	12.4	5.4	14.5
Not a college graduate	100.0	4.7	2.1	3.6	4.2	40.3	6.5	10.7	6.7	21.2
Bachelor's degree or more	100.0	1.4	3.4	3.3	3.6	42.1	13.4	13.7	7.4	11.7

Note: Millennials are aged 18 to 35; Generation Xers are aged 36 to 47; Baby Boomers are aged 48 to 66; Older Americans are aged 67 or older.
Source: Survey Documentation and Analysis, Computer-assisted Survey Methods Program, University of California, Berkeley, General Social Survey, 1972–2012 Cumulative Data Files, Internet site http://sda.berkeley.edu/cgi-bin/hsda?harcsda+gss12; calculations by New Strategist

Table 7.25 How Close to Whites, 2012

"In general, how close do you feel to whites?"

(percent of people aged 18 or older responding by selected characteristics, 2012)

	total	1 not at all close	2	3	4	5 neither	6	7	8	9 very close
Total people	100.0%	1.7%	0.8%	1.3%	2.3%	32.6%	8.1%	13.4%	12.1%	27.7%
Men	100.0	0.3	0.9	1.9	1.1	33.0	9.8	15.6	13.5	24.0
Women	100.0	2.8	0.8	0.8	3.3	32.3	6.7	11.5	11.0	30.8
Millenials	100.0	0.8	0.9	1.2	1.1	31.8	11.3	13.0	11.9	27.9
Generation Xers	100.0	1.9	0.6	2.7	3.0	28.1	8.4	12.8	15.0	27.4
Baby Boomers	100.0	2.4	0.8	0.1	2.3	34.8	5.9	13.9	11.4	28.4
Older Americans	100.0	1.5	1.0	1.5	4.0	36.8	5.9	12.5	10.2	26.6
Black	100.0	4.1	2.6	1.2	7.7	36.5	10.0	8.5	3.4	26.0
Hispanic	100.0	4.4	1.7	1.7	2.0	37.9	10.2	9.7	11.3	21.0
Non-Hispanic white	100.0	0.5	0.3	1.0	0.8	29.7	6.1	15.3	15.2	31.1
Northeast	100.0	1.1	1.1	4.1	4.9	33.3	6.9	16.0	11.4	21.1
Midwest	100.0	0.6	1.2	1.8	1.8	28.1	6.2	12.6	16.9	30.9
South	100.0	2.0	0.6	0.4	2.0	33.7	8.4	11.1	11.0	30.8
West	100.0	2.7	0.6	0.1	1.3	34.7	10.5	16.0	9.9	24.3
Not a college graduate	100.0	1.9	1.1	0.9	2.5	32.8	8.5	12.8	10.1	29.2
Bachelor's degree or more	100.0	1.0	0.0	2.3	1.8	32.1	7.2	14.7	17.5	23.6

Note: Millennials are aged 18 to 35; Generation Xers are aged 36 to 47; Baby Boomers are aged 48 to 66; Older Americans are aged 67 or older.
Source: Survey Documentation and Analysis, Computer-assisted Survey Methods Program, University of California, Berkeley, General Social Survey, 1972–2012 Cumulative Data Files, Internet site http://sda.berkeley.edu/cgi-bin/hsda?harcsda+gss12; calculations by New Strategist

Diversity: Historical Trends

Table 7.26 Reason for Racial Differences: Discrimination, 1977 to 2012

"On the average (blacks/African Americans) have worse jobs, income, and
housing than white people. Do you think these differences
are mainly due to discrimination?"

(percent distribution of people aged 18 or older by response for selected years)

	total	yes	no
2012	100.0%	34.9%	65.1%
2010	100.0	37.7	62.3
2008	100.0	34.5	65.5
2006	100.0	34.6	65.4
2004	100.0	33.5	66.5
2002	100.0	34.8	65.2
2000	100.0	38.1	61.9
1998	100.0	36.8	63.2
1996	100.0	38.9	61.1
1994	100.0	42.1	57.9
1993	100.0	42.4	57.6
1991	100.0	41.6	58.4
1990	100.0	41.9	58.1
1989	100.0	43.3	56.7
1988	100.0	44.6	55.4
1986	100.0	44.4	55.6
1985	100.0	45.6	54.4
1977	100.0	41.2	58.8

Source: Survey Documentation and Analysis, Computer-assisted Survey Methods Program, University of California, Berkeley, General Social Survey, 1972–2012 Cumulative Data Files, Internet site http://sda.berkeley.edu/cgi-bin/hsda?harcsda+gss12; calculations by New Strategist

Table 7.27 Reason for Racial Differences: Inborn Ability, 1977 to 2012

"On the average (blacks/African Americans) have worse jobs, income,
and housing than white people. Do you think these differences
are because most have less inborn ability to learn?"

(percent distribution of people aged 18 or older by response for selected years)

	total	yes	no
2012	100.0%	9.8%	90.2%
2010	100.0	10.5	89.5
2008	100.0	10.8	89.2
2006	100.0	8.3	91.7
2004	100.0	8.3	91.7
2002	100.0	11.9	88.1
2000	100.0	12.4	87.6
1998	100.0	9.8	90.2
1996	100.0	9.2	90.8
1994	100.0	13.1	86.9
1993	100.0	12.3	87.7
1991	100.0	15.2	84.8
1990	100.0	18.0	82.0
1989	100.0	17.2	82.8
1988	100.0	18.9	81.1
1986	100.0	19.9	80.1
1985	100.0	21.1	78.9
1977	100.0	26.0	74.0

Source: Survey Documentation and Analysis, Computer-assisted Survey Methods Program, University of California, Berkeley, General Social Survey, 1972–2012 Cumulative Data Files, Internet site http://sda.berkeley.edu/cgi-bin/hsda?harcsda+gss12; calculations by New Strategist

Table 7.28 Reason for Racial Differences: Education, 1977 to 2012

"On the average (blacks/African Americans) have worse jobs, income, and housing than white people. Do you think these differences are because most don't have the chance for education that it takes to rise out of poverty?"

(percent distribution of people aged 18 or older by response for selected years)

	total	yes	no
2012	100.0%	42.0%	58.0%
2010	100.0	47.7	52.3
2008	100.0	46.3	53.7
2006	100.0	44.7	55.3
2004	100.0	41.8	58.2
2002	100.0	43.8	56.2
2000	100.0	45.7	54.3
1998	100.0	44.4	55.6
1996	100.0	44.8	55.2
1994	100.0	50.0	50.0
1993	100.0	53.7	46.3
1991	100.0	52.9	47.1
1990	100.0	53.8	46.2
1989	100.0	55.4	44.6
1988	100.0	55.0	45.0
1986	100.0	51.6	48.4
1985	100.0	53.5	46.5
1977	100.0	51.2	48.8

Source: Survey Documentation and Analysis, Computer-assisted Survey Methods Program, University of California, Berkeley, General Social Survey, 1972–2012 Cumulative Data Files, Internet site http://sda.berkeley.edu/cgi-bin/hsda?harcsda+gss12; calculations by New Strategist

Table 7.29 Reason for Racial Differences: Lack of Will, 1977 to 2012

"On the average (blacks/African Americans) have worse jobs, income, and housing than white people. Do you think these differences are because most just don't have the motivation or willpower to pull themselves up out of poverty?"

(percent distribution of people aged 18 or older by response for selected years)

	total	yes	no
2012	100.0%	50.2%	49.8%
2010	100.0	49.4	50.6
2008	100.0	51.6	48.4
2006	100.0	49.8	50.2
2004	100.0	48.4	51.6
2002	100.0	49.6	50.4
2000	100.0	48.9	51.1
1998	100.0	46.5	53.5
1996	100.0	51.1	48.9
1994	100.0	52.7	47.3
1993	100.0	51.9	48.1
1991	100.0	58.7	41.3
1990	100.0	61.4	38.6
1989	100.0	58.4	41.6
1988	100.0	58.9	41.1
1986	100.0	61.2	38.8
1985	100.0	58.1	41.9
1977	100.0	64.7	35.3

Source: Survey Documentation and Analysis, Computer-assisted Survey Methods Program, University of California, Berkeley, General Social Survey, 1972–2012 Cumulative Data Files, Internet site http://sda.berkeley.edu/cgi-bin/hsda?harcsda+gss12; calculations by New Strategist

Table 7.30 Are Blacks Hardworking or Lazy, 1990 to 2012

"On a seven-point scale on which the characteristics of people in a group can be rated, a score of 1 means that you think almost all of the people in that group are hardworking. A score of 7 means that you think almost everyone in the group is lazy. A score of 4 means that you think that the group is not towards one end or another, and you may choose any number in between that comes closest to where you think people in that group stand. Are blacks hardworking or do they tend to be lazy?"

(percent distribution of people aged 18 or older by response for selected years)

	total	1 hardworking	2	3	4 neither	5	6	7 lazy
2012	100.0%	1.8%	3.5%	12.0%	49.1%	21.1%	8.7%	3.9%
2010	100.0	3.6	4.5	12.5	48.0	19.9	9.0	2.6
2008	100.0	2.1	4.2	11.2	49.0	21.3	9.0	3.2
2006	100.0	2.7	3.4	11.7	48.1	21.4	8.8	4.0
2004	100.0	3.0	4.9	12.7	51.3	17.8	7.5	2.9
2002	100.0	3.5	5.1	14.2	44.0	22.3	7.3	3.6
2000	100.0	3.2	5.6	13.7	42.7	21.0	10.2	3.6
1998	100.0	1.7	5.0	13.9	46.1	20.8	9.3	3.2
1996	100.0	2.3	5.1	10.9	46.8	22.0	10.3	2.6
1994	100.0	3.8	7.1	11.8	34.8	23.2	13.1	6.2
1990	100.0	3.8	4.8	12.4	35.3	23.7	13.9	6.0

Source: Survey Documentation and Analysis, Computer-assisted Survey Methods Program, University of California, Berkeley, General Social Survey, 1972–2012 Cumulative Data Files, Internet site http://sda.berkeley.edu/cgi-bin/hsda?harcsda+gss12; calculations by New Strategist

Table 7.31 Are Whites Hardworking or Lazy, 1990 to 2012

"On a seven-point scale on which the characteristics of people in a group
can be rated, a score of 1 means that you think almost all of the people in that
group are hardworking. A score of 7 means that you think almost everyone
in the group is lazy. A score of 4 means that you think that the group
is not towards one end or another, and you may choose any number in
between that comes closest to where you think people in that group
stand. Are whites hardworking or do they tend to be lazy?"

(percent distribution of people aged 18 or older by response for selected years)

	total	1 hardworking	2	3	4 neither	5	6	7 lazy
2012	100.0%	6.4%	10.3%	21.0%	49.4%	9.7%	2.1%	1.1%
2010	100.0	5.1	8.9	23.6	48.0	9.9	3.2	1.2
2008	100.0	7.1	9.9	22.3	48.2	9.6	2.0	0.9
2006	100.0	5.7	10.5	25.4	46.8	8.6	2.0	1.1
2004	100.0	4.7	10.2	21.4	51.9	8.9	1.5	1.5
2002	100.0	8.2	12.8	27.7	42.1	8.0	0.7	0.5
2000	100.0	7.2	14.1	25.2	42.4	8.3	2.2	0.7
1998	100.0	4.4	10.9	24.8	47.3	8.7	3.0	0.9
1996	100.0	4.2	10.3	25.9	45.1	11.7	2.0	0.9
1994	100.0	8.2	18.6	25.7	38.6	5.9	1.8	1.1
1990	100.0	9.3	18.4	29.0	37.2	4.4	1.3	0.4

Source: Survey Documentation and Analysis, Computer-assisted Survey Methods Program, University of California, Berkeley, General Social Survey, 1972–2012 Cumulative Data Files, Internet site http://sda.berkeley.edu/cgi-bin/hsda?harcsda+gss12; calculations by New Strategist

Table 7.32 Are Blacks Unintelligent or Intelligent, 1990 to 2012

"On a seven-point scale on which the characteristics of people in a group can be rated, a score of 1 means that you think almost all of the people in that group are unintelligent. A score of 7 means that you think almost everyone in the group is intelligent. A score of 4 means that you think that the group is not towards one end or another, and you may choose any number in between that comes closest to where you think people in that group stand. Do blacks tend to be unintelligent or intelligent?"

(percent distribution of people aged 18 or older by response for selected years)

	total	1 unintelligent	2	3	4 neither	5	6	7 intelligent
2012	100.0%	0.0%	2.8%	10.6%	57.3%	18.8%	7.5%	2.9%
2010	100.0	0.6	2.7	9.9	56.2	19.8	6.9	3.9
2008	100.0	1.1	2.2	12.0	55.8	18.5	6.8	3.7
2006	100.0	0.7	2.3	11.6	55.4	19.5	6.7	3.7
2004	100.0	1.1	2.3	8.9	58.2	18.2	7.4	3.9
2002	100.0	1.2	3.3	14.8	49.4	20.8	6.9	3.7
2000	100.0	1.3	5.3	15.1	48.2	17.9	7.8	4.4
1998	100.0	0.7	4.1	11.6	52.8	19.4	8.6	2.9
1996	100.0	0.4	4.2	13.2	54.0	20.0	6.0	2.2
1990	100.0	2.4	7.0	19.0	46.0	16.1	6.3	3.1

Source: Survey Documentation and Analysis, Computer-assisted Survey Methods Program, University of California, Berkeley, General Social Survey, 1972–2012 Cumulative Data Files, Internet site http://sda.berkeley.edu/cgi-bin/hsda?harcsda+gss12; calculations by New Strategist

Table 7.33 Are Whites Unintelligent or Intelligent, 1990 to 2012

"On a seven-point scale on which the characteristics of people in a group can be rated, a score of 1 means that you think almost all of the people in that group are unintelligent. A score of 7 means that you think almost everyone in the group is intelligent. A score of 4 means that you think that the group is not towards one end or another, and you may choose any number in between that comes closest to where you think people in that group stand. Do whites tend to be unintelligent or intelligent?"

(percent distribution of people aged 18 or older by response for selected years)

	total	1 unintelligent	2	3	4 neither	5	6	7 intelligent
2012	100.0%	0.5%	1.8%	5.3%	47.9%	25.1%	13.6%	5.8%
2010	100.0	0.6	2.6	5.8	46.7	23.4	14.2	6.7
2008	100.0	0.7	1.5	7.7	47.0	22.2	13.3	7.6
2006	100.0	0.7	2.0	5.6	45.9	24.5	14.4	6.8
2004	100.0	1.0	0.9	4.4	47.1	25.0	15.1	6.5
2002	100.0	0.3	1.9	8.3	40.9	25.1	16.7	6.8
2000	100.0	0.5	2.1	4.6	40.5	26.9	17.3	8.1
1998	100.0	0.5	2.3	7.6	44.7	22.9	16.3	5.7
1996	100.0	0.7	2.6	8.4	44.0	25.0	15.5	3.7
1990	100.0	0.9	2.1	4.2	33.6	26.8	22.1	10.3

Source: Survey Documentation and Analysis, Computer-assisted Survey Methods Program, University of California, Berkeley, General Social Survey, 1972–2012 Cumulative Data Files, Internet site http://sda.berkeley.edu/cgi-bin/hsda?harcsda+gss12; calculations by New Strategist

Table 7.34 Are Blacks Rich or Poor, 1990 to 2012

"On a seven-point scale on which the characteristics of people in a group can be rated, a score of 1 means that you think almost all of the people in that group are rich. A score of 7 means that you think almost everyone in the group is poor. A score of 4 means that you think that the group is not towards one end or another, and you may choose any number in between that comes closest to where you think people in that group stand. Are blacks rich or poor?"

(percent distribution of people aged 18 or older by response for selected years)

	total	1 rich	2	3	4 neither	5	6	7 poor
2012	100.0%	0.3%	1.5%	6.3%	29.7%	40.3%	18.7%	3.3%
2010	100.0	0.6	1.3	6.5	31.4	39.1	17.3	3.8
2008	100.0	0.1	1.9	6.0	27.7	43.5	17.2	3.7
2006	100.0	0.4	1.0	5.6	26.0	41.4	20.7	4.9
2004	100.0	0.1	1.2	6.4	26.2	43.1	19.6	3.5
2002	100.0	0.7	0.8	6.6	28.1	39.2	21.0	3.7
2000	100.0	0.4	1.4	6.4	26.6	39.6	20.8	4.9
1998	100.0	0.5	1.8	7.0	24.1	41.5	22.1	3.0
1996	100.0	0.2	2.5	6.3	24.1	40.5	22.3	4.1
1994	100.0	0.3	1.3	3.3	20.2	42.9	25.4	6.7
1990	100.0	0.2	1.3	3.3	21.3	36.5	29.0	8.3

Source: Survey Documentation and Analysis, Computer-assisted Survey Methods Program, University of California, Berkeley, General Social Survey, 1972–2012 Cumulative Data Files, Internet site http://sda.berkeley.edu/cgi-bin/hsda?harcsda+gss12; calculations by New Strategist

Table 7.35 Are Whites Rich or Poor, 1990 to 2012

"On a seven-point scale on which the characteristics of people in a group can be rated, a score of 1 means that you think almost all of the people in that group are rich. A score of 7 means that you think almost everyone in the group is poor. A score of 4 means that you think that the group is not towards one end or another, and you may choose any number in between that comes closest to where you think people in that group stand. Are whites rich or poor?"

(percent distribution of people aged 18 or older by response for selected years)

	total	1 rich	2	3	4 neither	5	6	7 poor
2012	100.0%	5.9%	7.6%	27.0%	51.8%	6.6%	0.9%	0.2%
2010	100.0	5.0	9.9	26.9	47.7	9.3	0.8	0.4
2008	100.0	5.5	6.1	28.5	50.9	7.8	0.8	0.5
2006	100.0	5.1	10.3	29.3	46.3	7.1	1.2	0.7
2004	100.0	5.6	9.0	26.9	50.8	6.7	1.0	0.0
2002	100.0	4.0	10.4	31.8	43.7	8.7	0.6	0.7
2000	100.0	5.5	12.0	30.5	42.1	8.1	1.6	0.3
1998	100.0	4.0	8.7	29.6	49.3	6.6	1.2	0.4
1996	100.0	4.4	6.7	27.3	52.1	8.3	0.9	0.2
1994	100.0	4.2	9.2	25.7	53.6	5.7	1.3	0.4
1990	100.0	4.4	6.7	30.6	52.4	5.4	0.3	0.1

Source: Survey Documentation and Analysis, Computer-assisted Survey Methods Program, University of California, Berkeley, General Social Survey, 1972–2012 Cumulative Data Files, Internet site http://sda.berkeley.edu/cgi-bin/hsda?harcsda+gss12; calculations by New Strategist

Table 7.36 Racial Makeup of Workplace, 1990 to 2012

"Are the people who work where you work all white, mostly white,
about half and half, mostly black, or all black?"

(percent distribution of people aged 18 or older by response for selected years)

	total	all white	mostly white	half and half	mostly black	all black
2012	100.0%	22.3%	43.8%	26.9%	6.0%	1.0%
2010	100.0	22.0	48.4	23.7	4.9	0.9
2008	100.0	21.4	43.1	29.0	5.4	1.0
2006	100.0	24.4	45.5	25.5	4.2	0.4
2004	100.0	29.2	42.9	23.2	4.3	0.4
2002	100.0	27.1	48.0	19.0	4.6	1.4
2000	100.0	26.2	48.4	20.3	4.4	0.8
1998	100.0	29.9	46.5	18.9	3.5	1.2
1996	100.0	26.7	49.6	19.7	3.3	0.6
1990	100.0	34.4	49.7	11.3	3.3	1.2

Source: Survey Documentation and Analysis, Computer-assisted Survey Methods Program, University of California, Berkeley, General Social Survey, 1972–2012 Cumulative Data Files, Internet site http://sda.berkeley.edu/cgi-bin/hsda?harcsda+gss12; calculations by New Strategist

Table 7.37 Blacks Should Overcome Prejudice without Favors, 1994 to 2012

"Do you agree strongly, agree somewhat, neither agree nor disagree, disagree somewhat, or disagree strongly with the following statement? Irish, Italian, Jewish and many other minorities overcame prejudice and worked their way up; blacks should do the same without any special favors."

(percent distribution of people aged 18 or older by response for selected years)

	total	agree strongly	agree somewhat	neither agree nor disagree	disagree somewhat	disagree strongly
2012	100.0%	41.7%	29.1%	14.5%	9.1%	5.5%
2010	100.0	41.1	30.7	13.1	8.5	6.5
2008	100.0	44.4	30.2	12.6	7.9	4.8
2006	100.0	44.6	29.0	13.0	8.4	5.0
2004	100.0	41.0	27.7	15.5	10.6	5.1
2002	100.0	47.7	26.5	12.7	7.5	5.6
2000	100.0	44.3	28.5	11.0	9.4	6.9
1998	100.0	42.4	30.7	12.8	8.4	5.8
1996	100.0	44.7	28.9	11.7	9.2	5.4
1994	100.0	44.7	30.1	10.1	9.7	5.4

Source: Survey Documentation and Analysis, Computer-assisted Survey Methods Program, University of California, Berkeley, General Social Survey, 1972–2012 Cumulative Data Files, Internet site http://sda.berkeley.edu/cgi-bin/hsda?harcsda+gss12; calculations by New Strategist

Table 7.38 Should Government Aid Blacks, 1975 to 2012

"Some people think that (blacks/African Americans) have been discriminated against for so long that the government has a special obligation to help improve their living standards. Others believe that the government should not be giving special treatment to (blacks/African Americans). Where would you place yourself on this scale?"

(percent distribution of people aged 18 or older by response for selected years)

	total	1 government should help	2	3 agree with both	4	5 no special treatment
2012	100.0%	7.7%	8.4%	29.6%	18.6%	35.6%
2010	100.0	9.0	9.1	30.2	20.2	31.5
2008	100.0	9.0	7.1	33.6	20.3	29.9
2006	100.0	9.4	7.3	33.8	19.1	30.3
2004	100.0	7.7	6.5	31.1	20.2	34.4
2002	100.0	8.6	8.4	30.8	20.5	31.7
2000	100.0	9.2	10.4	32.1	20.3	28.1
1998	100.0	6.3	10.2	32.5	22.1	28.9
1996	100.0	7.9	8.3	29.6	24.5	29.7
1994	100.0	8.5	7.6	30.3	24.4	29.3
1993	100.0	7.2	10.3	32.8	21.6	28.0
1991	100.0	10.3	12.0	31.6	18.5	27.6
1990	100.0	10.4	10.8	33.9	17.2	27.7
1989	100.0	9.2	10.6	26.9	19.3	34.1
1988	100.0	7.0	10.2	30.8	17.6	34.5
1987	100.0	10.6	10.3	29.1	18.6	31.4
1986	100.0	8.1	10.1	29.0	18.8	34.0
1984	100.0	10.5	8.8	31.0	18.4	31.4
1983	100.0	7.9	10.3	26.4	20.7	34.7
1975	100.0	17.0	8.3	22.0	12.9	39.8

Source: Survey Documentation and Analysis, Computer-assisted Survey Methods Program, University of California, Berkeley, General Social Survey, 1972–2012 Cumulative Data Files, Internet site http://sda.berkeley.edu/cgi-bin/hsda?harcsda+gss12; calculations by New Strategist

Table 7.39 Affirmative Action, 1994 to 2012

"Some people say that because of past discrimination, blacks should be given preference in hiring and promotion. Others say that such preferences in hiring and promotion of blacks is wrong because it discriminates against whites. What about your opinion—are you for or against preferential hiring and promotion of blacks?"

(percent distribution of people aged 18 or older by response for selected years)

	total	strongly support	support	oppose	strongly oppose
2012	100.0%	10.6%	8.3%	27.6%	53.5%
2010	100.0	11.3	8.2	27.6	53.0
2008	100.0	10.3	6.7	27.1	55.8
2006	100.0	9.1	6.1	27.3	57.4
2004	100.0	9.8	7.0	28.8	54.5
2002	100.0	8.8	7.1	27.8	56.3
2000	100.0	11.4	7.8	26.6	54.2
1998	100.0	8.3	6.8	24.7	60.3
1996	100.0	10.2	6.7	26.1	57.0
1994	100.0	9.9	7.3	25.0	57.8

Source: Survey Documentation and Analysis, Computer-assisted Survey Methods Program, University of California, Berkeley, General Social Survey, 1972–2012 Cumulative Data Files, Internet site http://sda.berkeley.edu/cgi-bin/hsda?harcsda+gss12; calculations by New Strategist

Table 7.40 Whites Hurt by Affirmative Action, 1990 to 2012

"What do you think the chances are these days that a white person won't get a job or promotion while an equally qualified black person gets one instead?"

(percent distribution of people aged 18 or older by response for selected years)

	total	very likely	somewhat likely	not very likely
2012	100.0%	16.7%	41.9%	41.4%
2010	100.0	15.2	45.7	39.0
2008	100.0	16.7	46.4	36.9
2006	100.0	18.2	48.1	33.8
2004	100.0	16.4	47.8	35.8
2002	100.0	19.9	50.6	29.6
2000	100.0	20.1	46.4	33.5
1998	100.0	20.3	47.6	32.1
1996	100.0	25.2	46.1	28.7
1994	100.0	28.0	43.1	28.9
1990	100.0	25.9	39.3	34.7

Source: Survey Documentation and Analysis, Computer-assisted Survey Methods Program, University of California, Berkeley, General Social Survey, 1972–2012 Cumulative Data Files, Internet site http://sda.berkeley.edu/cgi-bin/hsda?harcsda+gss12; calculations by New Strategist

Table 7.41 Blacks Living in the Neighborhood, 1972 to 2012

"Are there any (blacks/African Americans) living in this neighborhood now?"

(percent distribution of people aged 18 or older by response for selected years)

	total	yes	no
2012	100.0%	72.3%	27.7%
2010	100.0	69.9	30.1
2008	100.0	69.4	30.6
2006	100.0	67.5	32.5
2004	100.0	67.0	33.0
2002	100.0	70.6	29.4
2000	100.0	67.7	32.3
1998	100.0	65.8	34.2
1996	100.0	64.7	35.3
1994	100.0	63.9	36.1
1993	100.0	63.1	36.9
1991	100.0	55.0	45.0
1990	100.0	57.2	42.8
1989	100.0	54.5	45.5
1988	100.0	54.2	45.8
1987	100.0	49.1	50.9
1986	100.0	48.7	51.3
1985	100.0	50.7	49.3
1984	100.0	53.7	46.3
1983	100.0	48.9	51.1
1982	100.0	48.6	51.4
1980	100.0	47.6	52.4
1978	100.0	50.1	49.9
1977	100.0	39.1	60.9
1976	100.0	43.6	56.4
1975	100.0	33.7	66.3
1974	100.0	44.2	55.8
1973	100.0	41.5	58.5
1972	100.0	30.0	70.0

Source: Survey Documentation and Analysis, Computer-assisted Survey Methods Program, University of California, Berkeley, General Social Survey, 1972–2012 Cumulative Data Files, Internet site http://sda.berkeley.edu/cgi-bin/hsda?harcsda+gss12; calculations by New Strategist

Table 7.42 Open Housing Laws, 1973 to 2012

"Suppose there is a community-wide vote on the general housing issue.
There are two possible laws to vote on: One law says that a homeowner can
decide for himself to whom he sells his house, even if he prefers not to sell to
blacks/African Americans. The other law says a homeowner cannot refuse to sell
to someone because of their race or color. Which law would you vote for?"

(percent distribution of people aged 18 or older by response for selected years)

	total	owner decides	can't discriminate	neither
2012	100.0%	25.0%	72.3%	2.7%
2010	100.0	23.3	72.9	3.7
2008	100.0	25.2	70.9	3.9
2006	100.0	26.6	69.0	4.5
2004	100.0	33.1	66.9	0.0
1996	100.0	29.8	67.9	2.3
1994	100.0	32.7	64.6	2.7
1993	100.0	29.9	66.3	3.8
1991	100.0	34.7	62.7	2.7
1990	100.0	39.3	59.1	1.6
1989	100.0	37.2	60.8	2.0
1988	100.0	39.6	58.0	2.4
1987	100.0	43.9	54.4	1.7
1986	100.0	46.4	52.2	1.4
1984	100.0	45.8	51.9	2.3
1983	100.0	51.2	46.9	1.8
1980	100.0	53.8	44.6	1.5
1978	100.0	56.3	42.7	1.0
1976	100.0	63.3	35.0	1.7
1975	100.0	64.6	34.6	0.8
1973	100.0	63.8	34.7	1.6

Source: Survey Documentation and Analysis, Computer-assisted Survey Methods Program, University of California, Berkeley, General Social Survey, 1972–2012 Cumulative Data Files, Internet site http://sda.berkeley.edu/cgi-bin/hsda?harcsda+gss12; calculations by New Strategist

Table 7.43 Favor Living in Neighborhood Half Black, 1990 to 2012

"Please tell me whether you would very much favor, somewhat favor, neither favor nor oppose, somewhat oppose, or very much oppose living in a neighborhood where half of your neighbors were black?"

(percent distribution of people aged 18 or older by response for selected years)

	total	strongly favor	favor	neither favor nor oppose	oppose	strongly oppose
2012	100.0%	8.7%	18.4%	52.0%	14.1%	6.8%
2010	100.0	10.0	19.2	51.6	13.9	5.3
2008	100.0	9.5	18.0	53.4	13.6	5.5
2006	100.0	9.9	16.4	51.3	15.1	7.3
2004	100.0	7.7	19.1	52.2	15.7	5.2
2002	100.0	12.2	18.6	44.1	17.8	7.3
2000	100.0	10.8	16.8	45.7	17.2	9.5
1998	100.0	11.3	13.8	46.8	18.6	9.6
1996	100.0	10.2	16.5	46.2	18.2	8.9
1990	100.0	4.9	10.9	42.2	29.1	12.9

Source: Survey Documentation and Analysis, Computer-assisted Survey Methods Program, University of California, Berkeley, General Social Survey, 1972–2012 Cumulative Data Files, Internet site http://sda.berkeley.edu/cgi-bin/hsda?harcsda+gss12; calculations by New Strategist

Table 7.44 Favor Living in Neighborhood Half White, 2000 to 2012

"Please tell me whether you would very much favor, somewhat favor, neither favor nor oppose, somewhat oppose, or very much oppose living in a neighborhood where half of your neighbors were white?"

(percent distribution of people aged 18 or older by response for selected years)

	total	strongly favor	favor	neither favor nor oppose	oppose	strongly oppose
2012	100.0%	21.1%	23.4%	51.4%	3.0%	1.1%
2010	100.0	21.5	25.0	49.0	3.3	1.3
2008	100.0	19.6	24.5	50.0	4.5	1.3
2006	100.0	22.8	21.9	48.7	5.1	1.4
2004	100.0	19.9	22.1	50.7	5.9	1.5
2002	100.0	28.9	22.9	41.1	5.0	2.1
2000	100.0	31.0	21.6	40.6	5.2	1.6

Source: Survey Documentation and Analysis, Computer-assisted Survey Methods Program, University of California, Berkeley, General Social Survey, 1972–2012 Cumulative Data Files, Internet site http://sda.berkeley.edu/cgi-bin/hsda?harcsda+gss12; calculations by New Strategist

Table 7.45 Favor Relative Marrying an Asian American, 1990 to 2012

"What about having a close relative marry an Asian American? Would you
be very much in favor of it, somewhat in favor, neither in favor
nor opposed, somewhat opposed, or very opposed to it?"

(percent distribution of people aged 18 or older by response for selected years)

	total	strongly favor	favor	neither favor nor oppose	oppose	strongly oppose
2012	100.0%	18.0%	14.1%	55.8%	8.2%	3.9%
2010	100.0	18.6	17.3	51.6	8.1	4.4
2008	100.0	16.7	16.1	52.1	10.1	5.1
2006	100.0	14.7	16.7	51.3	11.0	6.3
2004	100.0	12.5	16.7	52.9	11.3	6.6
2000	100.0	15.8	17.8	45.7	12.0	8.7
1990	100.0	3.3	6.5	48.3	27.0	14.8

Source: Survey Documentation and Analysis, Computer-assisted Survey Methods Program, University of California, Berkeley, General Social Survey, 1972–2012 Cumulative Data Files, Internet site http://sda.berkeley.edu/cgi-bin/hsda?harcsda+gss12; calculations by New Strategist

Table 7.46 Favor Relative Marrying a Black Person, 1990 to 2012

"What about having a close relative marry a black person? Would you be very much in favor of it, somewhat in favor, neither in favor nor opposed, somewhat opposed, or very opposed to it?"

(percent distribution of people aged 18 or older by response for selected years)

	total	strongly favor	favor	neither favor nor oppose	oppose	strongly oppose
2012	100.0%	17.9%	12.5%	52.8%	8.3%	8.6%
2010	100.0	20.6	13.5	47.9	9.7	8.4
2008	100.0	16.6	14.6	47.3	11.1	10.4
2006	100.0	15.8	12.8	46.7	12.8	11.9
2004	100.0	14.4	12.0	47.1	14.5	12.0
2002	100.0	20.6	11.6	40.1	13.1	14.5
2000	100.0	17.9	12.5	39.4	13.1	17.0
1998	100.0	13.7	10.7	40.8	16.6	18.2
1996	100.0	13.5	10.8	39.5	16.6	19.6
1990	100.0	7.2	4.4	31.1	25.0	32.2

Source: Survey Documentation and Analysis, Computer-assisted Survey Methods Program, University of California, Berkeley, General Social Survey, 1972–2012 Cumulative Data Files, Internet site http://sda.berkeley.edu/cgi-bin/hsda?harcsda+gss12; calculations by New Strategist

Table 7.47 Favor Relative Marrying a Hispanic American, 1990 to 2012

"What about having a close relative marry a Hispanic American? Would you
be very much in favor of it, somewhat in favor, neither in favor
nor opposed, somewhat opposed, or very opposed to it?"

(percent distribution of people aged 18 or older by response for selected years)

	total	strongly favor	favor	neither favor nor oppose	oppose	strongly oppose
2012	100.0%	20.0%	14.3%	54.4%	7.0%	4.3%
2010	100.0	19.0	16.7	51.7	7.8	4.8
2008	100.0	18.0	16.4	50.3	9.6	5.7
2006	100.0	17.4	15.5	49.3	11.7	6.2
2004	100.0	14.6	15.6	52.3	11.0	6.5
2000	100.0	18.2	17.2	44.7	11.6	8.2
1990	100.0	5.1	6.7	48.4	24.6	15.2

*Source: Survey Documentation and Analysis, Computer-assisted Survey Methods Program, University of California, Berkeley,
General Social Survey, 1972–2012 Cumulative Data Files, Internet site http://sda.berkeley.edu/cgi-bin/hsda?harcsda+gss12;
calculations by New Strategist*

Table 7.48 Favor Relative Marrying a White Person, 2000 to 2012

"What about having a close relative marry a white person? Would you
be very much in favor of it, somewhat in favor, neither in favor
nor opposed, somewhat opposed, or very opposed to it?"

(percent distribution of people aged 18 or older by response for selected years)

	total	strongly favor	favor	neither favor nor oppose	oppose	strongly oppose
2012	100.0%	37.7%	12.5%	47.4%	1.5%	0.9%
2010	100.0	39.6	14.9	42.0	2.2	1.3
2008	100.0	39.6	15.4	42.1	1.9	0.9
2006	100.0	43.8	13.7	40.0	1.6	0.9
2004	100.0	43.4	13.8	39.3	2.1	1.4
2002	100.0	54.5	11.9	29.6	2.8	1.2
2000	100.0	53.5	12.1	31.3	2.1	1.0

Source: Survey Documentation and Analysis, Computer-assisted Survey Methods Program, University of California, Berkeley, General Social Survey, 1972–2012 Cumulative Data Files, Internet site http://sda.berkeley.edu/cgi-bin/hsda?harcsda+gss12; calculations by New Strategist

Table 7.49 How Close to Blacks, 1996 to 2012

"In general, how close do you feel to blacks?"

(percent distribution of people aged 18 or older by response for selected years)

	total	1 not at all close	2	3	4	5 neither	6	7	8	9 very close
2012	100.0%	3.8%	2.4%	3.5%	4.1%	40.8%	8.4%	11.6%	6.9%	18.6%
2010	100.0	4.7	2.6	4.5	3.5	39.8	8.8	13.6	5.5	17.0
2008	100.0	5.8	2.2	3.4	3.2	41.4	8.3	14.5	7.0	14.1
2006	100.0	5.3	1.9	2.5	3.4	47.0	8.4	12.5	4.6	14.4
2004	100.0	3.8	1.4	2.8	5.3	44.7	8.2	13.9	6.1	13.9
2002	100.0	5.0	1.6	3.5	4.6	45.2	9.6	9.5	6.1	14.8
2000	100.0	7.0	2.9	4.8	3.9	41.4	8.8	12.1	6.0	13.1
1998	100.0	6.5	4.6	5.2	4.2	43.4	7.7	10.8	5.1	12.6
1996	100.0	6.5	2.1	4.9	5.4	45.4	7.5	10.9	3.4	14.0

Source: Survey Documentation and Analysis, Computer-assisted Survey Methods Program, University of California, Berkeley, General Social Survey, 1972–2012 Cumulative Data Files, Internet site http://sda.berkeley.edu/cgi-bin/hsda?harcsda+gss12; calculations by New Strategist

Table 7.50 How Close to Whites, 1996 to 2012

"In general, how close do you feel to whites?"

(percent distribution of people aged 18 or older by response for selected years)

	total	1 not at all close	2	3	4	5 neither	6	7	8	9 very close
2012	100.0%	1.7%	0.8%	1.3%	2.3%	32.6%	8.1%	13.4%	12.1%	27.7%
2010	100.0	2.0	1.6	1.1	2.2	29.4	7.6	13.2	12.6	30.2
2008	100.0	1.8	1.2	2.3	1.9	31.5	7.0	14.7	12.0	27.5
2006	100.0	0.9	1.2	1.8	1.8	34.6	6.7	13.9	11.2	28.0
2004	100.0	0.8	0.3	0.8	1.3	33.5	6.5	14.6	13.9	28.2
2002	100.0	0.7	1.1	1.7	2.6	30.5	5.4	12.2	12.7	33.2
2000	100.0	1.5	1.0	0.9	1.6	28.5	4.6	13.3	13.8	34.8
1998	100.0	1.1	0.9	1.5	2.0	31.5	7.8	14.4	12.6	28.2
1996	100.0	1.1	0.6	1.7	2.0	33.0	5.8	14.6	11.8	29.5

Source: Survey Documentation and Analysis, Computer-assisted Survey Methods Program, University of California, Berkeley, General Social Survey, 1972–2012 Cumulative Data Files, Internet site http://sda.berkeley.edu/cgi-bin/hsda?harcsda+gss12; calculations by New Strategist

8

Personal Outlook

Most Americans are "pretty happy," and about one in three is "very happy." These figures have been relatively stable for decades. The average person does not trust others as much as he once did, however. The American outlook is shifting, and not always for the better.

Little or No Change

• **Time spent watching television has changed little.** Television viewing has not changed much in nearly four decades, with most people watching TV at least two hours a day.

• **Health status is unchanging, despite the aging population.** Three out of four Americans say their health is "good" or "excellent," virtually the same as in 1972.

Big Changes

• **Life is more exciting.** A growing share of the population thinks life is exciting, the figure rising from a low of 44 percent in the 1970s to 53 percent in 2012.

• **Trust has plunged.** The percentage of Americans who think other people can be trusted fell from close to 50 percent at times in the 1970s and 1980s to just 32 percent in 2012.

• **Newspaper readership is down.** Only 27 percent say they read a newspaper everyday, down from 69 percent 40 years ago. Among Millennials, just 15 percent read a daily newspaper and 28 percent never read the paper.

• **Gun ownership has declined.** Despite the ongoing debate about gun control, the percentage of Americans who own a gun has fallen from more than 50 percent in the early 1980s to just 34 percent in 2012.

Personal Outlook: 2012 Profiles

Table 8.1 Hours of Daily Television Viewing, 2012

"On the average day, about how many hours
do you personally watch television?"

(percent of people aged 18 or older responding by selected characteristics, 2012)

	total	none	one	two	three	four	five or more
Total people	**100.0%**	**6.6%**	**22.2%**	**26.4%**	**17.0%**	**12.5%**	**15.3%**
Men	100.0	6.2	22.2	27.8	16.7	11.9	15.2
Women	100.0	7.0	22.3	25.2	17.2	13.1	15.2
Millennials	100.0	8.1	24.9	25.7	18.4	10.4	12.5
Generation Xers	100.0	10.1	30.9	25.7	11.6	10.3	11.4
Baby Boomers	100.0	4.6	19.1	26.5	18.1	14.8	16.9
Older Americans	100.0	1.2	8.3	28.3	19.9	16.9	25.4
Black	100.0	6.4	10.1	14.2	18.5	21.7	29.1
Hispanic	100.0	4.9	26.7	36.4	9.3	9.4	13.3
Non-Hispanic white	100.0	6.6	23.7	26.9	18.7	10.7	13.4
Northeast	100.0	7.3	22.3	32.8	12.4	10.2	15.0
Midwest	100.0	7.0	20.3	23.5	23.5	11.6	14.1
South	100.0	8.2	19.7	23.1	16.6	13.5	18.9
West	100.0	3.3	27.9	30.0	14.3	13.5	11.0
Not a college graduate	100.0	5.2	18.2	25.4	18.3	13.9	19.0
Bachelor's degree or more	100.0	10.2	33.1	29.2	13.4	8.7	5.4

Note: Millennials are aged 18 to 35; Generation Xers are aged 36 to 47; Baby Boomers are aged 48 to 66; Older Americans are aged 67 or older.
Source: Survey Documentation and Analysis, Computer-assisted Survey Methods Program, University of California, Berkeley, General Social Survey, 1972–2012 Cumulative Data Files, Internet site http://sda.berkeley.edu/cgi-bin/hsda?harcsda+gss12; calculations by New Strategist

Table 8.2 Newspaper Readership, 2012

"How often do you read the newspaper—every day, a few times a week,
once a week, less than once a week, or never?"

(percent of people aged 18 or older responding by selected characteristics, 2012)

	total	every day	a few times a week	once a week	less than once a week	never
Total people	**100.0%**	**26.7%**	**16.3%**	**15.7%**	**16.5%**	**24.8%**
Men	100.0	27.8	16.9	14.5	16.6	24.3
Women	100.0	25.8	15.8	16.8	16.3	25.2
Millennials	100.0	14.8	18.0	19.3	20.3	27.6
Generation Xers	100.0	22.8	12.7	17.0	18.8	28.8
Baby Boomers	100.0	31.0	17.7	13.2	16.4	21.7
Older Americans	100.0	54.9	14.9	9.2	3.1	17.9
Black	100.0	16.0	20.4	23.2	19.7	20.7
Hispanic	100.0	14.3	17.6	15.6	19.8	32.6
Non-Hispanic white	100.0	32.4	15.1	13.9	15.5	23.1
Northeast	100.0	31.0	15.8	17.1	16.6	19.6
Midwest	100.0	32.4	18.4	15.5	13.3	20.4
South	100.0	23.0	17.2	15.8	18.6	25.5
West	100.0	24.0	13.3	15.0	16.3	31.4
Not a college graduate	100.0	21.3	16.1	18.0	17.9	26.6
Bachelor's degree or more	100.0	41.3	16.8	9.5	12.6	19.8

Note: Millennials are aged 18 to 35; Generation Xers are aged 36 to 47; Baby Boomers are aged 48 to 66; Older Americans are aged 67 or older.
Source: Survey Documentation and Analysis, Computer-assisted Survey Methods Program, University of California, Berkeley, General Social Survey, 1972–2012 Cumulative Data Files, Internet site http://sda.berkeley.edu/cgi-bin/hsda?harcsda+gss12; calculations by New Strategist

Table 8.3 Is Life Exciting, 2012

"In general, do you find life exciting, pretty routine, or dull?"

(percent of people aged 18 or older responding by selected characteristics, 2012)

	total	exciting	pretty routine	dull
Total people	**100.0%**	**52.7%**	**42.6%**	**4.7%**
Men	100.0	55.9	39.4	4.7
Women	100.0	50.0	45.3	4.7
Millennials	100.0	52.6	41.9	5.5
Generation Xers	100.0	56.9	40.2	3.0
Baby Boomers	100.0	53.6	40.7	5.7
Older Americans	100.0	42.9	53.7	3.4
Black	100.0	47.6	45.7	6.7
Hispanic	100.0	61.5	35.2	3.3
Non-Hispanic white	100.0	51.3	43.6	5.0
Northeast	100.0	57.0	40.5	2.5
Midwest	100.0	54.2	42.1	3.7
South	100.0	48.4	44.9	6.7
West	100.0	55.2	40.8	4.0
Not a college graduate	100.0	50.1	43.8	6.1
Bachelor's degree or more	100.0	59.4	39.6	1.1

Note: Millennials are aged 18 to 35; Generation Xers are aged 36 to 47; Baby Boomers are aged 48 to 66; Older Americans are aged 67 or older.
Source: Survey Documentation and Analysis, Computer-assisted Survey Methods Program, University of California, Berkeley, General Social Survey, 1972–2012 Cumulative Data Files, Internet site http://sda.berkeley.edu/cgi-bin/hsda?harcsda+gss12; calculations by New Strategist

Table 8.4 General Happiness, 2012

"Taken all together, how would you say things are these days—would you
say that you are very happy, pretty happy, or not too happy?"

(percent of people aged 18 or older responding by selected characteristics, 2012)

	total	very happy	pretty happy	not too happy
Total people	**100.0%**	**32.9%**	**54.2%**	**12.9%**
Men	100.0	31.4	55.7	12.9
Women	100.0	34.2	52.9	12.9
Millennials	100.0	33.4	55.1	11.5
Generation Xers	100.0	31.6	57.0	11.5
Baby Boomers	100.0	33.1	52.1	14.7
Older Americans	100.0	33.8	52.9	13.2
Black	100.0	23.3	57.5	19.2
Hispanic	100.0	27.7	57.3	15.0
Non-Hispanic white	100.0	35.8	52.7	11.5
Northeast	100.0	28.8	57.7	13.5
Midwest	100.0	32.9	56.8	10.3
South	100.0	32.3	53.7	14.0
West	100.0	37.0	49.8	13.2
Not a college graduate	100.0	31.5	53.6	14.8
Bachelor's degree or more	100.0	36.5	55.5	7.9

Note: Millennials are aged 18 to 35; Generation Xers are aged 36 to 47; Baby Boomers are aged 48 to 66; Older Americans are aged 67 or older.
Source: Survey Documentation and Analysis, Computer-assisted Survey Methods Program, University of California, Berkeley, General Social Survey, 1972–2012 Cumulative Data Files, Internet site http://sda.berkeley.edu/cgi-bin/hsda?harcsda+gss12; calculations by New Strategist

Table 8.5 Health Status, 2012

"Would you say your own health, in general, is excellent, good, fair, or poor?"

(percent of people aged 18 or older responding by selected characteristics, 2012)

	total	excellent	good	fair	poor
Total people	**100.0%**	**28.9%**	**46.4%**	**19.0%**	**5.7%**
Men	100.0	31.9	43.2	19.2	5.7
Women	100.0	26.4	49.0	18.9	5.7
Millennials	100.0	34.3	46.3	16.2	3.3
Generation Xers	100.0	29.8	50.1	16.1	4.0
Baby Boomers	100.0	27.7	42.8	22.8	6.8
Older Americans	100.0	17.9	48.1	21.9	12.0
Black	100.0	22.1	49.8	23.1	5.0
Hispanic	100.0	27.9	43.4	23.9	4.9
Non-Hispanic white	100.0	30.0	47.0	16.7	6.3
Northeast	100.0	36.9	40.9	17.0	5.2
Midwest	100.0	27.2	49.3	19.4	4.1
South	100.0	26.1	44.8	21.0	8.0
West	100.0	29.0	50.3	16.8	3.8
Not a college graduate	100.0	25.9	45.6	21.5	7.1
Bachelor's degree or more	100.0	36.8	48.4	12.6	2.2

Note: Millennials are aged 18 to 35; Generation Xers are aged 36 to 47; Baby Boomers are aged 48 to 66; Older Americans are aged 67 or older.
Source: Survey Documentation and Analysis, Computer-assisted Survey Methods Program, University of California, Berkeley, General Social Survey, 1972–2012 Cumulative Data Files, Internet site http://sda.berkeley.edu/cgi-bin/hsda?harcsda+gss12; calculations by New Strategist

Table 8.6 Afraid to Walk at Night in Neighborhood, 2012

"Is there any area right around here—that is, within a mile—
where you would be afraid to walk alone at night?"

(percent of people aged 18 or older responding by selected characteristics, 2012)

	total	yes	no
Total people	**100.0%**	**33.7%**	**66.3%**
Men	100.0	20.4	79.6
Women	100.0	45.0	55.0
Millennials	100.0	36.2	63.8
Generation Xers	100.0	30.2	69.8
Baby Boomers	100.0	33.6	66.4
Older Americans	100.0	33.3	66.7
Black	100.0	40.8	59.2
Hispanic	100.0	44.8	55.2
Non-Hispanic white	100.0	29.6	70.4
Northeast	100.0	28.9	71.1
Midwest	100.0	28.8	71.2
South	100.0	33.9	66.1
West	100.0	42.0	58.0
Not a college graduate	100.0	36.1	63.9
Bachelor's degree or more	100.0	27.5	72.5

Note: Millennials are aged 18 to 35; Generation Xers are aged 36 to 47; Baby Boomers are aged 48 to 66; Older Americans are aged 67 or older.
Source: Survey Documentation and Analysis, Computer-assisted Survey Methods Program, University of California, Berkeley, General Social Survey, 1972–2012 Cumulative Data Files, Internet site http://sda.berkeley.edu/cgi-bin/hsda?harcsda+gss12; calculations by New Strategist

Table 8.7 Helpfulness of People, 2012

"Would you say that most of the time people try to be helpful, or that they are mostly just looking out for themselves?"

(percent of people aged 18 or older responding by selected characteristics, 2012)

	total	helpful	look out for self	depends
Total people	**100.0%**	**46.5%**	**45.7%**	**7.8%**
Men	100.0	45.3	48.2	6.5
Women	100.0	47.5	43.6	8.9
Millennials	100.0	38.3	50.7	11.0
Generation Xers	100.0	44.9	48.3	6.8
Baby Boomers	100.0	49.5	45.2	5.3
Older Americans	100.0	59.8	32.1	8.1
Black	100.0	40.7	51.1	8.1
Hispanic	100.0	36.7	58.4	4.9
Non-Hispanic white	100.0	50.6	40.7	8.7
Northeast	100.0	44.7	43.5	11.8
Midwest	100.0	50.4	42.8	6.8
South	100.0	44.6	47.3	8.0
West	100.0	47.1	47.5	5.4
Not a college graduate	100.0	41.1	51.5	7.4
Bachelor's degree or more	100.0	59.6	31.5	8.9

Note: Millennials are aged 18 to 35; Generation Xers are aged 36 to 47; Baby Boomers are aged 48 to 66; Older Americans are aged 67 or older.
Source: Survey Documentation and Analysis, Computer-assisted Survey Methods Program, University of California, Berkeley, General Social Survey, 1972–2012 Cumulative Data Files, Internet site http://sda.berkeley.edu/cgi-bin/hsda?harcsda+gss12; calculations by New Strategist

Table 8.8 Fairness of People, 2012

"Do you think most people would try to take advantage of you
if they got a chance, or would they try to be fair?"

(percent of people aged 18 or older responding by selected characteristics, 2012)

	total	take advantage	be fair	depends
Total people	**100.0%**	**43.4%**	**50.0%**	**6.6%**
Men	100.0	42.3	52.1	5.6
Women	100.0	44.3	48.2	7.5
Millennials	100.0	54.5	38.4	7.1
Generation Xers	100.0	44.0	50.4	5.6
Baby Boomers	100.0	39.0	54.5	6.4
Older Americans	100.0	28.0	64.4	7.6
Black	100.0	53.8	39.3	6.9
Hispanic	100.0	51.4	41.8	6.8
Non-Hispanic white	100.0	39.1	53.9	7.0
Northeast	100.0	41.1	51.4	7.5
Midwest	100.0	37.4	57.1	5.5
South	100.0	48.4	44.3	7.3
West	100.0	42.7	51.3	6.0
Not a college graduate	100.0	51.2	42.1	6.7
Bachelor's degree or more	100.0	24.1	69.3	6.6

Note: Millennials are aged 18 to 35; Generation Xers are aged 36 to 47; Baby Boomers are aged 48 to 66; Older Americans are aged 67 or older.
Source: Survey Documentation and Analysis, Computer-assisted Survey Methods Program, University of California, Berkeley, General Social Survey, 1972–2012 Cumulative Data Files, Internet site http://sda.berkeley.edu/cgi-bin/hsda?harcsda+gss12; calculations by New Strategist

Table 8.9 Trust in People, 2012

"Generally speaking, would you say that most people can be trusted
or that you can't be too careful in life?"

(percent of people aged 18 or older responding by selected characteristics, 2012)

	total	can trust	cannot trust	depends
Total people	**100.0%**	**32.2%**	**64.2%**	**3.7%**
Men	100.0	34.5	62.5	3.0
Women	100.0	30.2	65.6	4.3
Millennials	100.0	21.2	75.2	3.6
Generation Xers	100.0	32.5	64.6	2.9
Baby Boomers	100.0	39.9	56.5	3.6
Older Americans	100.0	38.0	56.8	5.2
Black	100.0	17.6	78.8	3.6
Hispanic	100.0	15.8	82.4	1.8
Non-Hispanic white	100.0	39.0	56.8	4.2
Northeast	100.0	33.5	62.7	3.8
Midwest	100.0	36.2	61.2	2.6
South	100.0	28.2	66.9	4.8
West	100.0	33.5	63.7	2.8
Not a college graduate	100.0	23.9	72.5	3.5
Bachelor's degree or more	100.0	52.3	43.7	4.0

Note: Millennials are aged 18 to 35; Generation Xers are aged 36 to 47; Baby Boomers are aged 48 to 66; Older Americans are aged 67 or older.
Source: Survey Documentation and Analysis, Computer-assisted Survey Methods Program, University of California, Berkeley, General Social Survey, 1972–2012 Cumulative Data Files, Internet site http://sda.berkeley.edu/cgi-bin/hsda?harcsda+gss12; calculations by New Strategist

Table 8.10 Ever Been Locked Up, 2012

"Have you ever spent any time in prison or jail?"

(percent of people aged 18 or older responding by selected characteristics, 2012)

	total	yes	no
Total people	**100.0%**	**14.0%**	**86.0%**
Men	100.0	21.2	78.8
Women	100.0	7.9	92.1
Millennials	100.0	18.6	81.4
Generation Xers	100.0	14.1	85.9
Baby Boomers	100.0	11.9	88.1
Older Americans	100.0	6.8	93.2
Black	100.0	21.2	78.8
Hispanic	100.0	15.2	84.8
Non-Hispanic white	100.0	12.4	87.6
Northeast	100.0	7.4	92.6
Midwest	100.0	15.7	84.3
South	100.0	16.8	83.2
West	100.0	12.8	87.2
Not a college graduate	100.0	17.2	82.8
Bachelor's degree or more	100.0	6.5	93.5

Note: Millennials are aged 18 to 35; Generation Xers are aged 36 to 47; Baby Boomers are aged 48 to 66; Older Americans are aged 67 or older.
Source: Survey Documentation and Analysis, Computer-assisted Survey Methods Program, University of California, Berkeley, General Social Survey, 1972–2012 Cumulative Data Files, Internet site http://sda.berkeley.edu/cgi-bin/hsda?harcsda+gss12; calculations by New Strategist

Table 8.11 Ever Received a Traffic Ticket, 2012

"Have you ever received a ticket, or been charged by the police,
for a traffic violation—other than for illegal parking?"

(percent of people aged 18 or older responding by selected characteristics, 2012)

	total	yes	no
Total people	**100.0%**	**63.7%**	**36.3%**
Men	100.0	70.6	29.4
Women	100.0	57.7	42.3
Millennials	100.0	61.8	38.2
Generation Xers	100.0	65.7	34.3
Baby Boomers	100.0	65.8	34.2
Older Americans	100.0	59.6	40.4
Black	100.0	55.5	44.5
Hispanic	100.0	49.9	50.1
Non-Hispanic white	100.0	69.1	30.9
Northeast	100.0	52.1	47.9
Midwest	100.0	68.4	31.6
South	100.0	63.8	36.2
West	100.0	67.3	32.7
Not a college graduate	100.0	59.9	40.1
Bachelor's degree or more	100.0	72.7	27.3

Note: Millennials are aged 18 to 35; Generation Xers are aged 36 to 47; Baby Boomers are aged 48 to 66; Older Americans are aged 67 or older.
Source: Survey Documentation and Analysis, Computer-assisted Survey Methods Program, University of California, Berkeley, General Social Survey, 1972–2012 Cumulative Data Files, Internet site http://sda.berkeley.edu/cgi-bin/hsda?harcsda+gss12; calculations by New Strategist

Table 8.12 Ever Been Arrested, 2012

"Were you ever picked up, or charged, by the police, for any reason whether or not you were guilty?"

(percent of people aged 18 or older responding by selected characteristics, 2012)

	total	yes	no
Total people	**100.0%**	**20.4%**	**79.6%**
Men	100.0	29.1	70.9
Women	100.0	13.0	87.0
Millennials	100.0	27.8	72.2
Generation Xers	100.0	22.4	77.6
Baby Boomers	100.0	15.1	84.9
Older Americans	100.0	10.4	89.6
Black	100.0	23.5	76.5
Hispanic	100.0	25.8	74.2
Non-Hispanic white	100.0	19.2	80.8
Northeast	100.0	16.5	83.5
Midwest	100.0	22.6	77.4
South	100.0	21.7	78.3
West	100.0	19.2	80.8
Not a college graduate	100.0	22.3	77.7
Bachelor's degree or more	100.0	15.9	84.1

Note: Millennials are aged 18 to 35; Generation Xers are aged 36 to 47; Baby Boomers are aged 48 to 66; Older Americans are aged 67 or older.
Source: Survey Documentation and Analysis, Computer-assisted Survey Methods Program, University of California, Berkeley, General Social Survey, 1972–2012 Cumulative Data Files, Internet site http://sda.berkeley.edu/cgi-bin/hsda?harcsda+gss12; calculations by New Strategist

Table 8.13 Can You Speak a Language Other than English, 2012

"Can you speak a language other than English?"

(percent of people aged 18 or older responding by selected characteristics, 2012)

	total	yes	no
Total people	**100.0%**	**30.4%**	**69.6%**
Men	100.0	32.3	67.7
Women	100.0	28.7	71.3
Millennials	100.0	37.7	62.3
Generation Xers	100.0	34.5	65.5
Baby Boomers	100.0	24.9	75.1
Older Americans	100.0	18.8	81.2
Black	100.0	20.7	79.3
Hispanic	100.0	60.4	39.6
Non-Hispanic white	100.0	22.3	77.7
Northeast	100.0	37.2	62.8
Midwest	100.0	23.3	76.7
South	100.0	28.0	72.0
West	100.0	36.0	64.0
Not a college graduate	100.0	27.6	72.4
Bachelor's degree or more	100.0	37.7	62.3

Note: Millennials are aged 18 to 35; Generation Xers are aged 36 to 47; Baby Boomers are aged 48 to 66; Older Americans are aged 67 or older.
Source: Survey Documentation and Analysis, Computer-assisted Survey Methods Program, University of California, Berkeley, General Social Survey, 1972–2012 Cumulative Data Files, Internet site http://sda.berkeley.edu/cgi-bin/hsda?harcsda+gss12; calculations by New Strategist

Table 8.14 Visited an Art Museum, 2012

"How often did you visit an art museum last year?"

(percent of people aged 18 or older responding by selected characteristics, 2012)

	total	none	once	two or more times
Total people	**100.0%**	**67.2%**	**17.1%**	**15.7%**
Men	100.0	71.4	17.0	11.6
Women	100.0	63.5	17.1	19.4
Millennials	100.0	68.2	17.4	14.4
Generation Xers	100.0	66.9	17.5	15.6
Baby Boomers	100.0	65.2	17.7	17.1
Older Americans	100.0	71.6	13.8	14.6
Black	100.0	70.9	18.6	10.5
Hispanic	100.0	65.0	22.4	12.6
Non-Hispanic white	100.0	66.9	15.8	17.3
Northeast	100.0	61.3	18.3	20.4
Midwest	100.0	71.1	19.1	9.8
South	100.0	70.3	15.6	14.1
West	100.0	63.2	16.4	20.4
Not a college graduate	100.0	76.8	13.8	9.4
Bachelor's degree or more	100.0	42.6	25.5	31.9

Note: Millennials are aged 18 to 35; Generation Xers are aged 36 to 47; Baby Boomers are aged 48 to 66; Older Americans are aged 67 or older.
Source: Survey Documentation and Analysis, Computer-assisted Survey Methods Program, University of California, Berkeley, General Social Survey, 1972–2012 Cumulative Data Files, Internet site http://sda.berkeley.edu/cgi-bin/hsda?harcsda+gss12; calculations by New Strategist

Table 8.15 Visited a Natural History Museum, 2012

"How often did you visit a natural history museum last year?"

(percent of people aged 18 or older responding by selected characteristics, 2012)

	total	none	once	two or more times
Total people	**100.0%**	**72.7%**	**18.5%**	**8.8%**
Men	100.0	73.7	18.3	8.0
Women	100.0	71.8	18.8	9.4
Millennials	100.0	70.2	21.5	8.3
Generation Xers	100.0	65.3	22.1	12.6
Baby Boomers	100.0	74.5	16.3	9.2
Older Americans	100.0	84.0	12.7	3.3
Black	100.0	76.1	15.2	8.7
Hispanic	100.0	73.2	18.7	8.1
Non-Hispanic white	100.0	71.4	20.0	8.6
Northeast	100.0	71.1	18.5	10.4
Midwest	100.0	77.2	17.4	5.4
South	100.0	74.1	19.1	6.8
West	100.0	67.5	18.8	13.7
Not a college graduate	100.0	78.8	15.6	5.6
Bachelor's degree or more	100.0	57.0	26.2	16.8

Note: Millennials are aged 18 to 35; Generation Xers are aged 36 to 47; Baby Boomers are aged 48 to 66; Older Americans are aged 67 or older.
Source: Survey Documentation and Analysis, Computer-assisted Survey Methods Program, University of California, Berkeley, General Social Survey, 1972–2012 Cumulative Data Files, Internet site http://sda.berkeley.edu/cgi-bin/hsda?harcsda+gss12; calculations by New Strategist

Table 8.16 Visited a Zoo, 2012

"How often did you visit a zoo last year?"

(percent of people aged 18 or older responding by selected characteristics, 2012)

	total	none	once	two or more times
Total people	**100.0%**	**54.2%**	**26.3%**	**19.5%**
Men	100.0	53.5	26.9	19.6
Women	100.0	54.8	25.8	19.4
Millennials	100.0	44.2	27.8	28.0
Generation Xers	100.0	41.8	31.2	27.0
Baby Boomers	100.0	59.1	26.7	14.2
Older Americans	100.0	78.1	14.9	7.0
Black	100.0	62.7	22.6	14.7
Hispanic	100.0	49.0	30.8	20.2
Non-Hispanic white	100.0	53.9	26.0	20.1
Northeast	100.0	59.6	22.0	18.4
Midwest	100.0	50.7	27.7	21.6
South	100.0	57.6	25.2	17.2
West	100.0	47.8	30.1	22.1
Not a college graduate	100.0	59.2	24.0	16.8
Bachelor's degree or more	100.0	41.2	32.4	26.4

Note: Millennials are aged 18 to 35; Generation Xers are aged 36 to 47; Baby Boomers are aged 48 to 66; Older Americans are aged 67 or older.
Source: Survey Documentation and Analysis, Computer-assisted Survey Methods Program, University of California, Berkeley, General Social Survey, 1972–2012 Cumulative Data Files, Internet site http://sda.berkeley.edu/cgi-bin/hsda?harcsda+gss12; calculations by New Strategist

Table 8.17 Visited a Science Museum, 2012

"How often did you visit a science museum last year?"

(percent of people aged 18 or older responding by selected characteristics, 2012)

	total	none	once	two or more times
Total people	**100.0%**	**75.1%**	**17.3%**	**7.6%**
Men	100.0	74.7	18.5	6.8
Women	100.0	75.4	16.3	8.3
Millennials	100.0	70.4	20.2	9.4
Generation Xers	100.0	68.7	21.4	9.9
Baby Boomers	100.0	77.5	15.7	6.8
Older Americans	100.0	86.6	10.1	3.3
Black	100.0	81.3	12.2	6.5
Hispanic	100.0	76.5	17.9	5.6
Non-Hispanic white	100.0	74.4	17.7	7.9
Northeast	100.0	72.2	18.0	9.8
Midwest	100.0	76.3	19.1	4.6
South	100.0	77.6	14.6	7.8
West	100.0	72.0	19.4	8.6
Not a college graduate	100.0	82.2	13.2	4.6
Bachelor's degree or more	100.0	56.5	28.0	15.5

Note: Millennials are aged 18 to 35; Generation Xers are aged 36 to 47; Baby Boomers are aged 48 to 66; Older Americans are aged 67 or older.
Source: Survey Documentation and Analysis, Computer-assisted Survey Methods Program, University of California, Berkeley, General Social Survey, 1972–2012 Cumulative Data Files, Internet site http://sda.berkeley.edu/cgi-bin/hsda?harcsda+gss12; calculations by New Strategist

Table 8.18 Visited a Public Library, 2012

"How often did you visit a public library last year?"

(percent of people aged 18 or older responding by selected characteristics, 2012)

	total	none	once	two or more times
Total people	**100.0%**	**40.5%**	**10.6%**	**48.9%**
Men	100.0	50.2	11.4	38.4
Women	100.0	31.7	9.9	58.4
Millennials	100.0	39.1	11.6	49.3
Generation Xers	100.0	30.6	9.4	60.0
Baby Boomers	100.0	43.4	10.4	46.2
Older Americans	100.0	49.7	11.4	38.9
Black	100.0	35.5	9.6	54.9
Hispanic	100.0	38.0	17.2	44.8
Non-Hispanic white	100.0	41.2	9.5	49.3
Northeast	100.0	38.0	6.6	55.4
Midwest	100.0	40.5	11.1	48.4
South	100.0	43.4	11.1	45.5
West	100.0	37.7	12.5	49.8
Not a college graduate	100.0	43.5	11.4	45.1
Bachelor's degree or more	100.0	32.6	8.7	58.7

Note: Millennials are aged 18 to 35; Generation Xers are aged 36 to 47; Baby Boomers are aged 48 to 66; Older Americans are aged 67 or older.
Source: Survey Documentation and Analysis, Computer-assisted Survey Methods Program, University of California, Berkeley, General Social Survey, 1972–2012 Cumulative Data Files, Internet site http://sda.berkeley.edu/cgi-bin/hsda?harcsda+gss12; calculations by New Strategist

Table 8.19 Have a Gun in Home, 2012

"Do you happen to have in your home (or garage) any guns or revolvers?"

(percent of people aged 18 or older responding by selected characteristics, 2012)

	total	yes	no	refused
Total people	**100.0%**	**34.4%**	**63.6%**	**2.0%**
Men	100.0	38.8	59.1	2.1
Women	100.0	30.8	67.3	1.9
Millennials	100.0	26.7	72.5	0.8
Generation Xers	100.0	33.6	65.3	1.2
Baby Boomers	100.0	38.1	58.8	3.1
Older Americans	100.0	46.2	50.3	3.5
Black	100.0	22.2	76.3	1.5
Hispanic	100.0	19.7	78.8	1.5
Non-Hispanic white	100.0	42.8	54.7	2.4
Northeast	100.0	22.2	77.8	0.0
Midwest	100.0	36.1	63.1	0.9
South	100.0	42.0	64.6	3.4
West	100.0	29.6	68.2	2.2
Not a college graduate	100.0	34.7	63.3	2.0
Bachelor's degree or more	100.0	33.7	64.3	2.0

Note: Millennials are aged 18 to 35; Generation Xers are aged 36 to 47; Baby Boomers are aged 48 to 66; Older Americans are aged 67 or older.
Source: Survey Documentation and Analysis, Computer-assisted Survey Methods Program, University of California, Berkeley, General Social Survey, 1972–2012 Cumulative Data Files, Internet site http://sda.berkeley.edu/cgi-bin/hsda?harcsda+gss12; calculations by New Strategist

Table 8.20 Does Respondent or Spouse Hunt, 2012

"Do you (or does your husband/wife) go hunting?"

(percent of people aged 18 or older responding by selected characteristics, 2012)

	total	respondent	spouse	both	neither
Total people	**100.0%**	**10.8%**	**6.1%**	**2.8%**	**80.3%**
Men	100.0	19.8	0.3	2.9	77.0
Women	100.0	3.2	10.9	2.7	83.1
Millennials	100.0	12.6	5.4	3.9	78.2
Generation Xers	100.0	10.2	9.9	3.5	76.3
Baby Boomers	100.0	9.4	5.3	2.0	83.3
Older Americans	100.0	11.3	3.4	1.2	84.1
Black	100.0	4.3	2.2	0.0	93.5
Hispanic	100.0	7.3	3.1	0.9	88.7
Non-Hispanic white	100.0	13.8	7.8	4.2	74.2
Northeast	100.0	9.8	3.9	0.8	85.5
Midwest	100.0	12.5	7.8	3.2	76.6
South	100.0	12.9	6.3	3.3	77.5
West	100.0	6.2	5.7	3.2	84.8
Not a college graduate	100.0	12.2	5.6	3.6	78.5
Bachelor's degree or more	100.0	7.1	7.2	0.7	85.0

Note: Millennials are aged 18 to 35; Generation Xers are aged 36 to 47; Baby Boomers are aged 48 to 66; Older Americans are aged 67 or older.
Source: Survey Documentation and Analysis, Computer-assisted Survey Methods Program, University of California, Berkeley, General Social Survey, 1972–2012 Cumulative Data Files, Internet site http://sda.berkeley.edu/cgi-bin/hsda?harcsda+gss12; calculations by New Strategist

Personal Outlook: Historical Trends

Table 8.21 Hours of Daily Television Viewing, 1975 to 2012

"On the average day, about how many hours
do you personally watch television?"

(percent distribution of people aged 18 or older by response for selected years)

	total	none	one	two	three	four	five or more
2012	100.0%	6.6%	22.2%	26.4%	17.0%	12.5%	15.3%
2010	100.0	6.8	19.9	26.9	18.5	10.2	17.8
2008	100.0	6.2	20.5	29.7	16.0	13.4	14.1
2006	100.0	4.4	23.1	29.1	17.3	10.9	15.1
2004	100.0	5.9	27.1	26.5	14.7	12.0	13.8
2002	100.0	3.2	23.9	25.2	18.5	11.5	17.8
2000	100.0	5.4	21.4	27.8	17.1	12.7	15.6
1998	100.0	4.6	21.7	27.3	17.5	13.8	15.2
1996	100.0	4.5	20.4	30.2	17.4	12.9	14.7
1994	100.0	3.5	21.8	27.6	19.6	14.3	13.1
1993	100.0	3.8	21.2	28.6	19.7	11.9	14.8
1991	100.0	3.2	17.8	26.5	21.5	14.1	16.8
1990	100.0	2.7	22.2	29.0	18.7	12.1	15.3
1989	100.0	3.4	18.1	30.5	16.9	14.4	16.6
1988	100.0	2.6	19.7	25.7	19.6	13.0	19.6
1986	100.0	4.1	18.3	25.9	20.5	13.9	17.3
1985	100.0	5.2	17.1	28.0	19.9	12.7	17.2
1983	100.0	6.2	18.2	25.1	19.9	14.2	16.5
1982	100.0	4.2	20.3	25.8	19.0	14.1	16.6
1980	100.0	7.4	18.1	24.0	18.8	13.2	18.5
1978	100.0	5.1	21.0	27.2	19.9	12.2	14.6
1977	100.0	3.3	21.0	26.0	21.0	13.0	15.7
1975	100.0	3.3	17.0	27.5	19.9	14.9	17.4

Source: Survey Documentation and Analysis, Computer-assisted Survey Methods Program, University of California, Berkeley, General Social Survey, 1972–2012 Cumulative Data Files, Internet site http://sda.berkeley.edu/cgi-bin/hsda?harcsda+gss12; calculations by New Strategist

Table 8.22 Newspaper Readership, 1972 to 2012

"How often do you read the newspaper—every day, a few times a week, once a week, less than once a week, or never?"

(percent distribution of people aged 18 or older by response for selected years)

	total	every day	a few times a week	once a week	less than once a week	never
2012	100.0%	26.7%	16.3%	15.7%	16.5%	24.8%
2010	100.0	31.4	19.5	15.0	15.5	18.6
2008	100.0	32.3	22.9	17.3	14.3	13.2
2006	100.0	34.2	22.1	15.8	15.8	12.2
2004	100.0	40.2	25.4	14.0	13.0	7.4
2002	100.0	42.4	23.2	11.7	12.9	9.8
2000	100.0	36.6	25.5	14.6	14.8	8.7
1998	100.0	43.0	22.8	16.4	10.3	7.5
1996	100.0	42.5	24.2	15.9	11.4	6.0
1994	100.0	50.4	23.4	13.4	9.6	3.3
1993	100.0	46.7	26.3	13.0	8.9	5.1
1991	100.0	51.9	21.9	13.1	8.7	4.4
1990	100.0	52.7	22.4	10.4	10.1	4.5
1989	100.0	49.6	25.5	12.8	7.0	5.2
1988	100.0	50.9	23.8	12.2	8.6	4.5
1987	100.0	55.3	20.5	12.7	6.2	5.3
1986	100.0	54.0	20.7	12.3	7.5	5.5
1985	100.0	52.7	21.4	12.3	7.6	6.0
1983	100.0	55.7	20.5	11.0	8.4	4.4
1982	100.0	52.1	22.7	12.8	6.8	5.6
1978	100.0	58.0	20.5	9.3	7.3	4.9
1977	100.0	63.3	16.6	9.7	6.2	4.3
1975	100.0	66.7	16.4	8.1	5.0	3.9
1972	100.0	69.4	15.2	7.8	3.9	3.8

Source: Survey Documentation and Analysis, Computer-assisted Survey Methods Program, University of California, Berkeley, General Social Survey, 1972–2012 Cumulative Data Files, Internet site http://sda.berkeley.edu/cgi-bin/hsda?harcsda+gss12; calculations by New Strategist

Table 8.23 Is Life Exciting, 1973 to 2012

"In general, do you find life exciting, pretty routine, or dull?"

(percent distribution of people aged 18 or older by response for selected years)

	total	exciting	pretty routine	dull
2012	100.0%	52.7%	42.6%	4.7%
2010	100.0	52.1	43.3	4.6
2008	100.0	47.6	48.5	3.8
2006	100.0	51.2	43.9	4.9
2004	100.0	49.6	47.0	3.4
2002	100.0	52.3	44.2	3.5
2000	100.0	46.6	49.1	4.3
1998	100.0	45.2	49.9	4.9
1996	100.0	50.9	45.3	3.8
1994	100.0	48.2	48.3	3.5
1993	100.0	47.3	47.3	5.4
1991	100.0	44.8	52.0	3.1
1990	100.0	45.1	50.8	4.1
1989	100.0	45.0	50.2	4.9
1988	100.0	46.4	49.2	4.4
1987	100.0	45.6	50.9	3.5
1985	100.0	46.1	47.9	5.9
1984	100.0	45.2	50.2	4.6
1982	100.0	45.4	49.7	4.9
1980	100.0	47.6	47.1	5.3
1977	100.0	44.4	49.2	6.4
1976	100.0	45.1	51.7	3.3
1974	100.0	43.5	52.0	4.5
1973	100.0	46.1	49.0	4.8

Source: Survey Documentation and Analysis, Computer-assisted Survey Methods Program, University of California, Berkeley, General Social Survey, 1972–2012 Cumulative Data Files, Internet site http://sda.berkeley.edu/cgi-bin/hsda?harcsda+gss12; calculations by New Strategist

Table 8.24 General Happiness, 1972 to 2012

"Taken all together, how would you say things are these days—would you say that you are very happy, pretty happy, or not too happy?"

(percent distribution of people aged 18 or older by response for selected years)

	total	very happy	pretty happy	not too happy
2012	100.0%	32.9%	54.2%	12.9%
2010	100.0	28.8	57.0	14.2
2008	100.0	31.7	54.4	13.9
2006	100.0	32.4	55.9	11.7
2004	100.0	33.6	54.7	11.7
2002	100.0	32.9	55.8	11.3
2000	100.0	33.9	56.4	9.6
1998	100.0	33.3	55.9	10.9
1996	100.0	32.1	57.4	10.5
1994	100.0	30.5	58.2	11.3
1993	100.0	33.4	56.9	9.7
1991	100.0	32.5	58.0	9.5
1990	100.0	35.7	56.5	7.7
1989	100.0	34.5	56.7	8.8
1988	100.0	36.1	55.7	8.2
1987	100.0	33.6	55.2	11.2
1986	100.0	33.2	56.6	10.2
1985	100.0	29.4	60.3	10.3
1984	100.0	35.8	52.1	12.1
1983	100.0	31.7	55.8	12.5
1982	100.0	34.7	53.6	11.7
1980	100.0	36.0	52.0	12.0
1978	100.0	34.4	57.9	7.7
1977	100.0	35.7	53.2	11.0
1976	100.0	34.8	52.9	12.2
1975	100.0	33.4	53.6	13.0
1974	100.0	38.3	49.2	12.5
1973	100.0	36.8	50.9	12.3
1972	100.0	29.7	53.0	17.2

Source: Survey Documentation and Analysis, Computer-assisted Survey Methods Program, University of California, Berkeley, General Social Survey, 1972–2012 Cumulative Data Files, Internet site http://sda.berkeley.edu/cgi-bin/hsda?harcsda+gss12; calculations by New Strategist

Table 8.25 Health Status, 1972 to 2012

"Would you say your own health, in general, is excellent, good, fair, or poor?"

(percent distribution of people aged 18 or older by response for selected years)

	total	excellent	good	fair	poor
2012	100.0%	28.9%	46.4%	19.0%	5.7%
2010	100.0	27.0	45.8	21.4	5.8
2008	100.0	25.5	49.0	20.9	4.6
2006	100.0	29.0	46.1	19.8	5.2
2004	100.0	31.7	48.4	16.4	3.5
2002	100.0	30.8	47.2	17.1	4.9
2000	100.0	31.2	48.5	15.7	4.7
1998	100.0	31.9	47.9	15.8	4.5
1996	100.0	31.8	48.9	15.7	3.6
1994	100.0	32.3	46.2	17.5	4.1
1993	100.0	32.8	47.1	14.9	5.1
1991	100.0	32.2	45.5	18.6	3.7
1990	100.0	32.2	45.8	17.3	4.7
1989	100.0	34.3	45.8	16.0	3.9
1988	100.0	30.8	46.2	17.8	5.2
1987	100.0	34.5	43.1	17.3	5.1
1985	100.0	32.4	43.8	17.4	6.4
1984	100.0	29.8	49.5	16.8	3.9
1982	100.0	33.1	42.0	18.5	6.4
1980	100.0	33.6	41.3	18.8	6.3
1977	100.0	32.5	40.9	20.3	6.4
1976	100.0	32.5	41.8	19.0	6.6
1975	100.0	32.9	39.8	21.5	5.8
1974	100.0	33.3	40.6	20.3	5.9
1973	100.0	32.4	39.8	20.6	7.2
1972	100.0	29.6	46.0	19.8	4.7

Source: Survey Documentation and Analysis, Computer-assisted Survey Methods Program, University of California, Berkeley, General Social Survey, 1972–2012 Cumulative Data Files, Internet site http://sda.berkeley.edu/cgi-bin/hsda?harcsda+gss12; calculations by New Strategist

Table 8.26 Afraid to Walk at Night in Neighborhood, 1973 to 2012

"Is there any area right around here—that is, within a mile—
where you would be afraid to walk alone at night?"

(percent distribution of people aged 18 or older by response for selected years)

	total	yes	no
2012	100.0%	33.7%	66.3%
2010	100.0	32.7	67.3
2008	100.0	32.7	67.3
2006	100.0	35.1	64.9
2004	100.0	30.2	69.8
2002	100.0	31.0	69.0
2000	100.0	37.7	62.3
1998	100.0	39.2	60.8
1996	100.0	40.8	59.2
1994	100.0	45.4	54.6
1993	100.0	41.0	59.0
1991	100.0	42.9	57.1
1990	100.0	39.0	61.0
1989	100.0	38.5	61.5
1988	100.0	38.0	62.1
1987	100.0	37.3	62.7
1985	100.0	38.7	61.3
1984	100.0	40.8	59.3
1982	100.0	44.6	55.4
1980	100.0	42.4	57.6
1977	100.0	43.0	57.0
1976	100.0	42.3	57.7
1974	100.0	43.6	56.4
1973	100.0	39.9	60.1

Source: Survey Documentation and Analysis, Computer-assisted Survey Methods Program, University of California, Berkeley, General Social Survey, 1972–2012 Cumulative Data Files, Internet site http://sda.berkeley.edu/cgi-bin/hsda?harcsda+gss12; calculations by New Strategist

Table 8.27 Helpfulness of People, 1972 to 2012

"Would you say that most of the time people try to be helpful,
or that they are mostly just looking out for themselves?"

(percent distribution of people aged 18 or older by response for selected years)

	total	helpful	look out for self	depends
2012	100.0%	46.5%	45.7%	7.8%
2010	100.0	46.1	43.9	10.0
2008	100.0	45.7	45.1	9.2
2006	100.0	42.8	47.0	10.1
2004	100.0	49.4	40.3	10.3
2002	100.0	48.0	42.7	9.3
2000	100.0	45.9	45.4	8.7
1998	100.0	47.7	43.2	9.1
1996	100.0	42.9	50.2	6.8
1994	100.0	46.9	46.6	6.4
1993	100.0	52.5	41.9	5.6
1991	100.0	49.3	44.5	6.2
1990	100.0	51.6	43.0	5.5
1989	100.0	50.9	44.2	4.9
1988	100.0	49.6	46.1	4.3
1987	100.0	47.4	48.3	4.3
1986	100.0	56.3	38.4	5.2
1984	100.0	52.3	44.0	3.7
1983	100.0	58.3	38.3	3.5
1980	100.0	48.3	47.0	4.7
1978	100.0	59.8	35.4	4.8
1976	100.0	42.0	51.9	6.1
1975	100.0	56.7	36.9	6.3
1973	100.0	46.7	49.6	3.7
1972	100.0	45.9	47.9	6.2

Source: Survey Documentation and Analysis, Computer-assisted Survey Methods Program, University of California, Berkeley, General Social Survey, 1972–2012 Cumulative Data Files, Internet site http://sda.berkeley.edu/cgi-bin/hsda?harcsda+gss12; calculations by New Strategist

Table 8.28 Fairness of People, 1972 to 2012

"Do you think most people would try to take advantage of you if they got a chance, or would they try to be fair?"

(percent distribution of people aged 18 or older by response for selected years)

	total	take advantage	be fair	depends
2012	100.0%	43.4%	50.0%	6.6%
2010	100.0	39.4	52.1	8.6
2008	100.0	41.3	50.1	8.6
2006	100.0	38.8	48.6	12.5
2004	100.0	40.5	50.7	8.8
2002	100.0	39.9	49.8	10.3
2000	100.0	38.3	52.2	9.5
1998	100.0	38.8	52.7	8.6
1996	100.0	43.5	49.9	6.6
1994	100.0	39.6	53.5	6.8
1993	100.0	37.3	55.8	7.0
1991	100.0	37.5	57.1	5.4
1990	100.0	36.0	58.0	6.0
1989	100.0	35.3	59.2	5.4
1988	100.0	33.7	60.6	5.7
1987	100.0	37.5	59.1	3.4
1986	100.0	33.3	63.0	3.7
1984	100.0	35.0	62.3	2.7
1983	100.0	35.8	59.4	4.8
1980	100.0	34.0	61.3	4.7
1978	100.0	30.6	64.1	5.3
1976	100.0	36.6	59.4	4.0
1975	100.0	31.3	61.7	7.0
1973	100.0	37.6	57.5	4.9
1972	100.0	35.2	59.1	5.8

Source: Survey Documentation and Analysis, Computer-assisted Survey Methods Program, University of California, Berkeley, General Social Survey, 1972–2012 Cumulative Data Files, Internet site http://sda.berkeley.edu/cgi-bin/hsda?harcsda+gss12; calculations by New Strategist

Table 8.29 Trust in People, 1972 to 2012

"Generally speaking, would you say that most people can be trusted
or that you can't be too careful in life?"

(percent distribution of people aged 18 or older by response for selected years)

	total	can trust	cannot trust	depends
2012	100.0%	32.2%	64.2%	3.7%
2010	100.0	32.2	62.5	5.3
2008	100.0	31.9	63.9	4.3
2006	100.0	32.3	62.4	5.2
2004	100.0	35.5	58.9	5.6
2002	100.0	34.8	57.7	7.6
2000	100.0	35.2	58.5	6.3
1998	100.0	37.2	57.4	5.4
1996	100.0	33.7	61.4	5.0
1994	100.0	34.4	61.3	4.3
1993	100.0	35.3	60.6	4.1
1991	100.0	38.9	56.0	5.1
1990	100.0	38.4	57.4	4.2
1989	100.0	41.1	55.5	3.3
1988	100.0	39.5	56.1	4.4
1987	100.0	43.6	52.7	3.7
1986	100.0	37.7	59.5	2.7
1984	100.0	49.5	48.2	2.4
1983	100.0	34.8	61.2	4.0
1980	100.0	43.9	52.1	4.1
1978	100.0	40.2	55.6	4.3
1976	100.0	44.0	52.6	3.4
1975	100.0	39.7	56.1	4.2
1973	100.0	46.8	50.4	2.8
1972	100.0	46.3	50.0	3.8

Source: Survey Documentation and Analysis, Computer-assisted Survey Methods Program, University of California, Berkeley, General Social Survey, 1972–2012 Cumulative Data Files, Internet site http://sda.berkeley.edu/cgi-bin/hsda?harcsda+gss12; calculations by New Strategist

Table 8.30 Ever Received a Traffic Ticket, 1973 to 2012

"Have you ever received a ticket, or been charged by the police,
for a traffic violation—other than for illegal parking?"

(percent distribution of people aged 18 or older by response for selected years)

	total	yes	no
2012	100.0%	63.7%	36.3%
1984	100.0	55.7	44.3
1982	100.0	47.8	52.0
1980	100.0	52.3	47.7
1977	100.0	42.7	57.3
1976	100.0	40.9	59.1
1974	100.0	41.3	58.7
1973	100.0	42.8	57.1

Source: Survey Documentation and Analysis, Computer-assisted Survey Methods Program, University of California, Berkeley, General Social Survey, 1972–2012 Cumulative Data Files, Internet site http://sda.berkeley.edu/cgi-bin/hsda?harcsda+gss12; calculations by New Strategist

Table 8.31 Ever Been Arrested, 1973 to 2012

"Were you ever picked up, or charged, by the police, for any
reason whether or not you were guilty?"

(percent distribution of people aged 18 or older by response for selected years)

	total	yes	no
2012	100.0%	20.4%	79.6%
1984	100.0	12.5	87.5
1982	100.0	12.7	87.1
1980	100.0	13.2	86.7
1977	100.0	9.8	90.2
1976	100.0	8.7	91.4
1974	100.0	9.6	90.4
1973	100.0	11.0	88.9

Source: Survey Documentation and Analysis, Computer-assisted Survey Methods Program, University of California, Berkeley, General Social Survey, 1972–2012 Cumulative Data Files, Internet site http://sda.berkeley.edu/cgi-bin/hsda?harcsda+gss12; calculations by New Strategist

Table 8.32 Can You Speak a Language Other than English, 2000 to 2012

"Can you speak a language other than English?"

(percent distribution of people aged 18 or older by response for selected years)

	total	yes	no
2012	100.0%	30.4%	69.6%
2010	100.0	27.0	73.0
2008	100.0	27.8	72.2
2006	100.0	25.4	74.6
2000	100.0	26.4	73.6

Source: Survey Documentation and Analysis, Computer-assisted Survey Methods Program, University of California, Berkeley, General Social Survey, 1972–2012 Cumulative Data Files, Internet site http://sda.berkeley.edu/cgi-bin/hsda?harcsda+gss12; calculations by New Strategist

Table 8.33 **Have a Gun in Home, 1973 to 2012**

"Do you happen to have in your home (or garage) any guns or revolvers?"

(percent distribution of people aged 18 or older by response for selected years)

	total	yes	no	refused
2012	100.0%	34.4%	63.6%	2.0%
2010	100.0	32.3	64.1	3.6
2008	100.0	36.0	62.9	1.1
2006	100.0	34.5	63.8	1.7
2004	100.0	37.3	61.3	1.4
2002	100.0	36.4	62.7	0.9
2000	100.0	34.3	64.4	1.3
1998	100.0	36.7	63.0	0.4
1996	100.0	43.4	56.2	0.4
1994	100.0	43.9	55.1	0.9
1993	100.0	45.5	53.8	0.6
1991	100.0	43.7	55.1	1.2
1990	100.0	45.8	54.2	0.0
1989	100.0	48.9	51.1	0.0
1988	100.0	43.4	55.8	0.9
1987	100.0	48.1	51.3	0.6
1985	100.0	48.1	51.4	0.5
1984	100.0	47.4	52.0	0.6
1982	100.0	50.8	47.9	1.3
1980	100.0	51.6	48.2	0.1
1977	100.0	54.0	45.8	0.2
1976	100.0	49.6	49.1	1.2
1974	100.0	47.9	51.5	0.6
1973	100.0	49.1	49.9	1.0

Source: Survey Documentation and Analysis, Computer-assisted Survey Methods Program, University of California, Berkeley, General Social Survey, 1972–2012 Cumulative Data Files, Internet site http://sda.berkeley.edu/cgi-bin/hsda?harcsda+gss12; calculations by New Strategist

Table 8.34 Does Respondent or Spouse Hunt, 1977 to 2012

"Do you (or does your husband/wife) go hunting?"

(percent distribution of people aged 18 or older by response for selected years)

	total	respondent	spouse	both	neither
2012	100.0%	10.8%	6.1%	2.8%	80.3%
2010	100.0	12.6	4.3	1.3	81.7
2008	100.0	11.3	4.8	1.6	82.3
2006	100.0	10.1	5.1	2.0	82.8
2004	100.0	11.7	5.1	2.6	80.6
2002	100.0	14.7	3.3	2.2	79.8
2000	100.0	11.9	5.1	1.7	81.3
1998	100.0	11.5	6.0	1.8	80.7
1996	100.0	14.8	5.8	2.6	76.8
1994	100.0	13.7	5.9	2.4	77.9
1993	100.0	13.4	5.9	1.8	79.0
1991	100.0	14.4	6.3	2.4	77.0
1990	100.0	14.8	6.7	2.8	75.7
1989	100.0	12.9	6.8	3.7	76.6
1988	100.0	13.1	7.1	2.1	77.8
1987	100.0	13.3	7.7	4.1	74.8
1985	100.0	16.4	6.9	3.0	73.7
1984	100.0	14.3	9.6	2.5	73.6
1982	100.0	15.7	9.1	2.9	72.3
1980	100.0	14.2	9.3	4.0	72.6
1977	100.0	18.6	9.4	3.6	68.3

Source: Survey Documentation and Analysis, Computer-assisted Survey Methods Program, University of California, Berkeley, General Social Survey, 1972–2012 Cumulative Data Files, Internet site http://sda.berkeley.edu/cgi-bin/hsda?harcsda+gss12; calculations by New Strategist

CHAPTER

9

Sexuality

Some sexual attitudes and behaviors have changed greatly over the past half-century, while others have barely budged. General Social Survey questions that probe sexual activity support the notion that human beings are essentially monogamous, with some backsliding. The results also show that some "controversial" issues—such as whether sex education should be taught in the public schools—are not controversial at all.

Little or No Change

• **Support for abortion.** No one likes the idea of abortion, but most Americans support abortion in certain circumstances—attitudes that have not changed in decades. Only 43 percent of the public supports abortion for any reason, but 87 percent support abortion if a woman's health is endangered.

• **Sex education in the public schools.** The great majority of the public has supported sex education in the public schools for decades, with more than nine out of 10 in favor of it in 2012.

Big Changes

• **Premarital sex.** Big changes have occurred in attitudes toward premarital sex over the past several decades. In 1972, only 28 percent of the public said premarital sex is "not wrong at all." In 2012, the figure was 58 percent.

• **Attitudes toward homosexuality and gay marriage.** There has been a dramatic shift toward acceptance of gays and lesbians in the past two decades. The percentage of Americans who think sexual relations between adults of the same sex is "always wrong" dropped from 73 percent in 1973 to 46 percent in 2012. The percentage who think gays and lesbians should have the right to marry climbed from 12 percent in 1988 to 49 percent in 2012. Among Millennials, the 62 percent majority supports gay marriage. As younger people age and replace older, less tolerant generations, acceptance of gays and lesbians will continue to grow.

Sexuality: 2012 Profiles

Table 9.1 Sex Education in Public Schools, 2012

"Would you be for or against sex education in the public schools?"

(percent of people aged 18 or older responding by selected characteristics, 2012)

	total	favor	oppose
Total people	**100.0%**	**90.9%**	**9.1%**
Men	100.0	89.4	10.6
Women	100.0	92.3	7.7
Millennials	100.0	93.8	6.2
Generation Xers	100.0	94.5	5.5
Baby Boomers	100.0	89.3	10.7
Older Americans	100.0	80.9	19.1
Black	100.0	93.7	6.3
Hispanic	100.0	89.4	10.6
Non-Hispanic white	100.0	90.1	9.9
Northeast	100.0	91.6	8.4
Midwest	100.0	92.6	7.4
South	100.0	89.2	10.8
West	100.0	91.5	8.5
Not a college graduate	100.0	91.6	8.4
Bachelor's degree or more	100.0	89.0	11.0

Note: Millennials are aged 18 to 35; Generation Xers are aged 36 to 47; Baby Boomers are aged 48 to 66; Older Americans are aged 67 or older.
Source: Survey Documentation and Analysis, Computer-assisted Survey Methods Program, University of California, Berkeley, General Social Survey, 1972–2012 Cumulative Data Files, Internet site http://sda.berkeley.edu/cgi-bin/hsda?harcsda+gss12; calculations by New Strategist

Table 9.2 Birth Control for Teenagers, 2012

"Do you strongly agree, agree, or strongly disagree that methods of birth control should be available to teenagers between the ages of 14 and 16 even if their parents did not approve?"

(percent of people aged 18 or older responding by selected characteristics, 2012)

	total	strongly agree	agree	disagree	strongly disagree
Total people	**100.0%**	**24.1%**	**33.7%**	**25.1%**	**17.1%**
Men	100.0	19.9	34.5	25.1	20.6
Women	100.0	27.9	33.0	25.2	14.0
Millennials	100.0	28.7	36.3	21.4	13.7
Generation Xers	100.0	27.7	30.3	26.0	16.0
Baby Boomers	100.0	20.8	34.9	24.0	20.2
Older Americans	100.0	13.9	29.0	36.4	20.7
Black	100.0	28.5	33.2	25.3	13.0
Hispanic	100.0	19.3	35.4	26.8	18.4
Non-Hispanic white	100.0	24.2	33.4	24.9	17.4
Northeast	100.0	27.6	36.6	20.9	14.8
Midwest	100.0	22.6	32.0	27.6	17.7
South	100.0	21.4	32.9	27.4	18.4
West	100.0	27.4	34.4	22.2	16.0
Not a college graduate	100.0	24.0	34.6	24.6	16.8
Bachelor's degree or more	100.0	24.4	31.2	26.5	17.9

Note: Millennials are aged 18 to 35; Generation Xers are aged 36 to 47; Baby Boomers are aged 48 to 66; Older Americans are aged 67 or older.
Source: Survey Documentation and Analysis, Computer-assisted Survey Methods Program, University of California, Berkeley, General Social Survey, 1972–2012 Cumulative Data Files, Internet site http://sda.berkeley.edu/cgi-bin/hsda?harcsda+gss12; calculations by New Strategist

Table 9.3 Sexual Relations between Teenagers, 2012

"Do you think sex relations before marriage between people in their early teens, say 14 to 16, are always wrong, almost always wrong, wrong only sometimes, or not wrong at all?"

(percent of people aged 18 or older responding by selected characteristics, 2012)

	total	always wrong	almost always wrong	sometimes wrong	not wrong at all
Total people	**100.0%**	**66.9%**	**15.1%**	**11.9%**	**6.0%**
Men	100.0	63.0	16.6	14.0	6.4
Women	100.0	70.4	13.8	10.1	5.7
Millennials	100.0	51.2	20.3	20.8	7.7
Generation Xers	100.0	70.3	13.6	7.4	8.7
Baby Boomers	100.0	76.3	12.5	7.9	3.3
Older Americans	100.0	82.0	10.0	4.6	3.4
Black	100.0	74.6	9.4	12.0	4.0
Hispanic	100.0	66.1	12.1	12.2	9.7
Non-Hispanic white	100.0	65.6	17.1	11.6	5.7
Northeast	100.0	60.0	14.7	14.1	11.1
Midwest	100.0	72.4	16.1	9.0	2.5
South	100.0	72.4	14.7	9.3	3.5
West	100.0	57.9	15.1	17.2	9.8
Not a college graduate	100.0	69.1	13.7	11.3	6.0
Bachelor's degree or more	100.0	61.1	19.0	13.7	6.2

Note: Millennials are aged 18 to 35; Generation Xers are aged 36 to 47; Baby Boomers are aged 48 to 66; Older Americans are aged 67 or older.
Source: Survey Documentation and Analysis, Computer-assisted Survey Methods Program, University of California, Berkeley, General Social Survey, 1972–2012 Cumulative Data Files, Internet site http://sda.berkeley.edu/cgi-bin/hsda?harcsda+gss12; calculations by New Strategist

Table 9.4 Number of Sex Partners in Past Year, 2012

"How many sex partners have you had in the last 12 months?"

(percent of people aged 18 or older responding by selected characteristics, 2012)

	total	no partners	one partner	two or more partners
Total people	**100.0%**	**18.6%**	**68.1%**	**13.3%**
Men	100.0	17.4	65.7	16.9
Women	100.0	19.7	70.1	10.2
Millennials	100.0	13.3	63.3	23.4
Generation Xers	100.0	7.9	78.4	13.7
Baby Boomers	100.0	21.6	71.9	6.5
Older Americans	100.0	47.6	50.7	1.7
Black	100.0	25.1	57.6	17.3
Hispanic	100.0	11.7	73.3	15.0
Non-Hispanic white	100.0	18.9	68.7	12.4
Northeast	100.0	20.9	66.7	12.4
Midwest	100.0	18.5	68.0	13.5
South	100.0	18.7	69.7	11.6
West	100.0	17.1	66.5	16.4
Not a college graduate	100.0	20.6	65.9	13.5
Bachelor's degree or more	100.0	13.9	73.3	12.8

Note: Millennials are aged 18 to 35; Generation Xers are aged 36 to 47; Baby Boomers are aged 48 to 66; Older Americans are aged 67 or older.
Source: Survey Documentation and Analysis, Computer-assisted Survey Methods Program, University of California, Berkeley, General Social Survey, 1972–2012 Cumulative Data Files, Internet site http://sda.berkeley.edu/cgi-bin/hsda?harcsda+gss12; calculations by New Strategist

Table 9.5 Relationship with Last Sex Partner, 2012

"The last time you had sex, was it with someone that you were in an
on-going relationship with, or was it with someone else?
Remember that by 'sex' we mean only vaginal, oral, or anal sex."

(percent of people aged 18 or older responding by selected characteristics, 2012)

	total	in relationship	not in relationship
Total people	**100.0%**	**90.2%**	**9.8%**
Men	100.0	87.1	12.9
Women	100.0	93.0	7.0
Millennials	100.0	86.5	13.5
Generation Xers	100.0	93.4	6.6
Baby Boomers	100.0	91.9	8.1
Older Americans	100.0	91.9	8.1
Black	100.0	91.6	8.3
Hispanic	100.0	84.6	15.4
Non-Hispanic white	100.0	91.3	8.7
Northeast	100.0	91.2	8.8
Midwest	100.0	91.7	8.3
South	100.0	92.6	7.4
West	100.0	84.3	15.7
Not a college graduate	100.0	89.0	11.0
Bachelor's degree or more	100.0	93.2	6.8

Note: Millennials are aged 18 to 35; Generation Xers are aged 36 to 47; Baby Boomers are aged 48 to 66; Older Americans are aged 67 or older.
Source: Survey Documentation and Analysis, Computer-assisted Survey Methods Program, University of California, Berkeley, General Social Survey, 1972–2012 Cumulative Data Files, Internet site http://sda.berkeley.edu/cgi-bin/hsda?harcsda+gss12; calculations by New Strategist

Table 9.6 Condom Use, 2012

"The last time you had sex, was a condom used?
By 'sex' we mean vaginal, oral, or anal sex."

(percent of people aged 18 or older responding by selected characteristics, 2012)

	total	used	not used
Total people	**100.0%**	**21.5%**	**78.5%**
Men	100.0	24.6	75.4
Women	100.0	18.9	81.1
Millennials	100.0	34.3	65.7
Generation Xers	100.0	19.6	80.4
Baby Boomers	100.0	14.5	85.5
Older Americans	100.0	7.3	92.7
Black	100.0	33.6	66.4
Hispanic	100.0	36.7	63.3
Non-Hispanic white	100.0	14.5	85.5
Northeast	100.0	19.1	80.9
Midwest	100.0	19.2	80.8
South	100.0	20.5	79.5
West	100.0	27.0	73.0
Not a college graduate	100.0	23.0	77.0
Bachelor's degree or more	100.0	17.8	82.2

Note: Millennials are aged 18 to 35; Generation Xers are aged 36 to 47; Baby Boomers are aged 48 to 66; Older Americans are aged 67 or older.
Source: Survey Documentation and Analysis, Computer-assisted Survey Methods Program, University of California, Berkeley, General Social Survey, 1972–2012 Cumulative Data Files, Internet site http://sda.berkeley.edu/cgi-bin/hsda?harcsda+gss12; calculations by New Strategist

Table 9.7 Seen X-Rated Movie, 2012

"Have you seen an X-rated movie in the last year?"

(percent of people aged 18 or older responding by selected characteristics, 2012)

	total	yes	no
Total people	**100.0%**	**24.7%**	**75.3%**
Men	100.0	35.0	65.0
Women	100.0	15.9	84.1
Millennials	100.0	40.3	59.7
Generation Xers	100.0	31.4	68.6
Baby Boomers	100.0	13.6	86.4
Older Americans	100.0	7.0	93.0
Black	100.0	26.9	73.0
Hispanic	100.0	31.3	68.7
Non-Hispanic white	100.0	21.4	78.6
Northeast	100.0	28.2	71.8
Midwest	100.0	21.9	78.1
South	100.0	19.6	80.4
West	100.0	32.8	67.2
Not a college graduate	100.0	25.1	74.9
Bachelor's degree or more	100.0	23.7	76.3

Note: Millennials are aged 18 to 35; Generation Xers are aged 36 to 47; Baby Boomers are aged 48 to 66; Older Americans are aged 67 or older.
Source: Survey Documentation and Analysis, Computer-assisted Survey Methods Program, University of California, Berkeley, General Social Survey, 1972–2012 Cumulative Data Files, Internet site http://sda.berkeley.edu/cgi-bin/hsda?harcsda+gss12; calculations by New Strategist

Table 9.8 Laws against Pornography, 2012

"Which of these statements comes closest to your feelings about pornography laws? 1) There should be laws against the distribution of pornography whatever the age; 2) There should be laws against the distribution of pornography to persons under 18; 3) There should be no laws forbidding the distribution of pornography."

(percent of people aged 18 or older responding by selected characteristics, 2012)

	total	illegal to all	illegal under 18	legal
Total people	**100.0%**	**32.8%**	**64.0%**	**3.3%**
Men	100.0	26.0	69.4	4.6
Women	100.0	38.5	59.4	2.1
Millennials	100.0	20.7	74.7	4.6
Generation Xers	100.0	29.4	66.4	4.3
Baby Boomers	100.0	36.9	61.1	2.1
Older Americans	100.0	54.2	44.1	1.7
Black	100.0	26.7	69.7	3.5
Hispanic	100.0	34.3	62.3	3.3
Non-Hispanic white	100.0	33.9	63.3	2.8
Northeast	100.0	27.6	68.9	3.5
Midwest	100.0	33.6	63.1	3.3
South	100.0	37.3	60.5	2.1
West	100.0	28.4	66.7	4.9
Not a college graduate	100.0	32.9	63.6	3.6
Bachelor's degree or more	100.0	32.5	65.0	2.5

Note: Millennials are aged 18 to 35; Generation Xers are aged 36 to 47; Baby Boomers are aged 48 to 66; Older Americans are aged 67 or older.
Source: Survey Documentation and Analysis, Computer-assisted Survey Methods Program, University of California, Berkeley, General Social Survey, 1972–2012 Cumulative Data Files, Internet site http://sda.berkeley.edu/cgi-bin/hsda?harcsda+gss12; calculations by New Strategist

Table 9.9 Premarital Sex, 2012

"There's been a lot of discussion about the way morals and attitudes about sex are changing in this country. If a man and woman have sex relations before marriage, do you think it is always wrong, almost always wrong, wrong only sometimes, or not wrong at all?"

(percent of people aged 18 or older responding by selected characteristics, 2012)

	total	always wrong	almost always wrong	sometimes wrong	not wrong at all
Total people	**100.0%**	**21.9%**	**5.1%**	**15.5%**	**57.5%**
Men	100.0	20.1	4.1	15.7	60.1
Women	100.0	23.5	6.0	15.3	55.2
Millennials	100.0	13.7	4.0	16.6	65.7
Generation Xers	100.0	24.2	4.5	13.1	58.2
Baby Boomers	100.0	23.0	5.7	13.8	57.5
Older Americans	100.0	37.0	8.0	20.2	34.8
Black	100.0	26.5	5.5	14.1	53.9
Hispanic	100.0	25.0	6.2	14.0	54.8
Non-Hispanic white	100.0	21.1	4.7	15.3	58.9
Northeast	100.0	13.1	0.6	15.5	70.8
Midwest	100.0	21.1	6.5	15.5	56.9
South	100.0	30.4	5.6	15.5	48.6
West	100.0	15.8	6.2	15.4	62.6
Not a college graduate	100.0	21.6	5.5	15.8	57.2
Bachelor's degree or more	100.0	22.7	4.1	14.7	58.5

Note: Millennials are aged 18 to 35; Generation Xers are aged 36 to 47; Baby Boomers are aged 48 to 66; Older Americans are aged 67 or older.
Source: Survey Documentation and Analysis, Computer-assisted Survey Methods Program, University of California, Berkeley, General Social Survey, 1972–2012 Cumulative Data Files, Internet site http://sda.berkeley.edu/cgi-bin/hsda?harcsda+gss12; calculations by New Strategist

Table 9.10 Extramarital Sex, 2012

"What is your opinion about a married person having sexual relations with someone other than the marriage partner—is it always wrong, almost always wrong, wrong only sometimes, or not wrong at all?"

(percent of people aged 18 or older responding by selected characteristics, 2012)

	total	always wrong	almost always wrong	sometimes wrong	not wrong at all
Total people	**100.0%**	**81.9%**	**11.2%**	**5.6%**	**1.3%**
Men	100.0	76.4	15.0	6.7	2.0
Women	100.0	86.6	8.1	4.8	0.6
Millennials	100.0	83.2	11.0	4.2	1.7
Generation Xers	100.0	79.2	12.6	7.3	0.9
Baby Boomers	100.0	81.2	11.2	6.3	1.4
Older Americans	100.0	84.5	9.9	5.1	0.5
Black	100.0	84.6	10.3	5.1	0.0
Hispanic	100.0	86.5	7.7	4.0	1.8
Non-Hispanic white	100.0	81.3	11.8	5.5	1.4
Northeast	100.0	73.6	18.5	7.3	0.6
Midwest	100.0	85.1	10.0	4.6	0.3
South	100.0	85.8	8.0	4.8	1.4
West	100.0	78.3	12.3	6.8	2.5
Not a college graduate	100.0	85.6	8.5	4.8	1.1
Bachelor's degree or more	100.0	72.0	18.3	7.9	1.7

Note: Millennials are aged 18 to 35; Generation Xers are aged 36 to 47; Baby Boomers are aged 48 to 66; Older Americans are aged 67 or older.
Source: Survey Documentation and Analysis, Computer-assisted Survey Methods Program, University of California, Berkeley, General Social Survey, 1972–2012 Cumulative Data Files, Internet site http://sda.berkeley.edu/cgi-bin/hsda?harcsda+gss12; calculations by New Strategist

Table 9.11 Ever Had an Affair, 2012

"Have you ever had sex with someone other than your
husband or wife while you were married?"

(percent of ever-married people aged 18 or older responding by selected characteristics, 2012)

	total	yes	no
Total ever-married	**100.0%**	**14.6%**	**85.4%**
Men	100.0	19.0	81.0
Women	100.0	12.3	87.7
Millennials	100.0	10.5	89.5
Generation Xers	100.0	17.5	82.5
Baby Boomers	100.0	15.7	84.3
Older Americans	100.0	16.5	83.5
Black	100.0	18.6	81.4
Hispanic	100.0	12.6	87.4
Non-Hispanic white	100.0	15.6	84.4
Northeast	100.0	10.4	89.6
Midwest	100.0	14.6	85.4
South	100.0	17.4	82.6
West	100.0	15.7	84.3
Not a college graduate	100.0	14.8	85.2
Bachelor's degree or more	100.0	16.4	83.6

Note: Millennials are aged 18 to 35; Generation Xers are aged 36 to 47; Baby Boomers are aged 48 to 66; Older Americans are aged 67 or older.
Source: Survey Documentation and Analysis, Computer-assisted Survey Methods Program, University of California, Berkeley, General Social Survey, 1972–2012 Cumulative Data Files, Internet site http://sda.berkeley.edu/cgi-bin/hsda?harcsda+gss12; calculations by New Strategist

Table 9.12 Ever Paid for Sex, 2012

"Thinking about the time since your 18th birthday, have you ever had sex with a person you paid or who paid you for sex?"

(percent of people aged 18 or older responding by selected characteristics, 2012)

	total	yes	no
Total people	**100.0%**	**5.6%**	**94.4%**
Men	100.0	9.1	90.9
Women	100.0	2.7	97.3
Millennials	100.0	2.0	98.0
Generation Xers	100.0	5.4	94.6
Baby Boomers	100.0	8.1	91.9
Older Americans	100.0	10.2	89.8
Black	100.0	8.9	91.1
Hispanic	100.0	4.4	95.6
Non-Hispanic white	100.0	5.5	94.5
Northeast	100.0	5.5	94.5
Midwest	100.0	3.6	96.4
South	100.0	6.5	93.5
West	100.0	6.2	93.8
Not a college graduate	100.0	5.7	94.3
Bachelor's degree or more	100.0	5.5	94.5

Note: Millennials are aged 18 to 35; Generation Xers are aged 36 to 47; Baby Boomers are aged 48 to 66; Older Americans are aged 67 or older.
Source: Survey Documentation and Analysis, Computer-assisted Survey Methods Program, University of California, Berkeley, General Social Survey, 1972–2012 Cumulative Data Files, Internet site http://sda.berkeley.edu/cgi-bin/hsda?harcsda+gss12; calculations by New Strategist

Table 9.13 Same-Sex Sexual Relations, 2012

"What about sexual relations between two adults of the same sex—
do you think it is always wrong, almost always wrong,
wrong only sometimes, or not wrong at all?"

(percent of people aged 18 or older responding by selected characteristics, 2012)

	total	always wrong	almost always wrong	sometimes wrong	not wrong at all
Total people	**100.0%**	**45.7%**	**2.9%**	**7.7%**	**43.8%**
Men	100.0	50.9	3.5	10.4	35.3
Women	100.0	41.2	2.4	5.4	51.0
Millennials	100.0	32.3	2.7	10.2	54.8
Generation Xers	100.0	46.8	3.4	5.7	44.0
Baby Boomers	100.0	48.7	2.8	8.2	40.3
Older Americans	100.0	69.9	2.6	3.7	23.8
Black	100.0	61.4	1.8	7.3	29.5
Hispanic	100.0	45.6	6.0	7.0	41.3
Non-Hispanic white	100.0	42.1	2.3	7.3	48.4
Northeast	100.0	33.5	2.0	10.1	54.4
Midwest	100.0	45.1	4.0	6.0	44.9
South	100.0	57.6	2.7	7.5	32.2
West	100.0	34.9	2.7	7.9	54.5
Not a college graduate	100.0	50.5	3.4	7.7	38.3
Bachelor's degree or more	100.0	33.4	1.4	7.7	57.5

Note: Millennials are aged 18 to 35; Generation Xers are aged 36 to 47; Baby Boomers are aged 48 to 66; Older Americans are aged 67 or older.
Source: Survey Documentation and Analysis, Computer-assisted Survey Methods Program, University of California, Berkeley, General Social Survey, 1972–2012 Cumulative Data Files, Internet site http://sda.berkeley.edu/cgi-bin/hsda?harcsda+gss12; calculations by New Strategist

Table 9.14 Gay Marriage, 2012

"Do you agree or disagree: Homosexual couples should
have the right to marry one another?"

(percent of people aged 18 or older responding by selected characteristics, 2012)

	total	strongly agree	agree	neither agree nor disagree	disagree	strongly disagree
Total people	**100.0%**	**25.2%**	**23.7%**	**12.0%**	**14.2%**	**24.9%**
Men	100.0	20.7	22.3	12.2	15.7	29.2
Women	100.0	29.0	24.9	11.8	12.9	21.3
Millennials	100.0	35.0	27.2	13.0	10.1	14.6
Generation Xers	100.0	27.5	23.2	9.9	8.8	30.7
Baby Boomers	100.0	20.9	21.7	13.8	16.9	26.7
Older Americans	100.0	9.2	20.6	9.1	25.4	35.8
Black	100.0	21.1	22.3	13.0	15.7	27.9
Hispanic	100.0	26.9	25.0	16.0	12.8	19.4
Non-Hispanic white	100.0	26.4	23.7	9.5	15.2	25.2
Northeast	100.0	37.3	20.5	10.7	8.8	22.7
Midwest	100.0	25.8	26.8	11.1	16.1	20.3
South	100.0	16.5	22.3	11.2	17.9	32.2
West	100.0	29.8	25.8	15.3	10.2	18.9
Not a college graduate	100.0	21.4	23.2	12.9	14.7	27.8
Bachelor's degree or more	100.0	35.0	25.1	9.6	12.8	17.5

Note: Millennials are aged 18 to 35; Generation Xers are aged 36 to 47; Baby Boomers are aged 48 to 66; Older Americans are aged 67 or older.
Source: Survey Documentation and Analysis, Computer-assisted Survey Methods Program, University of California, Berkeley, General Social Survey, 1972–2012 Cumulative Data Files, Internet site http://sda.berkeley.edu/cgi-bin/hsda?harcsda+gss12; calculations by New Strategist

Table 9.15 Sexual Orientation, 2012

"Which of the following best describes you?"

(percent of people aged 18 or older responding by selected characteristics, 2012)

	total	gay, lesbian, or homosexual	bisexual	heterosexual or straight
Total people	**100.0%**	**1.5%**	**2.2%**	**96.3%**
Men	100.0	2.2	1.8	96.0
Women	100.0	0.8	2.6	96.6
Millennials	100.0	1.8	4.0	94.2
Generation Xers	100.0	2.1	2.4	95.4
Baby Boomers	100.0	1.0	0.7	98.3
Older Americans	100.0	0.6	0.9	98.5
Black	100.0	1.2	1.5	97.3
Hispanic	100.0	3.2	2.7	94.0
Non-Hispanic white	100.0	1.3	2.4	96.3
Northeast	100.0	0.6	0.6	98.8
Midwest	100.0	1.8	2.6	95.6
South	100.0	2.0	2.6	95.4
West	100.0	1.0	2.4	96.6
Not a college graduate	100.0	1.1	2.5	96.3
Bachelor's degree or more	100.0	2.4	1.5	96.2

Note: Millennials are aged 18 to 35; Generation Xers are aged 36 to 47; Baby Boomers are aged 48 to 66; Older Americans are aged 67 or older.
Source: Survey Documentation and Analysis, Computer-assisted Survey Methods Program, University of California, Berkeley, General Social Survey, 1972–2012 Cumulative Data Files, Internet site http://sda.berkeley.edu/cgi-bin/hsda?harcsda+gss12; calculations by New Strategist

Table 9.16 Sex of Sex Partners in Past Year, 2012

"Have your sex partners in the last 12 months been...?"

(percent of people aged 18 or older responding by selected characteristics, 2012)

	total	exclusively male	both male and female	exclusively female
Total people	**100.0%**	**53.1%**	**1.1%**	**45.8%**
Men	100.0	3.0	0.8	96.3
Women	100.0	96.7	1.4	1.9
Millennials	100.0	53.0	2.0	45.1
Generation Xers	100.0	55.1	1.2	43.7
Baby Boomers	100.0	53.3	0.3	46.4
Older Americans	100.0	43.6	0.0	56.4
Black	100.0	60.3	0.2	39.5
Hispanic	100.0	50.1	0.4	49.6
Non-Hispanic white	100.0	53.4	1.5	45.1
Northeast	100.0	52.8	0.5	46.6
Midwest	100.0	48.6	0.9	50.5
South	100.0	54.8	1.1	44.1
West	100.0	54.8	1.6	43.6
Not a college graduate	100.0	53.0	1.3	45.7
Bachelor's degree or more	100.0	53.3	0.7	46.0

Note: Millennials are aged 18 to 35; Generation Xers are aged 36 to 47; Baby Boomers are aged 48 to 66; Older Americans are aged 67 or older.
Source: Survey Documentation and Analysis, Computer-assisted Survey Methods Program, University of California, Berkeley, General Social Survey, 1972–2012 Cumulative Data Files, Internet site http://sda.berkeley.edu/cgi-bin/hsda?harcsda+gss12; calculations by New Strategist

Table 9.17 Sex of Sex Partners since Age 18, 2012

"Since the age of 18, have your sex partners been...?"

(percent of people aged 18 or older responding by selected characteristics, 2012)

	total	only men	some women, but mostly men	equally men and women	some men, but mostly women	only women	no sex partners
Total people	**100.0%**	**49.5%**	**3.1%**	**0.6%**	**1.1%**	**42.1%**	**3.6%**
Men	100.0	2.3	0.9	0.7	1.2	91.0	3.8
Women	100.0	89.9	4.9	0.6	1.0	0.2	3.3
Millennials	100.0	44.2	4.3	0.9	1.5	41.5	7.5
Generation Xers	100.0	52.3	3.0	0.9	1.7	41.0	1.0
Baby Boomers	100.0	52.9	2.6	0.2	0.6	42.2	1.4
Older Americans	100.0	48.8	0.7	0.4	0.2	47.3	2.6
Black	100.0	59.7	3.4	0.2	0.3	34.0	2.4
Hispanic	100.0	47.9	2.4	1.2	0.2	45.7	2.7
Non-Hispanic white	100.0	48.4	3.5	0.7	1.6	41.9	3.9
Northeast	100.0	46.9	2.4	0.0	0.3	47.2	3.2
Midwest	100.0	45.7	3.4	0.0	2.3	45.0	3.6
South	100.0	52.8	3.0	1.3	1.1	39.4	2.3
West	100.0	49.5	3.3	0.6	0.5	40.2	5.7
Not a college graduate	100.0	48.9	3.3	0.8	1.1	41.8	4.2
Bachelor's degree or more	100.0	51.0	2.5	0.3	1.1	43.1	2.0

Note: Millennials are aged 18 to 35; Generation Xers are aged 36 to 47; Baby Boomers are aged 48 to 66; Older Americans are aged 67 or older.
Source: Survey Documentation and Analysis, Computer-assisted Survey Methods Program, University of California, Berkeley, General Social Survey, 1972–2012 Cumulative Data Files, Internet site http://sda.berkeley.edu/cgi-bin/hsda?harcsda+gss12; calculations by New Strategist

Table 9.18 Same-Sex Female Couple Can Raise a Child Well, 2012

"To what extent do you agree or disagree with the following statement? A same-sex female couple can bring up a child as well as a male-female couple."

(percent of people aged 18 or older responding by selected characteristics, 2012)

	total	strongly agree	agree	neither agree nor disagree	disagree	strongly disagree
Total people	**100.0%**	**10.1%**	**37.3%**	**11.4%**	**25.9%**	**15.4%**
Men	100.0	7.4	32.9	10.8	30.0	18.9
Women	100.0	12.4	41.2	11.9	22.2	12.2
Millennials	100.0	15.1	43.8	9.9	19.8	11.4
Generation Xers	100.0	11.1	40.0	11.4	24.2	13.2
Baby Boomers	100.0	6.2	32.5	13.6	29.2	18.5
Older Americans	100.0	3.6	26.2	10.8	37.6	21.9
Black	100.0	7.1	37.4	7.3	32.2	16.1
Hispanic	100.0	13.9	31.8	13.2	29.3	11.8
Non-Hispanic white	100.0	10.2	38.8	11.8	23.9	15.3
Northeast	100.0	13.8	53.1	6.5	14.9	11.8
Midwest	100.0	9.6	37.2	12.6	26.6	14.0
South	100.0	6.9	30.8	10.8	33.8	17.7
West	100.0	12.7	36.6	14.5	20.7	15.6
Not a college graduate	100.0	9.5	34.5	11.5	28.5	16.1
Bachelor's degree or more	100.0	11.6	45.0	11.0	18.8	13.5

Note: Millennials are aged 18 to 35; Generation Xers are aged 36 to 47; Baby Boomers are aged 48 to 66; Older Americans are aged 67 or older.
Source: Survey Documentation and Analysis, Computer-assisted Survey Methods Program, University of California, Berkeley, General Social Survey, 1972–2012 Cumulative Data Files, Internet site http://sda.berkeley.edu/cgi-bin/hsda?harcsda+gss12; calculations by New Strategist

Table 9.19 Same-Sex Male Couple Can Raise a Child Well, 2012

"To what extent do you agree or disagree with the following statement? A same-sex male couple can bring up a child as well as a male-female couple."

(percent of people aged 18 or older responding by selected characteristics, 2012)

	total	strongly agree	agree	neither agree nor disagree	disagree	strongly disagree
Total people	**100.0%**	**9.6%**	**34.0%**	**12.0%**	**26.9%**	**17.6%**
Men	100.0	7.2	28.2	10.8	31.5	22.2
Women	100.0	11.6	39.1	13.0	22.7	13.5
Millennials	100.0	14.4	40.3	10.7	21.6	13.0
Generation Xers	100.0	10.4	36.6	12.9	25.9	14.2
Baby Boomers	100.0	6.1	29.9	13.8	28.4	21.9
Older Americans	100.0	3.1	21.6	10.0	40.1	25.2
Black	100.0	6.6	34.1	7.5	33.4	18.3
Hispanic	100.0	13.6	28.4	12.7	28.6	16.7
Non-Hispanic white	100.0	9.6	35.7	12.9	24.9	17.0
Northeast	100.0	12.4	52.6	7.7	15.0	12.3
Midwest	100.0	9.7	32.7	13.9	27.7	16.0
South	100.0	6.1	26.6	11.1	34.6	21.6
West	100.0	12.7	33.8	14.2	22.6	16.7
Not a college graduate	100.0	8.7	31.6	11.5	29.5	18.7
Bachelor's degree or more	100.0	12.0	40.5	13.1	19.9	14.6

Note: Millennials are aged 18 to 35; Generation Xers are aged 36 to 47; Baby Boomers are aged 48 to 66; Older Americans are aged 67 or older.
Source: Survey Documentation and Analysis, Computer-assisted Survey Methods Program, University of California, Berkeley, General Social Survey, 1972–2012 Cumulative Data Files, Internet site http://sda.berkeley.edu/cgi-bin/hsda?harcsda+gss12; calculations by New Strategist

Table 9.20 Abortion if Chance of Serious Defect in Baby, 2012

"Do you think it should be possible for a pregnant woman to obtain a legal
abortion if there is a strong chance of serious defect in the baby?"

(percent of people aged 18 or older responding by selected characteristics, 2012)

	total	yes	no
Total people	**100.0%**	**73.3%**	**26.7%**
Men	100.0	74.8	25.2
Women	100.0	72.1	27.9
Millennials	100.0	69.1	30.9
Generation Xers	100.0	74.9	25.1
Baby Boomers	100.0	75.5	24.5
Older Americans	100.0	76.8	23.2
Black	100.0	68.9	31.1
Hispanic	100.0	69.0	31.0
Non-Hispanic white	100.0	75.4	24.6
Northeast	100.0	76.3	23.7
Midwest	100.0	75.3	24.7
South	100.0	69.4	30.6
West	100.0	75.8	24.2
Not a college graduate	100.0	71.3	28.7
Bachelor's degree or more	100.0	78.2	21.8

Note: Millennials are aged 18 to 35; Generation Xers are aged 36 to 47; Baby Boomers are aged 48 to 66; Older Americans are aged 67 or older.
Source: Survey Documentation and Analysis, Computer-assisted Survey Methods Program, University of California, Berkeley, General Social Survey, 1972–2012 Cumulative Data Files, Internet site http://sda.berkeley.edu/cgi-bin/hsda?harcsda+gss12; calculations by New Strategist

Table 9.21 Abortion if Woman's Health Is Seriously Endangered, 2012

"Do you think it should be possible for a pregnant woman to obtain a legal abortion if the woman's own health is seriously endangered by the pregnancy?"

(percent of people aged 18 or older responding by selected characteristics, 2012)

	total	yes	no
Total people	**100.0%**	**86.7%**	**13.3%**
Men	100.0	85.5	14.5
Women	100.0	87.7	12.3
Millennials	100.0	84.6	15.4
Generation Xers	100.0	86.7	13.3
Baby Boomers	100.0	89.2	10.8
Older Americans	100.0	86.6	13.4
Black	100.0	87.1	12.9
Hispanic	100.0	81.2	18.8
Non-Hispanic white	100.0	88.5	11.5
Northeast	100.0	86.5	13.5
Midwest	100.0	91.7	8.3
South	100.0	84.2	15.8
West	100.0	86.2	13.8
Not a college graduate	100.0	85.0	15.0
Bachelor's degree or more	100.0	91.0	9.0

Note: Millennials are aged 18 to 35; Generation Xers are aged 36 to 47; Baby Boomers are aged 48 to 66; Older Americans are aged 67 or older.
Source: Survey Documentation and Analysis, Computer-assisted Survey Methods Program, University of California, Berkeley, General Social Survey, 1972–2012 Cumulative Data Files, Internet site http://sda.berkeley.edu/cgi-bin/hsda?harcsda+gss12; calculations by New Strategist

Table 9.22 Abortion if Married and Wants No More Children, 2012

"Please tell me whether or not you think it should be possible for a
pregnant woman to obtain a legal abortion if she is married
and does not want any more children."

(percent of people aged 18 or older responding by selected characteristics, 2012)

	total	yes	no
Total people	**100.0%**	**44.9%**	**55.1%**
Men	100.0	45.0	55.0
Women	100.0	44.7	55.3
Millennials	100.0	40.9	59.1
Generation Xers	100.0	49.9	50.1
Baby Boomers	100.0	49.2	50.8
Older Americans	100.0	35.8	64.2
Black	100.0	45.9	54.1
Hispanic	100.0	35.7	64.3
Non-Hispanic white	100.0	46.6	53.4
Northeast	100.0	52.3	47.7
Midwest	100.0	44.2	55.8
South	100.0	37.9	62.1
West	100.0	52.0	48.0
Not a college graduate	100.0	38.4	61.6
Bachelor's degree or more	100.0	61.6	38.4

Note: Millennials are aged 18 to 35; Generation Xers are aged 36 to 47; Baby Boomers are aged 48 to 66; Older Americans are aged 67 or older.
Source: Survey Documentation and Analysis, Computer-assisted Survey Methods Program, University of California, Berkeley, General Social Survey, 1972–2012 Cumulative Data Files, Internet site http://sda.berkeley.edu/cgi-bin/hsda?harcsda+gss12; calculations by New Strategist

Table 9.23 Abortion if a Family Cannot Afford More Children, 2012

"Please tell me whether or not you think it should be possible for a pregnant woman to obtain a legal abortion if the family has a very low income and cannot afford any more children."

(percent of people aged 18 or older responding by selected characteristics, 2012)

	total	yes	no
Total people	**100.0%**	**42.4%**	**57.6%**
Men	100.0	42.4	57.6
Women	100.0	42.5	57.5
Millennials	100.0	41.6	58.4
Generation Xers	100.0	45.9	54.1
Baby Boomers	100.0	44.1	55.9
Older Americans	100.0	34.9	65.1
Black	100.0	44.4	55.6
Hispanic	100.0	31.0	69.0
Non-Hispanic white	100.0	44.5	55.5
Northeast	100.0	52.0	48.0
Midwest	100.0	42.2	57.8
South	100.0	34.7	65.3
West	100.0	48.5	51.5
Not a college graduate	100.0	36.9	63.1
Bachelor's degree or more	100.0	56.8	43.2

Note: Millennials are aged 18 to 35; Generation Xers are aged 36 to 47; Baby Boomers are aged 48 to 66; Older Americans are aged 67 or older.
Source: Survey Documentation and Analysis, Computer-assisted Survey Methods Program, University of California, Berkeley, General Social Survey, 1972–2012 Cumulative Data Files, Internet site http://sda.berkeley.edu/cgi-bin/hsda?harcsda+gss12; calculations by New Strategist

Table 9.24 **Abortion in Case of Rape, 2012**

"Do you think it should be possible for a pregnant woman to obtain
a legal abortion if she became pregnant as a result of rape?"

(percent of people aged 18 or older responding by selected characteristics, 2012)

	total	yes	no
Total people	**100.0%**	**75.8%**	**24.2%**
Men	100.0	75.5	24.5
Women	100.0	76.0	24.0
Millennials	100.0	76.1	23.9
Generation Xers	100.0	78.5	21.5
Baby Boomers	100.0	74.1	25.9
Older Americans	100.0	75.1	24.9
Black	100.0	74.1	25.9
Hispanic	100.0	65.8	34.2
Non-Hispanic white	100.0	79.6	20.4
Northeast	100.0	76.0	24.0
Midwest	100.0	80.3	19.7
South	100.0	72.1	27.9
West	100.0	77.6	22.4
Not a college graduate	100.0	72.8	27.2
Bachelor's degree or more	100.0	83.1	16.9

Note: Millennials are aged 18 to 35; Generation Xers are aged 36 to 47; Baby Boomers are aged 48 to 66; Older Americans are aged 67 or older.
Source: Survey Documentation and Analysis, Computer-assisted Survey Methods Program, University of California, Berkeley, General Social Survey, 1972–2012 Cumulative Data Files, Internet site http://sda.berkeley.edu/cgi-bin/hsda?harcsda+gss12; calculations by New Strategist

Table 9.25 Abortion if a Woman Is Not Married, 2012

"Please tell me whether or not you think it should be possible
for a pregnant woman to obtain a legal abortion if she is
not married and does not want to marry the man."

(percent of people aged 18 or older responding by selected characteristics, 2012)

	total	yes	no
Total people	**100.0%**	**41.1%**	**58.9%**
Men	100.0	40.9	59.1
Women	100.0	41.3	58.7
Millennials	100.0	37.3	62.7
Generation Xers	100.0	47.4	52.6
Baby Boomers	100.0	43.0	57.0
Older Americans	100.0	36.3	63.7
Black	100.0	40.3	59.7
Hispanic	100.0	28.3	71.7
Non-Hispanic white	100.0	43.9	56.1
Northeast	100.0	49.8	50.2
Midwest	100.0	41.4	58.6
South	100.0	33.3	66.7
West	100.0	47.9	52.1
Not a college graduate	100.0	35.3	64.7
Bachelor's degree or more	100.0	56.5	43.5

Note: Millennials are aged 18 to 35; Generation Xers are aged 36 to 47; Baby Boomers are aged 48 to 66; Older Americans are aged 67 or older.
Source: Survey Documentation and Analysis, Computer-assisted Survey Methods Program, University of California, Berkeley, General Social Survey, 1972–2012 Cumulative Data Files, Internet site http://sda.berkeley.edu/cgi-bin/hsda?harcsda+gss12; calculations by New Strategist

Table 9.26 Abortion for Any Reason, 2012

"Please tell me whether or not you think it should be possible for a pregnant woman to obtain a legal abortion if the woman wants it for any reason."

(percent of people aged 18 or older responding by selected characteristics, 2012)

	total	yes	no
Total people	**100.0%**	**42.7%**	**57.3%**
Men	100.0	40.9	59.1
Women	100.0	44.3	55.7
Millennials	100.0	40.7	59.3
Generation Xers	100.0	51.0	49.0
Baby Boomers	100.0	42.9	57.1
Older Americans	100.0	34.1	65.8
Black	100.0	43.1	56.9
Hispanic	100.0	31.5	68.5
Non-Hispanic white	100.0	45.6	54.4
Northeast	100.0	53.7	46.3
Midwest	100.0	42.0	58.0
South	100.0	35.7	64.3
West	100.0	46.9	53.1
Not a college graduate	100.0	36.8	63.2
Bachelor's degree or more	100.0	58.1	41.9

Note: Millennials are aged 18 to 35; Generation Xers are aged 36 to 47; Baby Boomers are aged 48 to 66; Older Americans are aged 67 or older.
Source: Survey Documentation and Analysis, Computer-assisted Survey Methods Program, University of California, Berkeley, General Social Survey, 1972–2012 Cumulative Data Files, Internet site http://sda.berkeley.edu/cgi-bin/hsda?harcsda+gss12; calculations by New Strategist

Sexuality: Historical Trends

Table 9.27 Sex Education in Public Schools, 1974 to 2012

"Would you be for or against sex education in the public schools?"

(percent distribution of people aged 18 or older by response for selected years)

	total	favor	oppose
2012	100.0%	90.9%	9.1%
2010	100.0	89.9	10.1
2008	100.0	91.9	8.1
2006	100.0	89.2	10.8
2004	100.0	89.5	10.5
2002	100.0	87.9	12.1
2000	100.0	87.2	12.8
1998	100.0	87.1	12.9
1996	100.0	87.3	12.7
1994	100.0	88.0	12.0
1993	100.0	86.4	13.6
1991	100.0	87.5	12.5
1990	100.0	90.1	9.9
1989	100.0	87.7	12.3
1988	100.0	87.6	12.4
1986	100.0	84.8	15.2
1985	100.0	84.8	15.2
1983	100.0	85.3	14.7
1982	100.0	85.0	15.0
1977	100.0	78.5	21.5
1975	100.0	79.7	20.3
1974	100.0	82.0	17.4

Source: Survey Documentation and Analysis, Computer-assisted Survey Methods Program, University of California, Berkeley, General Social Survey, 1972–2012 Cumulative Data Files, Internet site http://sda.berkeley.edu/cgi-bin/hsda?harcsda+gss12; calculations by New Strategist

Table 9.28 Birth Control for Teenagers, 1986 to 2012

"Do you strongly agree, agree, or strongly disagree that methods of birth control should be available to teenagers between the ages of 14 and 16 even if their parents did not approve?"

(percent distribution of people aged 18 or older by response for selected years)

	total	strongly agree	agree	disagree	strongly disagree
2012	100.0%	24.1%	33.7%	25.1%	17.1%
2010	100.0	24.1	34.0	25.5	16.4
2008	100.0	23.1	33.9	21.4	21.6
2006	100.0	25.2	29.1	24.4	21.3
2004	100.0	23.3	29.8	25.2	21.7
2002	100.0	30.7	26.1	19.7	23.6
2000	100.0	28.6	30.7	19.9	20.8
1998	100.0	26.8	30.9	21.0	21.3
1996	100.0	29.4	30.3	21.4	18.8
1994	100.0	26.6	30.4	21.8	21.2
1993	100.0	27.1	31.4	23.2	18.3
1991	100.0	26.9	34.5	20.3	18.3
1990	100.0	28.6	32.2	23.9	15.3
1989	100.0	27.6	28.3	24.2	19.9
1988	100.0	28.3	31.0	23.3	17.4
1986	100.0	22.8	34.6	25.4	17.2

Source: Survey Documentation and Analysis, Computer-assisted Survey Methods Program, University of California, Berkeley, General Social Survey, 1972–2012 Cumulative Data Files, Internet site http://sda.berkeley.edu/cgi-bin/hsda?harcsda+gss12; calculations by New Strategist

Table 9.29 Sexual Relations between Teenagers, 1986 to 2012

"Do you think sex relations before marriage between people in their early teens,
say 14 to 16, are always wrong, almost always wrong, wrong
only sometimes, or not wrong at all?"

(percent distribution of people aged 18 or older by response for selected years)

	total	always wrong	almost always wrong	sometimes wrong	not wrong at all
2012	100.0%	66.9%	15.1%	11.9%	6.0%
2010	100.0	67.2	15.5	11.7	5.6
2008	100.0	71.8	15.6	8.1	4.5
2006	100.0	72.6	15.0	8.3	4.1
2004	100.0	70.9	15.3	10.2	3.6
2002	100.0	72.8	14.5	8.7	4.0
2000	100.0	72.3	15.1	9.2	3.5
1998	100.0	72.2	16.2	8.2	3.4
1996	100.0	69.7	15.9	10.1	4.3
1994	100.0	70.0	17.6	8.7	3.7
1993	100.0	68.5	18.0	9.8	3.7
1991	100.0	68.0	19.1	8.9	4.0
1990	100.0	69.1	16.8	10.9	3.3
1989	100.0	70.2	16.5	9.2	4.1
1988	100.0	68.5	16.4	11.6	3.5
1986	100.0	67.1	18.9	10.8	3.1

Source: Survey Documentation and Analysis, Computer-assisted Survey Methods Program, University of California, Berkeley, General Social Survey, 1972–2012 Cumulative Data Files, Internet site http://sda.berkeley.edu/cgi-bin/hsda?harcsda+gss12; calculations by New Strategist

Table 9.30 Number of Sex Partners in Past Year, 1988 to 2012

"How many sex partners have you had in the last 12 months?"

(percent distribution of people aged 18 or older by response for selected years)

	total	no partners	one partner	two or more partners
2012	100.0%	18.6%	68.1%	13.3%
2010	100.0	19.2	67.5	13.4
2008	100.0	18.0	68.8	13.2
2006	100.0	19.8	68.0	12.1
2004	100.0	15.7	71.8	12.5
2002	100.0	18.8	67.7	13.5
2000	100.0	18.2	69.2	12.6
1998	100.0	17.4	70.6	12.0
1996	100.0	15.0	71.3	13.7
1994	100.0	18.4	70.5	11.1
1993	100.0	17.4	72.0	10.6
1991	100.0	18.3	70.8	10.9
1990	100.0	16.3	70.1	13.6
1989	100.0	19.0	68.2	12.8
1988	100.0	19.8	66.5	13.7

Source: Survey Documentation and Analysis, Computer-assisted Survey Methods Program, University of California, Berkeley, General Social Survey, 1972–2012 Cumulative Data Files, Internet site http://sda.berkeley.edu/cgi-bin/hsda?harcsda+gss12; calculations by New Strategist

Table 9.31 Relationship with Last Sex Partner, 1996 to 2012

"The last time you had sex, was it with someone that you were in an on-going
relationship with, or was it with someone else? Remember that
by 'sex' we mean only vaginal, oral, or anal sex."

(percent distribution of people aged 18 or older by response for selected years)

	total	in relationship	not in relationship
2012	100.0%	90.2%	9.8%
2010	100.0	91.5	8.5
2008	100.0	92.2	7.8
2006	100.0	90.9	9.1
2004	100.0	92.1	7.9
2002	100.0	93.1	6.9
2000	100.0	90.3	9.7
1998	100.0	89.9	10.1
1996	100.0	92.3	7.7

Source: Survey Documentation and Analysis, Computer-assisted Survey Methods Program, University of California, Berkeley, General Social Survey, 1972–2012 Cumulative Data Files, Internet site http://sda.berkeley.edu/cgi-bin/hsda?harcsda+gss12; calculations by New Strategist

Table 9.32 Condom Use, 1996 to 2012

"The last time you had sex, was a condom used?
By 'sex' we mean vaginal, oral, or anal sex."

(percent distribution of people aged 18 or older by response for selected years)

	total	used	not used
2012	100.0%	21.5%	78.5%
2010	100.0	22.7	77.3
2008	100.0	24.0	76.0
2006	100.0	23.0	77.0
2004	100.0	18.7	81.3
2002	100.0	21.8	78.2
2000	100.0	20.6	79.4
1998	100.0	18.8	81.2
1996	100.0	20.4	79.6

Source: Survey Documentation and Analysis, Computer-assisted Survey Methods Program, University of California, Berkeley, General Social Survey, 1972–2012 Cumulative Data Files, Internet site http://sda.berkeley.edu/cgi-bin/hsda?harcsda+gss12; calculations by New Strategist

Table 9.33 Seen X-Rated Movie, 1973 to 2012

"Have you seen an X-rated movie in the last year?"

(percent distribution of people aged 18 or older by response for selected years)

	total	yes	no
2012	100.0%	24.7%	75.3%
2010	100.0	25.6	74.4
2008	100.0	24.2	75.8
2006	100.0	22.4	77.6
2004	100.0	26.2	73.8
2002	100.0	23.6	76.4
2000	100.0	24.5	75.5
1998	100.0	24.8	75.2
1996	100.0	27.2	72.8
1994	100.0	22.8	77.2
1993	100.0	20.3	79.7
1991	100.0	25.0	75.0
1990	100.0	23.7	76.3
1989	100.0	24.1	75.9
1988	100.0	27.6	72.4
1987	100.0	28.5	71.5
1986	100.0	25.2	74.8
1984	100.0	23.9	76.1
1983	100.0	19.3	80.7
1980	100.0	15.4	84.6
1978	100.0	16.1	83.9
1976	100.0	19.1	80.9
1975	100.0	19.2	80.8
1973	100.0	26.3	73.7

Source: Survey Documentation and Analysis, Computer-assisted Survey Methods Program, University of California, Berkeley, General Social Survey, 1972–2012 Cumulative Data Files, Internet site http://sda.berkeley.edu/cgi-bin/hsda?harcsda+gss12; calculations by New Strategist

Table 9.34 Laws against Pornography, 1973 to 2012

"Which of these statements comes closest to your feelings about pornography laws? 1) There should be laws against the distribution of pornography whatever the age; 2) There should be laws against the distribution of pornography to persons under 18; 3) There should be no laws forbidding the distribution of pornography."

(percent distribution of people aged 18 or older by response for selected years)

	total	illegal to all	illegal under 18	legal
2012	100.0%	32.8%	64.0%	3.3%
2010	100.0	30.9	65.0	4.1
2008	100.0	32.5	64.0	3.4
2006	100.0	38.7	58.1	3.2
2004	100.0	38.3	57.6	4.0
2002	100.0	39.1	56.4	4.5
2000	100.0	35.2	61.7	3.1
1998	100.0	37.8	58.6	3.6
1996	100.0	37.0	59.3	3.7
1994	100.0	36.5	60.5	3.0
1993	100.0	40.8	55.8	3.3
1991	100.0	40.5	55.1	4.3
1990	100.0	40.7	53.9	5.4
1989	100.0	40.7	54.6	4.7
1988	100.0	43.8	51.2	5.1
1987	100.0	39.7	56.0	4.3
1986	100.0	42.1	54.7	3.2
1984	100.0	40.8	55.2	3.9
1983	100.0	42.6	52.0	5.4
1980	100.0	40.8	52.7	6.5
1978	100.0	43.3	49.6	7.1
1976	100.0	40.1	51.7	8.2
1975	100.0	40.8	48.2	11.0
1973	100.0	41.6	48.7	9.7

Source: Survey Documentation and Analysis, Computer-assisted Survey Methods Program, University of California, Berkeley, General Social Survey, 1972–2012 Cumulative Data Files, Internet site http://sda.berkeley.edu/cgi-bin/hsda?harcsda+gss12; calculations by New Strategist

Table 9.35 Premarital Sex, 1972 to 2012

"There's been a lot of discussion about the way morals and attitudes about sex
are changing in this country. If a man and woman have sex relations
before marriage, do you think it is always wrong, almost always
wrong, wrong only sometimes, or not wrong at all?"

(percent distribution of people aged 18 or older by response for selected years)

	total	always wrong	almost always wrong	sometimes wrong	not wrong at all
2012	100.0%	21.9%	5.1%	15.5%	57.5%
2010	100.0	21.3	7.8	17.8	53.1
2008	100.0	22.6	7.2	15.4	54.8
2006	100.0	25.6	8.9	19.8	45.7
2004	100.0	27.2	9.6	19.0	44.1
2002	100.0	27.7	8.2	19.9	44.1
2000	100.0	27.7	8.6	21.4	42.2
1998	100.0	27.0	8.7	21.1	43.2
1996	100.0	24.1	9.8	22.6	43.6
1994	100.0	25.9	10.1	20.5	43.5
1993	100.0	26.9	10.0	21.8	41.4
1991	100.0	27.7	10.3	19.6	42.4
1990	100.0	24.8	11.3	24.5	39.5
1989	100.0	27.7	8.8	23.1	40.4
1988	100.0	26.2	10.2	22.2	41.4
1986	100.0	28.2	8.8	22.8	40.2
1985	100.0	27.5	8.6	20.1	43.7
1983	100.0	28.8	10.3	24.8	36.1
1982	100.0	28.9	9.1	21.4	40.6
1978	100.0	28.2	11.5	20.2	40.1
1977	100.0	30.8	9.9	23.0	36.3
1975	100.0	30.6	12.4	25.2	31.7
1974	100.0	33.4	12.9	23.9	29.8
1972	100.0	35.7	11.4	25.2	27.7

Source: Survey Documentation and Analysis, Computer-assisted Survey Methods Program, University of California, Berkeley, General Social Survey, 1972–2012 Cumulative Data Files, Internet site http://sda.berkeley.edu/cgi-bin/hsda?harcsda+gss12; calculations by New Strategist

Table 9.36 Extramarital Sex, 1973 to 2012

"What is your opinion about a married person having sexual relations with someone other than the marriage partner—is it always wrong, almost always wrong, wrong only sometimes, or not wrong at all?"

(percent distribution of people aged 18 or older by response for selected years)

	total	always wrong	almost always wrong	sometimes wrong	not wrong at all
2012	100.0%	81.9%	11.2%	5.6%	1.3%
2010	100.0	79.4	12.3	6.3	2.0
2008	100.0	84.2	9.2	5.3	1.3
2006	100.0	82.0	10.9	5.4	1.7
2004	100.0	82.1	11.6	4.6	1.7
2002	100.0	81.3	12.6	4.1	2.0
2000	100.0	79.4	10.9	7.3	2.4
1998	100.0	80.5	11.7	5.5	2.3
1996	100.0	78.5	14.9	5.0	1.6
1994	100.0	79.7	12.3	6.0	2.0
1993	100.0	78.5	13.9	5.2	2.4
1991	100.0	77.2	13.5	6.2	3.0
1990	100.0	79.0	12.5	6.7	1.8
1989	100.0	78.5	12.3	7.5	1.6
1988	100.0	80.7	12.3	5.1	1.9
1987	100.0	74.4	15.5	8.0	2.1
1985	100.0	76.0	12.9	8.3	2.7
1984	100.0	71.2	17.5	9.5	1.8
1982	100.0	74.1	14.0	9.7	2.1
1980	100.0	71.4	15.9	9.3	3.4
1977	100.0	73.9	13.5	9.9	2.8
1976	100.0	68.7	16.5	10.7	4.0
1974	100.0	73.2	12.5	11.8	2.5
1973	100.0	69.8	14.8	11.7	3.8

Source: Survey Documentation and Analysis, Computer-assisted Survey Methods Program, University of California, Berkeley, General Social Survey, 1972–2012 Cumulative Data Files, Internet site http://sda.berkeley.edu/cgi-bin/hsda?harcsda+gss12; calculations by New Strategist

Table 9.37 Ever Had an Affair, 1991 to 2012

"Have you ever had sex with someone other than your
husband or wife while you were married?"

(percent of ever-married people aged 18 or older responding by selected characteristics, 2012)

	total ever-married	yes	no
2012	100.0%	14.6%	85.4%
2010	100.0	16.3	83.7
2008	100.0	15.4	84.6
2006	100.0	17.8	82.2
2004	100.0	16.6	83.4
2002	100.0	17.0	83.0
2000	100.0	17.7	82.3
1998	100.0	15.7	84.3
1996	100.0	18.2	81.8
1994	100.0	15.2	84.8
1993	100.0	16.3	83.7
1991	100.0	15.3	84.7

Source: Survey Documentation and Analysis, Computer-assisted Survey Methods Program, University of California, Berkeley,
General Social Survey, 1972–2012 Cumulative Data Files, Internet site http://sda.berkeley.edu/cgi-bin/hsda?harcsda+gss12;
calculations by New Strategist

Table 9.38 Ever Paid for Sex, 1991 to 2012

"Thinking about the time since your 18th birthday, have you ever had sex with a person you paid or who paid you for sex?"

(percent distribution of people aged 18 or older by response for selected years)

	total	yes	no
2012	100.0%	5.6%	94.4%
2010	100.0	6.3	93.7
2008	100.0	9.0	91.0
2006	100.0	7.6	92.4
2004	100.0	7.0	93.0
2002	100.0	7.3	92.7
2000	100.0	7.9	92.1
1998	100.0	7.3	92.7
1996	100.0	8.8	91.2
1994	100.0	8.3	91.7
1993	100.0	8.4	91.6
1991	100.0	8.5	91.5

Source: Survey Documentation and Analysis, Computer-assisted Survey Methods Program, University of California, Berkeley, General Social Survey, 1972–2012 Cumulative Data Files, Internet site http://sda.berkeley.edu/cgi-bin/hsda?harcsda+gss12; calculations by New Strategist

Table 9.39 Same-Sex Sexual Relations, 1973 to 2012

"What about sexual relations between two adults of the same sex—
do you think it is always wrong, almost always wrong,
wrong only sometimes, or not wrong at all?"

(percent distribution of people aged 18 or older by response for selected years)

	total	always wrong	almost always wrong	sometimes wrong	not wrong at all
2012	100.0%	45.7%	2.9%	7.7%	43.8%
2010	100.0	45.7	3.7	7.9	42.7
2008	100.0	52.4	3.1	6.7	37.8
2006	100.0	56.2	4.9	6.7	32.3
2004	100.0	58.2	4.8	6.9	30.1
2002	100.0	55.8	5.2	7.3	31.7
2000	100.0	58.7	4.4	8.1	28.8
1998	100.0	58.5	5.9	7.3	28.3
1996	100.0	61.0	5.1	6.0	27.9
1994	100.0	67.6	3.7	5.9	22.8
1993	100.0	66.1	4.2	7.8	21.9
1991	100.0	77.4	3.8	4.0	14.9
1990	100.0	76.4	5.0	5.8	12.9
1989	100.0	74.4	4.0	6.3	15.3
1988	100.0	77.4	4.4	5.5	12.7
1987	100.0	77.3	4.2	6.5	12.0
1985	100.0	74.8	4.2	7.0	14.0
1984	100.0	75.9	4.6	6.4	13.1
1982	100.0	74.1	5.0	6.8	14.1
1980	100.0	74.4	5.5	5.7	14.4
1977	100.0	72.9	5.8	7.5	13.7
1976	100.0	70.3	6.3	7.9	15.5
1974	100.0	69.4	5.6	8.5	12.9
1973	100.0	72.5	6.7	7.7	11.2

Source: Survey Documentation and Analysis, Computer-assisted Survey Methods Program, University of California, Berkeley, General Social Survey, 1972–2012 Cumulative Data Files, Internet site http://sda.berkeley.edu/cgi-bin/hsda?harcsda+gss12; calculations by New Strategist

Table 9.40 Gay Marriage, 1988 to 2012

"Do you agree or disagree: Homosexual couples should
have the right to marry one another?"

(percent distribution of people aged 18 or older by response for selected years)

	total	strongly agree	agree	neither agree nor disagree	disagree	strongly disagree
2012	100.0%	25.2%	23.7%	12.0%	14.2%	24.9%
2010	100.0	21.1	25.4	12.8	15.6	25.1
2008	100.0	15.4	23.9	13.0	15.6	32.2
2006	100.0	15.1	20.2	13.5	15.8	35.3
2004	100.0	11.9	18.9	14.0	20.4	34.8
1988	100.0	2.8	8.9	15.1	26.1	47.2

*Source: Survey Documentation and Analysis, Computer-assisted Survey Methods Program, University of California, Berkeley,
General Social Survey, 1972–2012 Cumulative Data Files, Internet site http://sda.berkeley.edu/cgi-bin/hsda?harcsda+gss12;
calculations by New Strategist*

Table 9.41 Sex of Sex Partners in Past Year, 1988 to 2012

"Have your sex partners in the last 12 months been...?"

(percent distribution of people aged 18 or older by response for selected years)

	total	exclusively male	both male and female	exclusively female
2012	100.0%	53.1%	1.1%	45.8%
2010	100.0	50.3	0.4	49.3
2008	100.0	50.4	0.6	49.1
2006	100.0	53.2	0.8	45.9
2004	100.0	53.1	0.3	46.7
2002	100.0	51.5	0.5	48.0
2000	100.0	51.7	1.0	47.3
1998	100.0	53.8	1.0	45.3
1996	100.0	50.5	0.7	48.8
1994	100.0	52.3	0.4	47.3
1993	100.0	53.4	0.4	46.2
1991	100.0	55.2	0.4	44.5
1990	100.0	52.2	0.5	47.3
1989	100.0	52.0	0.4	47.6
1988	100.0	53.2	0.2	46.7

Source: Survey Documentation and Analysis, Computer-assisted Survey Methods Program, University of California, Berkeley, General Social Survey, 1972–2012 Cumulative Data Files, Internet site http://sda.berkeley.edu/cgi-bin/hsda?harcsda+gss12; calculations by New Strategist

Table 9.42 Abortion if Chance of Serious Defect in Baby, 1972 to 2012

"Do you think it should be possible for a pregnant woman to obtain a legal
abortion if there is a strong chance of serious defect in the baby?"

(percent distribution of people aged 18 or older by response for selected years)

	total	yes	no
2012	100.0%	73.3%	26.7%
2010	100.0	73.9	26.1
2008	100.0	73.7	26.3
2006	100.0	72.7	27.3
2004	100.0	71.5	28.5
2002	100.0	77.1	22.9
2000	100.0	77.9	22.1
1998	100.0	77.5	22.5
1996	100.0	81.1	18.9
1994	100.0	81.9	18.1
1993	100.0	79.9	20.1
1991	100.0	83.4	16.6
1990	100.0	81.2	18.8
1989	100.0	81.5	18.5
1988	100.0	78.6	21.4
1987	100.0	79.1	20.9
1985	100.0	79.3	20.7
1984	100.0	80.1	19.9
1983	100.0	77.1	22.9
1982	100.0	85.0	15.0
1980	100.0	82.8	17.2
1978	100.0	81.6	18.4
1977	100.0	85.5	14.5
1976	100.0	84.1	15.9
1975	100.0	82.4	17.6
1974	100.0	84.4	15.6
1973	100.0	84.2	15.8
1972	100.0	78.7	21.3

Source: Survey Documentation and Analysis, Computer-assisted Survey Methods Program, University of California, Berkeley, General Social Survey, 1972–2012 Cumulative Data Files, Internet site http://sda.berkeley.edu/cgi-bin/hsda?harcsda+gss12; calculations by New Strategist

Table 9.43 Abortion if Woman's Health Is Seriously Endangered, 1972 to 2012

"Do you think it should be possible for a pregnant woman to obtain a legal abortion if the woman's own health is seriously endangered by the pregnancy?"

(percent distribution of people aged 18 or older by response for selected years)

	total	yes	no
2012	100.0%	86.7%	13.3%
2010	100.0	86.4	13.6
2008	100.0	88.6	11.4
2006	100.0	86.6	13.4
2004	100.0	85.2	14.8
2002	100.0	91.1	8.9
2000	100.0	88.5	11.5
1998	100.0	87.6	12.4
1996	100.0	91.5	8.5
1994	100.0	90.4	9.6
1993	100.0	89.8	10.2
1991	100.0	91.1	8.9
1990	100.0	92.6	7.4
1989	100.0	90.6	9.4
1988	100.0	88.7	11.3
1987	100.0	89.1	10.9
1985	100.0	90.3	9.7
1984	100.0	90.4	9.6
1983	100.0	89.4	10.6
1982	100.0	91.7	8.3
1980	100.0	90.7	9.3
1978	100.0	90.5	9.5
1977	100.0	90.7	9.3
1976	100.0	90.9	9.1
1975	100.0	90.8	9.2
1974	100.0	92.5	7.5
1973	100.0	92.0	8.0
1972	100.0	87.4	12.6

Source: Survey Documentation and Analysis, Computer-assisted Survey Methods Program, University of California, Berkeley, General Social Survey, 1972–2012 Cumulative Data Files, Internet site http://sda.berkeley.edu/cgi-bin/hsda?harcsda+gss12; calculations by New Strategist

Table 9.44 Abortion if Married and Wants No More Children, 1972 to 2012

"Please tell me whether or not you think it should be possible for a
pregnant woman to obtain a legal abortion if she is married
and does not want any more children."

(percent distribution of people aged 18 or older by response for selected years)

	total	yes	no
2012	100.0%	44.9%	55.1%
2010	100.0	47.7	52.3
2008	100.0	43.7	56.3
2006	100.0	41.3	58.7
2004	100.0	40.8	59.2
2002	100.0	42.3	57.7
2000	100.0	39.9	60.1
1998	100.0	41.2	58.8
1996	100.0	46.2	53.8
1994	100.0	47.7	52.3
1993	100.0	46.4	53.6
1991	100.0	43.6	56.4
1990	100.0	44.4	55.6
1989	100.0	44.7	55.3
1988	100.0	39.9	60.1
1987	100.0	41.6	58.4
1985	100.0	41.4	58.6
1984	100.0	42.8	57.2
1983	100.0	37.6	62.4
1982	100.0	47.1	52.9
1980	100.0	46.3	53.7
1978	100.0	39.9	60.1
1977	100.0	45.7	54.3
1976	100.0	45.9	54.1
1975	100.0	45.2	54.8
1974	100.0	46.9	53.1
1973	100.0	48.3	51.7
1972	100.0	40.2	59.8

*Source: Survey Documentation and Analysis, Computer-assisted Survey Methods Program, University of California, Berkeley,
General Social Survey, 1972–2012 Cumulative Data Files, Internet site http://sda.berkeley.edu/cgi-bin/hsda?harcsda+gss12;
calculations by New Strategist*

Table 9.45 Abortion if a Family Cannot Afford More Children, 1972 to 2012

"Please tell me whether or not you think it should be possible for a
pregnant woman to obtain a legal abortion if the family has a
very low income and cannot afford any more children."

(percent distribution of people aged 18 or older by response for selected years)

	total	yes	no
2012	100.0%	42.4%	57.6%
2010	100.0	44.9	55.1
2008	100.0	42.3	57.7
2006	100.0	41.8	58.2
2004	100.0	40.1	59.9
2002	100.0	42.8	57.2
2000	100.0	41.0	59.0
1998	100.0	43.0	57.0
1996	100.0	45.7	54.3
1994	100.0	49.7	50.3
1993	100.0	49.0	51.0
1991	100.0	47.7	52.3
1990	100.0	47.5	52.5
1989	100.0	47.4	52.6
1988	100.0	41.9	58.1
1987	100.0	45.4	54.7
1985	100.0	44.4	55.6
1984	100.0	46.4	53.6
1983	100.0	41.3	58.7
1982	100.0	50.1	49.9
1980	100.0	51.0	49.0
1978	100.0	47.3	52.7
1977	100.0	52.6	47.4
1976	100.0	52.7	47.3
1975	100.0	52.2	47.8
1974	100.0	54.7	45.3
1973	100.0	53.5	46.5
1972	100.0	48.9	51.1

Source: Survey Documentation and Analysis, Computer-assisted Survey Methods Program, University of California, Berkeley, General Social Survey, 1972–2012 Cumulative Data Files, Internet site http://sda.berkeley.edu/cgi-bin/hsda?harcsda+gss12; calculations by New Strategist

Table 9.46 Abortion in Case of Rape, 1972 to 2012

"Do you think it should be possible for a pregnant woman to obtain
a legal abortion if she became pregnant as a result of rape?"

(percent distribution of people aged 18 or older by response for selected years)

	total	yes	no
2012	100.0%	75.8%	24.2%
2010	100.0	79.1	20.9
2008	100.0	75.6	24.4
2006	100.0	77.2	22.8
2004	100.0	75.2	24.8
2002	100.0	77.9	22.1
2000	100.0	79.8	20.2
1998	100.0	80.1	19.9
1996	100.0	83.7	16.3
1994	100.0	83.2	16.8
1993	100.0	82.2	17.8
1991	100.0	86.5	13.5
1990	100.0	84.7	15.3
1989	100.0	83.0	17.0
1988	100.0	81.1	18.9
1987	100.0	80.4	19.6
1985	100.0	81.2	18.8
1984	100.0	79.4	20.6
1983	100.0	80.6	19.4
1982	100.0	87.1	13.0
1980	100.0	82.6	17.4
1978	100.0	83.1	16.9
1977	100.0	83.9	16.1
1976	100.0	83.8	16.2
1975	100.0	83.3	16.7
1974	100.0	86.4	13.6
1973	100.0	83.6	16.4
1972	100.0	79.1	20.9

Source: Survey Documentation and Analysis, Computer-assisted Survey Methods Program, University of California, Berkeley, General Social Survey, 1972–2012 Cumulative Data Files, Internet site http://sda.berkeley.edu/cgi-bin/hsda?harcsda+gss12; calculations by New Strategist

Table 9.47 Abortion if a Woman Is Not Married, 1972 to 2012

"Please tell me whether or not you think it should be possible
for a pregnant woman to obtain a legal abortion if she is
not married and does not want to marry the man."

(percent distribution of people aged 18 or older by response for selected years)

	total	yes	no
2012	100.0%	41.1%	58.9%
2010	100.0	41.9	58.1
2008	100.0	40.3	59.7
2006	100.0	38.4	61.6
2004	100.0	40.6	59.4
2002	100.0	40.0	60.0
2000	100.0	38.0	62.0
1998	100.0	41.1	58.9
1996	100.0	44.3	55.7
1994	100.0	47.0	53.0
1993	100.0	47.3	52.7
1991	100.0	44.3	55.7
1990	100.0	45.3	54.7
1989	100.0	44.9	55.1
1988	100.0	39.2	60.8
1987	100.0	41.4	58.6
1985	100.0	42.1	57.9
1984	100.0	43.0	57.0
1983	100.0	37.2	62.8
1982	100.0	47.1	52.9
1980	100.0	46.6	53.4
1978	100.0	41.8	58.2
1977	100.0	48.7	51.3
1976	100.0	49.7	50.3
1975	100.0	47.8	52.2
1974	100.0	50.0	50.0
1973	100.0	48.9	51.1
1972	100.0	43.8	56.2

Source: Survey Documentation and Analysis, Computer-assisted Survey Methods Program, University of California, Berkeley, General Social Survey, 1972–2012 Cumulative Data Files, Internet site http://sda.berkeley.edu/cgi-bin/hsda?harcsda+gss12; calculations by New Strategist

Table 9.48 Abortion for any Reason, 1977 to 2012

"Please tell me whether or not you think it should be possible for a pregnant woman to obtain a legal abortion if the woman wants it for any reason."

(percent distribution of people aged 18 or older by response for selected years)

	total	yes	no
2012	100.0%	42.7%	57.3%
2010	100.0	42.9	57.1
2008	100.0	41.2	58.8
2006	100.0	39.2	60.8
2004	100.0	39.3	60.7
2002	100.0	41.1	58.9
2000	100.0	38.9	61.1
1998	100.0	39.9	60.1
1996	100.0	44.6	55.4
1994	100.0	45.8	54.2
1993	100.0	44.7	55.3
1991	100.0	42.2	57.8
1990	100.0	43.3	56.7
1989	100.0	40.2	59.8
1988	100.0	36.4	63.6
1987	100.0	39.9	60.1
1985	100.0	38.5	61.5
1984	100.0	37.9	62.1
1983	100.0	32.6	67.4
1982	100.0	39.7	60.3
1980	100.0	40.3	59.7
1978	100.0	33.6	66.4
1977	100.0	36.7	63.3

Source: Survey Documentation and Analysis, Computer-assisted Survey Methods Program, University of California, Berkeley, General Social Survey, 1972–2012 Cumulative Data Files, Internet site http://sda.berkeley.edu/cgi-bin/hsda?harcsda+gss12; calculations by New Strategist

Appendix

For those who want to explore the General Social Survey questions shown in this book, below are the variable names of each 2012 question by chapter and table number. To access the General Social Survey data extraction tool, visit the Computer-assisted Survey Methods Program of the University of California, Berkeley at http://sda.berkeley.edu/cgi-bin/hsda?harcsda+gss12.

Chapter 1. Public Arena

1.1	Confidence in Executive Branch of Government	confed
1.2	Confidence in Legislative Branch of Government	conlegis
1.3	Confidence in the United States Supreme Court	conjudge
1.4	Confidence in Banks and Financial Institutions	confinan
1.5	Confidence in Major Companies	conbus
1.6	Confidence in Organized Labor	conlabor
1.7	Confidence in the Scientific Community	consci
1.8	Confidence in Medicine	conmedic
1.9	Confidence in Education	coneduc
1.10	Confidence in Organized Religion	conclerg
1.11	Confidence in the Military	conarmy
1.12	Confidence in the Press	conpress
1.13	Confidence in Television	contv
1.14	Federal Income Tax Level	tax
1.15	Should Marijuana Be Made Legal	grass
1.16	Favor or Oppose Gun Permits	gunlaw
1.17	Courts Deal Too Harshly with Criminals	courts
1.18	Favor or Oppose Death Penalty for Murder	cappun
1.19	Allow Patients with Incurable Disease to Die	letdie1
1.20	Expect World War in 10 Years	uswary
1.21	Allow Antireligious Book in Local Library	libath
1.22	Allow Someone Who Is Against Religion to Speak	spkath
1.23	Allow Someone Who Is Against Religion to Teach College	colath
1.24	Allow a Communist's Book in the Local Library	libcom
1.25	Allow a Communist to Speak	spkcom
1.26	Allow a Communist to Teach College	colcom
1.27	Allow a Homosexual's Book in the Local Library	libhomo
1.28	Allow a Homosexual to Speak	spkhomo
1.29	Allow a Homosexual to Teach College	colhomo
1.30	Allow a Militarist's Book in the Local Library	libmil
1.31	Allow a Militarist to Speak	spkmil
1.32	Allow a Militarist to Teach College	colmil
1.33	Allow a Racist's Book in the Local Library	librac
1.34	Allow a Racist to Speak	spkrac
1.35	Allow a Racist to Teach College	colrac
1.36	Suicide if Person Has an Incurable Disease	suicide1
1.37	Suicide if Bankrupt	suicide2
1.38	Suicide if Person Has Dishonored Family	suicide3
1.39	Suicide if Ready to Die	suicide4

Chapter 2. Government and Politics

2.1	Political Leanings	polviews
2.2	Political Party Affiliation	partyid
2.3	Average Citizen Influence on Politics	polefy3
2.4	How Much Say about What Government Does	polefy11

Chapter 3. Science and Information

Chapter 4. Religion

Chapter 5. Work and Money

Chapter 6. Family and Friends

Chapter 9. Sexuality

Index